D1156271

THE LEISURE AGE

THE LEISURE AGE

ITS CHALLENGE TO RECREATION

Norman P. Miller
University of California
Los Angeles

Duane M. Robinson
George Williams College

Wadsworth Publishing Company, Inc.
Belmont, California

L. C. Cat. Card No.: 63-8485
Printed in the United States of America

PREFACE

In industrial society, and particularly in the United States, one of the principal sources of self-fulfillment for the individual has been his work. This was most obvious when man worked long hours and when the pressures, forces, and social values of the American culture made work and production into idols to be worshiped. Now, however, through the unprecedented advances in science, medicine, and economics, man is approaching the point where socially necessary work for many no longer demands such time commitments nor provides major satisfactions or means of self-fulfillment.

The twentieth century finds man turning more and more to his increasing free time to fulfill himself. It is during leisure time and through play and recreation that increasing numbers of people find the means for creative self-expression. The effect of this movement has made the present day a leisure age for new masses of people.

Mankind can, if it chooses, achieve in its culture greater heights than it has ever known before, and lead a richer, fuller life through this process. Certainly one of the real strengths of a free society is the amount of "discretionary time" individuals have at their disposal. But as it is a strength, it can also be a weakness. Where and how are individuals to use this time? The quality of resources and opportunities available for the pursuit of leisure and the quality of the choices exercised will largely determine whether the path toward a leisure society is a wise one.

In America, concern for this question has resulted in a countless variety of recreation and leisure pursuits, available for individuals and groups under a variety of auspices, organized and unorganized. An institutionalized structure and a fledgling profession have emerged, committed to the development of a philosophy of leisure and recreation and of more adequate resources for helping the individual in his search for the full life through leisure and recreation.

The purpose of this book is to help the reader better to understand both the historical context and the forces affecting leisure in America, and to suggest principles or guidelines for action that may facilitate the orderly development of the recreation profession. This book is written primarily for the individual considering entering the recreation profession, for the person preparing for professions allied to leisure and recreation (education, group work, ministry, medicine, etc.), and for the recreation worker now in the field. Its content is such, however, that we believe many general readers will find it of interest too, and, we hope, thought-provoking. We have brought together what we consider to be the basics of leisure and recreation. Primarily it describes concepts and principles more applicable in the United States than elsewhere, although we believe many of those suggested apply anywhere.

The book is divided into six parts. Part One seeks to document the idea that man has constantly striven for leisure and recreation expression—that he is recreation-bent—and that some of his basic values can be achieved through leisure and recreation. The chapters review leisure and recreation throughout history and examine the efforts of theorists and philosophers to understand their place in the goals and value structure of man. Some of these values are aesthetic and deal with the experiencing of beauty; others are ethical and relate to what man thinks of himself and of others, and how he relates to others. Recreation is a means of enhancing such values; it is a powerful instrument for individual self-fulfillment and is a significant instrument of social policy.

Part Two is an analysis of the present-day social milieu in which leisure and recreation are found and presents an examination of the forces that influence and interact with recreation. Just as the social environment operates on the individual and his leisure, so it is necessary that we see how this relates to the nature of the organization and provision of leisure and recreation services.

Part Three describes the ways people have come together and organized for their leisure and recreation. The chapter outlines the settings in which recreation is organized, but it does not attempt an expansive treatment of any one. This is done in other literature in the field in a much more comprehensive fashion. The purpose here is to describe these settings and to identify trends, issues, and problems of which the professional person should be aware. The areas covered include the public recreation agency, the school, the voluntary agency, the commercial agency, and other settings such as the church, industry, trade unions, cultural arts organizations, and state and federal governments.

Part Four studies the individual at various stages of growth and life and identifies biological-psychological-social needs that have meaning for leisure and recreation. This chapter should help the reader understand how recreation can contribute to the meeting of basic needs and drives and thus enhance his opportunity for self-fulfillment through leisure experiences. Some needs and drives are individual, but as man also fulfills himself in relationship to others and thus seeks others, so part of this study focuses on relationship needs and the role leisure and recreation can play. It is particularly important for the recreation professional to understand these processes if he is to be successful in helping people to achieve self-fulfillment through organized leisure and recreation.

Part Five reviews recreation as a profession and presents an analysis of its philosophy and present status. An attempt is made to summarize the scientific foundations of its professional method, to define and to delineate the method employed in working with recreation groups and recreation-bent individuals, and to show how this method is related through programs to fulfill major objectives of leisure and recreation services.

Part Six is an attempt to look ahead and identify significant problems, issues, and trends, and to lay down a challenge for the future of the recreation profession and of leisure and recreation.

Key guiding generalizations have been formulated throughout the book. These represent conclusions, descriptive concepts, assumptions, and principles proposed by the authors. For emphasis and to assist the reader they are set in *italics*.

We would like to express our sincere appreciation to a number of our professional colleagues representing several fields of scholarship who have helped us in many ways in the preparation of this manuscript, which deals with knowledge from a range of fields. We especially would like to acknowledge the thoughtful suggestions and criticisms, growing out of conscientious reading of various of our materials, of the following persons: Charles K. Brightbill, Camille Brown, Reynold E. Carlson, Rosalind Cassidy, Donald Clayton, John Ferstead, John L. Hutchinson, Betty Latimer, Alexander Reid Martin, Ross Quillian, Marjorie Robinson, William Schwartz, Robert L. Stanley, and Nelson Wieters.

We also want to thank the members of our family whose love for leisure culture is matched by their sophistication in its cultivation, and who gave up countless hours of family recreation in order that this book might be written.

N. P. M.
D. M. R.

CONTENTS

PART 2
RECREATION IN MODERN AMERICAN LIFE

PART 3
RECREATION AS A SOCIAL INSTITUTION

PART 4
RECREATION AND HUMAN NEEDS

PART 5
RECREATION AS A PROFESSION

Chapter 13
Contributions from Related Disciplines

Chapter 14
Working with People in Recreation

PART 6
THE CHANGING PERSPECTIVES IN LEISURE AND RECREATION

Chapter 15
Trends and Problems

INDEX

PART 1

HISTORY AND PHILOSOPHY OF LEISURE AND RECREATION

1

LEISURE AND RECREATION

Of the evolution of human civilization, one cause is outstanding: that man's hopes and ambitions have led him to struggle for a better life. As Dickens might say, "He has great expectations." Inextricably bound up with the concept of a better life has been the search for leisure. The effect of this search is dramatically portrayed throughout history by the leisure achievements that are held as ideals by historians, philosophers, politicians, sociologists, and the like. The thesis of these scholars is that the quality of any society's leisure activity sets the tone of that society and, in effect, measures the level of its civilization.

The average American today finds himself in what may well be described as the "Age of Leisure." For the first time in history, leisure belongs to the masses and not only to the few. Never have so many men and women had so many hours available for achievement in all realms, from gambling to fine art, nor so many means for that achievement. As *Life* magazine suggests, the opportunities are so unprecedented that the "American civilization ought to be freer and bolder than the Greek, more just and powerful than the Roman, wiser than the Confucian, richer in invention and talent than the Florentine or Elizabethan, more resplendent than the Mongol, prouder than the Spanish, saner than the French, more responsible than the Victorian, and happier than all of them together." [1]

Certainly concern for and interest in the impact of increased free time upon the progress of man—particularly of the American man—is no idle matter. The scores of published articles and books dealing with the problem of leisure emphasize its complexity and its importance in modern society. The elements of American culture that operate to create more and more free time—lengthening life expectancy, earlier retirement, increasing mechanization and automation, shorter work day, rising standard of living, improved communication and transportation—continue to operate at an accelerating pace. As Paul Douglass, the former President of American University, says, "the assimilation of leisure into our ways of living may become as disconcerting in the decades ahead as was the impact of science upon religion and life habits in the first decades of this century." [2]

For the first time in man's history leisure may become more important than work in giving meaning to life. This shift in emphasis gives no evidence of being temporary. The panorama of recreation in action, and the specifics of community planning and economic production for recreation, become more and more apparent as the twentieth century unfolds. Man stands on a threshold in time at which the potential and opportunity for the good life through increased leisure time is unparalleled.

How man has reached this point, what factors have created this issue, what are its salient characteristics, and what man is doing about it, form the basic content of this book. Since one of man's principal uses of leisure time is his recreation, it is only natural that the words

---

[1] Editorial, *Life,* Vol. 47, No. 26 (December 28, 1959), p. 62.

[2] Paul Douglass, "The Administration of Leisure for Living," *Bulletin of the American Recreation Society,* Vol. 12, No. 3 (April 1960), p. 11.

(*leisure* and *recreation*) are identified and linked together as the basic content for this book—not exactly a *new* idea, certainly, since man has played and recreated since earliest days and has used his leisure time for this purpose. But today the factors and forces creating time for leisure place new emphasis upon, and require new understanding of, the role played by recreation in the enrichment and enhancement of man's life and of his civilization.

DEFINITION OF TERMS

At this point it is essential to define a number of important terms, which will occur frequently throughout the following pages, as they will be used in this book. These several terms have been given different interpretations by different writers through the years. Although, perhaps, the following definitions will not survive numerous years of use in an age marked by great change, they are offered as working definitions for this book. Among these definitions are important relationships and common elements of meaning; they are not intended to be mutually exclusive.

The first of these is "free time." Dr. Alexander Reid Martin of the American Psychiatric Association calls it the latest and greatest freedom of all.[3] Huge new amounts of such time are being provided in our highly technological age. This is a quantitative concept, measurable in the number of hours free from necessary work and other survival duties, hours that individuals can expend freely, in a variety of ways. Some writers have added the economic context ("time sold is work, time unsold is free"). Others have used the term "discretionary time." The question of *how* this time is spent is not a question of definition.

Free time: time available to the individual after necessary work and other survival duties are accomplished, to be spent at the discretion of the individual.

The second term is "leisure time." A very simple means of differentiating between this kind of time and free time is to define leisure time as that part of free time devoted to activities undertaken in pursuit of *leisure,* which may, through recreative processes and playful activities, or may *not,* be attained. For leisure itself, as we shall define it in

[3] Alexander Reid Martin, *Urgent Need for a Philosophy of Leisure in an Aging Population,* unpublished manuscript, 1961.

a moment, is not a quantitative thing measured in terms of minutes or hours doing something that you don't have to do, but a qualitative thing, a matter of fulfillment of a human capacity for inner experience. Leisure time simply defines the time spent in pursuit of leisure values, whether or not they are attained.

Leisure time: that portion of available free time devoted to the pursuit of leisure values.

The third concept, "leisure," is to be understood, and its meaning identified, in the *quality* of leisure-time experience; that is, in the nature of the self-fulfilling values achieved by an individual as he uses his leisure time, as he chooses what he does, and attains relaxation from tension, freedom, satisfaction, pleasure, and creativity; and thus recreates himself to the degree that he attains these values. Chapter 5 will include much more analysis of this idea and of its significance in modern times. Let us emphasize at this point that we are concerned with the fulfillment of the capacity of the self for leisure, by means of the condition of leisure. We identify leisure as an inner or subjective experience. In reading citations from other sources throughout the book the reader will soon discover that many writers think of and use "leisure" in a context for which we shall employ the term "leisure time." We will reserve for "leisure" a broader, more meaningful concept, defined as follows:

Leisure: the complex of self-fulfilling and self-enriching values achieved by the individual as he uses leisure time in self-chosen activities that recreate him.

To view recreation from several perspectives reveals some of its dimensions and aspects, but it is necessary to undertake a formal definition, even though some confusion exists among those who have attempted such definition. Sapora and Mitchell list twenty-five different definitions of play and recreation, ranging from what one does, to the attitude with which one engages in activity.[4] The essential confusion is over whether recreation is an objective reality of activities and forms of human relationships, or is a subjective thing of feelings of pleasure and satisfaction. Slavson says, in defining the second view,

---

[4] Allen V. Sapora and Elmer D. Mitchell, *The Theory of Play and Recreation,* Third edition (New York: The Ronald Press Company, 1961), pp. 114-115.

"Recreation does not consist of *what* one does; it is rather the motive, attitude, and value of the doing to the individual that gives an activity a recreational significance."[5] The title of Romney's book, *Off the Job Living,* suggests the objective point of view.[6]

Other writers have undertaken to reconcile the philosophical differences by suggesting that recreation is both a pattern of activities specific to a certain area of life and a set of feelings. Butler undertakes this compromise:

> Expressed in terms of activities, recreation, in the author's opinion, may be considered as any activity which is not consciously performed for the sake of any reward beyond itself, which is usually engaged in during leisure, which offers man an outlet for his physical, mental, or creative powers, and in which he engages because of inner desire and not because of outer compulsion. . . . recreation is *any form of leisure-time experience or activity in which an individual engages from choice because of the enjoyment and satisfaction which it brings directly to him.*[7]

To those who think in scientific terms, one might define recreation as a pattern of culture, a complex of widely diverse, yet traditional and socially recognized, activities undertaken by individuals or groups in their leisure time, and recognized as being engaged in as a means of spending leisure time pleasurably. Persons involved in recreation usually are striving for personal satisfaction; their attitudes reflect and depend upon the objective conditions surrounding and involved in the activities, the leisure-time situation, the degree to which the activities are self-chosen, their creativity, and similar variable factors.

Recreation: the process of engaging in activities during leisure time, with a set of attitudes that makes possible the attainment of leisure values.

The nature of the set of attitudes necessary will be explored in later chapters. We shall explore also the relationship of these attitudes to the psychological process of relaxation from stress, of recreativity and

---

[5] S. R. Slavson, *Recreation and the Total Personality* (New York: The Association Press, 1948), p. 2.

[6] G. Ott Romney, *Off the Job Living* (New York: A. S. Barnes and Company, 1945).

[7] George D. Butler, *Introduction to Community Recreation,* Third edition (New York: McGraw-Hill Book Company, 1959), p. 10.

renewal, recognizing that for many people the values obtained are minimal. Recreation values are, therefore, variable. It is sufficient to say at this point, for the reader's clarification, that we refer to attitudes recognized in the words "fun," "noncompulsory," "happy," "playful."

Since the word "play" is so frequently related to and used in context with "recreation," it is necessary to understand distinctions between the two words in usage. The cultural anthropologist uses the word "play" to mean the pattern of recreational activities found in society—the "play of men." The sociologist thinks of "man playing" and finds the play element in almost all human activities. The psychologist uses it to theorize about a special form of child behavior. Since we will be discussing foundation material and employing terminology from these areas, the words "play" and "recreation" assume similar meanings, particularly in the anthropological and historical sense.

One minor distinction relating to function can be drawn for the purpose of putting "play" in perspective with "leisure" and "recreation" as defined above. In popular parlance, "play" is used to describe the activities of children and "recreation" to describe those of adults. This may represent a cultural bias. Actually the play of children and the recreation of adults can be practically the same thing, only serving different functions. The play of children provides for a somewhat different and more important group of developmental needs, whereas play for adults may function to "re-create" physically, psychologically, or emotionally after the wear and tear of other activities. The concept "recreation" includes more of the idea of leisure values and self-fulfillment goals related to activity—the re-creative, relaxing, creative, renewing and restoring function—than the concept "play" does. "Play," like "playful," carries the meaning of free, happy, joyous, full of fun and natural expression; play is made up of activities and attitudes with these qualities, which have, for the child, developmental significance.

Play: activities engaged in purposely with free, happy, natural attitudes, full of fun and expression.

Throughout this book the terms "recreation," "play," and "leisure" will be used with the above definitions in mind. Because other authors in the field have proposed definitions different from these, and because usage in the field is not standardized, the reader might want to recheck the definitions given to assure himself that he understands our meaning of these words.

Each of the definitions has been presented in terms of its application to the individual and his life. Recreation is also a social phenomenon based upon collective representations of the many individual phenomena. In order to understand the true nature of leisure and recreation, therefore, it will be necessary to examine them from several points of scientific and philosophical vantage, in both their individual and their social contexts. These several points of vantage will, in the chapters following, be the bases for different analyses of recreation. From these examinations the foundation knowledge of leisure and recreation can be outlined. The paragraphs immediately following provide brief summary statements of certain concepts and assumptions that underlie the organization of these chapters. These statements reflect the several different contexts, or systems of relationships, within which recreation may be analyzed. They are offered here only as a working approach, which we hope will be meaningful and useful to the reader.

In Part One, underlying Chapters 1-3, which have to do with the general background, history, and description in modern times of leisure and recreation, are the concepts (1) that leisure and recreation are cultural universals, being found as common elements in the behavior of individuals in all societies, and (2) that recreation is a social function, an integral element invariably present in the social organization necessary to all societies. These two basic concepts are developed further and enhanced by the assumption that leisure and recreation possess basic ethical and aesthetic values. Chapters 4-6, then, have generally to do with the theories and philosophies of leisure and recreation.

The rationale behind the ideas in Part Two is the concept that recreation is a complex of social forces and dynamic social processes interacting with other social forces (Chapters 7-10).

Part Three takes a look at recreation as a social institution (in Chapter 11), and is based on the concept that the institutionalization of recreation has created, in various societies, major systems of organized activities and customs by which men obtain basic common leisure values.

Part Four (Chapter 12) is based on the concept that leisure and recreation are means of self-actualization and of meeting individual needs in realizing that self-actualization.

Part Five (Chapters 13-15) discusses the profession of recreation. It deals with the concept that recreation is a professional field, with a special group of individuals authorized by the society to function officially in the institutionalized segment of recreation, with an emerging science, philosophy, and methodology.

LEISURE AND RECREATION AS CULTURAL UNIVERSALS

Anthropologists contribute an important insight about recreation in its many forms. Although there is no complete evidence that organized, formalized, or institutionalized recreation exists in every society, anthropologists indicate that athletics, sports, dancing, bodily adornment, games, music, folklore, and such are found in some form in every culture known to history and ethnology. These are common elements of universal and basic patterns emerging in response to a set of essential common needs, or *cultural universals.*[8] Anthropologists and psychologists have been engaged in efforts to determine what underlying identities between all peoples are responsible for these universal elements. As Murdock says, efforts to explain these universal culture patterns begin with the assumption "that all peoples now living or of whom we possess substantial historical records, irrespective of differences in geography and physique, are essentially alike in their basic psychological equipment and mechanism, and that the cultural differences between them reflect only the differential responses of essentially similar organisms to unlike stimuli or conditions."[9]

All mankind is presumed to behave as he learns to behave in his culture; that is, he solves his problems of survival, meets his hungers, and resolves his other psychobiological drives and tensions through behavior deeply influenced and determined by the culture of the group of which he is a member. The wide variety of forms in which cultural patterns are found do not deny the fundamental identity of such cultural universals as athletic sports, use of paints and cosmetics on the body, decorative clothing, dancing, decorative art, folklore, games, hair styles, joking, music, mythology, visiting, and

---

[8] George P. Murdock and others, *Outline of Cultural Materials,* Yale Anthropological Studies, Volume 2, Second edition (New Haven, Conn.: Yale University Press, 1945).

[9] George P. Murdock, "The Common Denominator of Cultures" in *The Science of Man in the World Crisis,* ed. Ralph Linton (New York: Columbia University Press, 1945), p. 126.

others. Anthropologists have undertaken to explain the functional association between the peculiar forms in which these customs are found and the social factors, forces, and conditions that influence these variations.

Recreation—not in its formal and organized, but in its informal and often casual, forms—is found among all peoples, meeting deeply fundamental needs, and satisfying basic interests and human demands.

RECREATION AS A SOCIAL FUNCTION

Like government or public education, recreation can be identified as an important form of social organization. However, recreation is broader than institutional forms, and broader yet than that vast complex with which the recreation profession is concerned. George Hjelte, one of the leading recreation authorities in America, has said, "Recreation finds its definition in the vast collection of activities which are voluntarily engaged in by all the people, young and old, rich and poor, urban and rural, cultured and uneducated. It comprises activities in all the fields of individual and group expression from the simplest and most natural to the artificial and most complicated forms of human experience." [10] In this sense recreation becomes an important part of the life of every person throughout his entire lifetime. Not only in its institutional forms, its organized governmental and agency functions, its commercial and industrial and informal organization manifestations, but also in the informal, personal, intimate pleasures of the family and of the individual gaining respite, release, and relaxation from study and toil, in both casual and intensive forms, is recreation a part of everyone's life.

A social function might be defined simply as any activity that is an integral part of the life of any society and one that is invariably present in social relationships and organizations. Recreation meets these criteria. It is an integral part of the life of every known society. The forms vary widely according to the rigors of the life of the people, the resources of leisure time, and the cultural traditions of

---

[10] George Hjelte, "Recreation" in *Developing Democratic Human Relations,* Yearbook of the American Association for Health, Physical Education, and Recreation, a Department of the National Education Association (Washington, D.C.: The Association, 1951), p. 90.

the particular society. But in some form recreation will be found. In modern American society recreation is found as a function of government and of other agencies serving the common welfare. A huge amusement industry catering to leisure-time interests of the population indicates the importance of this particular function.

Later on we shall study in more detail how the recreation of a people will reflect basic patterns of group life. But ponder for a moment how modern mass production of amusement for a mass audience, advertised and promoted as a big business, characterizes to some degree the picture in the United States where big industry, big cities, big auditoriums and stadiums, big movies, and so forth, are so common. And try to understand what the great baseball and football games, with their frantically cheering and booing and debris-throwing audiences, reflect in the culture of our country and in our customs of emotional expression. The Neumeyers point out in their pioneering sociological treatise on leisure and recreation that the British people are known for their great interest in sports and for their emphasis on sportsmanship and fair play. This attitude has been compared to the boisterous and seemingly sadistic behavior of sports crowds in the United States by students of this subject.[11]

In any event, the folk dances of many countries, the pleasures of recreation arising out of the indigenous resources of an area, and the large patterns as well as the more intimate patterns of leisure-time enjoyment, help to make clear the importance which recreation has as a basic part of the functioning of all societies, and the way in which people meet their particular needs for recreation in ways peculiar to themselves and influenced by other aspects of their lives. Meyer and Brightbill describe this in pointing out that "At every turn one sees clearly the growing importance of recreation as a fundamental element in life of the people of this nation. The vast host of Americans who play, who travel, who participate in sports, who enjoy athletic, musical, and dramatic spectacles, who seek the out-of-doors, who find expression in the arts and crafts, and who read for the joy of it—these Americans symbolize an era of recreation." [12]

---

[11] Martin H. Neumeyer and Esther S. Neumeyer, *Leisure and Recreation: A Study of Leisure and Recreation in Their Sociological Aspects,* Third edition (New York: The Ronald Press Company, 1958), pp. 100-105.

[12] Harold D. Meyer and Charles K. Brightbill, *Community Recreation: A Guide to Its Organization* (Englewood Cliffs, N.J.: Prentice-Hall, Inc., 1956), p. 38.

Focusing on the physical, psychological, and social characteristics of the human individual, we recognize that recreation is an important means of meeting some of his self-actualizing needs. For the wholesome development of the child, and for the maintenance of the well-being of the adult, recreation has almost boundless resources of which only a portion are being used. Special values of recreation lie in the powerful motivation of all human beings to play. With a foundation of skills and interests in recreational activities, individuals and groups, often with help and guidance from a qualified professional person, can satisfy many of their social and individual needs. The question will be considered of how, at different points in individuals' lives, their good health and well-being—physical, mental, aesthetic, and social—may best be furthered by thoughtfully designed individual and group activities and relationships. This particular exploration is attracting more and more conscientious educators and recreation researchers who sense the superb values of recreation to the individual, and the unique opportunity afforded in the intrinsic interests and motivations of play.

RECREATION AND AESTHETIC VALUES

Only in modern times has there been the thought that in the pursuit of happiness all men equally might share in the deep pleasures and satisfactions of aesthetic experiences. Aesthetics in earlier days was for the select few who perhaps "understood" the arts, and who could afford to be their patrons. Of course, a concept of aesthetics which equated it with the fine arts would be too narrow, for in much of nature, in the simple creativity of the craftsman or the folk group, or in many forms of human relations at their finest, one finds beauty. Aesthetics is concerned with the nature and quality of beauty in man's life.

Much of recreation is a search for beauty, the creative use of oneself and working materials, or the pleasure of contemplating the results of creative activities by others. Joseph Lee is credited with stating, among the *Nineteen Recreation Principles,* the following: "Every man should be helped to learn how to make something of beauty in line, form, color, sound, or graceful use of his own body. At least he should find pleasure in what others do in painting, woodworking, sculpture, photography, if he cannot himself use these forms of expression." [13] These forms of creative artistic expression, along with reading, music, social relationships, and many others, constitute a source of profound satisfaction for almost all persons, although within a wide range of variability. They meet what apparently are deeply seated needs of the human being. The pursuit of happiness must be understood as the pursuit of beauty in as many aspects of life as possible, in elegant mathematical solutions as well as in the arts, in contemplation, in play, and so on. Thus aesthetics is concerned with the nature of all human existence, with the infusion of beauty into every phase of life.

Recreation, more than most of man's daily activities, is immediately directed toward pleasurable feeling, happiness, joy of living. One may view leisure time as the major opportunity and recreation as the major means that most men possess to express themselves creatively, to exercise artistic skills and pursue cultural interests as they please. Such a view assumes that aesthetic values are the prime objectives of life itself. Mechanical and automated aspects of life frustrate many men's sharing of these values and deny to many persons the opportunity to develop the skills to implement adequately their creative interests. One may judge the level of civilization by the criterion, among others, of the opportunity afforded all groups and individuals in the population to enjoy aesthetic pleasures—and by the use these individuals make of this opportunity. In our own country we must view very critically our resources for creative recreation when we contrast them with the influences that debase or vulgarize the tastes of the people. Recreational and cultural workers, on aesthetic grounds, must strive to increase the opportunity for all members of our society to enjoy a rich cultural life.

RECREATION AND ITS SOCIAL FORCES

Sociologically defined, a "social force" is a movement, a situation-in-change, a consciously conceived, planned, and organized, or perhaps an unwilled, common social effort or dynamic social process,

---

[13] Joseph Lee, *Nineteen Recreation Principles,* The National Recreation Association, New York (published in several different forms during recent years).

which influences broader areas of social relationships and social change. Sociological analysis would discover the existence of social forces in the operation of social institutions and the motivations of individuals who together strive for satisfaction of their common needs and organize for that purpose. Social movements might create social forces as they develop action to solve problems or meet needs.

We shall consider that recreation creates such social forces particularly as institutionalized recreation develops and interacts with the social forces represented by institutionalized organizations such as business, government, or religion. We shall examine also the impact on recreation of the operation of other fundamental forces such as population and technological change, the forces represented in physical and geographical conditions and changes.

There is the philosophical view, based upon some consideration of the values in recreation, that recreational forces operate in response to human needs and operate as forces for well-being. Meyer and Brightbill believe that recreation is not only a fundamental element in the life of the people in this nation, but also "a major force in social well-being. Recreation takes its place . . . as an essential process molding individual personality and creating abundant community living . . . [contributing to] the design of the good life." [14]

In the final analysis recreation must contribute to, rather than take away from, the total social welfare. Those disturbed by the apparent threat that debasing and vicious uses of leisure time pose for social good might disagree with the argument that recreation creates, largely, forces for social good. Even those who believe in recreation as a positive force in the lives of many people must take cognizance of the development of cheap and passive entertainments and amusements and other recreations with questionable or clearly negative values to the individual. However, modern leisure and recreation may be assumed to have a potential as a force for social well-being, and this assumption must be examined systematically.

RECREATION AS A SOCIAL INSTITUTION

Recreation can be viewed, in some of its organized parts, as a major institutionalized culture complex, as one of the great systems

---

[14] Meyer and Brightbill, *Community Recreation,* p. 37.

of activities and customs into which some of social life is organized and by which men seek to meet some basic common needs. Social institutions have been defined by social scientists as systems of activities carried on by members of a society, often helped by designated groups of special people, operating under a set of historical and custom-supported sanctions, within a framework of social values and group mores. These values and mores define not only the persons who shall carry on the institutional functions but the rules, rituals, and standards governing their work. Often elaborate material apparatus, physical equipment, and the like, are required. As Helen Witmer says, "Institutions have four main elements: activities, personnel, a charter and norms, and a material apparatus, all of which are organized and systematized for the fulfilling of some social function." [15]

Recreation can be found to have these institutional characteristics. There are many organized recreational activities ranging from the programs of the municipal and school agencies to those of the many voluntary agencies of local and national sponsorship. There are the activities of industrial establishments; the great commercial recreation ventures; the highly popular mass media of radio, movies, and television; the state, regional, and nationally sponsored activities for tourists, sportsmen and outdoor enthusiasts. These make up part of the cluster of related activities by which the institutionalization of some parts of the recreational culture patterns may be identified.

The "specifically designated persons" responsible for carrying on institutionalized functions are found in the growing recreation profession. Their several national professional organizations and agencies, such as the American Recreation Society, the American Camping Association, the American Association for Health, Physical Education and Recreation, and the National Recreation Association, among others, are developing the beginnings of professional standards and encouraging the growth of a new profession.[16]

The third aspect Witmer mentions, an institution's fundamental structure of social sanctions, legal foundations, standards and sup-

---

[15] Helen L. Witmer, *Social Work: An Analysis of a Social Institution* (New York: Farrar and Rinehart, Inc., 1942), p. 19.

[16] For a complete and descriptive listing of professional organizations and agencies related to recreation, see Downey, Davis, McCann, and Stitt, *Exploring Physical Education* (Belmont, Calif.: Wadsworth Publishing Company, Inc., 1962), Chapter 11.

porting mores, are found in the widespread establishment of governmental bodies to administer programs, the growing significance of the leisure time educational and adult-educational-recreational function of the public schools, the existence of great national youth-serving and "character-building" organizations built around guided recreational activities, and the huge industry built around commercial recreational activities.

The final element, the material apparatus, is identified in the great systems of playgrounds, community centers, neighborhood settlements, state and national parks, commercial recreation establishments, and the play facilities which are found in most communities as the tangible evidence of the place of recreation in the lives of all the people.

An independent test of the assumption that recreation has these basic social institutional characteristics can be made by applying a criterion from social anthropology. Anthropologists have studied the great variety of customs and culture patterns that are found in various societies, both ancient and contemporary, with the purpose of understanding the ways in which these cultures are alike and different. They have studied the wide range of forms through which people express their lives together and the manner in which the customs of any society function in the lives of the individuals who make up that society.

Anthropologists believe that institutionalization of cultural patterns found in all societies have a common base: the need of major or dominant groups in the societies to work out means of satisfying their basic needs or interests. These institutional patterns will vary, but their basic purposes will be much alike for several societies. They might not be equally significant and useful to all groups in a society, but recreation appears to be an institutional means through which most members of human societies have always undertaken, in varying ways, to meet some of their needs. There is a wide range of forms through which people express their recreational interests, and these forms may become associated with the religion, the economic activities, and other institutional forms. But recreation seems to have an independent identity as the source of satisfaction of basic pleasure motives, creative and aesthetic interests, and need for self-expression.

Anthropological study thus suggests that recreation has many institutionalized forms, found in all societies, organized in different patterns, but basic to the lives of the people and a source of deep common interests of mankind.

RECREATION AS A PROFESSION

Recreation can be viewed as a profession. In the institutional system of any society, and the American society of our day as well, certain groups of individuals in these institutional systems are given the special responsibility of providing needed services requiring a high degree of technical training and knowledge and a developed sense of social responsibility. A profession has as its prime object the service it can render to the society. Often the area of professional service is regulated, and the standards and practices limited and protected by legal controls. But generally the professional groups are active in developing their own codes of professional ethics, standards of professional practice, programs of professional education, and areas of professional function.

The profession would define the responsibilities of the practitioner to the client, to other professional persons in their own and other professions, and to the public in general. For example, in the medical profession, relations with the patients cover matters of diagnosis, obligations to answer calls, and willingness to care for the indigent sick without fees. The relations with other members of the profession deal with consultation practices, fee-splitting, criticism of each other, sharing of new medical discoveries and important improvements, carrying on of health education programs, and so on. Relations with the public deal with such matters as advertising, personal conduct, and the confidentiality of professional relations.

Some professions—like the medical and legal—have a history of organization going back several centuries. Other professions—like engineering and teaching—have a long but not as ancient a lineage. Then there are relatively young professions such as that of social work, and others related to the modern social welfare institution.

In several professions that have grown up in relatively modern times the practitioners are concerned with working with individuals and groups, utilizing processes that involve giving help in personal growth and affecting more adequate adjustment with the social environment. These professions, building their professional method primarily upon the knowledge and use of human relationships and helping skills, have been identified together as a family of *helping professions*. Recreation is beginning to take its place as one of these helping professions.

As a profession, recreation has the basic purpose of helping individuals and groups to make the most constructive and wholesome use of their leisure time in creative, pleasurable, and satisfying play activities and relationships. To this end the professional recreation workers make use of a specific and growing fund of knowledge about individuals' needs for leisure-time pleasure, and of a set of skills in helping individuals to get the maximum values out of their recreational activities and their relationships with others engaged in these activities. Through sensitive and proficient use of his activity and relationship skills, the recreation worker contributes worthwhile values to the persons and groups with whom he works, and thus to human welfare itself.

Writers in the recreation field have used several titles to describe the person working in recreation. The term *recreation leader* was used for many years to describe the persons working with recreation groups. The word *recreationist* was coined and used for a time. Lately, the word *recreator* has been experimented with by some in the field. The *recreation administrator,* the *recreation specialist* and the *recreation therapist* have become identifiable persons and subgroups functioning within the growing profession. But a term to identify adequately the generic professional worker has not gained broad acceptance in the field to this date. For the purpose of this book, to describe the generic professional worker, the member of the profession, or the worker with professional aspirations and identifications, we shall use the term *recreation worker*. This, hopefully, will provide an image of the professional practitioners who make up the core group of the profession. To this core group may be added the many practitioners who are not yet fully equipped by education and professional training to function fully professionally but who identify with the profession, strive to fulfill their ethical and their other obligations professionally, and strive to increase their professional knowledge and skill as a means of perfecting their method and attaining authentic status as members of the profession.

THE STATUS OF RECREATION PHILOSOPHY

The foregoing paragraphs have been directed toward providing the reader with a set of definitions and reference points as tools to use in examining the foundations, and in developing a philosophy of leisure and recreation. The modern recreation field has produced few philosophers to speak for it. As a field grows and develops its philosophy grows and develops with it. But in recent years the great strides recreation has made have not been matched by the development of philosophies or interpretations of recreation that reflect man's growing scientific knowledge. There is need for philosophical writings that will continue to integrate the scientific knowledge bearing on the recreation field, the concepts of social ethics and modern aesthetics, and the facts concerning modern recreation in relation to individuals, their needs and their potentials, in our present day. The chapters that follow are an attempt to synthesize simply some considerable historical and scientific knowledge about recreation and some modern philosophical insights into man, his nature and his needs, and to focus this knowledge upon this important field of man's welfare. We will deal briefly with recreation's history and with several important philosophical questions in the field, and will analyze briefly several contributions to the growing body of knowledge about recreation. We will examine some theories of play, several interpretations of modern leisure and its relation to recreation, some speculations on recreation and a balanced life, and formulate a philosophy of leisure and recreation for the student.

Questions for Study and Discussion

1. *How do the definitions stated by the authors compare with those of other writers? What differences exist among the various definitions? Do you agree or disagree with the authors? With the other writers? Why?*
2. *Is there a recreation profession? Explain.*
3. *What are cultural universals? How would you justify considering leisure and recreation as cultural universals?*
4. *What is your own philosophy of recreation?*
5. *What part of recreation would you define as institutionalized recreation?*

Selected Readings

Meyer, Harold D., and Charles K. Brightbill, *Community Recreation: A Guide to Its Organization* (Englewood Cliffs, N.J.: Prentice-Hall, Inc., 1956).

Neumeyer, Martin H., and Esther S. Neumeyer, *Leisure and Recreation: A Study of Leisure and Recreation in Their Sociological Aspects,* Third edition (New York: The Ronald Press Company, 1958).

Slavson, S. R., *Recreation and the Total Personality* (New York: The Association Press, 1948).

Witmer, Helen L., *Social Work: An Analysis of a Social Institution* (New York: Farrar and Rinehart, Inc., 1942).

2

A LOOK AT THE HISTORY OF LEISURE AND RECREATION

It is our present task to undertake a brief review of the history of recreation from its earliest appearance in the life of man up to modern times. We will find out about the recreational life of men at different eras in man's history. We will learn with what basic point of view or philosophy they undertook to explain the meaning and significance of play in man's life. We will strive to carry out at the same time study of the life that went on in different historical periods, in order to discover the foundations and developments of modern philosophies of play. In this way it may be possible to bring meaning to earlier philosophies, which necessarily have to be understood in terms of the conditions confronting man, the environmental situation in which he existed, at the time particular philosophies came into being.

RECREATION IN PRELITERATE SOCIETIES

The person who undertakes to search for the historic origins of play, if he searches diligently, may find a wealth of data showing that *play has always been an integral part of man's life*. As we saw in Chapter 1, scientists have discovered that as far back as we can trace the existence of groups of men we can find evidences that individuals and groups took time for and engaged in play activities. Many of these activities were closely related to the survival activities of food-getting and many were related to religious worship, which also seems to have existed universally among early peoples.

Archeologists have uncovered and carefully examined the material artifacts that belonged to the earliest known groups of human beings. These artifacts tell us something about the way these groups lived. Thousands of years ago, the evidence tells us, early man lived in caves in the hillside, in rough tree houses, or on platforms built upon stilts over the waters. The evidence tells us also that he made efforts to bring beauty and fun into his life when he had a few moments for pleasure. Carved miniature weapons and other toys for children, delicate workmanship of hand axes, paintings or engravings upon the walls of caves, and adornment of clothing, tools, and weapons, attest to early efforts at creative artistic expression. The skillfully executed paintings and drawings found upon the walls of the Aurignacian caves in southern France point back twenty thousand years to early primitive people who, we think, made strong hunting magic and told stories by means of these pictures. Excavations in Europe, Africa, and Asia uncovered similar remains of groups who lived perhaps as long ago as a quarter of a million years, and whose simple stone and bone implements show artistic beauty in workmanship and design.

The anthropologists, in their explorations of the cultures of these early peoples, may have discovered the reasons behind the remarkable likenesses, and sometimes the apparently unexplainable variety, in the customs of different societies.

It is recognized that in all early societies there had to be solved the primary problems of providing food, shelter, and clothing. Depending upon whether climate and other natural conditions were favorable or not, the pursuit of food varied from a sharp struggle for mere survival, such as that among the Eskimos and the Zuñi Indians, to the comparatively easy acquisition of food by such groups as the Samoan Islanders. But, even for the most primitive man, there was leisure time, and it was during this time that he played and created the objects by which we know him. Thus, from earliest beginnings, man's leisure, recreation, and play have been integrated with the arts and creative expression.

Religion and Art

In addition to providing for basic needs, primitive societies paid much attention to what we now call religion. We find in most societies a great concern for a proper relationship to the spirits and deities so that either their generous and loving protection would be continued or their punishments and displeasure would be averted. The recreation and the religion of these societies were almost always closely intertwined. There was much reverence for spiritual forms in the play, the festivals, the dances and pageants and songs, the stories and poetry, with which men amused themselves and enjoyed social relationships. And, like religion, the play of the groups took on the same forms as the rest of their pattern of life. Thus the children of cooperative societies might be found enjoying the imitative and group games with little or no competition in them, while the adults would join together in collective sports and games and festivities whose social features far outweighed the competitive ones.

In the competitive or individualistic societies the pattern is found often to be much different, stressing competitive struggles and showing some of the attitudes characteristic of modern athletic programs. We can find examples of such in both ancient and modern primitive societies. Some Eskimos have a singing competition called a *drum match*, which is described by Mirsky as their chief pastime.[1] Two persons may for several years come together on occasion before an audience of village members and sing songs taunting and deriding and insulting each other, the songs accompanied by insulting gestures and even physical combat.

> For each new meeting the parties prepare and practice new songs, in which the crimes are vastly exaggerated, or, if they

[1] See Jeannette Mirsky, "The Eskimo of Greenland" in *Cooperation and Competition Among Primitive Peoples,* ed. Margaret Mead (New York: McGraw-Hill Book Company, 1937), pp. 63-69.

> can find no new material that is suitable, they may father new crimes on their opponents or reproach them for deeds which may have been merely intended but never committed. . . . The opponents stand facing one another. They sing one at a time while the other party stands quietly and listens. The singer mocks the other in a number of ways. . . . Drum songs start out in a competitive mood, each competitor striving to gain a definite point, to swing the opinion of the onlookers to his side. But from this competitive start the drum matches . . . [may] degenerate into a cooperative act in which the two principals and the onlookers all enjoy the "show." [2]

The forms play took were functionally closely related to the rest of life in primitive societies. There was infinite variety in the games and sports and creative activities found through studies of primitive peoples. Woody points out that in most cultures, whether life was easy or hard, great pains were taken in the manufacture of tools, toys, and totems: "The bow and arrow, spear, boat, snowshoes, all of which serve the chase; the ball-club, snow snake, ring-and-pin, and other implements used in sports; the trinkets for adornment; . . . all these reveal man, the lover of activity and creation, impelled by necessity, yet often inspired with an aesthetic sense which produced a beautiful industrial art." [3] The extremely beautiful, complex, and difficult painting, design, and ornamentation found in many cultures testifies to the significance of this form of "play," for play is what it is.

The skillful artists of scores of thousands of years ago were refining the shapes and proportions of flint knives and spearheads, decorating them, possibly with lines representing the animals they were supposed to strike down. Stone, ivory, and horn objects were engraved delicately. Using paints made from natural materials, the artist decorated skins and cave walls with both naturalistic and highly stylized and vigorous paintings. Truly, the artist of today has a heritage as old as man.

Dance, Storytelling, and Games

The same creativity, as well as often the most painstaking copying of old art or activity forms and rituals, is found in the almost

---

[2] Mirsky, pp. 68-70.

[3] Thomas Woody, *Life and Education in Early Societies* (New York: The Macmillan Company, 1949), p. 12.

universal religious and recreational customs of dancing. Modern students of the arts recognize that American Indian dances and ceremonies are one of the great forms of art produced on this continent, an art telling its story in the beautiful medium of the human body. Grace in the movement and gestures of the limbs and head and the rest of the body expressed mood and emotion, and told a story with vividness and imagination. The dances and the tales they told so rhythmically and poetically were passed on from generation to generation, the oldest and wisest members of the tribe often watching over the purity of the tale so retelling would not vary, vulgarize, or tarnish it.

The dances were ceremonies rich with religious meaning, a communication with the gods, prayers in pageantry, not so often created by the individual to express himself but concerning the tribe and executed with careful and serious attention to tradition and ritual requirement. The audience was closely involved as the story, prayer, or supplication was delivered because it might affect them all. Thus war dances, hunting, planting and harvest dances, courtship dances and love rites, rain dances, birth and death dances, puberty and initiation rites, and the like, were important in the lives of primitive groups, indicating the deep and common satisfaction human beings derive from rhythmic bodily expression, and the use to which this form of expression is put in primitive religious and recreational life. Musical instruments were invented to make noise and accentuate the rhythm, expressing by these means and in song the powerful emotions that the dances also helped to express.

Meeting some of the same needs is the wide range of games found in such communities. There are recorded literally thousands of kinds of games different groups invented to entertain themselves. Many of these involved athletic skill or dexterity, and included a broad range of ball games, races, contests of strength, skill, poise, or stamina in wielding weapons or in swimming, riding, running, archery, and so on. Many were individual competitions and contests, or just social games in which no winner was sought. Then there were a multitude of larger group activities ranging from the most informal and simple to those of a very complex nature. The famous lacrosse game played by the Choctaw Indians sometimes lasted a whole day or longer and involved up to a thousand young men. The game was preceded by numerous intensive challenges which were sent throughout the participating tribes, by gambling between members in which practically all things of any use were bet on the outcome, and by night-long dancing and singing. The game itself would last many hours, until one hundred points were scored by one side, whereupon all bets would be collected and the party would end in merrymaking.[4]

Storytelling, closely related to singing and dancing, is found in abundance, both as a form of recreation and as an educational process whereby children are informed of the folklore and traditions of the group. In many societies, courtship and wooing take on the character of games. The game of love, often a serious and beautiful affair, usually is an attractive pursuit of all age groups, but perhaps especially of those in the marriageable years. Such games are enriched with giving of gifts, with songs, music, tales of great feeling, devotion and romance, and a wide range of physical expression, depending upon the sexual customs of the group.

Among many modern literate and nonliterate groups there are still celebrated some of the festivals whose origins, apparently, were in the centuries of primitive life when agriculture and hunting were relied upon for food. These societies, for endless centuries, have celebrated the end of winter, the coming of spring and the time of planting, and the harvest time, with suitable rituals. In the spring, the demons of darkness and gloom are frightened away with fires and shouting, and the lengthening days are welcomed. In the fall, the harvest is celebrated with rural feastings and dancing, killing and eating the animals or fowls, which then are in their prime, and having the last fling before the harsh winter closes in.[5]

Woody gives us a basis for examining these data about primitive peoples in relation to their significance in understanding the role of play in human societies. He points out his belief that certain fundamental general tendencies or needs in man constitute always the basis for his activities and for the organization of his society. Let us relate his six central tendencies to patterns of play we have identified.

1. Tendencies to satisfy hunger.	1. Games, dances, songs and stories, feasting ceremonies and rituals, etc., connected with hunting, fishing, and agriculture.

[4] Described in George Catlin, *Letter and Notes on the Manners, Customs, and Conditions of the North American Indians,* two volumes (London: The Author, 1841).

[5] For detailed materials on festivals see Dorothy G. Spicer, *The Book of Festivals* (New York: The Woman's Press, 1937).

2. Drives that minister to self-preservation when opposed or pursued by foes.	2. Manifold activities of the same nature connected with war, combat, and peace.
3. Drives operational in mating and propagation.	3. Many of the same, especially dances connected with courtship, wooing, marriage and mating, conception, and childbirth.
4. The bent toward a degree of random and satisfying manipulation of brain and brawn.	4. The vast range of creative and artistic pursuits using graphic materials or using music, dance, and storytelling forms and all of the above.
5. An inclination to fear the strange, the untried, the unknown.	5. The same kinds of activities directed toward religious ends.
6. A preference for gregarious behavior.	6. The whole gamut of play activities become significant as they are seen as part of man's fundamentally social nature, for it was in groups for the most part that these were carried on.

Woody points out that each of these tendencies and patterns is completely involved in intricate interrelations with the others.

This brief analysis helps to explain why play, as a social institution, has existed from the earliest days of mankind. The nature of man's play activities is related to the group's particular response to the environment and to the particular process of the group's development of culture and social structuring. These activities vary widely and indicate the interacting influence of powerful and diverse forces in the society. But they seem still to have a number of basic elements in common which it will be good to identify further as we proceed to examine later eras in man's history.

In primitive societies of both ancient and modern times, individual and social play behavior has been an integral element in the life of individuals and has reflected the unique customs and culture of each society.

LEISURE OF ANCIENT CIVILIZATIONS

Archeologists studying early civilizations uncovered traces of another phenomenon of utmost significance: written language. The invention of writing, probably growing out of the need to keep records in the expanding economic life, marked the change from preliterate to literate societies. Some scientists have tried to classify societies as "civilized" or "primitive" according to the presence or absence of written communication, although there are difficulties connected with the use of such categories. With the emergence of written language, it became possible for men to keep records that are of great value today. Historians usually have to begin their studies with the literate societies, because this important tool of communication—written language—permitted groups to record the data of their existence, and permitted later scholars to gain insights into the lives of these early societies, insights far surpassing those to be gained from other material artifacts.

The Class System

More basic to the emergence of what we like to call "civilization," however, than the growth of written language, was the gradual development of agricultural pursuits so that societies could give up hunting and fishing as the key source of food and rely upon domestically cultivated plants and the breeding of domesticated animals for the major food supply. Fixed villages and cities could grow up. As the land-tillers developed productive skills sufficient to create a surplus of food, as they learned to fertilize and manure, to plow, to sow and irrigate, and to harvest and store, then production increased. This meant that some members of the group could readily live on the surplus created, and devote full time to producing magic, making tools, making war, or enjoying themselves. There developed in most societies, in addition to the peasants, other social classes: the craftsmen, the priests, the warriors, and the nobles. Such an economic order, along with the class system, political system, and social relations based upon it, was found four to six thousand years ago in Egypt, Babylonia, Assyria, India, China, and other countries.

Woody points out that this functional stratification of society into classes resulted in the priests and the military rulers occupying the favored places: "Next to the wise men in importance were the strong men, the king (sometimes also priest) and his soldiers, who trained themselves to do his bidding. Supporting the spiritual and physical rulers was a basic class of workers—agriculturalists, herdsmen, artisans."[6] Childe says, "The surplus produced by the new economy was, in fact, concentrated in the hands of a relatively small class."[7] The rulers of these societies took for themselves a large share of the wealth produced. They perpetuated themselves in power by claiming to be related to the gods. By the swords of their soldiers, and with the cooperation of the priests, they held the commoners in a form of semi-slavery while they ruthlessly exploited them.

Woody quotes words first written thousands of years ago and translated by the modern scholar, Maspero. These words describe the Egyptian lower classes:

> Egyptian toilers appear to have been made of resilient stuff; though they labored hard, they sang at their work and feasted and drank at payday. But though spirits were brave, bodies were calloused, broken, bent, and diseased by inhuman labor, from which there was seldom any relaxation. The dolorous lot of artisans is pictured darkly by an ancient scribe: the smith's hands, "rugged as the crocodile"; the weaver "squatting, his knees against his chest"; the mason, his arms "worn out with work," since "he has no other bread than his fingers"; the dyer, "his fingers reeking, his eyes weary, his hand never at rest"; . . . In the country it is no better. The peasant works hard for others first, and himself when he can . . . "Worms have destroyed half of the crop; hippopotami have eaten the rest; there are swarms of rats in the fields, the grasshoppers alight there, the cattle devour, the little birds pilfer . . . [then the tax collectors come] crying: 'Come now, corn!' There is none, and they throw the cultivator full length upon the ground; bound, dragged to the canal, they fling him in head first; his wife is bound with him, his children are put into chains; the neighbors in the meantime, leave him and fly to save their grain."[8]

---

[6] Woody, *Life and Education in Early Societies,* p. 5.

[7] Gordon Childe, *What Happened in History* (New York: Penguin Books, Inc., 1941), p. 92.

[8] Woody, *Life and Education in Early Societies,* pp. 51-52, quoting as his source G. Maspero, *The Dawn of Civilization: Egypt and Chaldaea* (London: The Society for Promoting Christian Knowledge, 1901).

The Leisure Class

Before examining the play and the amusements of the commoners of these ancient times, let us look briefly at the pattern of life for the upper, leisure classes. Veblen has contributed a keen analysis of the use of leisure by these ancient aristocracies of wealth and power.[9] In these societies, said Veblen, the ruling class used its power to exploit the peasants and artisans, to drive them to ceaseless toil and to expropriate from them a large portion of the fruits of their toil. Then the rulers proceeded to an assiduous cultivation of the arts of leisure, along with a vast culture representing their effort to show off their wealth in the most ostentatious manner possible, in a manner to invite invidious comparison from their peers. There was an active cultivation and patronizing of the arts of painting, sculpture, music, the sciences, each of value to the degree that it clearly demonstrated the leisurely status of the patron.

Veblen argued that these were perversions of the basic "instinct of workmanship," which he believed motivated every normal person to create beauty of form and soundness of function in all that he did. This ostentatious display and conspicuous consumption of wealth, and the perverted use of leisure, was castigated by him as a basic impiety, a form of social perversion, and a vulgarity to be avoided by civilized peoples.

There are many evidences of the validity of Veblen's analysis. The construction of the pyramids and temples in Egypt and Babylonia at a fabulous cost in lives and labor was a means of glorifying the great kings and contributing to their status. In the cultural field, the nobles paid for the services of multitudes of musicians, singers, and dancers. Weaving of tapestries and cloth, painting, sculpturing, pottery, metal filigree work, and similar arts, were arts carried on for the nobility, to add to his display and thus to his glory.

In China in the earlier centuries the rulers and scholars were the leisured ones, and status was associated with classical scholarship. The well-known custom of Chinese scholars of growing fingernails to an astonishing length was as convincing as anything could be that their life was one of intellectual excellence, of contemplation, totally divorced from use of the hands for work.

---

[9] Thorstein Veblen, *Theory of the Leisure Class* (New York: The Macmillan Company, 1899).

We find many of the nobles and soldiers hunting, riding, contesting in sports, pursuing the arts of music, painting, and the dance, largely as patrons. Provision of lavish banquets and parties, and the entertainment of guests with professional musicians and dancers, was a favorite pastime of the wealthy. The house of the aristocrat "was equipped with well-designed furniture and utensils of wood, ivory, glazed pottery, metal, and many kinds and colors of stone; his costume was of linen with abundant jewelry . . . limestone and sandstone from the Nile cliffs and granite from the great dikes at the cataracts; alabaster and the hard diorite, porphyry and breccias, valuable for the color, texture, and striation, from the nearby deserts; abundant gold from Numidia; copper from Sinai.[10] All of these were made into things of beauty by the slave craftsmen for the pleasure of the royalty and the nobility. The palaces were things of beauty. Furniture was superbly designed and skillfully constructed. Beautiful terraces and luxuriant gardens filled with exotic plants testified to the artistic skill of landscape artists and gardeners.

In China, Confucius favored the serious use of music, and great study was made by scholars of music and instrumentation. It is said that the founding of bells was brought to Europe from China. And the Chinese nobility enjoyed literature, poetry, and the active pleasures of hunting, dueling, combat sports, and games, as well as gambling. In India and other early societies the ruling classes also developed parallel leisure-time arts while "standing on the backs of the commoners."

The Common Folk

What did the common folk do for fun in these ages? One important fact we find is that the common folk could *not* be deprived of some time and resources for leisure, despite their burden of work for the leisure class. Many societies enjoyed many days during the year that were, by public policy, proclaimed as days of rest and play. Often these were scheduled in relation to religious or traditional festival days. Burns says,

> In ancient Egypt, it seems, holidays amounted to one fifth of the year; in ancient Athens there were fifty to sixty days of festival in the year; and in Tarentum in the days of its pros-

[10] Helen Gardner, *Art Through the Ages* (New York: Harcourt, Brace & World, 1936), p. 20.

perity there were more holidays than working days. In ancient Rome about one third of the days of the year were *nefasti,* unlucky for work, and in the later Empire, the "games" and other festivals were largely extended.[11]

The big public festivals in Egypt attracted thousands of persons who assembled with pipes and castanets, coming in boats and landing to dance, sing, and celebrate. Dancing was without restraint, often took on licentious and extravagant themes, with buffoonery and ludicrous stunts and great gaiety. There were many of these during the year, and in addition, there was much fishing and hunting for small game, mainly for supplementary food but also for sport. They also had feasts, sports contests such as jousting, ball games, and feats of strength and skill. Children played with toy dolls, ducks, boats, balls, marbles, tops and all the paraphernalia of active games. These might be very elaborate for those with money and very simple for those without. But children, as always, had toys.

We do not have in the literature of these ancient societies much that refers specifically to recreation and play. When the ancient empires gradually declined, giving way to those of Greece and Rome and then, centuries later, to western European dominance, their economic life changed; it became dominated more by feudalistic agricultural and pastoral pursuits, and the nobles and leisurely upper classes, naturally, shared in the depression. The arts and sciences lost some of their vigor. In reconstructing what we might guess was a philosophy of recreation that typified these civilizations, we have to rely upon the best estimates of later writers.

Veblen provides one of the best analyses of the ideologies which emerged to justify the exploitation of the common people by the nobility, those favored of the gods and divinely chosen to rule. The priests and scribes were readily able to prove that this system was desirable by proving the superiority of the well-born over the common mass. The nobility were nobles because they were noble, of finer qualities, "cut from finer cloth," the gentle ladies and gentlemen were gentle as well as noble, and it was possible quickly to explain that many of us who were built of common clay properly ought to devote our lives, literally, to the service of such nobility in order that they might glorify the gods with lives that would in some manner reflect the splendor and

---

[11] C. DeLisle Burns, *Leisure in the Modern World* (New York: The Century Company, 1932), p. 260.

beauty in which it was imagined that the gods themselves lived. We find in the writing of philosophers from the earliest times to the most recent justification for the elevation of an elite to a position above the masses, from which position of vantage the privileged class would be able to rule wisely, keep order, protect all from enemies, live beautifully, and thus do god's will.

The Hebraic-Christian Tradition

We have not spoken much of the early Hebrews, but from Hebrew literature have come some important concepts that have influenced western civilization through the centuries. The second chapter of Genesis describes how the Lord, having labored for six days in the creation of the earth, then devoted the seventh day to rest and contemplation of his work as a thing of beauty. The Hebraic-Christian tradition has been built upon this belief, that one day a week must be devoted to rest from work, and this day is spent in worship and appropriate leisure pursuits. (We shall not dwell now upon the great changes that have occurred in the idea of "appropriateness.") In the Garden of Eden, it is related, there were not only trees that would bear good food, but also trees that would be pleasant to see, an aesthetic note of interest.

The Jews were a serious people, whose sabbath was a time for recreation of mind and body, which included bathing and maintenance of cleanliness. School for all children was an important objective and play for them was guided by the scholars, teachers, and rabbis. There were many occasions for dancing, singing, and instrumental music, both on religious and festive occasions. Dancing especially was a highly important and popular activity, both for religious and cultural expression. The Kinneys summarize some biblical allusions to show that this art was held in high respect. " 'Praise the Lord . . . praise him with timbrel and the dance,' is commanded . . . To honor the slayer of Goliath, the women came out from all the cities of Israel, 'singing and dancing . . . with tabrets, with joy and with instruments of music' . . . 'Thou shalt again be adorned with thy tabrets, and shall go forth in the dances of them that make merry' (Jeremiah 31:4) 'Then shall the virgin rejoice in the dance' (Jeremiah 31:13) 'and David danced before the Lord with all his might' (2 Samuel 6:14)." [12] Similarly, music is

---

[12] Troy Kinney and Margaret Kinney, *The Dance: Its Place in Art and Life* (New York: Frederick A. Stokes Company, 1914), p. 5.

referred to often as an important element in worship and in play of the Hebrews.

There was stern criticism of vulgar, improper, pagan, and idle pursuits. This criticism, based upon religious grounds, has been likened to the criticisms by the early Christians against the recreational excesses of the Romans. Thus in the earliest times there were undoubtedly both the apologists for the rulers, who justified their deeds upon one ground or another, and those critics who demanded a more adequate social order, the elimination of the evils and vices and a more humanistic approach to the welfare of the people. However, such a philosophy had to wait for centuries to find an opportunity for active expression.

GREECE IN THE GOLDEN AGE

The contribution of Greece to the history of leisure and play is a great one, partly because of the heights reached by Athenian civilization and partly because in the history of Greece two radically contrasting views of play contended for a period. One view was a "military attitude" toward play—play being used as a means of training for the accomplishment of desired military objectives. A somewhat modern counterpart of early Sparta, with its thoroughly military organization of all social life, was Nazi Germany. The highly attractive activities of the Hitler Youth Organization, for example, the outdoor games, conditioning hikes, practice at war, group singing, and great youth festivals, were powerful means of influencing the children and youth toward the fascist ideals and popularizing the Nazi way of life. The second view, the "art attitude," found its earliest recorded expression in Athens. Let us look first at Sparta.

Spartan Life

Sparta was a military state of the strictest sort, the rulers maintaining themselves by military might against outsiders and against the subjugated people they exploited, as well as waging aggressive wars of conquest. Cultural development was frustrated; the national songs and dances and games were those mainly of a great military barrack. Education and play of young and old were dedicated to perfecting the skills of battle and preparing the Spartan man or woman to fight bravely and with the utmost of courage and steadfastness, as well as to die willingly for the state.

From boyhood to manhood the male was trained on austerity of living, severity of discipline, harshness and sternness of physical education, and puritanical and nationalistic arts and morals. No wonder that down to this age have come such terms as "Spartan-like simplicity" and "laconic speech." Spartan girls had almost as exacting a training, so that they might become mothers of stalwart sons. Their games were athletic ones, they marched in religious processions, participated in choruses, and danced at certain festivals. Life was indeed harsh and unpleasant, although after twenty or thirty, when adulthood had been reached, some pleasures like hunting, riding, gymnastics, and dancing, as well as choral singing and participating in the great national and religious festivals, games, and ceremonies, provided recreation for adults.

It is hard to draw conclusions from the experience of Sparta. One is tempted to agree that the perversion of the needs of man for play, relaxation, fun and amusement into the stern discipline of war-making and militarization of all phases of life might lead to internal contradictions, despair of many, and the progressive brutalization of many, accompanied by cultural decline and decline of the very strength the policy is supposed to guarantee. Of interest is the philosophy this system spawned, characterized by the Stoicism of the philosopher Zeno and others, that virtue lies in service, loyalty, and duty to the state, the foregoing of bodily pleasures and the practicing of moderation and simplicity of life.

Quite opposed to the Stoic philosophy that bodily pleasures should be foregone was the philosophy of Epicurus, follower of the materialist Democritus, the advocate of democracy. Epicurus, a contemporary of Zeno, believed that the good life is marked by a rational utilization of sense pleasures. He believed that the aim of man is to attain a tranquillity of soul which is gained by knowledge and freedom from fear, and a reasonable and rational enjoyment of the pleasures which our many senses and our intellect can appreciate. He warned against pleasures that excite and disturb the soul, which they should quiet and appease, bringing tranquillity, equanimity, repose of mind; he urged us not to avoid pleasures, but to select them wisely. The stark contrast between the bright "pursuit of happiness" of epicureanism and the demand for sober self-denial of the pleasures of life of stoicism, and the conflict between these two views, has continued in some measure until the present time.

Athens

Historians have agreed in general that the Athens of Socrates, Plato, and Aristotle, during the "Golden Age of Pericles" from 500 to 400 B.C., reached the highest peak of civilization to that time, and the foundations were laid for much of the scientific, philosophical, and cultural growth of later centuries. The society of Athens during the years of her greatness provides a dramatic contrast to Spartan society, and is very instructive to the historian of recreation. In her concepts of leisure and recreation, as in other fields, there is much to interest the recreationist.

The Athenian state during this period was closer to a democracy, perhaps, than any other state theretofore had been. Yet slaves and foreigners outnumbered the citizens perhaps two or three to one at different times. Although in the Athenian state many types of labor were respected as worthy of free men, and the majority of the citizens were artisans, farmers, and the like, these classes of citizens were permitted only limited rights to vote and to participate in the affairs of state. Wealth, prestige, and power went hand in hand. Poor workers and peasants suffered losses of jobs and property, ending up as slaves, much as in other civilizations of the time. Many of the slave class, however, were prisoners, the spoils of military conquest, brought home to be kept or sold.

The Athenian ideal of life, a balance of moral, mental, physical, and aesthetic living, along with civic participation and moderation in all things, was the foundation of much of the education of the youth of means, and of life for the adults. A warm family life centered about the home-bound mother. The children were entertained at home with a variety of amusements, toys, games, storytelling, as well as with pets, dancing, and music. Children of the well-born went to the palaestra and gymnasium and the music school for several years of study. At some points broader groups were served by public gymnasiums. Woody says, "A balance of mental and physical education was sought at Athens. The palaestra (wrestling place) and the music school were to give that training in music and literature for the soul and exercise for the body which was thought essential for freeborn youth." [13] Plato was credited with saying that one should not use compulsion in

---

[13] Woody, *Life and Education in Early Societies,* p. 300.

schools, but let early education be a sort of amusement. Knowledge that is acquired under compulsion obtains no hold on the mind. Interestingly enough, the Greek word for leisure is *skol* from which we have derived our word *school*.

Many youths learned to read and write, and both youths and adults enjoyed the classical literature, as well as a great production of drama, poetry, and music-poetry. Greek poetry, beginning with Homer, was studied and read widely. The works of the Greek tragedians and comedians were presented in the great hillside theaters and at festival times and were enjoyed by large groups.

Gardner points out that all the citizens, men and women, young and old, came to and participated in leisure-time activities, the great festivals and plays, and developed a considerable critical sense.

> At the dramatic performances of Aeschylus and Sophocles . . . the audience of citizens approved with silence or applause, or condemned with a shower of figs and olives. The comedies of Aristophanes were enjoyed to the utmost when they satirized the great figures of the day with a daring that would be tolerated in no city not truly democratic. Quality was demanded in these plays by an audience that was composed of a people of all classes who were not art critics or theorizing esthetes but who as an everyday matter of fact knew good drama from bad.[14]

Modern students of the dance have suggested that in Athens there may have been reached a peak of cultural development of the dance not since shared by any society. The Kinneys point out that

> . . . we find choreography luxuriant, perhaps, as it never has been since; protected by priesthood and state, practiced by rich and poor, philosopher and buffoon. Philosophers taught it to pupils for its effect on body and mind; it was a means of giving soldiers carriage, agility and health, and cultivating *esprit de corps*. To the development of dancing were turned the Greek ideals of beauty, which in their turn undoubtedly received a mighty and constant uplift from the beauty of harmonized movements of healthy bodies . . . the variety of emotional and aesthetic motives that dancing was made to express, all com-

---

[14] Gardner, *Art Through the Ages,* p. 127.

> bine to give Greece a rank never surpassed as a dancing nation.[15]

The use of dances ranged from the sublime and reverent to the ridiculous and the gay, from the gentle or amorous to the military. People danced to be serious and danced for fun, to while away the time.

The Athenians combined religious worship and athletic and cultural events in a large number of annual festivals occupying perhaps seventy days of the year, which were the Greek days of rest, recreation, patriotism, and religious devotion. Plato is credited with the statement that the holy festivals were ordained by the gods, who pitied the labors of men and who sought thereby to alternate their labors with rest. Many of these festivals emphasized athletic games, and modern track meets, boxing and wrestling matches, and horse and sulky racing, take on much of the character of their Athenian ancestry.

Foot Race at the Olympic Games

Athens helped to sponsor the most famous of the great games, the Olympiad, held every four years as a great national festival, during which a "Truce of God" was declared, and all else was set aside while

[15] Kinney and Kinney, *The Dance,* pp. 6-7.

those of wealth or nobility participated or watched. Poets and singers would come and sing odes to the victors, who at first received simply the olive wreath of victory, but eventually rich prizes as well, in the later years when professionalism entered in. This influence, among other things, eventually ruined the games.

The culture of Athens was not limited to sports, dance, drama, music, and literature. In the arts of the sculptor, painter, architect, ceramist, silversmith, and goldsmith, Greece also had a golden age, which reflected a demand for beauty of form and design among broad groups of the citizens. Childe points out, "Greek artists were the first (save perhaps for the authors of some doubtful sculptures from the Indus cities) to present the human figure in a naturalistic manner; they were allowed to treat even the Gods in the same spirit. . . . Architects . . . created architectural forms that . . . are still things of ineffable beauty even when in ruins." [16]

Although these artists and craftsmen were usually slaves or humble workers they produced vast amounts of artistic objects for everyday use by the public, from temples and gymnasia to beautifully designed and decorated ceramic objects, metal work, and woodwork. Perhaps therein lies the means of summing up Athenian life from the point of view of its recreational cultural characteristics. A Greek proverb credited to Aristotle ran "There is no leisure for slaves." Education and leisure and the beautiful life were for the well-born, and certainly there was often grace and beauty in their lives, modest and moderate in all things, participating as they did in civic life, athletics and sports for their pleasure and health, in drama, music, and poetry for their soul, and in frequent festivals and religious occasions for worship through play and social life. They also had their share of feasting, banqueting, and parties, entertained by musicians, dancers, and *hetaerae,* who were pictured generally as talented entertainers and prostitutes with whom Greek men amused themselves.

But for the laboring class one hears of no such leisured existence. As Woody says, "Those who labored long in mine, quarry, or mill had little or no surplus energy to give to other physical exercise. For them labor was enough—indeed, too much—and they lightened it by chanteys of boatmen, songs of the vintners, flailmen, and grinders at the mill. Even beggars lightened their labor with the song of the crow:

---

[16] Childe, *What Happened in History,* pp. 220-221.

Or a well-kneaded loaf or an obolos give,
Or what you will, for the crow must live.[17]

Yet the commoners shared in many of the festival days, at least, because some of the work ceased on those days. They shared in the beauties of the city itself; some participated as creative persons in the great arts of the day; and, as the artists, helped to create the beauty for which Greece is renowned.

Plato And Aristotle

The two most famous Greek philosophers are Plato and Aristotle, both of whom were concerned with recreation. Plato planned a Utopia, an ideal state. His Republic is a class-differentiated aristocracy ruled by "philosopher-kings." The rulers would be truly wise men. Then there would be guards, pure of heart and spirit, who would defend the welfare of the state. Finally there would be the artisans and husbandmen who would do the work. The education of the guards and of the rulers would include both gymnastics and military sports, and virtuous music and poetry eulogizing bravery, courage, endurance, purity of spirit, and temperance.

> On these accounts it is that we attach such supreme importance to a music education; because rhythm and harmony sink most deeply into the recesses of the soul, and take most powerful hold of it. . . . Gymnastic will hold the next place to Music in the education of our young men. . . . This is my view of the case: —not that a good body will necessarily make the soul good: but that a good soul will by its proper virtue render the body as perfect as it can be. We must therefore first administer the requisite treatment to the mind, and then charge it with the direction of the body.[18]

Aristotle was a scientist and intellectual giant whose contribution in bringing together a large part of the existing physical and biological knowledge was matched by acute examination of ethics and aesthetics as well. As Will Durant says, he "almost creates the study of esthetics, the theory of beauty and art. . . . [S]ays Aristotle . . . the aim of art is to represent not the outward appearance of things, but their inward significance . . . for this . . . is their reality. . . . The noblest art appeals

---

[17] Woody, *Life and Education in Early Societies,* p. 329.

[18] Plato, *The Republic,* translated by William Whewell (London: The Macmillan Company, 1861), p. 203.

to the intellect as well as to the feelings . . . and this intellectual pleasure is the highest form of joy to which a man can rise." [19]

Aristotle's attitude toward work and leisure was that "nature requires us not only to be able to work well but also to idle well." Idleness or leisure for Aristotle was the principle of the universe. Man worked in order to have leisure: "Leisure is preferable to work, it is the aim of all work." This teaching, however, applied to the free man, the citizen of Greece, who did not have to work for a living, and who thus, as Huizinga says, "had leisure to pursue his life's aim in noble occupations of an educative nature." [20]

A philosophy of recreation and play has much to gain from ancient Greece. The epicurean concept of sense pleasures as the aim of life; the concept that education through play and voluntary games is as valuable as education through compulsion and discipline; the concept that leisure is of worth and its constructive use valuable to the spirit of man; the concept that all might share in some of the values of leisure; the concept that beauty and aesthetic pleasures are important in man's pursuit of happiness; the concept that play is a way to health; all of these concepts, even though sometimes expressed in confused and contradictory form, represent elements of a philosophy of play that undergirded a development of recreation surpassing that reached by any known society up to the modern era, and perhaps surpassing many modern societies. Unfortunately, Greece did not produce, neither at that time nor for some time to come, philosophers to speak for the rights of the common man. As yet there seemed not to be any basis for assuming that all men might equally enjoy the fruits of leisure, and all voices seemed to speak for the perpetuation of privilege for the few, as the means of approaching the ideal society. Yet, in the final analysis, it was primarily this weakness in the Greek concept of democracy that led to the decline of Greece.

ROME—BREAD AND CIRCUSES

The Roman Empire took many centuries to expand to its widest limits. From the seventh century B.C. to the first century B.C., Rome

---

[19] Will Durant, *The Story of Philosophy,* New revised edition (New York: Simon and Schuster, Inc., 1926), pp. 84-85. Copyright © 1926, 1933, 1961 by Will Durant. By permission of Simon and Schuster, Inc.

[20] Johan Huizinga, *Homo Ludens: A Study of the Play Element in Culture* (London: Routledge & Kegan Paul, Ltd., 1955), p. 161.

grew from tribal community to city to center of an independent empire. In the first century A.D., it was estimated that the Roman Empire might have totaled eighty to one hundred million people, with the city of Rome having perhaps a million population. The empire included most of what is now Europe, much of the Middle East, and parts of Africa. The rough-hewn agricultural democracy of early Rome, the Republic, with all Romans as citizens and freemen, changed through the years until in the later centuries, as an empire, it presented a picture far different from the democratic ideal from which it sprang.

There was wealth, profiteering, and the garnering of huge incomes by the rulers and by a group of unscrupulous entrepreneurs; this "economics" was based upon exploitation, levying of tribute, and robbery of the vast provinces conquered by military might. A huge urban indigent group was maintained in semi-idleness. There persisted a group of workers and craftsmen organized into guilds, and, during the later empire, reduced to compulsory labor and enslaved by the government. There were some independent farmers, but more often farming was done by slaves, and then by *coloni,* or tenants bound to the land and paying rent for its use. The use of slaves was widespread in both city and country, until later years; at one point there may have been one for every two or three freemen in Rome.

The Exploitation of Leisure

It was upon such an economic and class system that Roman social and recreational life was based during the empire. The wealthy class valued its leisure, without which liberal education and a cultured life would be impossible. Some of the members cultivated the arts. There were many great philosophers, writers, and poets in the empire, such as Cicero, Virgil, Quintilian, Seneca, and others. But the prevalent debauchery of the later rulers and classes, the despotism of and persecution by government, resulted in a stultification and decline of scholarship, philosophy, and literature, which apparently need the wind of freedom to stir them to life.

The wealthy classes might be patrons of the arts; rulers might endow and build great libraries. But more often Roman recreation would take more sensuous forms. Enjoyment of the Roman gymnasia and baths, which often were combined, became a major recreation both for the favored classes who constructed luxurious private baths, and for the public. The rulers late in the Republic, and the emperors later on, built great public baths. Seneca, the cynical and conservative satirist, is quoted by Woody in his protest against this extravagance.

> We think ourselves poor and mean if our walls are not resplendent with large and costly mirrors; if our marbles from Alexandria are not set off by mosaics of Numidian stone, if their borders are not faced over on all sides with difficult patterns, arranged in many colours like paintings; if our vaulted ceilings are not buried in glass; if our swimming pools are not lined with Thasian marble, once a rare and wonderful sight in any temple—pools into which we let down our bodies after they have been drained weak by abundant perspiration; and finally if the water has not been poured from silver spigots . . . with what masses of water that fall crashing from level to level. We have become so luxurious that we will have nothing but precious stones to walk upon.[21]

The bath became the social and athletic club of the Roman citizens, and for the leisured class the daily routine of exercise, bathing, and eating was the usual order.

The old military tradition continued to dictate some of the recreational customs of the wealthy, although paid armies of mercenaries, and armies made up largely of poorer citizens, became prevalent in later centuries. The vigorous athletic sports of hunting, fishing, boating, wrestling, and gymnastic exercise remained popular, not for the purpose of maintaining one's fitness for army service, but as pleasurable ends in themselves. Woody points out,

> The Roman's love of play is variously displayed in hunting, running, ball games, swimming, wrestling, riding, . . . crowding festivals, horse races, play in light arms, play with ball and hoop, and well-oiled young men bathing in the waters of the Virgo. The time came, indeed, when, by Seneca's account, some Romans spent their whole life in play at chess, at ball-play, and baking themselves in the sun. When not indulging in play of some kind himself, the wealthy Roman who had put on

---

[21] Woody, *Life and Education in Early Societies,* pp. 649-650, quoted from Epistle LXXXVI, 6-7. Seneca, *Epistulae Morales,* translated by B. M. Gunmere. The Loeb Classical Library, quoted by permission of Harvard University Press, Cambridge, Mass.

> the new life of luxury, loved to entertain his guests with acrobats, musicians, dancers and other artists.[22]

It was an age of spendthrift luxury, extravagance, and frantic lust for wealth and pleasures. Conspicuous display of riches gave social standing. Critics and philosophers railed in vain against the shamelessness, bribery, rapacity, avarice, lust for power and money, and crime, that were found in Rome. The emperor Caligula, trying to outdo everybody in extravagance, threw money to the crowds for several days, bathed in hot and cold perfumed oils, drank pearls dissolved in vinegar, and laid loaves and meats of gold before his guests. Galleys with ten banks of oars, gem-set sterns, and colored sails were provided with spacious baths, banquet halls, colonnades, and even vines and fruit trees, so that he might sail and feast at pleasure.

The Roman Games

But perhaps the most fantastic extravagance of ancient Rome was the games. As in other societies, these ostensibly began mainly as religious celebrations, but to these dates were added festivals in honor of heroes, victories, and so on. The number was astounding. At the time of the first emperors, there were ninety festival days. Three hundred years later, there were twice that many, plus many special celebrations. These games were free, and attracted huge crowds. It was said that the Circus Maximus at the time of Caesar would seat 260,000 persons, and gradually was enlarged through the centuries to a capacity of 385,000. The Colosseum could accomodate nearly 90,000 spectators. There were many other great arenas, forums, circuses, and amphitheaters constructed throughout the empire as the games increased in popularity.

Rulers and persons of wealth increased their popularity with the masses through the giving of games and fantastic sums were spent, costs at times mounting to ruinous heights. They bankrupted both public treasuries and private fortunes, and required new and heavy tribute from allies and subject peoples. Caligula was said to have come to power with two or three billion sesterces in the treasury, and was in dire straits within a year or two because of his lavish expenditures on spectacle-making.

The games included circuses, gladiator contests, fights between beasts, even sea battles. Circuses featured chariot races and other

---

[22] Woody, p. 660.

equestrian events. The gladiatorial games featured combats between gladiators, and others, in pairs or larger groups, using all forms of weapons, on foot, on horse, or in chariots, to the death. In the *venationes* beasts were pitted against beasts, against humans who were armed and destroyed them, or were unarmed and whom they destroyed. In the *naumachiae,* sea battles were fought in artificially contrived lakes in the arenas between fleets of ships in which sometimes thousands of fighters were involved.

Often athletic contests and special shows of all kinds were added to the other spectacles to satisfy the jaded appetites of the Romans. Hundreds or thousands of animals might be slaughtered in a single spectacle; scores of human deaths in a day of gladiatorial combat were not unusual; at one naval battle staged by Domitian a storm came and, because the emperor was unwilling to stop the battle and to permit the audience to leave, most of the participants and many of the audience died by drowning.

The brutality, blood, lust, and horror of these games were bitterly criticized by Romans of more noble sensitivities during the years, and frequent attempts were made to reform them. But as the empire declined the vulgarity, inhumanity, and cruelty of the games and of the crowds witnessing them increased, and mass debauchery, corruption, and perversion of spirit and morals seems to have taken place. It has to be remembered that for the mobs of indigent poor in Rome the games and public baths were the main recreations. For survival there were doles of corn and bread, and to appease the grumbling of such a mass of lumpen proletariat there were games. The slogan of "bread and circuses" has portrayed the means whereby tyrants there and elsewhere have kept the masses from revolting. The folk saying "Roman holiday" literally means a bacchanalia of corrupt amusement, celebration, and cruelty.

The Decline of the Empire

With the disintegration of the empire came the end of the custom of holding such extravaganzas, and with depression came reduction of expenditures and some reforms—although even in the sixth century A.D. bloody games were still being held.

With such an environment, it is understandable how the Roman philosophers turned cynic, stoic, or depressed defeatist, and how a philosophy might be developed with strong negative overtones. Earlier philosophers like Cicero hopefully praised the ideal of the virtuous and active citizen-soldier, loyal to country and democratic in spirit, and in music and song giving honor to the gods. Seneca, living in a later period, reflects a deep despair and cynicism concerning civilization. He inveighs against the luxury and greed of man, the wickedness of men in all positions. His is a philosophy of disillusionment and pessimism, and a plea to give up the vices and pleasures that corrupt and rot away the spirit of man. Seneca was in some measure the prophet of Roman decline. His problem was that he had no hope, and therefore no plan for reform for a better life. His stoicism, and that of others, became the dominant philosophy of critical Rome.

The Christians became sharp critics of the Roman life during these declining centuries. They continuously attacked the games of the arena and circus as pagan, vicious, and pernicious. As Christianity gained in strength, the leaders of the church and the monks who directed its activity played a more active role both in influencing the rulers to abolish some of the more serious of the vices connected with the games, and in influencing the masses of the people toward a more serious and pious attitude toward life.

Roman recreation included much that was wholesome and healthy and much that was corrupt, debased, and debauched. That "circuses" became the central element of the philosophy of recreation for the masses of dispossessed farmers and lumpen proletariat instead of more wholesome work and play is a fact. This was of course the strategy of a corrupt and declining imperial system in contrast with a more noble concept of human welfare and pursuit of happiness with which the Republic began. It was still too early in history, perhaps, for any other system to develop than that of a privileged aristocracy living upon the labor of workers, slaves, serfs, and subject peoples.

So it was that Rome, weakened and bankrupt from excess, a discouraged, disillusioned empire, was unable to resist attack from within or without. Christianity grew in strength, and its attack upon "pagan ways" left little doubt that the old ways of empire were disintegrating. It remained only for Attila and the Huns to complete the scourge, looting, burning, pillaging, scattering the bonds of empire to the four winds. The curtain of empire rang down, leaving the way clear for feudalism to flourish, and the Catholic church to rise as a force binding people together.

Still, all that was *Antica Roma* did not perish and fade. Caught forever in graceful columns and marble figures, part of the beauty that was Rome still lives—proof for the artist, architect, writer, student, and traveler that beauty really does, after all, transcend man's baser expressions.

Among the craftsmen, the members of the workers' guilds, the simple artists, and the remnants of the rural peasantry, there was much that was conservative of traditional folk life. Families still worked and played together; children still were told stories, learned games and songs, hunted for rabbits in the fields; village groups still got together for dancing, music and merriment, and insisted upon their "days off." And, while the Roman Empire collapsed and a rural feudal order came upon many parts of the civilized world, the term "dark ages" does not portray correctly its nature.

Childe points out that the "cultural capital," the vast gains in technical and social development accumulated during the rise and development of the ancient civilizations and centered in Rome, was not by any means annihilated in the collapse of the Roman Empire. He says:

> Many refinements, noble and beautiful, were swept away. But for the most part these had been designed for and enjoyed by only a small and narrow class. Most achievements . . . that had become firmly established on a genuinely popular footing by the participation of wider classes were conserved, even if temporarily fossilized. . . . City life, with all of its implications, still continued. Most crafts were still plied with all the technical skill and equipment evolved in Classical and Hellenistic times. . . . Writing was not forgotten . . . scientific and literary texts were studiously copied and preserved. . . . The new arts and crafts introduced in the empire were not extinguished. For instance, descendants and apprentices of the Syrian glassworkers kept the Norman and Rhenish furnaces going all through the Dark Ages.[23]

The current flowed on to fertilize a new science, a new technology, a fresh economy, new experiments in government, a new humanistic philosophy, and a new recreation, in a western European environment.

The dominant leisure groups in classical civilizations were the upper classes, who built an elaborate leisure culture, small parts of which were enjoyed as well by the working masses. A philosophy of recreation emerged to justify and rationalize an aristocratic concept of leisure values.

---

[23] Childe, *What Happened in History,* pp. 273-274.

LIFE, LABOR, AND LEISURE IN THE MIDDLE AGES

The (roughly) one thousand years between the invasion of Rome by the barbarians from the north and the discovery of America by Columbus has been called the "middle ages" of western civilization. This period ended with the industrial revolution and the gradual emergence of capitalism and modern social life. Dealing somewhat casually with dates, let us examine briefly the contributions of the middle ages to our understanding of the growth of recreation and a philosophy to support it.

Medieval Feudalism

At first look, one might think there was little in this period to suggest either that recreation was important in the lives of people or that philosophers of the time concerned themselves with play and its significance. The feudal system was organized around the castle or house of the nobleman, who by virtue of his military strength held sway over a particular region. The noble family, the retainers or hangers-on, and the serfs who tilled the soil on his estates made up the community. The serf was bound to the soil, and thus to the service of the nobleman, and he in turn was presumed to be the protector of his serfs. It was essentially an agricultural economy, although weavers, blacksmiths, and other craftsmen plied their trades at the manor house or the castle, also in the service of the nobleman.

While a very large portion of the medieval population lived on the feudal estates the cities and towns which had grown up over a period of several thousand years before still existed as trading and manufacturing centers. Merchants, traders and sea captains, maintaining trade throughout the Mediterranean area, and travelers carrying merchandise and news from place to place, kept the western and eastern worlds in contact. Along the main arteries of trade new towns grew up, where craftsmen and merchants plied their trades, often only nominally influenced and dominated by feudal or church rule. It was in these feudal cities, which grew gradually to greater importance, that the craftsmen workers and the merchants maintained their guilds and organizations of free producers and often largely governed the towns.

A new force also grew up in the middle ages to dominate life in western Europe: the ecclesiastical and monastic system of the Christian church. The church found its first supporters among craftsmen, laborers, and slaves. Its revolutionary affirmation of human rights was welcomed by the oppressed. The doctrine nourished dangerous discontents and provided new and effective channels of organization for the lower classes. The new religion gained followers rapidly among all classes, however, and rooted itself in the cities, as well as consolidating itself over a period of several hundred years as the dominant religion in Europe.

The church gradually gained more and more power through the economic organizations of the monastery system, which controlled much of the trade and industry of the medieval era. The monasteries developed agriculture and organized the industrial production of metal workers, woodcarvers, shoemakers, weavers, and furriers. The bishops and monks combined in this manner the functions of pastor, landlord, employer, and master. The monastic system of land ownership and economic production grew very rapidly and to a tremendous position of power during the middle ages. Monasteries were large-scale enterprises and business organizations, and they developed a strong hold on international trade and industry.

The medieval class system had four main elements. At the top was the feudal nobility. The noble was a military ruler, on a small scale usually, who exacted tribute from his serfs and what slaves he might have, exacted tribute from what villages and towns he might exploit, and lived a life of rough and rural leisure in his moated castle. About him he gathered a group of lower nobility and knights. The latter were a class of professional fighters, some of presumed noble background. They attached themselves to a lord and ran the risks of battle for the sake of the board and room, and the booty from successful conquest of his neighbors.

The second main element in the class system was the church authority—the hierarchy of bishops, members of the monastic orders, and the local priesthood. They were, in addition, entrepreneurs, industrialists, and merchants, and levied tribute from the towns over which they maintained varying degrees of spiritual and temporal authority.

The third element in the class system was the urban worker in the cities, whose struggle for subsistence led to the expansion of industry. The craftsman, owning his skills and his tools and protected by his guild, had a degree of freedom and maintained the cities as centers of economic life. An element closely related to the workers were the urban merchants, the *burghers* in early Germany or the French *bourgeoisie*. These men, who owned their own goods and worked in trade or finance, fought for and gradually obtained more and more freedom from the oppressive taxes, levies, and tributes paid to feudal lords, and from the authority of the church. The craftsmen and burghers first cooperated against the landlords and, second, fought each other for a dominant place in the city's life. The burghers, with their greater economic power, usually won.

At the base again, forming the productive base of feudalism, was the serf, bound to the soil, taxed and exploited. The land was his only source of livelihood, unless he wished to join the wandering poor and take his chances in the cities, an alternative at first without much promise but later more attractive.

The recreation of the medieval nobility included the traditional activities of a predatory leisure class—the hunting, riding, and play at combat. The stories of famous medieval knightly jousts and tournaments at arms have been passed down from early times in literature and song. The castle was the center of social life for these groups. Songs, stories, and performances by traveling dancers and bards entertained the nobles and their knights. The early training of the nobleman's son involved learning the arts of chivalry, many of which were involved in athletic skills of all kinds, such as archery, wrestling, swordsmanship, horsemanship, and so on, as well as familiarity with the games of chess and backgammon, and playing the harp or lute. He participated in the tournaments along with other young nobles and gentlemen.

There developed during this period a folk poetry and balladry, presented sometimes in the formal Latin of the religious orders but more often in the vernacular and folk tongues of the people. Troubadours sang gay, romantic, sentimental, and martial songs at banquets, festivals, or castle gatherings. The *Meistersingers* formed a German guild of trained singers in medieval times and sang for festivals in the market places and in the feudal courts. A free and secular music thus was maintained outside the staid and stately church.

In Wales, a medieval performance of court musicians and bards was celebrated as a national cultural celebration having its roots back in the centuries before the Roman conquest. Gantvoort says that among the Celts, "bards, or minstrels, were sought after and honored. . . . They sang legends and stories of martial adventure, accompanying themselves upon primitive harps."[24] An annual festival, the *Eistedd-*

[24] A. J. Gantvoort, *Familiar Talks on the History of Music* (New York: G. Schirmer, Inc., 1923), p. 55.

fod, has been perpetuated until this day as a festival of competition in harp playing, solo and choral singing, dramatic presentations and poetic compositions, with honors and prizes to the winners. In Ireland, "in the day of Druidism, the Irish nation celebrated an annual feast lasting six days, a *Feis.* It was the custom . . . for the nobles of Ireland, and their ladies, and bards and harpists from far and near, to gather at the castle of the king; and there for six days there were competitions in all kinds of music and dancing." [25]

The Influence of the Church

To understand the recreational life of the groups other than the feudal nobility we must understand the powerful influence of the church in regulating the lives of most people. To understand this we must recall the violent reaction of the Christian church to the pleasure-loving paganism and debauchery of Rome. In medieval times work was needed; easygoing life had to be given up, and toil had to be unremitting, if the soul were to be free.

In following up this idea, the church waged constant war against pagan rites and festivals, especially the traditional festival days. During the medieval period, the church replaced the Greek-Roman festival days by saints' days, and added additional religious significance to the Jewish tradition of the sabbath day. The number of Greek-Roman festivals was reduced so that in modern times in the western world there were about sixty days of public holidays in a year, only about half the number that were common in Greece, Rome, and other civilized societies in the past. The war was only partly won, for the traditional seasonal festivals remained, whether named after a saint or not, a time for all folks to come together for rest and pursuit of traditional forms of celebration.

The medieval guardians of the people's morals became much concerned with the struggle between the noble spirit and the sinful flesh: "The Flesh lusteth against the Spirit, and the Spirit against the Flesh; and these are contrary the one to the other; so that ye cannot do the things that ye would," stated the Apostle Paul (Epistle to the Galatians, Chapter 5, verse 17). Man was to work, to apply himself diligently to his labors, and forego seductive pleasures, which were plainly of the devil. Here was a philosophy that sharply negated the philosophy of Epicurus, and one that spiritual and temporal rulers tried to

[25] Kinney and Kinney, *The Dance,* p. 177.

impose upon the working folk of the land for the profit of the ruling groups. It became a powerful support of Calvinism and Puritanism at a later date, became a part of the American tradition, and is still highly influential in our lives today.

The Neumeyers say that the monks "looked upon play as not only useless but evil. They felt that it turned men's minds away from God and the higher values of life. So, according to this view, all kinds of amusements were sinful. To indulge in them was to forfeit eternal salvation. Intellectual and political leaders during the Middle Ages and years later joined hands with the religious forces to suppress sports, games, and other forms of entertainments." [26] Many of the monks also seriously practiced what they preached, including celibacy, although there were many tales of pleasures of the flesh practiced by those who preached the ascetic doctrines, among the clergy and otherwise. The delightful tale of Friar Tuck in the English fable *Robin Hood* is one example; Boccaccio's *Decameron* gives others, as does Chaucer's *Canterbury Tales.*

We do not know how truly influential such attitudes were in the lives of the feudal masses. Certainly the feudal lords and the church worked together to uphold the feudal system of exploitation of the rural serfs. The history of the later centuries of feudalism was a history of revolts, armed and otherwise, against the authority of the church and the feudal lords by both the cities and the peasants.

The influence of the Christian concepts of industry, sobriety, and sinless life ought not to be underestimated, nor should it be overestimated. The wealthy families did not cast aside the luxuries and lecheries of "sinful" life readily, and we find about the nobles and kings of all the centuries of this age tales of extravagant living and generous sampling of all the pleasures available to those with means.

The young city dweller of sufficient means might go to the medieval university, where asceticism was carried over into university policy. Leonard and Affleck point out that "Provision for lawful amusements was rarely made in the University statutes, which appear frequently to regard harmless attempts at pleasure with more hostility than they display toward actual vice and crime. The sports of chivalry were not considered seemly for the student, even if he had the means

---

[26] Martin H. Neumeyer and Esther S. Neumeyer, *Leisure and Recreation: A Study of Leisure and Recreation in Their Sociological Aspects,* Third edition (New York: The Ronald Press Company, 1958), p. 55. Copyright 1958 The Ronald Press Company.

to indulge in them. Dancing was seldom countenanced in any form. 'Playing with a ball or bat' is sometimes found included in the list of 'insolent' games, and other prohibitions make mention of 'profane games, immodest runnings and horrid shoutings." [27] Yet the young men found relaxation from serious study in vigorous games, as well as in drinking, gambling, and other forms of vice, much after the pattern of student ancestors in Rome eight hundred years earlier, and some moderns eight hundred years later.

Urban Life

The medieval cities were centers for important cultural developments. Among their cultural achievements must be mentioned the cathedrals, which were erected as monuments to the church and as centers of worship and religious life, but were cooperative artistic productions as well. The crafts of the architects, stoneworkers, carpenters, and sculptors found their medieval expression in the construction and equipment of these great cathedrals. The church called upon the artists for "fine fabrics for costumes and for hangings; jeweled ornaments; books, which, to suit current tastes, might be written in gold letters upon purple-tinted vellum or decorated with bright miniatures on gold grounds, and bound in gold, ivory, enamel, and jewels; vessels for the service, which must be of the finest materials and workmanship to be worthy of the church." [28] The forests of northern Europe produced great oak timbers for massive construction as well as finely carved furniture and the art of the woodworkers. A vigorous Gothic art and architecture emerged, as well as painting, metalwork, weaving, enameling, and the exquisite art of the worker in stained glass who created the fabulous designs of the leaded windows of the cathedrals. The church provided a center for large groups of urban craftsmen, and many others participated as producers and consumers in this cultural movement.

Medieval dancing, drama, and festivals reflected both religious and secular influences. Dancing was used in the morality play, in the rituals of worship, in the great pantomimes, as well as the processions, maskings, and mummings incidental to the religious festivals. The church, in a confused way, vacillated between proscribing all dancing

---

[27] Fred E. Leonard and George B. Affleck, *A Guide to the History of Physical Education* (Philadelphia: Lea and Febiger, 1947), p. 47.

[28] Gardner, *Art Through the Ages,* p. 230.

and approving certain forms for religious uses. The morality plays were often elaborate spectacles with scenery, floats, chariots, bands of dancers in choreographic processions, and large casts of performers. Some were quite solemn and pious, but "Performers no less than authors were sometimes guilty of ribaldry ranging from the frivolous to the impious." [29]

The growing demand of urban groups in the medieval period for independence from ecclesiastical interference in the town's life was expressed in their cultural life. A growing literature became available in the thirteenth and fourteenth centuries. It permitted writers other than the clergy to find an audience, and other than religious themes to be developed. The church used liturgical drama as a means of popularizing religious themes. Now the urban theater guilds grew up, popularizing the scriptures and other stories for entertainment in the market places. Companies of ballad singers and actors produced dramas on festival and holiday occasions. Some groups, called "Fools' Companies," played comedy that was satirical and sharply critical of the church. The famous Feast of Fools, a New Year revel, was used for this purpose throughout Europe. Eventually such bold drama could be used for profit as well. The Feast of Fools helped to break the spell of religious ritual. The crude pantomime in the streets seemed closer to the people, something they could seize and use for their own ends. Not since the Greek satirical comedy had drama been used so boldly for mass entertainment.

In the countryside, the serfs still had their folk entertainments inherited from the centuries past. Seasonal celebrations retained their hold on rural communities, and were simplified in games and dances. Martin says that the dancing of the rural and urban common folk, in its beginnings, "was the lusty and uninhibited emotional expression of crude and unpolished peoples. Its attitude toward sex was likely to be altogether frank, and the many varieties of couple dances that evolved were openly designed for purposes of courtship. . . . But if these were honest and healthy dances, they were not notable for reticence or refinement." [30]

With music, the peasantry also developed and clung to a folk expression that was all their own. Vital and beautiful songs and dances

---

[29] Kinney and Kinney, *The Dance*, p. 34.

[30] John Martin, *The Dance* (New York: The Tudor Publishing Company, 1946), pp. 28-29.

sprang up by common consent, were perfected by common effort, and persisted by mere tradition, having a powerful effect upon the music of the church, the troubadours, the opera, the ballet, and other music for the upper classes.

English Folk Dancing

When the serfs were involved in one of their frequent and desperate struggles against their overlords (as happened in Luther's time, in England in the time of Piers Plowman, and at other times) they used these occasions, as well as secret night-time meetings, the Feast of Fools, and such, to express their protest. Such perhaps is the earliest example of protest drama, which along with protest literature has been a means of expressing dissatisfaction with conditions and of calling men to action ever since. Chambers repeats the vivid description of one of the Feast of Fools celebrations by the scandalized theology professors of the University of Paris:

> Priests and clerks may be seen wearing masks and monstrous visages at the hours of office. They dance in the choir dressed as women, panders or minstrels. They sing wanton songs. They eat black pudding at the horn of the altar while the celebrant

> is saying mass. They play dice there. They (make incense) with stinking smoke from the soles of old shoes. Finally they drive about the town and rouse the laughter of their fellows and the bystanders in infamous performances, with indecent gestures and verses scurrilous and unchaste.[31]

A form of popular celebration somewhat like the Feast of Fools which may have originated or received its impetus about the same time, is the Carnival, the Mardi Gras, which is found in France, Italy, Poland, Portugal, Spain, Syria, and elsewhere. It seems to have arisen in response to the church insistence upon the observance of Lent, during which sobriety, piety, abstinence, and dietary self-denial were to be practiced. So there grew up the custom of a "last fling," where the festivities included much eating and drinking, gambling, bullfights, parties, dances, and so on. Gay masqueraders paraded through the streets singing. Horseplay, obscene jokes, and other expressions of license were popular. Amid boisterous hilarity, clowns, buffoons, and pranksters carried on in the streets and at great parties and balls.

Middle Eastern and Oriental Patterns

Brief note should be made of the parallel development of cultural and recreational life in the societies of other parts of the world. The vitality and skill in conquest shown by the Moslem rulers of the east brought to them great riches, which were expended partly upon gracious living and the arts. The Koran decreed puritanically against sumptuousness and license of all kinds. Yet, especially in the later period, the rulers, the Mamelukes, "with their Oriental love of color, of fine silks, jewels, and richly inlaid vessels, managed in various ways to circumvent these decrees. With great wealth at their command they adorned their homes, and even their traveling tents of gold-shot silk, with rich hangings, fine rugs and, at least, a few exquisite utensils; and they clothed themselves in the most splendid apparel. In spite of many fastings, prayers, and pilgrimages demanded by the Koran, life was gay with festivals, feasts, and sports." [32]

The architecture, stucco and stone carving and ornamentation, carved wood panels and doors, elaborate decoration of walls of mosques, palaces, and wealthy houses, the vivid painting, mosaics,

---

[31] E. K. Chambers, *The Medieval Stage,* Vol. 1 (Oxford: The Clarendon Press, 1903), pp. 320-321.

[32] Gardner, *Art Through the Ages,* p. 250.

metalwork, glasswork, tapestries and fabrics and rugs, testified to a high development of the work of artists and craftsmen of the east. They attest to the vitality and inventiveness of the artist and the pleasure and joy in his creation by the small group that could enjoy the artist's work. The music and the dance of Mohammedan and Arab cultures were very highly developed, borrowing freely of all the countries they conquered and enriching them with many indigenous contributions to create a great popular art.

In Persia, even in several periods of conquest by both Oriental east and Islamic west, there continued among the rulers the encouragement and perpetuation of the life of leisure and gentility, patronage of the fine arts, and pursuit of the arts of war. The Persian sculptors, architects, silversmiths, and weavers, especially silk weavers, created an extraordinary art for the period.

In the north, the Russians showed the impact of Oriental, Byzantine, Hellenic, Gothic, and other influences upon their religious life, and an art was produced which developed a Russian character uniquely synthesizing the many influences.

Far to the east, the Chinese, whose civilization as a whole was not subject to the shocks of rapid change such as the west experienced, were living through two great "golden ages" of culture. During the Tang dynasty (618–907 A.D.), painting, sculpture, metalwork, poetry, dancing, music and other arts flourished and were shared by much of the population as part of leisure-time living. Then a brief period of revolution resulted in the destruction of much of the cultural life. The Sung dynasty (960–1280 A.D.) was a second great period, analogous to the western Renaissance, with statesmen, philosophers, poets, artists and painters sustaining a second era of cultural development.

Two more dynasties in four hundred years maintained much of the development of this cultural movement. Highly developed arts included painting, especially with inks on silk, sculpture, unsurpassed bronze work, jade carving, and porcelain work that was traded around the world, admired as highly treasured works of art, and purchased by those who could afford it for the last five hundred years.

A similar portrait of the life in India can be traced. The "pious craftsmen" of the temples developed superb skills in the arts, especially sculpture, metalwork, and weaving. These arts helped to enrich the lives of the fortunate ones of India's masses.

We have made the point before that cultural interchange was active during all civilized ages, and this is no less true of the middle ages. To the degree to which orient, middle east, and west exchanged ideas and artifacts, the cultures in each were enriched. Historians have told us something of the lives, leisure, and arts of the wealthy, and we must assume that to a limited degree some of the fruits of luxury filtered through to the lower classes in these societies—although the evidence is sparse. In the main, in the medieval as well as the ancient period, all of the beauties, riches, and pleasures that might enrich human life were for the masses only promises, promises yet to be fulfilled.

The Religious View

The medieval period produced another human experience of interest to the student of recreation. It was the effort to establish a "religious view" of recreation; play in most of its forms, as well as the usual use of leisure time, became not noble but ignoble and sinful. The church held that true virtue lay in diligent labor, abstinence from the pleasures of the flesh, and sober application of oneself to work.

Under this view, play, art, and music were condoned only if they were religious in context and form. Otherwise, leisure should be devoted to more work or in meditation on spiritual and ascetic matters. The impact of this concept is reflected in the predominance of religious content in play and art forms during the middle ages in most of Southern Europe.

This view was influential, although it was honored only in the breach by many of the ruling nobility and some of the ruling clergy. It was resisted and only partly obeyed by the urban classes, and was perhaps only a little more effective among the labor-bound and oppressed peasantry.

As the gradual stimulation of continued interchange with all peoples of the world continued, and the cities gained more and more freedom to develop uniquely modern forms of living, there began to emerge in western Europe the beginnings of three great developments: (1) the rise of science and learning—the Renaissance; (2) the increasing development of technological and industrial knowledge applied to economic production—the industrial revolution; and (3) the development of capitalism, which brought with it the rise to dominance of a new economic class, the bourgeoisie, and a new political system—modern democracy.

The world's feudal systems have supported a recreation-bent aristocracy living on the labor of serfs. The latter were forced to struggle both against a religious asceticism which fought play as sin, and against their feudal lords and masters, in order to gain leisure-time to enjoy recreation and the arts.

THE RENAISSANCE AND THE REFORMATION

Two events occurred in history roughly four centuries ago that helped to mark the change from the medieval to the modern period. One of these is called the Renaissance, the other, the Reformation. The Renaissance has been thought of mainly as a cultural movement, as an awakening in science, philosophy, literature, and the arts. It was a period marked by great confusion, instability, struggle, and a degree of intellectual liberation. Leading the way were the cities and the active and growing economic classes that dominated city life. The increase in urban manufacturing and trade created new wealth for the urban bourgeoisie. With it came the more powerful position of city administration in national life, and opportunity for more active pursuit of the culture that leisure time affords, than had been possible before that time. The medieval nobility gradually tended to lose its position of power. The growth of national states, based upon the power of the rising capitalist class, was a new and very important trend.

In the field of science and philosophy there were important developments. This was the age of Copernicus, Galileo, Servetus, Vesalius, and Francis Bacon, and of great developments in science and philosophy. A mechanical invention second to none in its influence on future cultural development was the invention of printing processes and the borrowing of papermaking from the Chinese and Moslems. Printing permitted a veritable revolution in the reading habits of the people. The demand for education, for books and for other reading, resulted in the rise to new heights of prestige of scholars, writers, and playwrights.

The Renaissance was marked as well by a trend in philosophy toward humanism, a movement to free mankind from the fetters of medievalism and scholasticism and to emphasize the rights and values of human personality. Humanism aspired to free morality from the ascetic standards of medieval Christianity and to defend the epicurean concept of the right of the healthy exercise of the physical senses and emotions. Among the humanist philosophers were Dante, Boccaccio, Erasmus, and Thomas More, who criticized and satirized the old, and presented utopian views of a more ideal life for mankind.

THE RISE OF THE ARTS

In the field of the arts—painting, sculpture, architecture, craftsmanship, the dance, drama, and music—the Renaissance was truly a fertile era. The fabulously wealthy families who ruled the cities and states of Italy, and the popes who ruled at Rome, became the patrons of Raphael, Michelangelo, Leonardo, Titian, Botticelli, Cellini, and others. Renaissance arts, especially the architecture of the period, spread to France and Germany, and to the other European states. But it was in Italy that the arts flourished under the stimulus not only of patronage but also of an enthusiasm and striving both for technical perfection and for aesthetic expression to match the intellectual awakening of the times.

Renaissance art was a fresh and vigorous use of the classical form developed in Greece and Rome and revived by Renaissance architects, sculptors, and painters. Artists such as Michelangelo and Leonardo were brilliant in all three media, but most artists excelled in only one or two. Of the painters there were Raphael (also an architect), Titian, El Greco, Dürer, and Holbein. In sculpture there were Ghiberti, Donatello, and Della Robbia. In architecture there was Cellini, an artist who worked superbly in gold, silver, and bronze as well, and whose work in these media is unsurpassed; and there were ceramists, weavers, engravers, and others, all of whom enjoyed the active encouragement and support of wealthy patrons.

In the field of music, the Renaissance also quickened and broadened appreciation and stimulated the development of a modern music with realism, emotional vitality, and a secular quality not bound by ecclesiastical formalism. Music printing began, itself an extremely important event. The manufacture of better instruments paved the way for better and more flexible composition. The child of the cultured family might be expected to study music as assiduously as he studied fencing, riding, or the dance. The Renaissance secular music, created for the stage, the music room, the court, and the chapel, as Hull says, was in these beginnings "an aristocratic art, and it depended for its support for over two centuries . . . entirely on a system of private patronage. Born in Italy in the palaces of the wealthy nobles, it was nurtured in their elegant chapels and presence chambers." [33]

---

[33] A. Eaglefield Hull, *Music, Classical, Romantic and Modern* (New York: E. P. Dutton and Company, 1927), pp. 15-16.

Students of the dance point out that the Renaissance in the dance featured the adaptation by the new aristocracy of the crude and unpolished folk dances which peasants had been dancing since medieval times and earlier. The new bourgeois

> . . . was still a crude, mannerless lout, who ate like an animal, walked like a clodhopper, and generally comported himself like a peasant. . . . [So] Scholars and tutors were attached to the individual courts to remedy individual shortcomings, but of equal importance were the dancing masters who were brought in to remedy the gross defects of carriage and deportment. . . . Clearly the old dances of the countryside were both impracticable and utterly unsuitable in manner and style . . . [Therefore] The dancing masters took as the basis for the elegant routines they evolved for the courtiers *these very dances of the common people* [our italics], toned them down and made them intricate and complicated. In fact, so void of spontaneity and spirit did they ultimately become—so lacking in the elements of basic dance—that courtiers frequently skipped away quietly and joined the dances of the much despised common people, where they could really find some outlet for their emotional exuberance.[34]

Folk dances became the social dances of the court, and from there became popular among broad groups of the upper and middle classes. It must be noted that these events did not touch the peasantry, who went on dancing as they had always done, unbothered by refinements and bourgeois gentility.

The modernists in a similar way adopted and refined the minstrelsy of the city streets to the tastes of the wealthy patrons in their salons and parlors through the madrigal and other musical-dramatic forms. The opera also found its beginning at about this time. Hundreds of urban opera houses were built in Italy and elsewhere. There appear to have been written at least seven hundred operas by many composers, mostly Italians, up to 1700. In fact, several hundred composers, producing thousands of individual works, found their places during this century—truly a productive period greater than any other like period in history to that point.

Finally, the literature of the Renaissance flourished, spurred on

---

[34] J. Martin, *The Dance,* pp. 29-32.

by Gutenberg's press and stimulated by the wide audience and the great interest in reading for both knowledge and amusement. There was a great outpouring of religious works, including translations of the Bible into the vernacular tongues, translations of the Greek and Latin classics, a flow of controversial religious literature reflecting the Reformation agitation, much political literature such as Machiavelli's works, and so on. The names of Rabelais, Montaigne, Cervantes, Edmund Spenser, Hans Sachs, and Shakespeare are famous in the literature of this period.

The Renaissance saw an effort to make education more vital to those receiving it and to break away from the pattern of medieval scholarship. New universities and academies, lavishly supported by merchant princes and wealthy bankers, sprang up in many parts of Europe to pursue the new learning and to teach the sons of the many families of wealth.

Leonard and Affleck tell of the great Italian schoolmaster, Vittorino, whose school for the boys of the great wealthy families of the peninsula's city-states, in addition to teaching Latin, Greek, and classical archeology, also taught riding, swimming, fencing, archery, ball games, and many other games. He took the boys on trips and excursions on foot into the surrounding country and acquainted them with the beauties of nature and the love of adventure.[35] Educators, philosophers, and physicians wrote on the great values of athletic sports such as running, jumping, wrestling, and fencing in maintaining the health and vigor of youth.

The Rise of the Bourgeoisie

The centers of the Renaissance were the cities. It was in the cities, as well, that the major struggles between the nobility, the bourgeoisie, and the commoners, were going on. The class that was rising to power was the class that controlled the economic life and were the leaders in the rising capitalist order. The ruling families were great manufacturers, bankers, and traders. A struggle went on between the old nobility and the new bourgeoisie, the feudal princes and nobles trying to hold on to the privileges that were rapidly slipping from their grasp, and the rising bourgeoisie and wealthy class demanding and obtaining more and more freedom from them.

New national states were rising, and the feudal order was slip-

[35] Leonard and Affleck, *History of Physical Education,* pp. 49-50.

ping away. In most places the king was tending to become an absolute monarch. The feudal nobles were less powerful and owed allegiance to the king. The great struggles that were to take place in the next centuries in the development of these countries would be between the monarchs and the major class groups making up the population. During the Renaissance the first stirrings of these struggles were seen.

Hayes explains the alliance of kings and bourgeoisie as follows:

> This class comprised a rapidly increasing number of men of wealth and brains. The kings catered to it, and it served—and worshipped—the kings. The middle class furnished the kings with lawyers and most useful officials, with more and more money for the mounting expenses of central government, and with reliable men for national armies; and in return the kings bestowed commercial monopolies and other financial favors upon the middle class. . . . The monarch . . . became the real head of a big national business in which the middle class was an important stockholder.[36]

The cultural upsurge of the Renaissance represented, in part, one aspect of the restless movement of the rising bourgeoisie to free themselves both economically and intellectually from feudal restrictions and to find a larger place for their values and aspirations as well as a larger share of the world's goods for themselves. Their recreational and cultural life expressed the philosophy of humanism, the right of man to the healthy exercise of the physical senses and emotions, in opposition to the stoicism and asceticism of medieval Christianity. Chaucer's *Canterbury Tales,* written in the 1300's, pictures the English bourgeoisie, the "burgeys," as he calls them, the merchants, salesmen, shop owners, and craftsmen, with their robust humor and worldliness, frankly anticlerical in their views, bold, and loving the luxuries of good food, ale, and entertainment.

The Renaissance was a movement somewhat removed from the life of the peasants and urban workers. They were as yet relatively submerged and nonvocal elements of the population who could participate little in the intellectual awakening of science and the arts; their life was hard, barren of many pleasures, and marked by infrequent

---

[36] Carlton J. Hayes, *A Political and Cultural History of Modern Europe,* Vol. 1 (New York: The Macmillan Company, 1933), p. 26.

enjoyment of a few moments of rest and relaxation from toil. Yet the new enlightenment and the new concept of the pursuit of happiness were to be the goals for later struggles of much broader groups among the people. Their struggles for these objectives took on more significance after the industrial revolution and the rise of modern capitalism had laid the foundation for a leisure that could extend to all the people.

The Reformation

The Protestant Reformation had combined several of these strivings toward a better life. It also was an important factor in the rise of the middle classes to power and their striving against the old order. The church was by far the largest landholder, industrialist, and merchant in Europe, and was deeply corrupt as well. Some of the kings, merchant-princes, and other business elements such as manufacturers and landlords saw the possibility of wresting some of this power away from the church and sharing it among themselves.

The spirit of social revolution and unrest was very strong among the peasantry and artisans as well, whose grievances against the old order for the ruthlessness of its demands upon them were infinitely greater than those of other classes. These grievances gave rise to a long series of revolts, rebellions, and religious heresies, in which peasants and workers had shared and which in general had been ruthlessly suppressed, with masses of rebels executed, and usually with great cruelty.

The course of the Reformation was much the same in many countries: in Germany under Luther's leadership; in England at the time of King Henry the Eighth; in the Scandinavian states at the same time; under Calvin and Zwingli's leadership in Switzerland; in Scotland under John Knox. There was propaganda against the abuses of the Catholic church, there were political uprisings and revolts against whatever ruler defended the church. These uprisings were led by the merchant princes and urban burghers, and were fought by the artisans and peasants. Church properties and lands were seized by the Protestant elements, the princes, or the kings. Then the victorious princes and bourgeois classes usually turned around and suppressed the peasants, who had been revolting not only against the church but against exploitation by the lay lords and nobles as well.

The peasant revolts were symbols of the mass resistance of the peasants and workers to their oppression, growing out of their desperate need and miserable conditions. Workers' revolts in Flanders, the

Wat Tyler rebellion in England, the establishment of the workers' government at Tabor in Bohemia, the revolts of the peasants and Cossacks in Russia, the rising of the Jacquerie in France, the agitations of the Lollards, and numberless other revolts, occurred all over the western world during the thirteenth to sixteenth centuries.

The Reformation played an important role in freeing the rising middle classes in Europe from the repressive control of the church, and encouraged the development of national monarchies. It did not make possible gains for the suppressed and exploited workers and peasants. In fact, as Hayes says, "the monarchs and lay landlords exploited them as much as the church, the suppression of monasteries cut off a main source of charity for them, the reduction of religious holidays and stricter rules of capitalism meant for employees a lengthening of the time for hard labor and a lessening of the opportunity for the recreation and quaint diversions which formerly had solaced labor. . . . [T]he peasants had exchanged oppressors and found themselves in a worse condition than before." [37] Hayes may be a little gloomy. Peasant rebellions and threats gained concessions in many places in Europe. But significant mass gains were yet to be won.

PURITANISM

The effect of the Reformation upon life, leisure, and the pursuit of happiness was very significant. Under Calvin there was established in Geneva an unbending puritanism, a solemn and severe austerity as the basis for social life. "Purity of conduct" was insisted upon, which meant the forbidding of gambling, card playing, dancing, wearing of finery, singing of gay songs, feasting, drinking and the like. There were to be no more festivals, no more theaters, no more ribaldry, no more light and disrespectful poetry or display. Works of art and musical instruments were removed from the churches. The folk festivals and drama were discouraged or banned, because of the opportunity these offered for groups to express revolutionary ideas and thinly veiled protest and to lampoon the sobriety and strictness of the church and its rule over people's lives.

The Protestants recognized the value of music in the churches, and, while eliminating the artistic richness of Catholic musical forms, continued and enlarged congregational hymn singing. Yet, in England, for example, Protestant church music suffered "degeneration under the

[37] Hayes, p. 217.

sway of Puritanism, which was responsible for the destruction of much of England's best music." [38]

Catholics for centuries had customarily celebrated Sunday Mass and thereafter engaged in leisure-time amusements and merrymaking. The Protestants abolished most of the special holidays, repudiating the veneration of saints in whose honor the holidays had been celebrated for centuries, and because they begrudged the economic losses resulting from idleness on so many days. An example comes from Scotland where the Calvinists saw that a new law was passed prohibiting Sabbath Day gaming, playing, and visiting of taverns and alehouses.

Despite the rigorous efforts to control the lives of the people with stern regulations against the sins of gay revelling and fun the people of all classes in most countries of Europe found many ways to enjoy themselves. Woodward pictures England in the 1500's as a lusty and brawling place.

> People made merry; ale was drunk; songs were bawled, and there were dances to the music of shawms and timbrels. It was a time of rude joys, of laughter and singing, of wrestling and fornication. Cheap traveling shows, with all their marvels, came plodding over the wretched roads.... And there were fights.... The civilization had lustiness and gusto.... Men threw dice and played cards.... Every village had its Maypole and its Morris dancers.... They played dozens of different kinds of card games... and their names were even stranger than the names of the dances.... Among them were: Whip Her Jenny, Tickle Me Quickly, and Post and Pair.[39]

This is a far cry from the solemnity of the Mass and the sober industry of the toiler at the bench or at the plow.

Contributions to a Fuller Life

An assessment of the contributions of this important period in history to the foundations of recreation must consider several very vital facts. One of these facts is that the Renaissance stimulated the arts to new heights of technical and aesthetic perfection. This was done primarily for the pleasures of the wealthy classes. A second fact is that

---

[38] Gantvoort, *Familiar Talks on Music,* p. 211.

[39] W. E. Woodward, *A New American History* (New York: Garden City Publishing Company, 1939), pp. 12-13.

the literary arts were stimulated immeasurably by the invention of the printing press and the beginning of widespread distribution of the writings of philosophers, scientists, poets, dramatists, and others. Now scores of thousands could read what only scores could read before. Education to read took on a completely different significance, and reading as a recreation could become for the first time a priceless possession. A very broad group of urban dwellers of middle and upper class ranks could gain an education, enjoy the arts, attend the theater, and enjoy the recreations formerly enjoyed only by a very small group of feudal lords.

A third fact is that the underlying reason for the great upsurge in the arts was the greater interest in them by larger and growing groups who could support these activities. The contribution the common folk made to this great cultural movement was unique and, to some, surprising; it was the folk dances, drama, and the basic artisanship and workmanship of the artists who were of common origin; these folk arts were the basic source for the dances of the ballet, the songs of the troubadours and meistersingers, and the themes of the operas. The vitality, beauty, and naïve charm of the folk culture was borrowed to make art for the upper classes.

A fourth fact is the impact of the Reformation on the lives of members of the different classes. It would be a mistake to misjudge the effect of this religious conflict on the lives of different groups, for the effect varied quite widely. In the countries that remained largely Catholic under the impact of the reforms that swept through the Catholic church itself, life went on somewhat as before. In the Protestant countries, while there were stern puritanical principles set up as guides, the leisure time and cultural activities of the several classes did not necessarily conform to the demands of the dominant religious and authoritarian groups.

The demand of pastors, priests, princes, landlords, and employers that life be devoted mainly to serious work and serious worship was resisted by the peasants and townsfolk who defended and perpetuated their right to some leisure time for folk festivals, laughter, and communal pleasures. The puritan philosophy of play, which is, in essence, anti-play, and which has had a profound effect in American society up to today, should be understood as having had considerable influence since its inception. But it in no wise destroyed the underlying pleasure-loving philosophy of the common people. This philosophy was, partly, a means of expressing resistance to, and resentment of, the exploitation, the speeding up and stretching out of productivity, of which they were medieval victims. Partly it was an expression of the irrepressibility of motivations to play, a philosophy in which man found the elements of a happy and pleasing existence. They showed that even the lowly would fight for the right to enjoy life.

The Renaissance and the Reformation marked a change in western civilization from feudalism to the modern era. The upsurge of cultural and recreational expression reflected struggles of the middle-class and lower-class groups to break away from the repressions of feudalism and to reach out for a fuller life.

Questions for Study and Discussion

1. *Select a period of history and contrast the recreations of the various social classes of that time.*
2. *What is the evidence that creativity is a human trait that seeks expression in all cultures?*
3. *What was the impact of the Renaissance on the recreation of the common people?*
4. *Do you think it probable that religion grew out of a need for deeply meaningful recreation? Defend your answer.*
5. *Why has the church striven to influence, guide, and control the leisure-time activities of man?*

Selected Readings

Durant, Will, *The Story of Philosophy* (New York: Simon and Schuster, Inc., 1926).

Hayes, Carlton J., *A Political and Cultural History of Modern Europe,* Vol. 1 (New York: The Macmillan Company, 1933).

Leonard, Fred E., and George B. Affleck, *A Guide to the History of Physical Education* (Philadelphia: Lea and Febiger, 1947).

Woody, Thomas, *Life and Education in Early Societies* (New York: The Macmillan Company, 1949).

3

LEISURE AND RECREATION IN MODERN TIMES

The technological-industrial-economic revolution that gave birth to modern times has dramatically changed the political, social, and recreational life of most of the world's peoples. A brief study of the history of recreation in the United States in the light of these revolutionary changes will help us to understand this country's recreational past and will provide a basis for a short description of recreation in the twentieth century as a basis for later, more detailed study of some of its characteristics and as a foundation for the philosophical study to follow.

THE INDUSTRIAL REVOLUTION, CAPITALISM, AND DEMOCRACY

The industrial revolution is the name given to a rapid and continuing development of large-scale production based upon power-driven machines. It had its roots in the technical and economic developments of four hundred years ago, and has continued since then. Two things characterize this revolution: (1) *automatic machines* were invented to take the place of human labor; (2) water, steam, oil, and electric *power* were developed and put to innumerable uses, as atomic power may be in the future. Great technical inventions led the way to fundamental industrial changes. Many European nations changed from agricultural to industrial societies.

Two outcomes of the industrial revolution have had utmost significance for recreation. One of these outcomes was the demand of big industry for large groups of workers to man the plants; therefore, industrial societies became urban societies. Recreation for urban folk is, and must be, quite different from recreation for rural folk. The second outcome was that man, with machines, for the first time reached the point of economic development where, potentially, he could produce material plenty for all and still have leisure for all. It took several generations before men realized that it was possible to provide not only the favored few, but the entire population, with enough of the world's goods for subsistence and comfort, at a fraction of the expenditure of time and effort required previously for mere survival.

This significant technological fact gradually became clear to larger groups in all countries. It changed the idea of the "pursuit of happiness" completely. Although "happiness" may mean different things to each of us, we may agree that two of its elements are *sufficiency of material things* to meet our needs, and *leisure time* to enjoy ourselves. The industrial revolution was bringing both of these within the reach of all men. Lest this sound too lyrical, let us hasten to point out that this promise has been realized only imperfectly so far, and for the centuries we are studying here no such utopia emerged. Life, for the most part, was a continuing grim struggle, even though efforts were made to organize economic and social relationships upon a productive and sound basis.

The industrial revolution got its best start in England, and then spread to the European countries and to America. Modern capitalism stimulated technological changes and put them into operation; and capitalism in turn was immeasurably stimulated to expansion and growth by the new possibilities for mass production.

Great corporations grew up, financial institutions were created, capitalists pooled their resources in order to expand. There was unending competition of all kinds between capitalists of large and small influence; this competition extended even into the international field. Imperialism increased and great fortunes were made in exploiting the resources and the peoples of the Americas, Asia, the Indies, India, and Africa.

All of this important economic development undermined the power of the old aristocracy who until modern times had ruled the countries of Europe. The aristocrats had two choices to make in this period: to become capitalists themselves and share in the expanding capitalism, or to cling to the king, and become a kind of parasitic ornament of his court. At any rate, during this time the nobility declined as the dominant class and was replaced by the bourgeoisie.

The factory system bred the factory city. Workers moved near the factory. They lived in congestion, squalor, disease, and filth; they were oppressed by starvation wages and frightened by recurrent unemployment; they were trapped by monotonous and prolonged labor; they were degraded by their economic need to send their women and children into mines and mills to work. Hayes points out that the immediate economic effects of the industrial revolution in England were "to add enormously to wealth and capital and, on the other hand, to degrade the English masses, enlarging the urban proletariat and holding it to poverty as a permanent condition." [1] The same was true in other countries as well.

The industrialization of agriculture resulted in profits for owners, and in poverty and unemployment for the peasants. One solution, for a time, was to send numbers of the unemployed to the colonies as indentured servants. But the lower classes saw before their eyes the glaring discrepancy between the productivity of the factories and the poverty and want they experienced intimately day by day. This discrepancy led them to rebel, to make demands, and to organize to enforce their demands. From many sources, in both the working class and the peasantry and from religious and other groups, came demands for reforms, for recognition of labor's right to organize, for the growth

---

[1] Carlton J. Hayes, *A Political and Cultural History of Modern Europe*, Vol. 1 (New York: The Macmillan Company, 1933), p. 51.

of cooperative societies, all of which resulted in improving a few of the worst conditions of the laboring masses.

Parallel to the economic movements were political changes, as the philosophy of democracy was preached to the peoples of the world, and as various groups arose to fight for democratic government. In England and France during the eighteenth and nineteenth centuries there were revolutions and struggles that put bourgeois governments in power and provided an opportunity for workers and peasants to agitate actively for the improvement of their conditions. Democratic struggles against autocracy, militarism, and war led the way for social reforms and a larger place in social life for the masses of the common folk.

Let us offer the following generalization to describe this basic fact of history:

The industrial revolution and the economic and political organization based upon it brought new problems of living to human society, the new possibility of a sufficiency of material things to meet individual needs, and new resources of leisure time for recreation.

RECREATION AND CULTURAL GROWTH FROM THE SEVENTEENTH THROUGH THE NINETEENTH CENTURY

The Flowering of the Arts

What can be gleaned from these important and rapid-moving events in history that helps to illuminate the recreational past? One significant event is that along with the industrial revolution went an intellectual revolution that had great meaning for the people of the world. In the scientific fields—physics, biology, physiology, chemistry, and medicine—were made great discoveries. In philosophy and in the arts a similar progress occurred during this period.

Modern Spain had its era of leadership in the arts in the first part of the seventeenth century, but lost that supremacy to France during the reign of Louis XIV, an age of royal splendor in France. The court lavishly subsidized all of the arts—architecture, sculpture, painting, engraving, music, and literature. French speech, literature, manners, dress, and art became the model of civilized Europe.

The Renaissance classicism continued and developed in architecture, painting, and sculpture. The florid and exuberant architecture of the baroque was manifested in churches, palaces, and other buildings throughout Europe. Painters found increasingly broader interest in their work. From China were imported fascinating paintings, porcelains, lacquers, and embroideries whose delicate quality challenged European artists. The arts were enjoying increased popularity, signified by broader interest and patronage by more and more groups with money to purchase, and capacity to appreciate, the products of the artists.

The world of music enjoyed considerable growth during these centuries. Because the audience of music could be larger than those of other arts, musicians were somewhat more sensitive—and responsive—to the needs of new groups. Opera continued to be most fashionable, but a wide variety of other musical forms was created and presented to audiences throughout Europe at the royal courts, in the opera houses and concert halls, in the churches, salons, and music chapels, for countless occasions. Works were written for larger ensembles of instruments, although it was not until the nineteenth century that the modern symphony orchestra came into being. Pratt points out that in the eighteenth century "the rise of instrumental music turned attention to the public concert as a frequent social event, gave employment and stimulus to the independent virtuoso, and ultimately led to the organization of fixed orchestras. . . . [It] also tended to lift musical art to a place of greater dignity in popular estimation." [2] Many of the great composers of the period, such as Chopin, Liszt, and Mozart, were talented performers as well, and played to large and appreciative audiences throughout Europe. The period produced the greatest group of composers, in the shortest time, that the world has ever seen: Bach, Mozart, Beethoven, Brahms, Mendelssohn, Wagner, Dvořak, Grieg, Mussorgsky, Tchaikowsky, to name just a few.

In France, during revolutionary times, there was a flowering of music in great popular pageants and informal popular opera, as well as much folk music and other popular forms. But the romantic themes became the most dominant music in Europe during the nineteenth century. Such music satisfied an audience primarily of the middle classes, who tried to emulate aristocratic traditions; yet the folk music arising from the recreations of the people was needed to make the whole of music more palatable to this new power group; and it influenced the art of all Europe. Such music responded to the listeners'

---

[2] Waldo S. Pratt, *The History of Music* (New York: G. Schirmer, Inc., 1930), p. 332.

demand for freshness, beauty, and reality, a music close to the people's hearts. It reflected the wider audiences to which music was playing, the greater participation of the lower middle classes and other groups in music, and the expansion of folk music as a means of expressing the gaiety and playfulness of the common people in their leisure hours. Hull described Haydn's music as "applying Viennese polish over the surface of the folk music of his native land, Croatia. . . . This rich Croatian folk-song carried with it the smell of the fresh fields, the scent of the new-mown hay. . . . Haydn took the actual folk-tunes themselves into his music." [3]

Literature from the seventeenth to nineteenth centuries was truly in a golden age. In each country, it had its great periods and its less brilliant ones, its periods of creativity and vitality and its periods of sterility. A priceless treasure of literature flowed from the pens of a great company of writers; Bacon, Milton, Hobbes, Locke, Rousseau, Voltaire, Dickens, Burns, Zola, Tolstoy, Dostoevsky, Tennyson, Burns, Keats, Shelley, Goethe, Scott, and scores more wrote for millions of readers, their books being produced by great commercial publishing companies. Libraries, schools, and universities were developing, and for the first time in history it began to appear that everyone might be able to share alike in one of the great cultural resources, literature.

Drama also had a period of growth, with a development much like that of music. From Shakespeare's time, plays were written and produced, sometimes underwritten by the king or some wealthy person, sometimes produced as a profit-making enterprise. But plays attracted both the aristocrats and the urban common people. Playwrights could now write for broad audiences. There was, on occasion, drama that was powerful propaganda for the democratic revolution against the tyranny of monarchs or ecclesiastics. Other playwrights employed their literary talents on the side of the church or the king. At other times the plays were built around simple romantic plots where the social and political situation was avoided or dealt with very lightly.

Closely related to drama and music was the dance. The greatest patron of the dance was Louis XIV of France, during whose reign the ballet reached great heights. Martin says, "The king was an excellent dancer and delighted in exhibiting his gifts. However outstanding they may have been, they led him to engage and to encourage the most

---

[3] A. Eaglefield Hull, *Music, Classical, Romantic and Modern* (New York: E. P. Dutton and Company, 1927), p. 56.

brilliant of musicians, painters and poets to collaborate on his ballets." [4] Ballet became not only a pastime of the court but an independent theater art. In the first half of the nineteenth century ballet enjoyed its golden age with a high degree of technical skill and vitality and broad public interest. Later it declined and public interest lagged. Commercial theater managers made more profits out of colorful extravaganzas, the forerunners of the present-day burlesque, relying not upon artistic, but rather upon vulgar, suggestive sexual themes to satisfy the tastes of the audiences.

Dancing was a favorite recreation of all classes. The fashionable balls of the people of wealth featured stately and restrained social dances such as the quadrille and the minuet. The common people danced in their homes or in the streets as a major source of pleasure and sociability. Peasants and workers in England romped the carefree Morris dances; Spaniards, the gypsy dances and flamenco; French youth, LaBourré's; Italians, the farandole. In Scotland it was the highland fling; in Ireland, the reel and jig; in Hungary, the czardas; in Poland, the oberek; and in Germany, the waltz. Martin says:

> Man . . . by his very nature has to assemble with his kind every so often and rejoice in the kinship. . . . [I]t was a matter almost of survival for the people . . . [to] meet at some fairly central spot for a long and energetic session of dancing once in a while. In no other way could they remind themselves that they were members of a single community, with common interests and habits and tastes.[5]

In Arabia, dancing, not always as rustic and romping as some European folk forms, was a pleasurable pastime in homes, a means of telling stories. Egypt for centuries continued its custom of dancing. India, Turkey, Persia, Java, China, Japan, Hawaii and many other countries had unique and highly treasured folk and national dances which were important to leisure-time pleasures.

Education and Sports

Another development of great importance was the growth of education. Schools had been limited to those families who could afford

---

[4] John Martin, *The Dance* (New York: The Tudor Publishing Company, 1946), p. 37.

[5] Martin, p. 26.

private schools, but there was agitation to broaden the base of education. John Knox, the Scottish Presbyterian, called for an elementary school for every parish, a grammar school for boys (not girls) for every market town, and a university for every English city. England, Germany, and the Scandinavian countries endowed numerous schools during the 1700's and 1800's.

Rousseau in France fought for the right of all children to learn through joyful and playful experience. He said of the child, "Give his body continual exercise; let him work, and move about, and run and shout, and be continually in motion; let him be a man in vigor, and soon he will be such by force of reason . . . it is the happy constitution of the body which renders the operations of the mind facile and sure." [6] He, Pestalozzi, and Froebel urged the democratization of kindergarten and elementary school programs for children during the nineteenth century.

Paralleling the interest in dancing was a growing interest in athletic sports. Leonard and Affleck describe, for seventeenth century England, the wide range of sports and recreations "much in use, as ringing, bowling, shooting (archery) . . . kelpins, tronks, quoits, pitching bars, hurling, wrestling, leaping, running, fencing, mustering, swimming, westers (fencing with wooden swords), foils, football, balloon, quintain, etc., and many such which are the common recreations of the country folks." [7] Great attention to perfection of play and a high regard for sportsmanship characterized the holiday sports to which large groups among all classes of Englishmen were strongly attracted.

German schoolmasters in the 1700's were encouraging their boys to participate in riding, dancing, fencing, playing soldier, marching and other sports. During summer months there were outdoor excursions and camping in tents, bathing, hunting, fishing, boating, climbing, and jumping. About the beginning of the nineteenth century Guts Muths, one of a number of pioneers in German physical education and play, was beginning his work in gymnastics and vigorous games. So influential were his fifty years of teaching and writing, that his books were published in most European languages, used all through the nineteenth century, and reprinted in the twentieth century.

---

[6] J. J. Rousseau, *Emile,* translated by Barbara Foxley (New York: E. P. Dutton and Company, 1911), p. 82.

[7] Fred E. Leonard and George B. Affleck, *A Guide to the History of Physical Education* (Philadelphia: Lea and Febiger, 1947), pp. 200-201.

The man called the father of popular gymnastics in Germany was Jahn, who, early in the 1800's, stimulated the Turner movement. Boys and young men would come to the *Turnplatz,* or gymnastics place, afternoons and nights for athletic games and play on the gymnastic apparatus. Motivated by health, recreation, and patriotic aims, the *Turners* became great recreational and sports associations, and organizations for national cultural expression. In fact, they were so popular a means for mobilizing masses of the people around programs of recreation and fun that reactionary German governments intermittently tried to suppress them as radical and subversive, even jailing Jahn himself on one occasion.

The will of the German people finally prevailed, however, and Germany continued to develop and democratize its sports programs. It created an indigenous play and recreation for its people, sponsoring pioneer kindergarten and playground movements. In Sweden, Ling fathered a gymnastics and cultural movement much like that in Germany. Denmark had a similar movement under the leadership of the famous teacher, Nachtegall.

During the last part of the nineteenth century the athletics movement grew rapidly throughout Europe. In 1896, worldwide athletics were reconstituted through the Olympic games after many centuries of lapse. The sports and games, which were attracting participants and observers from all classes, represented one significant area of recreation that during the eighteenth and nineteenth centuries became democratized to a considerable degree.

Political Revolution

To understand what really happened in the recreation of people in Europe during these centuries, especially during the nineteenth century, events in the economic and political field have to be related to events in the field of leisure. The rise of industrial capitalism and imperialism created a rapidly growing middle class of some economic means and a larger working class, which often lived in the poorest of circumstances in urban slums. Early economic theorists argued that natural laws brought the workers to this state and they could blame only their own fecundity for their conditions. Any effort by the state to interfere with these natural laws would result only in ruin, so the state should do little beyond meager relief for the destitute poor.

In contrast to this view there was emerging a more democratic point of view, which held that the welfare of all the people was the responsibility of the state, and that each individual had the right to share in the benefits of an expanding economy. Workers demanded higher wages, protection against slums, depressions, poverty, disease, ignorance, education for their children, more leisure, and an opportunity to pursue happiness during that leisure.

The political revolutions that took place in England, France, and America were three of the great upheavals in which the bourgeoisie joined with the peasants and workers to overthrow the aristocratic rule of the nobility. In each case the result was to place the middle-class economic elements more firmly in control of both economy and government while the lower classes gained little that was tangible.

The revolutions that went on during the 1800's, especially in 1848, in France, Germany, Italy, Hungary, Denmark, Austria, and elsewhere, were more generally led by working class elements and guided by socialist political thought. These upheavals influenced the dominant classes in Europe to pay new attention to the needs of the workers and peasants for a greater share in the life of the times. Examples of the significant concessions won through such struggles were the broader programs of public education, some small improvements in economic welfare programs such as relief for destitute children and families, broader programs of playgrounds and sports activities, and encouragement of richer cultural and similar leisure-time programs.

Along with increases in production went modest economic gains won by trade unions for the workers. The average person had a few more pence in his pocket, and the result was a greater expenditure for recreation. The popular theater got a new lease on life with the expansion of the paying clientele. The same thing was true of other recreations. When broader groups had the means for the purchase of such things, expansion was stimulated. Not the least of these recreations was the enjoyment of reading. The stimulus to read and to write was reflected in the growth of education and enlightenment in general.

Play Developments

Eighteenth and nineteenth century philosophers were paying attention to theories of play and recreation. They included educators, biologists, and psychologists who observed the behavior of people, analyzed their needs, and saw the values in play. Sapora and Mitchell point out that in this period "writers like Rabelais and Montaigne in France, Mulcaster and Ascham in England, and Comenius in Germany, pleaded the necessity of play in the life of children." [8] The Neumeyers say, "Men like Rousseau, Guts Muths, Pestalozzi and Froebel stressed that play is a normal phase of life. . . . Children should be allowed freedom and opportunity for the expression of their natural desires." [9]

There were wide differences in the basic rationalizations for play of some of these men. Guts Muths was interested in using play and physical education to strengthen the bodies of young men and to increase their competence as soldiers for militaristic Germany. In contrast, Rousseau and Froebel thought of the child as a person not to be hurried into adulthood but as one who should be given the opportunity to grow and develop freely in an environment of beauty and happiness, the better to prepare him for adult life.

To summarize these facts, we can see that the industrial revolution and capitalism on the one hand created new problems of city crowding, poverty, and the wear and tear of industrial labor. On the other hand, a tremendously greater wealth could be produced and, potentially, shared by all, and a much greater leisure could be provided by the productivity of the machine. The contradiction between the promise of comfort and leisure and the stark reality of discomfort, poverty, and dreary labor became clearer to the poorer classes. They realized that a better world could be brought into being and that it is man's right and duty to work for such a better world and to share in its pleasure. Much of the turmoil and instability of these centuries was the result of efforts by the masses to seize a larger share of all those things that meant a good life.

Recreation in this period reflected the same class-determined differences that existed in earlier societies. The more favored economic groups enjoyed greater opportunities to participate in recreational and cultural pursuits, but the genteel sports and the arts of leisure were patronized more actively and by broader middle-class groups than ever before. The common folk, however, although they were deprived of opportunities for many of these pursuits, gained many more opportunities for recreation and play than they had ever enjoyed before.

---

[8] Allen V. Sapora and Elmer D. Mitchell, *The Theory of Play and Recreation* (New York: The Ronald Press Company, 1961), p. 20.

[9] Martin H. Neumeyer and Esther S. Neumeyer, *Leisure and Recreation: A Study of Leisure and Recreation in Their Sociological Aspects,* Third edition (New York: The Ronald Press Company, 1958), p. 57.

There was a broadening and enriching of many of the arts, such as literature, music, drama, and dance, the beginning of the modern sports movements, and an expansion of education.

The great development in the several arts was related to the rest of the changes in the society. The middle class became the main patrons of the arts. Literature developed—sensitive to the stirrings among the people for its themes. In music, drama, and dance, the creative artist responded to the growing democratic spirit of the times, borrowing from the national and folk art for his themes, and enjoying the opportunity to have his art enjoyed by broader and larger groups, both as participants and as audiences.

There persisted among the common people deeply laid folkways of play. People in the rural areas still celebrated the seasons with festivals, dances, and songs. They had traditional holidays and recreations that radical changes in their lives did not alter completely. Young folks took great pleasure, as always, in the sports and games and athletic contests by which they showed off their strength and agility and competed for prizes or prestige. The rapid expansion in sports, aided by community provision for facilities often available to everybody, stimulated and gave some new forms to activities which had always been popular and traditional.

Democratization characterized recreational and cultural change in the modern period of history, with broadening participation in leisure-time pursuits and the promise to still larger groups of a greater share in their values.

At the beginning of the twentieth century there seemed to be many of the potentialities for a great increase in leisure, and for the use of this leisure by the masses of the people for the pursuit of the arts and pleasures of recreation. Before we examine the impact of twentieth-century events upon the lives of people, let us backtrack for a brief period and trace the history of recreation in America.

A SHORT HISTORY OF RECREATION IN THE UNITED STATES

Recreation has had a highly interesting development in the United States, and to picture its growth with any degree of adequacy we would need to devote much more space than we can to the subject. Several histories in the field are available to the student of this subject.

Dulles indicates that two forces operated in this country to influence recreation from the start.

> The first is the continuing influence of an inherent puritanism, both rising from and enforcing a dogma of work born of economic circumstances . . . it has frowned severely upon what the early settlers called any "mispense of time." . . . The second factor is the paramount influence on recreation of the gradual transformation of our economy from the simplicity of the agricultural era to the complexity of the machine age. . . . The machine has greatly increased the leisure of the laboring masses, and it has at the same time made life less leisurely . . . with an ever-growing need for play that can effectively compensate for the intensity under which we must work.[10]

Frontier Life

The settlers in America in the early 1600's tried to establish colonies in the bleak wilderness of the north or the malaria-ridden swamps of the south. Here, harsh climate, unfriendly Indians, starvation, and disease combined to make life difficult, "all things stared upon them with a weather-beaten face." Merely to keep alive was a demanding experience. There was no place for loafing, genteel life, or play. Learning to produce food in the new country was difficult and years of poverty and famine faced the early settlers. They usually had been sent over by a speculating English corporation hoping to make a financial killing. The company demanded that profitable goods be returned right away to England from the settlements. The economic and religious ideas of capitalism and puritanism were, however, adaptable to such a demand. Strict regulations "in detestation of idleness" enforced work and prohibited unseemly play and amusements. But the free atmosphere influenced many to seek freedom to enjoy leisure as well.

At Merry Mount, near Plymouth colony, a few adventurers and servants started a settlement separate from that of the Pilgrims, traded profitably with the Indians, and enjoyed such revelry and good times

---

[10] Foster Rhea Dulles, *America Learns to Play* (New York: D. Appleton-Century Company, 1940), pp. viii-ix. Copyright, 1940, by D. Appleton-Century Co., Inc. Reprinted by permission of the publishers Appleton-Century-Crofts, an affiliate of Meredith Press. See also Clarence E. Rainwater, *The Play Movement in the United States* (Chicago: The University of Chicago Press, 1922).

that they shocked the Puritan fathers into repressive action. When these carefree settlers set up the traditional English Maypole and undertook to be gay with wine and dancing, the Governor of the Massachusetts Bay Colony ordered the Maypole cut down and threatened dire punishment for anyone spending his time idly or unprofitably. Laws were passed banning cards and games and such vices as tobacco smoking in public or other than at mealtime. Sunday was no day for frivolity; it was to be spent in worship and pious reflection, even by children.

But despite such energetic efforts, the colonists were not to be denied some relaxation from work. The tavern, with its drinking, card playing, and dancing, soon became one of the great colonial institutions, despite efforts of the theocratic rulers to abolish and then to limit it. Gradually, more in the southern and middle colonies than in Puritan New England, the desires of hard-working persons of all classes for recreation resulted in a considerable expansion of such activities. With the coming of the 1700's the economic stability of the colonial communities increased. Southern plantations, fishing, shipbuilding, agriculture, and commerce were prospering. Colonial recreational life prospered as well.

The more well-to-do classes entertained themselves in sumptuous style, with epicurean banquets, exclusive hunting and fishing excursions, gambling at the horse races, parties at their social clubs, attendance at exclusive resorts to which members would repair by carriage for picnics and entertainment "in the genteelest manner." Golf, sleighriding, concerts, the theater, parties, balls, and other gay entertainments added pleasure to the lives of those well-to-do who could get away from their puritanical consciences. An influential factor in all colonial life, but especially in the South, was that its industry and agriculture were based upon the slavery of both Negroes and whites. On the large plantations of the South, living on the labor of slaves, the owners were a leisured upper class who pursued their recreations with gaiety and finesse. Among the common people, the great mass of yeomanry who made up nine tenths of the population, the English love of games and sports asserted itself. Hunting, fowling, and fishing for plentiful game were very popular. Community people gathered for work and play at fairs, election days, house raisings, sheep shearings, corn huskings, and other cooperative work and play days.

Colonists would enjoy shooting contests, horse races, cockfights, ice skating and sleighing in the winter, and bowling. Ever popular with the youth was the pastime of "bundling" in which the young folk would share the same bed, fully clothed (of course), but nonetheless romantic.

There appears to have been a prodigious amount of drinking. Woodward reports an estimate made by Boston merchants that in 1763 an average of four gallons of rum for every man, woman, and child in the Massachusetts colony was consumed that year, plus huge amounts of hard cider, drunk by children and adults alike.[11]

Gay and boisterous square dances, jigs, and reels were popular with the country folk. The upper classes imitated the European gentry with their minuets and gavottes, but these were not the dances of the countryside. Dulles says of the latter, "The music . . . was . . . generally furnished by an ancient fiddler or Negro slave with strumming banjo. Farm boys and girls, in leather jerkins and homespun gowns, asked only that the tune be lively. Often they danced until dawn, and sometimes they appear to have spent all their substances on the flips and toddy so obligingly sold by the tavernkeeper." [12]

In the west, the frontiersmen moved restlessly onward, unceasingly, for decades. The frontiersman's recreation was a treasured period in a life of very hard work, and when the religious circuit riders' camp meetings or revivals, or the barbecues, log-rollings, or other occasions, came along they were celebrated mightily and with gusto, with raw whiskey, shooting matches, hunting expeditions, horse racing, feats of strength and agility, and rough-and-tumble wrestling that was really rough. As for eating, Dulles says,

> Dinner was a gargantuan feast: a barbecued beef or hog, roasted in a deep hole lined with hot stones; quantities of buffalo steaks, venison, baked possum or wild turkey; and always hominy, corn dodgers and wheatcakes fried in bear's oil. After dinner and general sports, the climax of every gathering was a dance. . . . As for the dances themselves, "None of your straddling, minding, sadying," wrote Davy Crockett, "but a regular sifter, cut-the-buckle, chicken flutter set-to. It is a good wholesome exercise; and when one of our boys puts his arm around his partner, it's a good hug, and no harm in it." [13]

---

[11] W. E. Woodward, *A New American History* (New York: Garden City Publishing Company, 1939), p. 102.

[12] Dulles, *America Learns to Play,* p. 59.

[13] Dulles, pp. 76-77.

Whenever folks got together to sit and gossip, tale telling and story swapping went on. Western legend and folklore constitutes part of the great literature of America, as interesting to read today as it was entertaining to groups gathered to listen a century or two ago. The American Revolution, although it was primarily an economic struggle for freedom from British mercantile and imperialist regulations and restrictions, was also a struggle for democracy and against British tyranny. The ballads and folk tales coming out of the revolutionary army and its long struggles, along with those of the rest of the people, became part of America's treasured folklore.

After the revolution was over and the new government was organized, the United States was launched upon new and uncharted ways. Without any long-established national tradition or any well-established pattern of class relations, a vigorous capitalism indigenous to the American continent began to develop. A vigorous and unique form of democracy began to develop as well. Economic, political, and social factors were highly influential in the recreational customs that developed.

The Nineteenth Century

American capitalism and urban civilization grew during the 1800's. The middle classes were "getting ahead" economically and the workers, as in Europe, were "enjoying" long hours, low pay, poor working conditions, and the strain of keeping pace with the machine. In America, escape from such boredom was sometimes at hand. One could follow Horace Greeley's advice to "Go west, young man, and grow up with the country." During frequent depression periods thousands of the unemployed became pioneers and moved toward the wide open spaces. Parallel to this westward expansion was the growth of labor unions. Hutchinson points out, "Unions began to struggle vigorously for their avowed rights early in the nineteenth century . . . for higher wages and shorter hours . . . to create an improved balance between the length of the work day and the amount of daily leisure. The part labor unions played in producing twenty more hours of leisure per week during the nineteenth century should not be underestimated." [14] Aggressive trade unionism during the century brought three important gains to the working class. One of these was the

---

[14] John L. Hutchinson, *Principles of Recreation* (New York: The Ronald Press Company, 1951), pp. 34-35. Copyright 1951 The Ronald Press Company.

increased leisure time gained by shorter work days and the eventual six-day week—or less, in later years. The second was increased wages, which netted families at least a modest income, above the bare minimum for survival, with which to purchase some recreation. The third was better working conditions, which permitted the worker to do better work, maintain greater dignity, have better health, and to return home after work not completely exhausted, unable to enjoy the little leisure he had. Improvements came slowly, with another century required before levels consistent with human decency could be claimed by the society for most of its members.

American cities began to grow. The larger ones for the most part were slum-ridden and congested, with few private yards for play, few public parks, and few provisions for recreation. Children played in the streets at some risk to themselves. Juvenile crimes and other problems increased steadily. Adults drifted toward a variety of cheap, inadequate, and often undesirable forms of commercial amusement because of the lack of any other forms and the absence of civic and community sponsorship of recreation.

Urban dwellers watched horse races, ball games, and similar sports events. The American tradition of spectator sports began to be established. Holidays were great occasions. The worker and his family could attend a parade or picnic, go to the amusement park, or go on a steamboat or train excursion. Especially in the eastern cities such as New York did this activity, once restricted to the upper classes, become popular with thousands of workers and shopkeepers and their families. Several million immigrants from European countries brought with them their native recreational and cultural customs, which in some respects enriched American urban life. Usually the second and later generations would gradually lose their European identity and merge with the urban culture.

Recreation for most people had to be passive, commercialized, and cheap. The popular theater might charge from ten to thirty cents a seat. Dulles described the opening of the new Bowery theater in New York in mid-century:

> In a smoke-laden atmosphere redolent of beer and sweat, this boisterous audience watched the play with an enthusiasm untempered by any polite conventions. . . . Criticism . . . might still be emphasized . . . by a barrage of eggs and rotten fruit.[15]

[15] Dulles, *America Learns to Play*, p. 214.

One playwright, producing ten or twenty melodramas a year, reached an audience of several millions. Burlesque shows were popular, as was vaudeville. There were farces, musical shows, comedies, and occasional serious drama, but the public was given mostly "silly buffoonery and vulgar nonsense."

Dime museums, dance halls, shooting galleries, beer gardens, bowling alleys, music halls, billiard parlors, saloons, and similar amusement resorts made up the world of entertainment. Drinking, gambling, and prostitution were popular where corrupt municipal government allied with vice elements to run the city. When the electric trolley came along and families could ride, for a few cents each, to the cities' edges to amusement parks and ball parks, city dwellers turned more to these recreations. Dulles summarizes well the problem of urban recreation for the century:

> Democracy had asserted in ever-stronger terms its right to play. America had become a pleasure-loving nation, but the character of its amusements, in so far as the urban population was concerned, could not but cause serious misgivings.[16]

Some groups, mainly those more well-to-do, sought out other, more cultured, recreations. Symphonic organizations existed in New York, Philadelphia, Boston, Chicago, and other cities. The legitimate theater had a very healthy life during the latter half of the nineteenth century, along with other cultural activities. Society actively supported the recreations of tennis, golf, polo, horse shows and racing, as well as intercollegiate football.

In the South the genteel plantation life went on with grace and dignity for the wealthy and misery for the poor until the slave system came to an end with the Civil War. From the Negro people of the South came America's richest and greatest indigenous music, their spirituals, folk music, and protest songs. This music was not only a means of expression for the Negro people and a solace and pleasure in the moments they were permitted such luxury; it also gave this country its first claim to distinction in the creation of great music.

A quite different recreational picture faced the traveler of the century who ventured into the West. Here the cow towns and mining camps had a life all their own, with recreations suitable to a population composed at first almost entirely of men. When work was over,

---

[16] Dulles, p. 229.

entertainment dominated the lives of miners or cowboys, and the saloons and honky tonks were the recreation centers. Drinking, gambling at faro, roulette, monte, and poker, fighting, and dancing with the dance-hall girls made up their recreation.

When the mining towns and cow towns became more settled, life tamed down somewhat, although the cow-town atmosphere has never left many small western communities entirely. But for the most part the small American towns in the 1800's developed a recreation that was typically and uniquely American. There were town dances to which all were likely to come, as they did to local ball games or amateur band concerts. The churches were active with Ladies' Aid socials, missionary society meetings, Sunday School picnics, church suppers, and bazaars. There was much singing around the piano in the homes and at parties. Lodges and fraternal societies were numerous and their social functions were important recreations. Women organized social clubs as well as art, book, dramatic, sewing, and other societies. These activities were witness to the tremendous need the average adult had for joining with his fellows in some manner to enjoy fellowship and socialization.

Rural recreational life, in nineteenth-century United States, was built around church activities and activities of the Grange, which was organized for economic and educational reasons but remained to fulfill a great recreational responsibility as the main social gathering place for rural groups. Grange dances, entertainments, and other get-togethers were a precious recreation for rural folk, when they could dance and be gay and the young could romance. Special holiday celebrations, annual fairs, and an occasional circus or traveling show were important events as well.

In the latter part of the century, the country saw an increase in sports participation and a growth of organized recreation. Baseball, as the "national sport," began to be played by thousands of youngsters wherever open spaces could be found, even in the city streets. Tennis, croquet, roller skating, and bicycling became popular. Dulles says, "With the gradual passing of so much of what the frontier had always stood for, sports provided a new outlet for an inherently restless people." [17]

Such active participation was welcomed by educators and health experts as a means of maintaining the vitality of the people. Educators

[17] Dulles, p. 199.

after some years of resistance began to build elementary and high school gymnasiums and to introduce physical education courses and extracurricular athletics. Colleges introduced gymnastics, rowing, baseball, football, and such sports. By the turn of the century, physical education, sports, and athletics had become firmly anchored into the schools of the land, as well as in the affection of people of all classes and groups.

An important cultural pursuit of all classes of people was reading. The challenge of America stimulated a large group of American poets and writers to produce a worthy body of literature. Paine, Bryant, Whittier, Poe, Longfellow, Emerson, Thoreau, Lowell, Stowe, Phillips, Clemens, and many others, were among these writers. Books were published and sold by the millions of copies. Extensive public education made most people readers, and reading became one of the great recreations of the times. Here was one of the arts that did not rest solely upon the European creative genius, but found roots in the American soil too.

There was created a modest native music, but in general the American public heard the music of European composers. They enjoyed the other arts, usually imported, only to a limited degree. A large group of dramatists and musicians busied themselves turning out transient and popular plays, songs, and cheap melodramas, but practically none of this survived as art, nor impressed audiences as such.

Recreation in early United States history was influenced by conflict between puritanism and the indigenous pioneer concept of democratic recreational freedom. The result was culturally unsophisticated, informal recreation, ranging from genteel pursuits of the rural and urban wealthy to rustic community activities of rural and pioneer folk and weekend commercial amusements of urban working classes.

Emergence of the Recreation Movement

The century also saw the recreation movement draw its beginnings out of a complex of positive developments. The community park and playground movement, the national and state parks and recreation areas, the adult education movement, the kindergarten and nursery movements, the settlement and youth-serving voluntary agency beginnings, the cultural and arts movements, and the rest occurred in parallel. Each supported the others in becoming more firmly established in the American scene as a foundation for the recreation movement of the twentieth century.

The Young Men's Christian Association, the first of the great national youth-serving organizations, was organized in Boston in 1851. With a program stressing fellowship for religious worship, the YMCA gradually enlarged its program to include recreational gymnastics and sports and other group activities, mainly for boys and young men, in hundreds of communities throughout the country.

Parallel to this development was that of the Young Women's Christian Association. The first organization by that name was begun in 1866 in Boston and several hundred associations existed by the end of the century. The YWCA program included education, training, job placement, housing, religious activities, wholesome social recreation, and cultural activities. Both the YMCA and the YWCA provided the socialization, fellowship, and opportunity for play that young people needed.

The settlement movement had its beginnings in this period. University Settlement was established in New York City in 1886 and Hull House in Chicago in 1889. They were followed by other settlements and neighborhood centers. Here neighborhood people could get together to better their conditions, strengthen family life, improve neighborhood relations, and enjoy social, recreational, religious, civic, and other activities.

The park movement had a modest beginning in the decades before the Civil War. A few parks were developed in the cities; they were usually formally designed beauty spots in the better neighborhoods. Then gradually their use became more democratized, like other recreations. Because of the huge natural spaces available to dwellers in the United States, only a few public parks were developed in its cities until the last half of the 1800's. Then city planners began to see the values of these spots both for beauty and quiet relaxation and for more active play. Public authorities at all levels of government began to establish parks and recreation areas, which increased in number and size. Along with increased interest in parks there emerged professional groups of planners and park administrators who gave the new park movement stimulation and leadership.

In Boston, in 1885, a voluntary organization, borrowing the idea from Germany, arranged for a pile of sand to be placed in the yard of the Parmenter Street Chapel. That summer, children came there, "dug in the sand with their little wooden shovels and made countless sand-pies, which were remade the next day with undismayed alacrity."[18] This little playground project is now recognized as the beginning of the organized recreation movement in the United States. The playground movement, which had had great growth in Europe several decades earlier, did not really get under way in the United States, however, until the twentieth century.

Related to this community action for recreation was another aspect of governmental action. The federal government in 1872 created the first great national park at Yellowstone. Later, Yosemite, Sequoia, Mount Rainier, and other national parks were established, as the national government went into the business of recreation.

A parallel movement in America gave recreation a strong assist: the adult education movement. It began in colonial times with schools for training adults in reading, writing, and vocational skills, particularly the mechanical skills called for by the industrial revolution. The lyceums of the 1800's, and later on the chautauquas, attracted millions of adults to their educational-recreational events. The involvement of the public educational authorities in adult education, however, awaited the coming of major events in the 1900's.

How may we summarize this rich history of recreation in our country? One fact influencing its development is that our country, which began under the auspices and strict supervision of the Puritan fathers, by the twentieth century had in a very large measure repudiated, or at least lost sight of, the teaching that play is "mispense of time and that idleness should be shunned as evil." Three centuries of American history had all but laid that concept to rest. The increase in leisure time that marked the period was accompanied by the development of a philosophy of play that would support the pleasurable use of this free time.

Another fact was that people demanded fun and play in their lives. In whatever situation, whether frontier, crowded city, cow town, farming area, or rural village, people played, enjoyed amusements, and entertained themselves with whatever means were at hand. There seemed to be a relationship between the growth of democracy and the growth of recreation. The more democratic and free the atmosphere, the more free and eager the recourse of the people to the recreations and pleasures of their choice. This had been demonstrated in other

---

[18] "Annual Report of the Massachusetts Emergency and Hygiene Association," as quoted in Rainwater, *The Play Movement in the United States,* p. 22.

parts of the world and at other times, but it seemed particularly true for the people of this country.

There was a paucity of the cultural pursuits that marked the recreation of other societies. Perhaps a country must build up a cultural tradition and the accompanying institutions over a considerable time. The United States of the eighteenth and nineteenth centuries was still too young and immature to build the institutions and organizations for such things as painting and sculpture, music, drama, the dance, and so on. It was only in literature that American intellectual culture flowered. Perhaps the story of people building a new society on a new continent could be told by literary artists, but could not be described by other artists in the time they had.

The demand grew through the 1800's for organizations and agencies to help people enjoy their leisure in constructive ways. The growth of lodges and fraternal groups, Granges, settlements and youth-serving organizations, and public recreation programs in schools and elsewhere attest to this demand. As this country moved into the twentieth century there was a rapid increase in the production and enjoyment of the varied arts of leisure, along with what some insist is a real "mispense of time." Perhaps leisure was increasing more rapidly than the people could build the institutions of leisure to use it.

The age of recreation was in the making during this period, and forms of recreation organization, under many different auspices, and suitable to the needs and character of the American people at that time, were being evolved and developed. There can be derived from this history one of the concepts to be considered in this book:

The American recreation movement is based on a complex of parallel and mutually supporting movements evolving in the nineteenth century, including parks and playgrounds, kindergartens and nurseries, adult education, settlements, youth agencies, sports, and commercial amusements.

RECREATION IN THE TWENTIETH CENTURY

In the first half of the twentieth century, industrial capitalism reached an advanced stage in many countries of Europe as well as in the United States. There was a high degree of industrialization, a development of gigantic corporations employing thousands of workers, a growth of monopolies and cartels that became international in scope, and world wars over division and redivision of colonies, conflicting economic aims, and political differences. The first world war, from 1914 to 1918, was such a war. The second world war was more complex, but some of the same economic and imperialist motivations drove fascism into its war adventures.

Capitalism also had crises of a fairly regular nature, but the one that hit the United States in 1929 and affected all of the world was the most violent. The federal government under the New Deal responded to the national magnitude of the problem and the growing protests of the citizens over the extent of their hardships in the face of industry's capacity to produce wealth. Among many programs the government set up to meet the country's needs were two of great importance to recreation. One was a vastly expanded public works program, which built and improved hundreds of outstanding recreation facilities throughout the country. The second was a very large recreation program to assist people in using the forced leisure of unemployment to advantage and to provide employment for artists, actors, writers, and others. The WPA theater, the writers' and artists' projects, and the recreation projects were examples. Other measures provided many recreation agencies, both public and voluntary, with workers to carry on greatly enlarged programs.

The first half of the century brought stormy events to the world: the destruction of World War I; the economic collapse of the world depression; violent political and economic struggles in many countries; the establishment of fascism with its complete domination of a country by its most powerful industrialists in league with a political dictator; the second and even more devastating World War II; and the development of a new socialist sector of the world.

World War II called on the United States for a mobilization of all of its resources. Not only were the materials of war to be produced in giant quantities, but millions of citizens in the military forces and in production were to be provided with certain important elements in their life. One of these elements was recreation. In the armed forces, the recreation profession found heavy demand for its services in maintaining recreation and fitness programs for military personnel. The USO was founded by seven voluntary organizations to serve the recreational and other needs of servicemen. USO centers were built throughout the United States and overseas, staffed by professional recreation workers and thousands of volunteers. The USO continued after the war to meet peacetime recreation needs of servicemen, and scores of USO centers became community recreation centers.

In the years since the end of World War II, the world has seen a continuance of stresses and strains among the world's nations and peoples. The colonial peoples of Asia and Africa have striven for freedom from foreign rule. Intermingled with these struggles have been economic, political, and military skirmishes and a cold war between the East and West. Efforts continue to fend off other, more horrendous conflicts, in which the use of the ultimate weapons of automatic missile delivery and atom and hydrogen bombs might destroy whole civilizations. Even so, within this period of profound movement, change, and crisis, man lives and strives for a better future, and for solutions to the problems that confront him.

Along with the economic and political events of the century have come changes in the living arrangements of man. In the United States the big cities have continued to grow until at present half the population is crowded into one or another great metropolis, and all the stigmata of urbanism have become more aggravated. One example will suffice. When children were forced to leave the rural area or small town and live in the city, they lost their precious natural playground. The city streets became the children's playground. The children competed with the vehicles for which streets were originally built. But with the growth of rapid transportation, children could no longer play safely in the streets. So they in turn lost these playgrounds. The effect has been that children's play in some respects has changed greatly, and now city recreational and educational agencies must *create* playgrounds, if the right of children to a place to play is not to be further abridged.

The industrial revolution's tremendous movement has changed fundamentally man's basic struggle for survival. Technological and industrial production of material goods during the twentieth century has been phenomenal. The airplane, automobile, radio, television, telephone, home heating and air conditioning, food processing, and a myriad of other inventions have made life immeasurably easier, and necessary tasks are accomplished in remarkably few hours of work each week. Hutchinson says, "in a century and a half more than forty hours of leisure per week exist as an earned product resulting from man's ingenuity, and his desire to live with less of a struggle." [19]

To the degree that industrial organization has been able to utilize this fabulous increase in man-hour productivity and distribute it to the

---

[19] Hutchinson, *Principles of Recreation,* p. 40.

whole people, the welfare of the people has been increased. Now economists are talking about overproduction of goods, maldistribution of wealth, and technological unemployment as key problems. Leisure, instead of always being distributed equitably to all, as we shall see, may be forced on millions of workers in seasonal or cyclical periods of unemployment. Nevertheless, shorter working hours and higher pay have accrued to many millions of members of all classes in the more advanced industrial countries of the world as they variously share in the wealth of goods and leisure that modern power and machines produce.

We shall examine at a later point another effect of industrialism, the wear and tear on the physical and mental health of the worker. Just a brief look at the emergence of new illnesses that seem to be related to the strain of participating in high-powered industrial and commercial life, illnesses such as ulcers, cardiac disorders, nervous diseases, and mental and emotional disturbances, makes the serious student ask whether recreation can play a role in dealing with such a serious medical problem, the product of a machine civilization somewhere gone wrong.

The sciences have been enjoying rapid and highly productive development. The contributions to modern life of physics, chemistry, and biology, with their applications in agriculture, medicine, and so on, have been immense. But new sciences of psychology, psychiatry, sociology, and anthropology also have begun to make contributions of much significance to man and his recreation. Man's discoveries concerning his own mental, emotional, and physical nature are important to his understanding of the relationship of play and recreation to his health.

In later chapters this volume will deal with aspects of present-day society that are of importance to recreation, and will trace some of the developments in recent decades. At this point let us deal very briefly with a few areas of leisure and recreation, in order to view some parts of the current scene.

1. *The Cultural Arts*. In respect to twentieth-century literature, for example, mention must be made of the tremendous flood of modern recreational reading enjoyed by millions of people in this country. Many outstanding American writers have contributed significantly to modern literature—Dreiser, London, Faulkner, Dos Passos, Benét, Millay, Wolfe, Steinbeck, Hemingway, James, Fitzgerald, and many

others. American book companies and newspaper and magazine publishers are reaching millions. Libraries are doing "land-office" business.

Music through the 1900's has become more and more the means whereby millions of persons can enjoy beauty, both in performing and in listening. First, the phonograph became popular in the early 1900's. Dulles says, "The American people were spending more on phonographs and equipment, spurred on by an apparently limitless desire for new records, than they were on all other musical instruments, on all books and periodicals or on all sporting goods." [20]

Then the radio, movies, and television, as mass recreational media, brought radical changes in entertainment, especially musical entertainment. The actual opportunities to listen and enjoy music were multiplied. But the mass media threatened the custom of producing amateur music, of singing around the piano at home, of taking music lessons, and of planning a musical career. The advent of "canned" music struck a blow at the professional musician, for the canned product could be produced more cheaply, and thousands of musicians who used to play in hotel lobbies, restaurants, dance halls, concert halls, and saloons and salons now were replaced by juke boxes and recorded music.

Dancing, in the forms of both professional artistic endeavor and popular expression, has seen many changes. Modern ballet and modern dance are among the foremost expressive arts in Europe and America today. The movies and television interest the public in commercialized and popularized modern dance, but only a few talented dancers now reach mass audiences; and there is less opportunity for many other dancers to attract and reach smaller audiences. The little theater for drama, music, and dance production has taken hold, but the great mass media handicap the sharing of many creative efforts.

Dance, music, literature, and drama traditionally take some of their most vital themes from the everyday life and problems of the common people. Whether or not the creative and performing arts in the modern day can win the attention and interest of the masses of ordinary people who sit for hours with their eyes glued to the TV set, taking whatever quality of program is offered, and whether or not these arts can have a renaissance, and whether millions of people may be helped to find deeper pleasures in such creative endeavors as part of their leisure, are very important questions today.

---

[20] Dulles, *America Learns to Play,* p. 325.

2. *Getting Outdoors.* The pressure of people to get outdoors and away from the crowded city neighborhoods increased during the last half-century, partly because the automobile revolutionized outdoor recreation. Dulles says of the United States, "The entire face of the country was criss-crossed with highways of macadam and cement, lined with filling-stations, lunchrooms, curio stores, antique shops, hot-dog stands, tourist camps and sign-boards." [21] The automobile is important in countless recreations, both for transportation to the amusement places and for the pleasure of traveling. It opens up again the wide open spaces, encouraging picnics, outings, camping, and trips to the woods and mountains that were formerly inaccessible.

In some parts of the country, the building of roads, highways, superhighways, freeways, and tollways couldn't keep up with the traffic, and a large part of the Sunday outing was driving bumper-to-bumper for hours, breathing gas fumes, trying to get some place for fresh air. Still, every family tried to buy a car, and one of its most important uses was for family fun. The growing importance of recreational travel, the sport of "trailering," the expanding motel business, and other subjects will be considered in later chapters.

Travel has increased throughout the world; scores of thousands of people now journey through the several continents in a vast expanse of recreational travel. By air, ship, train, motorcar, and bicycle, a large number of tourists seek out the usual and the unusual features of each of the countries. For American travelers, Rome, Paris, Vienna, and other great cultural centers of the Old World continue to grow in popularity, along with more recent travel in Russia and the eastern countries.

3. *Sports.* Sports have become a dominant institution in most modern countries. In European countries, with many generations of sports traditions, there has been continued and growing interest. In the United States, interest in sports has increased. The habit of spectating in sports is now deeply ingrained, with millions of people watching and many betting on amateur and professional football, baseball, prize fighting, horse racing, basketball, and other sports. A string of national heroes, such as Jack Dempsey, Babe Ruth, Wilma Rudolph, and Mickey Mantle, have blazed a trail of glory for fans. Interest is growing in active participation in many sports. Bowling, skiing, and swim-

---

[21] Dulles, pp. 314-315.

ming take their place beside gardening and other simpler family recreational activities. The sports emphasis has had a profound effect upon education, with the virus of overemphasis on interscholastic and intercollegiate athletics worrying educators, with student athletes expelled from schools and occasionally sent to prison for underhanded dealing with gamblers who pay them to "shave points" or "throw games."

The Twist—an example of "fadism"

4. *Fads.* A whole saga could be told of the "fadism" of people of this country. In the field of popular music, ragtime, jazz, swing, bop, rock and roll, and the Twist successively attained popularity with millions. Weekly polls, "the top ten," and other similar devices are invented and manipulated by advertisers to register the momentary popularity of new songs and to push the sale of records. New games "catch on," such as mah-jong, crossword puzzles, miniature golf, monopoly, canasta, scrabble, bingo in the movies, and giveaway programs on radio or TV. Professional wrestling has had its day, in shows featuring a collection of flamboyant characters who commit their rehearsed mayhem on each other before thousands of hysterical fans and TV watchers.

5. *Organized Recreation.* There have been rapid developments in the fields of organized recreation. Hundreds of municipalities, following the example set by England, France, and other European countries several decades earlier, have begun to make provision for public parks, playgrounds, recreation centers, and specialized areas for the use of the whole population.[22] The recreation profession has begun to emerge in the United States: those administering programs discover that facilities and areas are not enough, and that skilled professional workers can help people to enjoy more fully these new resources. Schools by the thousands are moving away from the idea that their only task is classroom education, and are opening up playgrounds and buildings for afternoon, evening, weekend, and summer programs. The adult education movement that began in the 1930's mushroomed into the giant that it is today, contributing more to recreation than its founders ever guessed it would. There have developed several great national youth-serving agencies, such as Boys' Clubs, Scouts, Campfire Girls, "Y's," and a host of local ones. The churches threw themselves into recreation and helped to recapture flagging interest in church life. Recreation as a therapeutic tool is being used widely in hospitals, institutions, clinics, and programs of physical and mental health.

The twentieth century saw the United States developing a remarkably productive economy, emerging as a dominant world power, surviving economic and war crises and reacting to profound and rapid changes

---

[22] See George D. Butler, *Introduction to Community Recreation,* Third edition (New York: McGraw-Hill Book Company, 1959), for a fuller description of these developments.

occurring throughout the world. In America, there came a new leisure, a rapid expansion and change in recreation, mass communication and entertainment media, vastly increased transportation and travel, fadism, and great expansion of organized recreation by public, voluntary, and commercial organizations.

International Recreation

Viewing our subject from the international point of view, we may see that the outdoor life so attractive to Americans is equally attractive to the people of most other nations. In Germany, thousands of youths hike or cycle in the open country. Folk singing and folk dancing are very popular. English sports, characterized by the amateurism and sportsmanship that have been strongly traditional for many generations, have remained important in English life. Many organizations sponsor the arts, handicrafts, and folk-cultural activities throughout the British Isles and many of the areas in the British Empire. The winter sports of the Scandinavian countries have thousands of devotees.

The Olympic Games of 1960 showed the enthusiasm that people all over the world have for sports activities. Most of the countries of the world have built up interest and participation in sports, and have joined in the international event. Since 1896, the Olympic Games have been held every four years except for the period of the two world wars. These Games have greatly increased interest of millions of people throughout the world in the performances of the countries' finest athletes.

After several years of effort to bring the world's recreation organizations and leaders together in the interest of furthering recreation throughout the world, the International Recreation Association was organized in 1956. Its potential service to the recreation movements of the countries of the world is great. The first World Congress of Recreation was held in Los Angeles in 1932, at the time of the Olympic Games there. The Congress provided an important means of exchanging information on the recreation movements in the several countries, and contributed to international good will. Later congresses have been useful in furthering cooperation and understanding between nations as they find common goals in undertaking to strengthen this important function in the lives of their nations.[23]

---

[23] See Neumeyer and Neumeyer, *Leisure and Recreation,* pp. 99-141, for a useful summary of modern world trends in recreation.

Human Values

It is difficult to undertake a simple generalization that will describe the total interaction of recreation and life in the 1960's. Dulles points out that recreation pulled in many different directions, and a proper balance could not easily be struck in evaluating the total situation in terms of basic human values. Both wholesomeness and unwholesomeness were present. Who could estimate which more than the other?

> The movies tended to disrupt family life, but the radio kept people at home. Motoring took away from lawn games and informal back-yard sports; it also opened up larger opportunities for more ambitious outdoor activities. . . . Lodge night, the church social, the Grange picnic, and even the county fair, lost some of their old glory, but so did the pool-room, the beer-parlor, the burlesque show, and the shady entertainment palace of the metropolis. . . . The radio's incessant blare brought Beethoven as well as the Jazztown Rubes to its nationwide audience. . . . If conditions of urban life still placed a premium on passive indoor amusements, there was the underlying trend . . . toward a wider participation in sports than the country had ever known before.[24]

No more dynamic period ever has existed for recreation.

The impact of three major developments in the twentieth century led to the emergence of three main areas of philosophical inquiry. One of these developments was the growth of a modern science of man and his relations with others. With a better understanding of what physiological, psychological, and social needs man has, it has been possible to examine more adequately what role play should have in life, what contributions play can make. This suggests the need to examine theories of play.

Another development was the phenomenal increase in free time; with it came a tremendous challenge and, some believe, a threat, because of the vast amounts of free time man may now enjoy, and the potential that exists both for wholesome and truly recreational uses of that time, and for much less wholesome uses. Out of this comes our need to study a philosophy of leisure.

---

[24] Dulles, *America Learns to Play*, p. 371.

The third development has been an increasing understanding of the great values that man may capture for himself, the values in a good life, which are potentially, it seems, accessible to most of mankind, given some measure of success in organizing his economic and social life to permit him to survive and live at a level of comfort, decency, and dignity, and to pursue the arts of leisure with his basic needs secured. This more complicated problem of ethical and social values must concern us as we address ourselves to the question of recreation and a balanced life.

Questions for Study and Discussion

1. *Discuss the relative significance of the several forces bearing on United States recreational culture through its history.*
2. *What are the main impacts of the industrial revolution on the leisure of people in Western civilizations?*
3. *What do you think are the important things that happened in the arts during the eighteenth and nineteenth centuries, and what were their causes?*
4. *What is the promise of the twentieth century to man's leisure aspirations?*
5. *What effect has the great expansion of the mass-communication industries had on the use of leisure time by all classes?*

Selected Readings

Butler, George D., *Introduction to Community Recreation,* Third edition (New York: McGraw-Hill Book Company, 1959).

Dulles, Foster Rhea, *America Learns to Play* (New York: D. Appleton-Century Company, 1940).

Rainwater, Clarence E., *The Play Movement in the United States* (Chicago: University of Chicago Press, 1922).

Woodward, W. E., *A New American History* (New York: Garden City Publishing Company, 1939).

4

THEORIES OF PLAY

The foregoing historical review has, we hope, accomplished at least one thing: it has shown that play is fundamental to the life of man. Prehistoric man included play in his everyday life. People laughed and were gay even though life often was exceedingly precarious and the means of survival were limited. When civilizations began to arise in the ancient river valleys, pleasing pursuits were cultivated assiduously by the upper classes, the leisure arts proliferated and, in truth, made up much of the aesthetic culture of these societies. Common folk tenaciously clung to their few opportunities for play, and made the most of the simple pleasures they could afford.

We saw how the drive to play was turned to military purposes in Sparta and how it was vulgarized later in Rome, and how in the cultured atmosphere of Athens the arts of leisure were developed and nourished eagerly by all who shared in the benefits of the Golden Age. We observed how the medieval period clamped down with its grim demand for industry, and how the play spirit of the people nevertheless expressed itself in the romping, dancing, and playing at games, though both bishop and noble might frown and protest. We saw how the nobility and in more modern times certain leisure-class groups clung to the recreations of their class and pursued their gay way, often at some cost to others. We enjoyed the brash gaiety of the rising urban classes from the "burgeys" of Chaucer's England to the rebels at Merry Mount, whose eager self-seeking and lust for life led to incessant struggles both against religious asceticism and monarchical limitations and for freedom to pursue happiness as they saw fit. We recognized as similar to ourselves the revolutionary masses dancing in the streets of Boston or Paris. And we saw the enthusiasm with which all classes in modern times took the new free time and put it to recreational use.

We realize, therefore, that the play of a people is part of its basic life, part of its basic folkways and customs. There is need for us to ask the question, why is this so? What are the drives, the needs, the demands of the human individual and group that recreation uniquely meets? What is the place of play in the life of the individual? What is the relationship between social organization and play organization?

PLAY ATTITUDES AND THEORIES

Sapora and Mitchell identify five attitudes toward play [1] that have been expressed by different civilizations down through the ages: "(1) the *military* attitude, (2) the *art* attitude, (3) the *religious* attitude, (4) the *scientific* attitude, and (5) the *social* attitude." [2] They see the military attitude in Sparta, in Rome, and in the attitude of the rulers in the age of chivalry. The art attitude they think was dominant in ancient Athens. They think the Middle Ages, which they misname the "dark ages," was a time of the dominance of the religious attitude, and

---

[1] Allen V. Sapora and Elmer D. Mitchell, *The Theory of Play and Recreation,* Third edition (New York: The Ronald Press Company, 1961), pp. 13-23.

[2] Sapora and Mitchell, p. 14.

in the centuries since the Renaissance they see the development of the scientific attitude. They identify for present times what they believe is a view of more deep social understanding and appreciation of play and its importance in social life.

These five attitudes have been explored by students of recreation and such discussions have helped to broaden understanding of the varying uses to which recreation has been put by different societies at different times. Our brief historical study, however, should have indicated that these categories may represent an oversimplification of the historical facts. For example, religious attitudes toward play and cultural pleasures varied within a given society and among societies, from their glorification as spiritual experiences to their rejection as evils of the devil. Similar examples could be cited.

Sapora and Mitchell also undertook a brief evaluation of what they termed the five traditional theories of play: (1) the *surplus energy* theory, (2) the *recreation* theory, (3) the *instinct-practice* theory, (4) the *recapitulation* theory, and (5) the *catharsis* theory. They added the *relaxation* theory as a subtheory under the recreation theory. Then they developed their own theory, based on the earlier work of Mitchell and Mason. Finally, they analyzed briefly other explanatory approaches offered in modern years, among which are these: (1) the *psychoanalytic* approach, (2) the *genetic* approach, (3) the *learning process* approach, and (4) the *biosocial* approaches.[3]

There will be occasion to refer to Sapora and Mitchell later on. In the following pages we will pay attention to these several theories, as well as others, undertaking first an historical account of the emergence of several theories, and then an analysis of the elements of a modern theory of play.

We have seen how, through the centuries, some philosophers have spoken of play in terms of its essential values to man, how some others have decried play as something sinful and wasteful, and how rulers have even tried to legislate against it, without much success. Some of the conflict of views was represented in the philosophies of the Epicureans and the Stoics, and these have to be reconciled in some manner, for it would be difficult to accept both views. Further, we must recognize the insights of Plato, Aristotle, Pericles, and other great Athenians into the nature and values of play, which they have

---

[3] Sapora and Mitchell, pp. 77-112.

passed on to us. We can read the philosophies of the great educators through two thousand years and find much thought given to the playfulness of children and the need to stimulate that playfulness and guide it toward constructive ends in the name of education. Yet there were very few of these great thinkers who saw the place of play in life. Life in the early days was serious, at least to the philosophers. Seneca's disgust and fury with the playful excesses of the Romans did not lead him to formulate a deeper theory of play that would help to guide all mankind.

It was not until modern times, with the increase in scientific knowledge, with the increase in the concern of members of the human race for each other, and with the rise of an ethics of democracy, that scientists and philosophers could begin seriously to study the play needs of humans. We have seen how in the eighteenth century Rousseau spoke for the play needs of children. Earlier than that, Locke, Comenius, Rabelais, and others had described those same needs. These persons were striving to understand the nature of children, and to urge educational activity that was related to children's drives and needs for play.

NINETEENTH-CENTURY PLAY THEORIES

Froebel

Perhaps the person who contributed the most among the early students of children and play was Friedrich Froebel, whose work in the middle part of the nineteenth century marked the beginning of the kindergarten movement, and an important step in the education of young children. Froebel understood that to little children play is life itself. He urged that all of the vitality and happiness of playfulness go into the education of the child. He taught that the most important time in the life of the child is the early years, and that sound, sensitive help to the child through the medium of guided play activities is of prime significance to his healthy growth. Teachers must seek to release children's energies and to free their bodies and minds and voices, free them to frolic and question and search and explore. They must encourage spontaneity, guided by loving understanding. "There is often a high meaning in childish play," he said, and the frolicking of children is not mere exuberance and waste, but highly significant learning activity.

> Play is the highest phase of child-development—of human development at this period; for it is self-active representation of the inner—representation of the inner necessity and impulse.[4]

Knowing play to be essential to the child, Froebel created games, songs, and playful activities that had educational outcomes. He felt that whatever is necessary to be said or done to a young child may be said or done merrily or playfully. His keen insights and sensitive approach to children's needs challenged the stern and disciplinarian concepts of education too often held by educators. His teaching laid the foundation of the modern philosophy and method of the kindergarten and play school, and advanced the concepts of love, affection, kindness, and understanding, which are central in the education of the young.

Other educators and democratic philosophers added their judgments in support of Froebel's view. Pestalozzi in Switzerland, Guts Muths, Jahn, and Spiess in Germany, Ling in Sweden, Nachtegall in Denmark, and other great educators gradually brought to the attention of broader groups some of the importance of the free spirit of play, especially as a dynamic force in young people's lives. Earlier, some philosophers attempted in the 1800's to define the nature of play. One of these philosophers was Friedrich Schiller; another was Herbert Spencer.

The Surplus Energy Theory

Schiller, who wrote about the end of the 1700's, formulated the "surplus energy" theory of play, with the following analysis:

> No doubt nature has given more [energy] than is necessary to unreasoning being. . . . When the lion is not tormented by hunger, and when no wild beast challenges him to fight, his unemployed energy creates an object for himself; full of ardor, he fills the reechoing desert with his terrible roars and his exuberant force rejoices in itself, showing itself without an object. . . . The animal *plays* when the plenitude of force is this motor, when an exuberant life is excited to action.[5]

---

[4] See Friedrich Froebel, *The Education of Man* (New York: D. Appleton and Company, 1912). This selection and others are quoted in Robert Ulich, *Three Thousand Years of Educational Wisdom* (Cambridge: Harvard University Press, 1950), pp. 523-576.

[5] Friedrich Schiller, *Essays, Aesthetic and Philosophical* (London: George Bell and Sons, 1875), p. 112.

He pointed out that dogs and boys alike would fight in fun, not in anger, restraining the use of teeth or hands and playing make-believe at the most ferocious battle for survival. He also saw the imagination of man enjoying the use of its native vigor, power, and freedom through the exercise of art, which to him was a form of play. To him the expression of beauty and freedom in the make-believe and unreality of creative arts was for man the ideal expression of happiness, of ethical personality, of perfection of mankind. This was basic in his aesthetic theory of play.

Schiller's surplus energy theory of play, in particular, is interesting to us at this point; while it has meaning in describing one aspect of play, especially among children, it seems inadequate to explain all play. The forms that play takes, particularly the contemplative and sedentary ones, are not explained by this theory. The functions of play in helping persons relax from stress, escape from boredom or pressure, and re-create energies and spirits is not explained. The theory, however, is useful in portraying one aspect of play with which we must be concerned. Spencer elaborated a number of elements in addition to Schiller's ideas: the individual's need for activity and expression, children's imitative activities as learning experiences, and the individual's satisfaction with success in play as a substitute for success in other spheres.

EARLY TWENTIETH-CENTURY THEORIES

Preparation for Life Theory

The most famous play theorist of these early scholars was Karl Groos. His first book, *The Play of Animals,* published in 1898, was followed soon by a second book, *The Play of Man*. These represented the most serious research into the phenomena of play which had yet been undertaken, and were a major contribution to the theory of play. In common with other scientists of the period in which he wrote, he accepted the fundamental concept that human behavior, like animal behavior, is to be explained in terms of deeply rooted instincts that determine the major patterns of life. To support his view he marshaled a great deal of observational data concerning the wide range of play activities among children, basing his thesis upon anthropological studies of various cultures as well.

Groos was concerned primarily with the play of the young. He pointed out that play is a very important element in the development of children, being the means whereby they practice elements of the behaviors which help them to survive as adults. A child's play gives an opportunity, through the exercise of inborn dispositions, to strengthen and increase his inheritance in the acquisition of adaptations to his complicated environment, an achievement which would be unattainable by mere mechanical instinct alone. Thus play is practice for adulthood, through which one's "impulses" become socialized—that is, related to the realities of life in society with other human beings.

He discussed many kinds of play, identifying what he thought were catching, throwing, analytic, constructive, memory, imagination, rivalry, courtship, love, imitation, and other plays, which to him were indications of the child's struggles to exercise his capacities. He saw these play patterns appearing as "instinctive," urging the child to practice behaviors before he is required to exhibit them in the real situation of adult life. Thus, the child may play "school" or "marriage" or "work" long before life calls upon him to function in these respects, and valuable practice is had in these things. Groos recognized the importance of imitation, which he thought was a link between instinctive and intelligent conduct, as an active factor in influencing play behaviors. He also recognized the powerful tendencies toward association with others, which influence the group play behaviors of the young. This, of course, gives support to his thesis of play as preparation for life, especially for social life.

The instinct concept as a scientific approach was pushed aside by more productive and sound concepts in psychology later in the twentieth century. Groos himself suggested that the word *instinct* did not adequately describe the complex of associations and relations observed in play behavior, but in describing the many play activities he continued to use the term. In this description he included playful activity of the sensory apparatus and motor apparatus, the playful moving of foreign bodies, as well as imitative and social play. His effort to bring into the field of play the extensive range of activities and behaviors he observed gave to play theory extensive descriptive material. And his critique of the surplus energy and other theories to explain the phenomena of play was for his day very keen.

In his critique of play theories Groos dealt with the "surplus energy," "relaxation," and "preparation for life" views of recreation as follows:

> The first says: When a man is "quite fit," and does not know just what to do with his strength, he begins to sing and shout,

> to dance and caper, to tease and scuffle . . . [indicating] the necessity for some discharge of such superabundant vigor. The second view is diametrically opposed to this one, regarding play as it does in the light of an opportunity afforded for the relaxation and recreation of exhausted powers. As the strings of a zither and the cord of a bow should not always be taut if the instrument is to retain its usefulness, so do men need the relaxation of play. The third view emphasizes the teleological significance of play. Observation of men and animals forces us to recognize its great importance in the physical and mental development of the individual—that it is, in short, preparatory to the tasks of life. Every effort made to arouse and foster a feeling for play among our people is based on the conviction, "*pro patria est, dum ludere videmur.*" ["While we play, we serve our country."] [6]

He saw that each of these views contributed insights into the nature of play, although he relied heavily upon the concept that inborn impulses constitute the important foundation for play behavior, and that its purpose, among children especially, was preparation for the next steps in growth.

He analyzed the surplus energy theory rather critically, recognizing that although bubbling energy may be a great stimulus to play, it may not be a universal criterion of play, and that play comes from a number of urges and motivations other than simple excess energy. He stressed another aspect of play in his theory of relaxation and recreation that he felt had a special psychological significance.

> As soon as the individual has progressed far enough to realize the seriousness of life . . . the liberty of play signifies to him relief from this pressure. The more earnest is a man's life, the more will he enjoy the refuge afforded by play when he can engage in sham occupations chosen at will, and unencumbered by serious aims. There he is released from all the anxieties of life.[7]

This particular concept has become a central theme in the recreational philosophy of most writers in the last half century. The "preparation

---

[6] Karl Groos, *The Play of Man* (New York: D. Appleton and Company, 1901), p. 361.

[7] Groos, p. 383.

for life," or teleological, theory was closest to Groos's own central theory of play, explaining, as he believed, the major motivations for play and the patterns and forms it took, especially among children.

Analyzing play from the standpoint of its relation to aesthetics, Groos pointed out that artistic play permits the artist to satisfy his desires to make an impression and gain power and influence over the emotions through his artistic medium. There is pleasure in being able to create make-believe and illusion, to experiment. And he saw play and art as being closely identified with basic human drives or instincts to express one's self in self-exhibition, imitation, and decoration. These he saw as the three basic human arts. Groos also thought that play has much value in the ethical development of the child, that "play in itself contributes materially to the establishment of ethical individuality." [8] The role of the teacher or play leader is to guide the play so that its ethical values predominate.

Groos identified the social elements in play very simply and clearly.

> The effect of ordinary play is supported by social imitation. To do what others do, and so get the advantage of the stimulus which belongs to collective activity . . . to get out of the narrow circle of one's own desires and efforts—these the child learns with his playmates and the grown man in aesthetic sports and in festive gatherings.[9]

This also is an idea which has been elaborated and supported by later studies of man's social needs, and has become a central concept in the philosophy of recreation.

Two other concepts of Groos that should be mentioned briefly are: (1) the pleasurable effects, which he did not see as a universal criterion but usually present in play; (2) play movements of the child represent a very generalized form of preparation for life, preparation not in the long-range sense of a direct identification with adult activities but in the sense of growing readiness to undertake the next level of complexity of movement or activity, with play as practice in those elements of a situation that the child comfortably can master. Both of these ideas have been woven into the recreation writings of later philosophers such as Joseph Lee, Luther Gulick, L. P. Jacks, and others.

---

[8] Groos, p. 404.
[9] Groos, pp. 395-397.

Recreation and Relaxation Theory

Another aspect of play that has received consideration is its power to relax persons and give them release, from which arises the re-creational concept of recreation. Guts Muths argued this view, as did Lazarus, a German who lived a few decades later and argued that play recuperates and restores the mentally and physically tired, and that people should flee from empty idleness to active recreation in play. An elaborate, although somewhat inaccurate, analysis of the nature of relaxation through play was contributed some years ago by Patrick,[10] who pointed out that the modern work activities of many call for intensive use of mental powers and small muscles in exhausting and fatiguing activities. Play activities, he argued, in general do not call for the use of the same muscles or powers. They use instead the larger muscles and are easier, restful, and relaxing. He thought that these activities are older in the human race, come more naturally to persons, and are related to a kind of racial memory, or "deep-seated human instincts." He argued, also, that man becomes more fatigued using his higher mental powers—a point hard to prove. He more realistically pointed out that nervous tension and monotony in much of modern-day productive work puts a strain upon man not previously inflicted.

Sapora and Mitchell submit a helpful criticism of Patrick's theories, pointing out that, "In explaining the motivation of play in terms of 'deep-rooted human instincts,' 'race habits,' and a 'racial memory,' the theory is less satisfying. One soon seeks a definition of these terms that will square with proved, accepted psychological concepts." [11]

Patrick ignored the immense field of play which is represented in intellectual and mental activities; he does not provide a basis for analyzing the play of children, and in other respects his analysis is incomplete and inadequate. But he contributed an emphasis now recognized to be highly significant in his interesting and useful analysis of the special contribution of play to relaxation itself, and his clear explanation of the need for release from the tensions, boredom, and stern demands of modern life on the human organism. Later authors have developed this theme extensively.

---

[10] G. T. W. Patrick, *The Psychology of Relaxation* (Boston: Houghton Mifflin Company, 1916).

[11] Sapora and Mitchell, *Theory of Play and Recreation,* p. 83.

Recapitulation and Other Theories

A number of other views of play were expressed by interested scholars, with which the student of recreation should be acquainted. G. Stanley Hall undertook to argue that play at the various stages in a child's development is a recapitulation of the "cultural epochs" in the development of the human race. Thus, the child plays at savage, nomadic, agricultural, and tribal life, following by instinct these patterns of cultural behavior. Modern psychology has rejected completely any such concept of inheritance of the cultural patterns of an earlier age, even if all societies had gone through such stages, which they have not. Perhaps the effect of television shows on the play behavior of little children explains more adequately than Hall's instinctive notions why children imitate adult behavior in the manner that they see and understand it.

Another theorist, Appleton, centered her theory on an explanation of play as the aspect of growth that involves the developmental exercise of maturing functions. This theory is in some respects like Groos's teleological theory. Lehman and Witty interpret it as follows: "Growth, or the hunger for it, is the basic drive to play behavior. Play thus precedes the ability to function and gives rise to it." [12] Thus, play activity serves to satisfy the needs of the growing body. This theory is useful in explaining some of children's play, but not the play of adults.

Several writers have explained that play is a cathartic device, a safety valve for pent-up emotions. When a person feels the need to fight, and fighting type of play is available, to engage in such play has a specific cathartic effect, relieving the individual somewhat of these emotions. It is possible that the satisfactions from such forms of play will be deeper than cathartic ones. It is possible also that a pathological need for conflict or stormy struggle might be satisfied through aggressive play, only to whet one's appetite, or sharpen one's desire, for further conflict, unless other, more constructive influences are present. This subject has not been adequately explored, but it is hazardous to generalize that play by itself, by letting a person work out his aggressions and hostilities, will solve emotional problems. Some

---

[12] Harvey C. Lehman and Paul A. Witty, *The Psychology of Play Activities* (New York: A. S. Barnes and Company, 1927), p. 21.

problems are more involved than this point of view would suggest, and we shall consider this further at a later point.

Sigmund Freud, although he did not write directly on the subject of play, concerned himself with the psychology of group relations and suggested useful points of consideration by play theorists analyzing the social aspects of play. Writing in 1922, he formulated a concept of group psychology [13] that criticized the views of LeBon and the other "mob psychologists." LeBon's notion was that an individual in a group is caught by the contagion and suggestibility of group emotional feelings, loses his inhibitions, his will, and his rational self-discipline while he is an anonymous member of the group, and therefore behaves irresponsibly and irrationally, as he might never do if he were by himself. LeBon argued that a group never attains great heights of rational behavior, and is more likely to operate emotionally and irrationally than intelligently.[14]

In contrast to this, Freud argues that groups may be cruel, destructive, and extreme, but also may be influenced by suggestion to acts of high achievement and devotion to an idea.

> The group mind is capable of genius in intellectual creation, as is shown above all by language itself, as well as by folk-song, folk-lore and the like. It remains an open question, moreover, how much the individual thinker or writer owes to the stimulation of the group in which he lives, or whether he does more than perfect a mental work in which the others have had a simultaneous share.[15]

Freud argues that the individual, possessing important drives and needs related to his sexual function, is attracted to his fellows and enjoys friendship and emotional response from them. These warm, emotional relationships between individuals constitute the bonds holding the group together. He finds support for this hypothesis in two ideas:

> First, that a group is clearly held together by a power of some kind: and to what power could this feat be better ascribed than

---

[13] Sigmund Freud, *Group Psychology and the Analysis of the Ego,* The International Psycho-Analytic Library, No. 6 (New York: Liveright Publishing Corporation, 1951). Quotations from this work are by permission of Liveright, Publishers, N. Y. Copyright © 1951 by Liveright Publishing Corp.

[14] Gustave LeBon, *The Crowd* (London: Unwin, 1917).

[15] Freud, *Group Psychology,* p. 24.

> to Eros, who holds together everything in the world? Secondly, that if an individual gives up his distinctiveness in a group and lets its members influence him by suggestion it gives one the impression that he does it because he feels the need of being in harmony with them rather than in opposition to them—so that perhaps after all he does it "ihnen zu Liebe" . . . [for love of them] [16]

Freud's contribution to play theory has not been fully evaluated, although later writers, such as Slavson and Erikson, whose views will be examined, drew much from Freud's more well-known views on the powerful influence of psychic forces on behavior. Yet Freud's effort to clarify the nature of group interaction and the powerful attraction of groups for the individual, and his effort to criticize the reactionary views of psychologists who had stressed the "mob" character of groups, is of significance to recreation, which bases its method often on the use of guided group experiences as a means of providing persons with deep emotional satisfactions and psychic values, as well as valid experiences in cooperation and democracy.

The nineteenth and early twentieth centuries produced important pioneer theorists of play, whose theories found the bases of play in surplus energy, need for relaxation, preparation for life, or the recapitulation of racial history; each was based upon the instinct theory of the time and recognized the significance of play as a vital and necessary element in individual well-being.

Joseph Lee

Among modern philosophers of recreation Joseph Lee, former president of the National Recreation Association and called the "father of American recreation," was one of the most sensitive and creative thinkers. While he based his thinking on the work of Froebel and Groos and acknowledged his profound debt to them, he caught much of the spirit of the recreation movement in the United States and helped to give the recreation profession some important insights into the nature of play. His inability to visualize play in terms other than the "fulfillment of a play instinct" limited the value of his theory sharply. But his keen insights into the nature of the play of children were a very useful contribution.

Lee's book *Play in Education* emphasizes at the outset that play

[16] Freud, p. 40.

is a very serious matter with children; "it is the supreme seriousness of play that gives it its educational importance."[17] The complete enlistment of the child in his activity, and his seriousness, belie the casual view of adults that play itself is insignificant.

> In truth the play of children is in the main not play at all in the sense in which grown people use the word. It is play in the sense of being spontaneous, agreeable, undertaken for its own sake and not for an ulterior object. It is not play in the sense of being mere relaxation or diversion, or a thing of secondary importance. Of course children like to play; all good workmen like their work; but it is none the less serious on that account.[18]

Lee thought play was part of nature's law of growth. "Growth through play is simply an example of the general law of growth through action."[19] Though play trains the child for his life, "the function of play in growth is, then, to realize the potential body, and to supplement the impulses which the major instincts give in general terms by habits and reflexes, making them efficient to specific ends."[20] He thought there were some finer instincts involved in play, some "achieving instincts" in which the satisfaction of the drive is in doing and in the beauty of the thing done.

Another of Lee's theories is at odds with that of some modern philosophers of recreation who have visualized play as being uniquely an activity in which the pleasure of the activity itself is the main value. He points out that play, instead, is purposeful, that a person's desire is to produce results, to influence or create something.

> Play is almost always for an object. . . . If we say the satisfaction of the play is in the doing of it, we must also say that "it" is not the motions gone through, the process of the playing, but the end sought. It is on the end that the child's heart and mind are set. It absorbs his attention, gives meaning and motive. He is all intention: seeking the end of what he is doing, and the whole of it.[21]

---

[17] Joseph Lee, *Play in Education* (New York: The Macmillan Company, 1929), p. 3.

[18] Lee, p. 2.

[19] Lee, p. 6.

[20] Lee, p. 25.

[21] Lee, p. 247.

"... the supreme seriousness of play...."

The play purpose is not primarily the pursuit of pleasure, although such pleasure results from play. But the primary purpose is the doing of the thing, as he says, the self-forgetfulness and subordination, the playing of the game for all it is worth.

In contrast, he describes the self-entertainment motive in play: "The pursuit of pleasure is an egotistic, self-conscious, almost a morbid, state of mind, notoriously self-defeating." [22] Such is not the most wholesome approach to play. Play at its best is the challenge to the creative skills, ingenuity, and enthusiastic application of oneself to the tasks of accomplishment. To illustrate, there is much satisfaction on a hot day in feeling the cool water on one's body as one plunges in for a swim. But there may be more fulfilling satisfactions in the grace of one's movement in the water, the speed, smoothness, or beauty of one's swimming. This suggests the increase in the satisfactions and in the richness of the rewards of play, when with increasing skill and practice one's competence improves and one performs better the tasks set.

Lee also pointed to what he thought was the "belonging instinct." He felt that in team play and group activity this urge is satisfied at its fullest. To the person, losing himself in the team or group and merging his own individuality in the common consciousness is an exhilarating experience. Teamwork, acting together with a common purpose and consciousness, gives a person the deepest attainable experience of membership, and Lee felt this is of vital importance to the child, especially at the time when this is a powerful need for him, when, in Lee's own terms, "the belonging instinct . . . is establishing its dominion in the boy's heart." [23]

Lee, writing during the first world war, saw the need for persons to have an opportunity to have an overflow for their "fighting instinct," other than interpersonal conflict. While he thought there was such an instinct, he recognized that "war is in reality no longer a profitable expedient for its cultivation," [24] and suggested fishing, hunting, especially with a camera, sports, and, especially, creative activities: "The justification of peace is to make room for art. . . . It is in the piping times of peace that the arts flourish. But peace that has no time to pipe is barren." [25] And in this regard he emphasized the great aesthetic ideal of man:

> Art is the fulfillment of our creative instincts in richest and most elaborate ways; it twines and multiplies together its interpretations of the sense of form, of rhythm, of balance, of speed and space and mastery. . . . Art is play in its intensest, most sublimated form.[26]

---

[22] Lee, p. 255.
[23] Lee, p. 339.
[24] Lee, p. 464.
[25] Lee, p. 469.
[26] Lee, p. 469.

In these terms Lee explored, perhaps in a naïve and simple way, but with great sensitivity to the needs of modern folk in our society, what basic human values play may contribute to modern man. Although his theory of play was rooted in faulty psychological concepts of instinct, his analysis of the nature of play itself and its contribution to the growth and development of children has had a considerable influence on recreationists to this day.

LUTHER GULICK

The recreation movement in the United States had another important philosopher who contributed insights into the theory of play, Luther Halsey Gulick, Y.M.C.A. and public education leader. He, like Lee, wrote in a period when students of play based their thinking on instinct psychology. In analyzing the play of children at different ages, he did not define "stages" as firmly as did Lee, but he suggested the existence of powerful instincts determining the play behavior. In his book *A Philosophy of Play,* he gave at the outset his three conclusions concerning the nature of play:

> 1. The individual is more completely revealed in play than in any one other way; and conversely, play has a greater shaping power over the character and nature of man than has any one other activity. A man shows what he really is when he is free to do what he chooses;
> 2. A people most truly reveals itself in the character of its pleasures. . . . [T]he manner of its pleasures is the most character-determining force within a people. . . .
> 3. Certain great desires engulf the individual, directing his will, his purposes, to their own decided ends, with but slight regard for the benefit of the individual himself. . . . Each of these great waves or tides of desire raises the level of the psychic range and power of the individual, and makes the next one possible. . . . In this sense each individual recapitulates the history of his kind, both in individual growth and in social relations.[27]

Gulick analyzed the many forms of play, especially of children, and found in them the operation of basic instincts, which the process of

---

[27] Luther Halsey Gulick, *A Philosophy of Play* (New York: Charles Scribner's Sons, 1920), pp. xiv-xvi.

play powerfully develops as part of a person's growth. This analysis supported his first conclusion. His second conclusion was somewhat less necessary to his main argument. The third point, however, underlies his whole analysis, and serves to link him with those who earlier had developed a concept of recapitulation to explain play in man.

Like Lee, and Groos before him, Gulick undertook to analyze the different kinds of play of children and relate them to basic instincts of man. He argued that children's play at hunting and fighting were evidences of the necessary means of survival of man in primitive times. He thought such factors as courage, endurance, the willingness to hang on and finish when one is sorely punished, represented active and positive virtues that man has to develop to survive. He saw girls playing house and said that this activity is another of the child's preparations for life. He saw children fascinated over playing with fire and thought that this illustrated a deep feeling for fire.

> There must be some reason why these feelings have been preserved by natural selection—by the law that those tribes and species shall survive which have characteristics best fitting them to survive. . . . The sense of terror, the sense of protection, the sense of religious significance and of beauty attached to fire are part of our inheritance as human beings—a most valuable part, and closely related to our being here at all.[28]

He saw children playing together and developing teamwork and group loyalty, which he believed were based in a gang instinct. The spirit of loyalty to the group was basic to tribal survival. Fighting, hunting, and working in gangs was the only feasible survival pattern for man, so men had to stand together. Gulick even had women standing together somewhat less than men, and with more gentle virtues of love of home, kindness, sympathy, and forbearance, than the men, who were characterized by power, manhood, strength, and group loyalty.

Gulick's philosophy thus takes on a sort of mystical character, finding in the play patterns the expression of instincts that men acquired through natural selection during the ages of primitive struggle for survival. This was much like the instinctivist views of others, and was very influential among the first recreationists. It shows the strong influence of the Darwinian school of evolutionary thought, which was in vogue at the time. Modern students of anthropology have given us much more scientific insight into the processes of cultural transmission

---

[28] Gulick, p. 63.

and development, and of the acculturation of the individual in the society as a basis for a modern play theory.

Gulick at times seemed to criticize the recapitulation theory, which argued that children's play in some way recapitulates the cultural epochs through which man has gone. But he believed there was a progression in play from the simple movements of infancy to the complicated movements of childhood. Also he saw the child's play as individualistic at first, then competitive, then finally cooperative, featuring teamwork and group activity. He stressed the importance of play to physical growth, and to the education of the child's intellectual abilities. Finally, he saw through play a powerful influence toward the development of morality, which begins when the child develops a growing sense of fair play and defense of his own rights and then takes on a loyalty to his peers and a devotion to his group that may widen to be a true social altruism and social consciousness, if adequate guidance is given.

Gulick had a strong ethical sense concerning the nature of play. He saw play as in itself neither good nor bad, but the group relationships, and the loyalties and traditions developed, had for him deep ethical qualities, either positive or negative. In play he saw a form of freedom and its related responsibilities, which were different from those in family life or school life, because the child is free to leave the play situation if he chooses. So his controls are self-imposed to a considerable degree, not the result of an institutional authority that neglects self-control for obedience to external control.

> The playground alone affords to children the one great opportunity for cultivating those qualities that grow out of meeting others of like kind under conditions of freedom; it develops progressively . . . that sense of human relationships which is basal to wholesome living. Thus the playground is our great ethical laboratory. . . . Where there is no freedom there can be no self-control. . . . [F]reedom is necessary for morality. Self-control of the higher type is primarily developed under the conditions of the playground.[29]

Gulick saw play as being integral to a democracy. He saw the great growth in public education and science and welfare, and, side by side with this, "an unparalleled exploitation of the many by the

---

[29] Gulick, pp. 249-250.

few, with oftentimes a disregard for the law. And further, we see a tendency for popular, unthinking, uncontrolled action, which is shown in its worst form by the mobs. Both of these tendencies are fatal to the permanent life of a democracy." [30]

He saw as well a growing interdependence of groups and a need of a more sensitive civic conscience in a self-governed people. He felt that play, in its best forms, could provide for the experiences conducive to the development of the great virtues of social conscience and community feeling. "Democracy must provide . . . play and a good play tradition for every child on a playground. Without the development of the social conscience—which has its roots in the early activities of the playground—we cannot expect adults to possess those higher feelings, which rest upon the earlier social virtues developed during childhood." [31] And so a healthy play life for all children is the fundamental condition "without which democracy cannot continue, because upon them rests the development of that self-control which is related to an appreciation of the needs of the rest of the group and of the corporate conscience that is rendered necessary by the complex interdependence of modern life." [32]

In these and other statements Gulick showed his interest in play in terms of its basic sociological significance. Although we can recognize the inadequacies of the psychological framework of his theory, and the mystical quality of his generalizations concerning instincts, we can also see that his keen insights into basic ethical considerations constitute valuable contributions to play theory.

Two founders of American play theory, Lee and Gulick, devoted much attention to the significance of play behaviors in children's growth, attributing such behaviors to the operation of basic instincts, and seeing them as emerging at the proper points in the child's life, and guiding the development of his capabilities, social skills, and ethical judgment.

MODERN THEORIES OF PLAY

Physiological

In the modern day, students of play have been concerned with analyzing these phenomena with reference to basic physiological, psy-

---

[30] Gulick, p. 254.
[31] Gulick, pp. 264-265.
[32] Gulick, p. 265.

chological, social, and other capacities and needs. The universality of play, which led men earlier to explain the desires for play as a result of instinctive compulsions, has later on stimulated students to analyze the human person in relation to his physical, mental, and social self, and to be concerned with play in relation to these aspects of human personality.

John Dewey stated rather simply the biological basis of play in his suggestion that activity is basic to organic life, that one must recognize activity as necessary for all life. The organism is not in its natural state when it is quiet or still, nor is the stimulus of pain or unpleasantness necessary to movement.

> The fact of the case is that from intra-organic stimuli, the organism is in a constant state of action, activity indeed being the very essence of life. When the myth of natural quiescence is surrendered with its accompanying myth of the need of a special premium in order to arouse an inert agent, it ceases to be necessary to search for any special object in order to account for play. The only thing necessary is to state the conditions under which organic activity takes this or that form.[33]

The physiologists and the physical educators have contributed much concerning the relation of play to physiological growth and maintenance. Their analyses also begin with the basic fact that man is an active being, for whom energetic activity is a basic requirement of health itself. Physical health is looked upon as a fundamental value for man. As Nixon and Cozens put it, "man is much better fitted to thrive in an environment which calls for constant physical activity than in one that requires mental concentration and stress accompanied by physical inactivity. And there tends to be some agreement that normal humans, for efficient functioning and proper development, need some hours a day of vigorous muscular activity, depending upon the age and state of development of the individual."[34]

This muscular activity contributes to the entire functioning of the organism. Other factors such as food, fresh air, and rest are vital to the organism, but activity is the means of stimulating bodily functioning. The peculiar contribution of play, it is said, is in the interre-

---

[33] John Dewey, *A Cyclopedia of Education,* edited by Paul Monroe, Vol. 14 (New York: The Macmillan Company, 1925), p. 725.

[34] Eugene W. Nixon and Frederick W. Cozens, *An Introduction to Physical Education* (Philadelphia: W. B. Saunders Company, 1941), p. 13.

lation of these vigorous and stimulating activities with both the vital organs and the mind and emotions. Properly guided energetic play activities that involve big-muscle movement but do not overtax the body will stimulate growth, develop muscles, improve the posture, and stimulate better functioning of the vital organs.

The organic vigor of a person is benefited greatly, modern physiological study has shown, by correct amounts of physical exercise. In addition to the strengthening of the skeletal muscles, the muscular power and efficiency of the heart is increased with exercise, the heart being able to supply the body's organs with blood effectively during time of muscular exertion and then return to normal rapidly. The entire circulatory system is stimulated along with the heart, and the supply of fuel and oxygen for the muscles is carried to the muscles to maintain their functioning.

The lungs of an individual also benefit from vigorous play. A person who exercises actively and regularly builds up an efficient and strong respiratory system, permitting efficient oxygen intake without strain. The child or youth increases his chest capacity and his lung power, and the adult helps to maintain the lungs' active functioning, by these means. The increased heart and lung activity also stimulates the operation of the digestive system and eliminative system, both by maintaining general muscular tone and by maintaining active circulation. The intestines, kidneys, and other organs benefit from energetic use of the body, and sluggishness and poor functioning can be avoided. There is, finally, a wholesome effect on the nervous system, both from the relaxing and from the stimulating function of exercise.

The physiological benefits of relaxation, as well as the benefits of exertion, have been identified, and it is recognized that an adequate rhythm of activity and rest is necessary for good health. Play activities designed to provide this healthy balance of active demand upon the organism and rest from exertion are of basic value in meeting a person's physiological needs.

Selye contributes to this point a highly provocative analysis of stress as a physiological phenomenon of great significance. He points out that whatever we do and whatever is done to us causes stress—wear and tear. Stress, therefore, is a common feature of all biological activities. The general adaptation syndrome, he says, is the means our bodies have for helping to adjust us to the constant change in our lives. He points out the fact that many diseases are basically faulty adaptations or adjustments to stress, and he urges man to understand his stresses and to avoid overstress by reaching a healthy balance between work and rest and relaxation, in this balance having the opportunity to express one's innate vitality in the way nature foresaw for him.[35]

Modern physiology has established the values of vigorous play activities in developing and maintaining muscle tone, organic vigor, and vitality of body functioning.

Psychological

Psychological explanations of play have been closely related to the biological explanations of surplus physical energy, imitative physical movement, and so on. Early theorists supported their explanations in terms of instincts that compel these behaviors in the child, and provide the basis for adult habits. Contemporary writers are providing us with somewhat deeper insights into the psychology of play, stressing different aspects of the psychological experience. Some of these writers have based their views upon Freudian concepts of psychological dynamics, while others have expressed broader and opposing views. But Freud's theories of personality development, the concepts of the id, the ego, and the superego as the key elements of the self, the concept of the unconscious and its influence on behavior, and other of his ideas have been powerfully influential in modern psychology and the subject of endless discussion and no little controversy in recent years.

Lehman and Witty, discussing the psychology of play activities, felt that at least two of Freud's theories are important to this field. One is the theory that man is driven by the desire to gratify basic instincts such as sex and hunger. Any frustration of one of these instincts will lead to substitutive activities, but in each case the activity will be dominated by the desire to obtain pleasure; there is also an impulse toward the repetition of experiences, which may be much the same as the desire for familiar experiences, or simply habit formation. The two authors indicated confusion over some seeming inconsistencies between these two principles, the "pleasure principle" and the "repetition compulsion principle." [36] In general, modern psychologists have focused their attention on other aspects of Freud's work,

---

[35] Hans Selye, *The Stress of Life* (New York: McGraw-Hill Book Company, 1956).

[36] Lehman and Witty, *Psychology of Play Activities,* p. 22.

taking note of the powerful influence of basic drives which Freud called instinct and of the psychological processes he identified.

Among modern writers, S. R. Slavson has undertaken one of the most searching analyses of the psychological nature of play, basing his analysis upon Freudian concepts but seeing the individual as a psycho-organic-social unity. Like others he recognizes that play for the child is an important learning opportunity.

> Play is the means whereby the child, in fantasy, comes to know reality. The child scales down the world around him to simpler patterns that he can understand and master, gaining greater security and acquiring power as he does it. The adult world is to the small child threatening and forbidding, and in play he reduces its complexity to the level of his powers and understanding. As he grows and is able to deal with this world, his play activities gradually fuse with reality, until the latter becomes predominant.[37]

Play is visualized as a means of satisfying important inner needs, and a number of values are identified. He sees play, in our modern world of specialized and often monotonous and barren work, as a means of complementing, organically and emotionally, the rest of a person's life and helping to provide a balance. Further, recreation may compensate for emotional monotony by providing new experiences and varying stimuli, and often an opportunity to achieve success when the rest of one's life has been less successful and less satisfying.

Slavson, coming close to the instinctive psychologist's position, recognizes powerful "motives" as guiding behavior. He lists the need for movement, the need for change, the sex instinct, the death wish, sadistic drives, aggression, constructive trends, and regression as typical. And he identifies the types of play that result from these drives. He sees social recreations of various kinds as meeting basic sex needs, while dangerous sports unconsciously satisfy the death wish, and combative sports and games satisfy sadistic and aggressive motives. On the other hand are the creative and constructive "life-extending" urges, which are satisfied by creative and productive individual or group activities. Regression, "letting go" periodically, aids in establishing internal balance, a kind of emotional homeostasis.

---

[37] S. R. Slavson, *Recreation and the Total Personality* (New York: The Association Press, 1948), p. 3.

Very important to Slavson is the opportunity given in play to discharge aggressiveness. Aggressiveness is a basic law of survival of the species. For man to survive socially, however, these impulses have to be regulated and controlled, and the combative, competitive, and conflict-based sports and games serve to permit a person to express these aggressions in a socially accepted manner. The opportunity recreation gives the person to express his destructive and hostile feelings and to enjoy an emotional catharsis is thought by Slavson to be one of its major contributions. In this view Slavson gives a modern form to the similar speculations of earlier writers.

He sees also the value of recreation for an acceptable regression to more immature or infantile behavior, where one may let down the bars of dignity, decorum, and self-control, and enjoy temporarily a return to youthful enthusiasm, hilarity, and unrestrained happiness. Slavson does not consider the question of whether this is truly regression in many cases, or simply a freeing of oneself for spontaneous and uninhibited behavior which is often representative of a mature and creative individual; he seems more concerned with the pathological than with the normal expressions of enthusiasm and wholehearted pleasure in some recreation.

Slavson emphasizes the individual's need to escape the pressures of life's reality at times and to enjoy flights of fantasy and imagination. "One displaces the disturbing thoughts and anxieties with more pleasurable activities and fantasies. Satisfaction of the escape motive must be viewed as one of the major needs in the choice of recreation." [38] He groups together here the satisfactions of travel, fiction, movies, theater, fortune telling, gullible interest in magic, and such.

He recognizes the important role that recreation may play in satisfying social hunger, the need of association and group life, and points out the needs of persons at all ages for personal contacts in recreation situations to overcome feelings of loneliness and isolation. He sees also, however, that individuals need resources of individual recreation, finding a balance between the needs for companionship and one's wish to spend time alone.

Slavson, like Freud, suggests that the unconscious is the source of powerful drives, cravings, and influences on the individual. The Freudian view is that an individual forces many of his unsatisfied desires and wishes back into the unconscious where they create powerful

---

[38] Slavson, p. 14.

tensions and influence deeply the individual's behavior. These repressions need to be released in some manner, and Slavson sees the usefulness of play in this respect.

> Leisure-time occupations and hobbies, when they are freely chosen, balance and bring health to the total organism of man. Recreation provides discharge of repressed or hidden cravings and impulses in a manner approved by the group. Pleasure is derived from release of emotions as much as from what appears to be constructive use of one's powers and faculties. Pleasurable outcomes have a negative as well as a positive source.[39]

The repressing and inhibiting of spontaneous impulses to play is particularly harmful, especially to children. Also, the deprivations resulting from poverty and economic insecurity, anxiety, feelings of failure, excessive pressure of work, and physical congestion in the home or neighborhood, all aggravate feelings of distress and tension and interfere with healthy personality development and maintenance. Slavson sees in the freedom and spontaneity of recreation a prime opportunity to free the person from some of these pressures, to discharge some of the tension feelings, and to compensate for inadequacies elsewhere.

Slavson's concept of recreation and mental health is based upon an examination of the mental and emotional needs of man, as developed during the process of the socialization of the individual, bringing him into the pattern of group life, and controlling deviant behavior which might result from the natural expression of the individual's instinctual drives. Slavson is concerned with the inner tensions that are created by the strain of regulating oneself to meet social demands, and by the strain of our particular competitive and insecure modern life, which makes additional demands upon the individual. His hope that play and recreation are vital means of meeting these needs of the individual provides his major thesis.

A somewhat different analysis is given by Erikson in his book *Childhood and Society*. Erikson combines clinical psychoanalysis and cultural anthropology in his approach to the analysis of the child's problems of growing up in any society, and he assigns to play an important part in the growing-up process. "The play act . . . [is] a

---

[39] Slavson, p. 21.

function of the ego, an attempt to bring into synchronization the bodily and social processes of which one is a part even while one is a self." [40]

The individual, for the maintenance of his ego, to maintain a satisfactory degree of self-esteem, must master in some degree the various areas and problems of life. Play functions as an opportunity, through imaginative manipulations of one's personality and one's environment, to manage situations successfully. The infant's play begins with his own body, and next with a near person such as his mother. The child next ventures into the small world of manageable toys, and retreats to it, as Erikson says, when he needs to overhaul his ego. And finally, playfulness reaches into the world shared by others. Each sphere is endowed with its own sense of reality and mastery. Thus, he says, "the child's play is the infantile form of the human ability to deal with experience by creating model situations and to master reality by experiment and planning." [41]

He sees adult play as an activity chosen without being compelled by survival or other urgent interests, one in which the person is "on vacation from reality." For the adult, play "permits a periodical stepping out from those forms of defined limitations which are his reality." [42] Erikson suggests several dimensions of these:

> Take *gravity:* to juggle, to jump, or to climb adds unused dimensions to the awareness of our body. Play here gives a sense of divine leeway, of excess space.
>
> Take *time:* in trifling, in dallying, we lazily thumb our noses at this, our slave-driver. Where every minute counts, playfulness vanishes. . . .
>
> Take *fate* and *causality,* which have determined who and what we are, and where. In games of chance we re-establish equality before fate, and secure a virgin chance to every player willing to observe a few rules which, if compared with the rules of reality, seem arbitrary and senseless. . . .
>
> Take *social reality,* and our defined cubicles in it. In play-acting we can be what in life we could not or would not be. . . .
>
> Take our *bodily drives.* The bulk of the nation's advertis-

---

[40] Erik H. Erikson, *Childhood and Society* (New York: W. W. Norton and Company, 1950), p. 184.

[41] Erikson, p. 195.

[42] Erikson, p. 186.

> ing effort exploits our wish to play with necessity, to make us believe, for example, that to inhale and to eat are not pleasurable necessities, but a fanciful game with ever new and sensuous nuances. . . .
>
> Last but not least, in *love life* we describe as sex play the random activities preceding the final act, which permit the partners to choose body part, intensity and tempo. . . . Sex play ends when the final act begins, narrowing choice and giving rein to "nature." . . .
>
> This list of playful situations in a variety of human endeavors indicates the narrow area within which our ego can feel superior to the confinement of space and time and to the definitiveness of social reality, free from the compulsions of conscience and from impulsions of irrationality. Only within these limitations, then, can man feel at one with his ego; no wonder he feels "only human when he plays." [43]

Freud's concept of catharsis is put to use by Erikson in his analysis, with the recognition that play may permit the person to work off tensions and frustrations which trouble him. And the concept of repetition compulsion is dealt with likewise, recognizing the theme of child's play often as struggle to master a situation that originally had been too much for him to handle to his satisfaction.

Erikson approaches the problem of play from the point of view of one using play therapeutically, first to diagnose the anxieties and troubles of a child through observing the nature of his play, and second to help the child through his play to reach an understanding of his problem and of himself and to attain an adequate identity in the society. In this approach we can gain useful insights into the general nature of play.

The discussion of psychological aspects of play by Sapora and Mitchell, discussed earlier, contributes useful information to our knowledge on this subject. Their *self-expression* theory describes play as being motivated primarily by this desire of man for self-expressive activities of his own choosing, which are satisfying in themselves. They recognize that from the first the child adopts the behaviors learned in imitation of adults, and that around these behaviors habits are formed that themselves become motives, especially as the person gets satisfaction out of adequate performance of the activity.

---

[43] Erikson, pp. 186-187.

The environment, which is primarily social or man-made, *i.e.,* the cultural milieu, has, of course, a profound influence on this process. The child adopts the culture of his group, and his play patterns are those of the society of which he is a member. The authors deal very briefly with these factors of the social environment, and recognize as well the physical environmental influences on both the play habits and attitudes of the person.

They accept in general the concept that humans have in common certain basic *wishes.* These wishes they do not identify as instinctive, although earlier writers had ascribed to these wishes a basic instinctive foundation. They think instead that these wishes are a result of socially acquired experience, and in this way acquire values to the individual. They use as the basis for their classification of wishes the formulations of the sociologist W. I. Thomas, who postulated four desires: for new experience, for security, for response, and for recognition.[44] They add two additional ones: the wish for participation, and the wish for the aesthetic or beautiful.

Although social psychologists, and more directly, anthropologists, have been concerned with universal behavior patterns, or *cultural universals,* which appear in all human societies in one or another variation, there is less and less attempt to base these patterns on "human instincts" and more effort to explain them in terms of complex interaction of psychosomatic processes and needs arising in the course of individual development and the interaction with the environment or milieu.

Sapora and Mitchell treat briefly the compensatory aspect of play, pointing out that play offers the individual the opportunity for compensating for inferior feelings and failures in other areas of his life.[45] We have seen how several writers contributed much the same thought, that fantasy, competitive games, and the like have strong compensatory qualities. Sapora and Mitchell warn against overemphasizing compensation, speculating that much of play activity is natural and spontaneous expression and has little or no compensatory quality involved.

The self-expression theory of play that these two writers advance is based upon several important facts. One is that man is an active, dynamic creature. He also possesses a physiological and anatomical

---

[44] W. I. Thomas, *The Unadjusted Girl* (Boston: Little, Brown and Company, 1923).

[45] Sapora and Mitchell, *Theory of Play and Recreation,* pp. 98-101.

structure that predisposes him to certain kinds of activity. Also, his fitness, or resources of energy, and his psychological inclinations influence the types of activity he engages in. Being the kind of "animal" he is, "all that is necessary to explain play is the fact that he seeks to live, to use his abilities, to express his personality." [46] They consider a number of aspects of play, including: (1) the role of habit in play, (2) the role of social contact in the formation of play habits, (3) universal wishes, and (4) the compensatory aspect noted earlier.[47]

In arguing the advantages of the self-expression theory of play, these two writers suggest the following:

> It (the theory) emphasizes the conspicuous role of learned responses, of habits and attitudes.
>
> It utilizes the learning theory to explain individual differences in play.
>
> It accounts for the growing interest in types of play which one can master and the tendency of man to set goals of proficiency in play activities.
>
> It accounts for man's enthusiasm for thrilling and dangerous experiences.
>
> It accounts for the creative type of play, as a form of self-expression.
>
> It accounts for compensatory play.

These writers, like others, recognize the existence of those needs or drives in men which have been defined as "self-fulfilling" or "self-actualizing" drives, and undertake to comprehend this fact in their play theory.

The great importance of these several psychological views to a well-rounded theory of play suggests that it is necessary for students of recreation to study them carefully. But first it is desirable to examine two other approaches, the first of which is the sociological-anthropological.

Psychology has identified basic purposes of play: to discharge tensions and obtain catharsis, temporarily to escape reality through fantasy, to compensate for lack of success in other life activities, and to obtain the satisfaction of creative self-expression; for the child, in addition, there is the purpose of experimenting with some manageable elements of adult life.

---

[46] Sapora and Mitchell, pp. 89-90.

[47] Sapora and Mitchell, pp. 91-98.

Sociological-Anthropological

It was pointed out in the first chapter that, sociologically, recreation can be viewed in its institutionalized aspects as a social function and as a source of social forces. That brief description will suffice at present, although later on considerable attention will be paid to these subjects as we analyze some aspects of recreation in the modern community. But in advance of that, we must pay attention to certain social scientific facts that should be important foundation elements in a theory of play. The first of these, an anthropological fact, is that play is a cultural universal. In this same sense and as most anthropologists employ it, the word *play* is used in its fullest sense and is comparable to what we call *recreation.* Extensive studies by anthropologists of a large number of cultures, and cross-cultural studies, show that all human societies have play, in a wide range of forms, as a fundamental part of their ways of life. The forms in which play is found in the society are influenced very actively by the total culture of any particular society. In societies stressing cooperative forms of economic endeavor, the play activities also will take on cooperative forms, and in societies, conversely, in which competitive striving is at a premium the play of children and adults may be very competitive as well. In societies in which physical fitness is at a premium, to cope with a hostile natural environment or hostile human neighbors, the games will take on vigorous and combative forms related to the society's idea of what is best for survival. In important respects these several systems or sets of customs have equal validity for each of the peoples who possess them.

One of the most erudite spokesmen for the viewpoint that play is a cultural phenomenon is Huizinga. His contention is that culture arises in a form of play, that it is "played" from the beginning, and that through this process society expresses its interpretation of life and the world. Huizinga further contends that play is older than culture since animals play, and culture presupposes human society, but he makes this important point:

> . . . even in its simplest forms on the animal level, play is more than mere physiological phenomenon or psychological reflex. It goes beyond the confines of purely physical or purely biological activity. It is a *significant* function—that is to say, there is some sense to it. In play there is something at play which

> transcends the immediate needs of life and imparts meaning to the action. All play means something.[48]

Huizinga identifies as the first prerequisite of all play that it be voluntary. This quality of freedom is what sets play off from other natural processes. "Only when play is a recognized cultural function—a rite, a ceremony—is it bound up with notions of obligation and duty." [49] He goes on to describe play as order, being limited in time and space and being nonserious and outside of ordinary life, while at the same time absorbing the player intensely and utterly.

Anthropologists view play in modern society to be deeply influenced by the nature of present-day life. Neumeyer and Neumeyer vividly describe some of these influences as follows:

> Overspecialization, standardization, increased speed, the stress and strain of modern life, technological unemployment and the reduction of people to secondhand participants in their hours of recreation are some of the negative aspects of the machine age. . . . The machine has a tendency to destroy individuality and naturalness in play life by producing standardized models and patterns. It is a kind of steam roller of our present-day civilization, leveling off differences. It respects neither individuality nor personality. Though it may broaden our tastes, it has a tendency to flatten them also. The dangers of standardization can be overcome not by smashing the machine, but by building up a strong leisure life of the people.[50]

Hutchinson points out in an historical review of the growth of recreation in the United States how recreation developed in relation to and partly in response to the changing conditions and the changing ideologies of the various periods in our history. He suggests that the ideology of the twentieth century in this country reflected a considerable change from that of earlier periods, and that this had important effects upon attitudes toward play and recreation.

---

[48] Johan Huizinga, *Homo Ludens: A Study of the Play Element in Culture* (London: Routledge & Kegan Paul, Ltd., 1955), p. 1.

[49] Huizinga, p. 8.

[50] Martin H. Neumeyer and Esther S. Neumeyer, *Leisure and Recreation: A Study of Leisure and Recreation in Their Sociological Aspects,* Third edition (New York: The Ronald Press Company, 1958), pp. 152-153. Copyright 1958 The Ronald Press Company.

> New ideas had arisen in all fields bearing upon the social and cultural structure of the American people. The shackles of tradition had been broken; and at this point only time was needed to initiate action which would carry the ideas about leisure to their ultimate completion. The twentieth century lay ahead as the period in which recreation had an opportunity to develop as one of the social services people needed and desired.[51]

We have noticed how during certain historical periods the ideas and ideals of the period, influenced by the fundamental economic forces at the time, influence in turn the recreation and play of the people. These become part of the folkways and mores of a society, and folk conform to these as they do to other customs. Anthropologists, especially those following the functionalist's point of view, have explained the relation between the following: (1) the underlying organization of productive forces and relationships that grow out of the economic and survival needs of a society; (2) the other social institutions such as government, religion, and perhaps recreation; (3) the superstructure of ideologies and philosophies and mores that support, reinforce, and "explain" the existence and form of other social arrangements. Anthropologically based philosophers of recreation find much significance in the universal existence of play among all peoples, the wide range of forms it takes among different groups, and its relation to basic economic and social institutional forms. Play as an element in and of culture was Huizinga's main thesis. His analysis of play in relationship to language, contest, law, war, poetry, art, and philosophy should be reviewed by any student interested in evidence that play and recreation are woven through all human endeavor.

Meyer and Brightbill were perhaps the ones who first described recreation in respect to *social force*. They formulated the concept that recreation, education, health, religion, and work together constitute, in proper balance, the nucleus of total social stability, forces in social well-being, and essential processes in social life.

> Recreation's importance as an essential function, as increasingly evidenced in government actions, its sponsorship by

[51] John L. Hutchinson, *Principles of Recreation* (New York: The Ronald Press Company, 1951), pp. 38-39. Copyright 1951 The Ronald Press Company.

> religious organizations and educational organizations, its importance as a means of securing private income, its expanding use of industrial organizations, and its sponsorship in an impressive aggregation of voluntary youth-serving organizations, more and more is being recognized.[52]

The sociological view of recreation, within the framework of the concepts of society, social institutions, social structure, and social forces, sees it as having a place among the social institutions and an influence as a social force.

Sociologists are interested in the nature of social groups and the processes of social interaction which are found in groups. The Neumeyers describe recreation groups as meeting important needs in the lives of individuals, and the group aspects of recreation as being one of the powerful factors in its attractiveness. They point out that groups for human beings are necessary to their very survival, as well as profoundly important in molding personality and socializing the individual. They describe recreation groups as follows:

> Recreation groups are usually spontaneous ones, allowing freedom of action and a joyousness not to be found in most groups. . . . The joyful emotions are aroused in friendly competition and cooperation. The relationships are intimate and even naïve at times. Consequently, the influences that radiate from others are pronounced. One is controlled by them in a subtle and unique way. A spontaneity and naturalness of expression and a release from convention are present in most forms of recreation.[53]

They point out as well that recreation groups are often primary, or small, face-to-face groups which provide highly significant experiences for the individual, offering a means of identification, personal loyalty, and intimate friendship, which are of great value to him. They say of these groups, "Primary groups, because of the intimate contacts of persons composing them, have always exercised great social

---

[52] Harold D. Meyer and Charles K. Brightbill, *Community Recreation: A Guide to Its Organization* (Englewood Cliffs, N.J.: Prentice-Hall, Inc., 1956), p. 7.

[53] Neumeyer and Neumeyer, *Leisure and Recreation;* p. 254.

influence. This is true particularly of the play group in which the relationships are intimate and are relatively spontaneous. An interest is generated that absorbs attention and makes one susceptible to the influences emanating from the group itself." [54] There are many secondary groups, the larger, more impersonal groupings, in recreation, especially in mass recreation, both commercial and otherwise. It is recognized that there are different values, and perhaps less important ones, as well as some negative values, in a society that provides only such impersonal and transitory groups in play. The facts supporting this particular concept will be examined at a later point, but a philosophical point of view of recreation in modern-day life would be deeply concerned with these sociological concepts, especially the concepts of social value.

The Neumeyers explore a number of other sociological concepts concerning social processes involved in play and recreation. Competition and cooperation are analyzed, as well as conflict and destructive combat into which competitive play occasionally degenerates. Patterns of imitation are described, which help to explain the degree to which recreations gain popularity and in which temporary fads arise. Some aspects of crowd behavior are analyzed as they appear in recreation situations, and the effect on recreation as a social function of an increased emphasis on spectatoring has been studied. Nash's well-known book, *Spectatoritis,* contains an analysis of this particular sociological phenomenon.[55]

Modern recreationists are becoming more aware of the important contributions anthropology and sociology are making to a theory of play. It is apparent how important play always has been in the social life of man, how recreation functions as a social institution and as a universal cultural pattern, arising out of basic human needs and taking on forms which relate to the varying culture patterns of different groups. The impact of changing social conditions on recreation has been traced, using both an historical approach and some simple cross-cultural comparisons. We will study in more detail later the phenomena briefly noted here, that recreation is a social or group process, that individuals participate in recreation in groups, and the dynamics of groups have special meaning in the play setting.

---

[54] Neumeyer and Neumeyer, p. 256.

[55] Jay B. Nash, *Spectatoritis* (New York: A. S. Barnes and Company, 1932).

Sociology and anthropology have contributed to play theory the findings that play is a cultural universal, having a social function that produces institutional forms and social forces, and becomes a means whereby an individual's need for social relationships is met.

Aesthetic

While a consideration of the aesthetic view of play is included at this particular point instead of elsewhere it must not be thought of as necessarily a modern view, for a consideration of man's needs for aesthetic experiences was important in the philosophies of writers for many centuries. Even Plato, in his utopia *The Republic,* visualized the ruling class as having some training in such arts as music, poetry, and the dance. Philosophers of art have pointed out for a long time that creative and artistic pursuits are an essential part of man's striving for fulfillment of emotional and intellectual needs. An aesthetic theory of play may be formulated in these terms too: man's need for beauty in his life, and his use of play as a means of seeking beauty.

But we can gain some perspective on man's aesthetic needs by going back even further. In Childe's valuable little book at one point he discussed life among the hominoid ancestors of man, perhaps a quarter of a million years ago in the paleolithic or stone age (geologically, the middle Pleistocene era). He points out that the primitive stone axes, hammers, and scrapers "display extraordinary care and delicacy of workmanship. . . .Their authors were trying to make something not only useful but also beautiful. If so, the tools in question are really works of art, expressions of aesthetic feeling." [56] What deep urges to creative self-expression and beauty stimulated these early prehuman creatures in the dimmest prehistoric ages we can but guess. But it helps to define the depth and basic character of man's aesthetic drives and needs, these being just as demanding of fulfillment in modern as in ancient man.

If art has been important to man as long as we know man has existed, then we are dealing with something very fundamental. The importance of beauty in man's life, and the use of things of beauty to convey man's deepest emotional feelings and most profound thinking, has been apparent to students of aesthetics for centuries. We shall not undertake any history of aesthetics here, although later we will

[56] Gordon Childe, *What Happened in History* (New York: Penguin Books), p. 25.

examine a few working concepts of aesthetics. But modern play theorists from Froebel and Schiller on have noted that one of the profound satisfactions in play comes from expression in the arts, a seeking to create and to enjoy beauty and to use art as a spiritual language with which to express our most profound and basic values.

The aesthetician Lange maintained that man escapes from the boredom, the limits, the humdrum, of existence into the ideal world of play and art for his deepest pleasures and satisfactions. He saw

Play as the Art of Childhood

play as the art of childhood and art as the mature form of play, the two in his judgment being closely allied.

> The first characteristic which play and art have in common is their pleasure character and lack of a practical purpose. . . . [T]he intrinsic nature of the activity is the cause of the pleasure. . . . [W]e reserve the name play for those activities which are pursued with the conscious intent of realizing pleasure. . . .

> [T]his is likewise true in art. . . . [I]n this regard [there is] also a complete agreement between the two activities.[57]

He mentions many other ways in which play and art are related, such as in the satisfaction of sensuous pleasures of sight, hearing, and touch, of gaining of skill or virtuosity in performance, of competition with others, of influence and success, and so on.

From others having points of view like Lange have come the most thoughtful expression of the aesthetic view of play, that art and play are very intimately related, that aesthetic play is of value and significance in human life because through art may be expressed and communicated the highest values in man's experience. Brownell expresses a modern and, for recreationists, a challenging point of view when he says that art is not something to participate in. Art "is action in which we find inherent enjoyment, and the best way to get at it is doing what we enjoy. . . . It will produce play and recreation, games, athletics, hunting, fishing, gossip and kissing, music and dancing and home hobbies from burnt leather to gardening. Though the 'arts' are more maturely formulated than these enjoyable activities . . . the essential thing in all is the same, activity for the fun of it. . . . For that matter play is a kind of random art. . . . Play is [also] a prelude to art. . . . And by enjoyment I mean not necessarily pleasure but the inherent value and immediacy in actions, whatever that may be."[58] At another point he points out that instead of play being a prelude to art, it might properly be thought that art is a postscript to play. At any rate, play and art are very intimately related. Not only is play the means wherein art may become part of a person's life, but art is the activity from which the person draws the deep and profound satisfactions and self-sustaining contentment that freely chosen and creatively engaged in play pursuits can provide.

Anderson adds to this the social dimension, declaring that relationships between individuals offer an area for creative and aesthetic experiences. "Creativity in human relationships is a positive view of human behavior that admits the uniqueness and dignity of man. . . . [It] is a form or manner of reality to others which admits of one's own

---

[57] Konrad Lange, *Art as Play,* from *Das Wesen der Kunst,* 1901. Translated by Max Schertel and Melvin Rader in Melvin Rader, *A Modern Book of Esthetics* (New York: Henry Holt and Company, 1935), pp. 6-9.

[58] Baker Brownell, *Art Is Action* (New York: Harper & Row, Inc., 1939), pp. 33-34.

uniqueness and dignity and at the same time respects a uniqueness and dignity in others." [59]

The aesthetic view is that play is the chief means by which people may bring creativity and beauty into their lives. While art often is thought of in the narrow or specific sense of the graphic language, and movement arts and music, a broader concept is equally valid and helpful. Artistic experience may be seen in many phases of domestic life such as cooking and gardening, in many areas of human relationships, and in practically every activity of man. This broad concept goes hand in hand with the concept that aesthetic experience is not, as Plato suggested, only for the well-born or well-bred, but for everyone. There is, as leisure time increases, an opportunity for all people of all classes and cultures to share not only in the audience-receiving phases of cultural experiences but in the field of direct creative artistry itself. Artists and creative activities must come, says the democratic philosopher of play, from all ranks and groups. And the best of artistic experiences come from the lives of real people in real situations, the "common people." The deep hold upon the people in this country of certain forms of artistic expression represents not only, as some suggest, the influence of radio, television, and phonograph sales promotion, but urgent desires for forms of art that are familiar and that express feelings close to ordinary folk. The role of art is to express with special creative and vivid means the thoughts, the ideas, and the feelings of people.

The role of play as well is to provide a means for people to express these same thoughts, ideas, and feelings. As with play, art offers opportunity for "escape" from duties, responsibilities, and necessities, a person finding, as Frank says, "sheer delight in a wholly imaginary life. . . . [H]e finds release from burdens, relaxation of his exigent tensions, and freedom if only momentarily, from the continual anxieties he bears within him." [60] He goes on to say that art lures an individual "away into the world of phantasy from which he has returned with new vigor or endurance." [61] The individual "turns to

[59] Harold H. Anderson, "Creativity as Personality Development," in *Creativity and Its Cultivation,* ed. H. H. Anderson (New York: Harper & Row, Inc., 1959), p. 120.

[60] Lawrence K. Frank, *Society as the Patient* (New Brunswick: Rutgers University Press, 1948), p. 270.

[61] Frank, p. 270.

aesthetic experiences to console and sustain him against the strains and tasks of living."[62]

Art, or aesthetically creative endeavor, has another important role in the lives of people, and, as it functions as a form of play expression, it may contribute richly to the satisfactions of individuals. As art becomes meaningful to people, it functions to help them to understand their life and their society. It helps them to return to their workaday life with renewed spirit, understanding, and vigor, both to work better and to make life itself better. The problem is to make art meaningful, to understand how aesthetic life may become more directly the possession of all. This becomes a challenge for the whole people, to stimulate our search for the real beauty in life, to make of our play a creative and aesthetically satisfying thing which will be supporting and rewarding to us throughout our lives.

The goal defined for man, in the aesthetic sense, is to become freely creative, to enable this capability and potential in man to develop. Thus may the self-actualizing man, the inner-directed man, the mature personality, emerge. Maslow sought to point out some of the elements in this kind of person as part of the modern search for the means to cultivate creativity in human beings and thus enable them to enjoy greater self-fulfillment.

Human nature has been defined as partly a creative thrust. Maslow holds that fundamentally mature individuals, whom he calls "self-actualizing," are those in which real creativity is alive and continued. He says that the creativity of children is often frustrated and repressed during the process of growing up, and he was concerned with maintaining this quality as individuals grew up.

Maslow has seen in people with "self-actualizing creativeness" some special perceptiveness, spontaneity, and expressiveness, which flowed out easily and with less blocking and self-criticism. They could let themselves be flooded with emotion, effortlessly, free from stereotypes and clichés. They were "open to experience" with no fear of the unknown, the mysterious, and were free to puzzle over, be absorbed in, meditate on. "To the extent that creativeness is constructive, synthesizing, unifying, and integrative, to that extent does it depend in part on the inner integration of the person."[63]

---

[62] Frank, p. 272.

[63] Abraham H. Maslow, "Creativity in Self-Actualizing People," in *Creativity and Its Cultivation,* ed. H. H. Anderson (New York: Harper & Row, Inc., 1959), p. 88 and pp. 93-95.

This modern psychological-aesthetic view indicates, and it could be supported by scientific investigation, that in this area of man's search for the truth about himself there is an emerging field of scientific inquiry regarding the aesthetic part of man's being. This inquiry has much significance for play theory.

Aesthetic theory stresses the creative interest in man, and the function of play in bringing beauty into his life through a wide range of experiences, with the purpose of encouraging in him "self-actualizing creativeness."

Questions for Study and Discussion

1. *What were the strengths and shortcomings of nineteenth-century play theories?*
2. *Why did Froebel believe that play was life itself to little children?*
3. *What are the contributions of modern psychology to a philosophy of play?*
4. *Why did John Dewey state (1) that the organism is not in its natural state when it is quiet or still, and (2) that the stimulus of pain or unpleasantness is not necessary for movement? What importance has this view for recreation?*
5. *What definitions of the nature of play did the scientists Friedrich Schiller and Herbert Spencer contribute?*
6. *What were the main contributions to play theory of Karl Groos?*
7. *How would you evaluate the theories of Joseph Lee as a basic theory of play?*

Selected Readings

Freud, Sigmund, *Group Psychology and the Analysis of the Ego,* The International Psycho-Analytic Library, No. 6 (New York: Liveright Publishing Corporation, 1951).

Groos, Karl, *The Play of Man* (New York: D. Appleton and Company, 1901).

Huizinga, Johan, *Homo Ludens: A Study of the Play Element in Culture* (London: Routledge & Kegan Paul, Ltd., 1955).

Sapora, Allen V., and Elmer D. Mitchell, *Theory of Play and Recreation,* Third edition (New York: The Ronald Press Company, 1961).

Selye, Hans, *The Stress of Life* (New York: McGraw-Hill Book Company, 1956).

5

THEORIES OF LEISURE AND RECREATION

Having looked at the theories of play as foundations of a philosophy of leisure and recreation, we shall look next at the meaning of *leisure* and the meaning of *recreation,* beginning with the working definitions of these two terms that we formulated earlier.

We have defined *free time* in an economic sense as the time "off the job," time available after work is done, "unsold" time. It is man's disposable time, to do with as he wishes, his discretionary time, to spend according to his choice. It is his own time. We have defined *leisure time* as that portion of free time devoted to leisure pursuits. We have defined *leisure* as having something to do with being "leisurely."

These qualities of *tempo,* of self-determined pace, and of *focus* upon or attention to fulfilling and self-satisfying purpose are essential elements of leisure. Douglass says, "Everywhere on this globe man is redefining his habitual expectations in relationship to time. Leisure, defined as unhurried pleasurable living among one's spontaneous and educated enthusiasms, becomes a novel keystone in a new design of living." [1] Douglass then gives a definition of recreation.

> The content of this leisure is sometimes called recreation—defined as the voluntary, personal inwardly rewarding experience of enjoyment encountered within a framework of taste and values and contributing to personal growth and life-enrichment.[2]

In 1950, in connection with the Midcentury White House Conference on Children and Youth, the National Recreation Policies Committee issued "A Midcentury Declaration of Recreation Policy" in which they undertook to define recreation in terms that would be clear and helpful. The statement points out that modern times have created in America a condition wherein practically everyone enjoys considerable free time, some of which is utilized in some measure for the enrichment of living. Among the vast number of activities that occupy this free time are many that are recreational activities. As the conditions encouraging widespread leisure have developed,

> . . . the recreation activities of the people have grown in number and complexity. . . . Inventive genius and organizational skill . . . have been applied to our means of recreation as well. . . . Recreation has also changed its function and increased in its educational significance. Formerly the function of recreation was primarily to provide relaxation and refreshment from toil. . . . Work tended to satisfy the creative human instincts because it was varied and not highly specialized. . . . In this age . . . recreation becomes more important as a means of creative living. . . . Only recently have we tended to recognize these facts and to begin to plan for the organization of recreation as

---

[1] Paul Douglass, "The Administration of Leisure for Living," *Bulletin of the American Recreation Society,* Vol. 12, No. 3 (April 1960), p. 2.

[2] Douglass, p. 2.

> an instrument of liberal education and as a method for the promotion of the general welfare.[3]

In a stirring challenge to basic values, the document says:

> Recreation in a sense is a fortress of our precious freedom. In an age of high organization the activities of economic and industrial life, including performance of civic duties and military service, are accompanied necessarily by regimentation of people. Recreation in striking contrast is free from regimentation and coercion. The free and voluntary character of our recreation life is an antidote and a saving grace. In leisure time people are free to give play to their imaginative impulses. They may voluntarily choose the activities through which they may pursue happiness. . . .
>
> The free spirit may be oblivious of others or may join with others in cooperative enterprises. He may persist in or break off these relationships as he chooses. He may live complacently or creatively, according to the drives of his inner nature. He may expand and multiply his capacities for human expression in his recreational life to the extent that he purposes to do so. . . . In short . . . the goal of a "more abundant life" is within the grasp of the American people if they can be brought to appreciate the recreational heritage which is theirs, and the opportunities to utilize leisure for the improvement of the quality of living and for the "pursuit of happiness." [4]

These paragraphs may suffice as working definitions of the two terms we wish to study. Both terms are under close scrutiny today because of the crucial significance to society of the area of life with which they are concerned.

THE NEW LEISURE—ITS CAUSES AND ITS SIGNIFICANCE

We have seen earlier that every known society has had in its culture some leisure time, some time for leisure pursuits. In all ages and all times, all peoples have stopped work to play. Ancient societies have left many records of play activities. And yet we have seen how

---

[3] National Recreation Policies Committee, *Midcentury Declaration of Recreation Policy* (Washington, D.C.: The Committee, 1950), p. 1.

[4] National Recreation Policies Committee, p. 2.

philosophers in different societies differed radically in their ideas, and how leisure was viewed either as the full-time privilege of the well-born, the opportunity for citizens to enjoy a beautiful life, a "detestation," a basic right of the citizen of means, or the right of all in the society.

At different times in history the particular level of development of economic life in relation to climate and other natural environmental factors, and the relation of particular groups in the economic system to the productive process, were influential in determining the amount of leisure time and the quality of leisure, as well as the amount of wealth, of each group.

Today technology, science, and automation, all products of human skill and creativity, have brought us to a new peak of productivity. One hour of work today will produce as much as twenty to one hundred hours of work would have produced two or three hundred years ago. People want many more things today, and so we are producing vastly more things to eat, wear, and enjoy; still, there are many more leisure hours for the average person than there were a few generations back.

Nash very vividly describes the technological base for the new leisure, pointing out that the leisure of ancient Greece was based upon slavery, and that our machines may operate as slaves to us. "The Greeks attempted to keep a proportion of about twelve slaves to each citizen. It is estimated in America that we have from fifteen to twenty slaves per individual. . . . They light our buildings, start our cars, run our machines, shine our shoes, curl our hair, wash our clothes, and even shave our faces without lather. There will be more of them." [5]

Kaplan presents another estimate, saying that "the average middle-class home in America has in it enough vacuum cleaners, waffle irons, air cleaners, dishwashers, clothes scrubbers, and other gadgets to equal the energy of 90 male servants." [6]

Many writers have described the phenomenon of decreasing hours of labor. The forces at work, the steady development of more and still more machines, the rising levels of production, the steady

---

[5] Jay B. Nash, *Spectatoritis* (New York: A. S. Barnes and Company, 1932), p. 4.

[6] Max Kaplan, *Leisure in America: A Social Inquiry* (New York: John Wiley and Sons, Inc., 1960), p. 295.

decrease in hours of labor, have been analyzed. The work day has gone from sixteen hours a day to twelve, from twelve to eight, from eight to six, and the end is not in sight. Many writers declare the possibility that this generation may well see the four-hour day.

Several million homemakers have not been left out in this development, as we have seen. Household appliances such as vacuum cleaners, electric irons, electric washing machines and dish washers, automatic stoves with clocks attached, refrigerators and deep freezes, prepared frozen and canned foods, laundry and diaper services, supermarkets, cleaning and pressing shops, and myriads of other social inventions have reduced the housewife's work markedly, depending on how many of these services each can buy with the family income. The use of automatic stokers, traveling gardeners, and the like have robbed boys and girls of their chores to some extent as well, and left them with more free time.

On the American scene, the five-day, forty-hour week has become the standard work week in recent decades, giving the average person two full days each week for leisure. The worker now has more than twice as much time free for recreational activities than he had a half-century ago. Over the course of a century average hours of labor had been almost halved and available leisure has been estimated to have increased from about ten hours weekly to some seventy. The significance of this fact for recreation can hardly be ignored.

Phenomenal advances in modern industrial and productive technology have brought men, women, and children more and more hours of leisure. But modern economic life has also inflicted upon millions of persons periods of depression, recession, technological and cyclical unemployment, enforced free time during which youths and adults have time on their hands without knowing what to do with it. They are oppressed by the torments of insecurity, poverty, lack of opportunity for constructive work, and guilt over their failure to be at work. It is inaccurate to think of such time as leisure time, in the sense in which we are considering it—that is, as the time earned by the person and available for him freely to employ in leisure pursuits of interest to him.

During the 1950's and so far during the 1960's the movement for a further reduction in the work week to four days has been growing in strength, stimulated by occasional periods of increasing unemployment, and bolstered by the historical evidence that earlier establishment of a six-day or five-day week contributed to economic stability and social welfare. It is argued that the reductions in hours of work have accelerated social and economic progress and that substantial increases in productivity and output have resulted from technical advances over the years. The recent advances in automation indicate that a further reduction in hours of work without loss of income is feasible, necessary, and desirable.

An assessment of the significance of this new leisure in man's design of life requires a consideration of two points, which, it is argued, are related: one is a distressing fact, the other a hopeful hypothesis. The distressing fact, Martin says, is that "the past decade gave us the forty-hour week, the long weekend, longer vacations with pay, increased longevity, but it also brought us, among other things, an increasing tempo of living, more duodenal ulcers, increasing deaths from coronary thrombosis, increasing annual budgets for mental disease, and increasing consumption of drugs for sleeplessness of psychological origins. . . .[W]e have to include increased accident-proneness, especially automobile accidents, many of which can be attributed to the inability to relax, and the compulsive need to keep going at all costs, and to get there first." [7] The apparent relationship between increased leisure time and the increase in many indices of personal and social disorganization has yet to be either proven or disproven. We shall examine this argument later.

Douglass states for us the hopeful hypothesis that he draws from present-day economic and social trends, that for the first time in human history "leisure rather than work has become the dominant time factor which integrates life. . . . To accept our leisure as seriously as we once did our work shifts a whole emphasis. The change necessitates new value systems as leisure makes life richer and more exciting." [8] He believes that the impact of the new leisure will make necessary a major reorganization in man's design for living, and a reformulation of his philosophy of leisure and recreation.

Riesman, analyzing the character structures of Americans, found in the new leisure an opportunity for the development of more autonomy in the character of individuals, of more capacity to be creative and free from over-conformity, of more ability to be self-realizing in some measure:

---

[7] Alexander Reid Martin, *Leisure Time as a Basic Health Resource,* mimeographed (New York: American Psychiatric Association, 1958), p. 4.

[8] Douglass, *"The Administration of Leisure for Living,"* p. 11.

> Play, far from having to be the residue sphere left over from work time and work feeling, can increasingly become the sphere for the development of skill and competence in the art of living. Play may prove to be the sphere in which there is still some room left for the would-be autonomous man to reclaim his individual character from the pervasive demands of his social character.[9]

Vastly increased leisure time makes necessary a change from man's current work ethic to the conception that leisure will be the basic integrating factor in life, and the major source of value, although it will still be dependent upon a worthy work life and adequate meeting of basic material needs.

CIVILIZED LOAFING

Harry Overstreet stated some time ago, "Almost overnight a new idea has come to us. It is the recognition that we are to have more time to live our lives as we please. . . . We have, to an extent, grown work-wise. In the future, we shall grow leisure-wise." [10] Like Veblen he decried both the "barbaric leisure" of an ancient privileged leisure class and the "enforced leisure" of the depression-struck unemployed. And he argued for a leisure that expresses the art of living gracefully, of going slowly enough to see and enjoy the beauty of life around one's self, of finding joy and loveliness in these things. He quoted Whitman as saying, "I loafe and invite my soul." He reminded us that Aristotle said, "The end of labor is to gain leisure," and that even God is said to have rested from his labors.

Originally entitled *The Art of Civilized Loafing,* Overstreet's book raised such protests and criticisms that he realized that in our country at that time it was almost impossible to dignify the term *loafing;* so, like Galileo, he recanted, and renamed his book *A Guide to Civilized Leisure*. Then, as Galileo was supposed to have whispered to himself, "but nevertheless, the earth *does* go around the sun," Overstreet in his Foreword insists that "civilized loafing" is truly what he means, that it "would seem to express what we mean when we try to

---

[9] David Riesman, *The Lonely Crowd* (New Haven: Yale University Press, 1950), pp. 326-327.

[10] Harry Overstreet, *A Guide to Civilized Leisure* (New York: W. W. Norton and Company, Inc., 1934), p. 9.

combine two ideas of doing what we really wish to do and doing it in ways that enhance the pleasure of our self respect." [11]

This idea gains support from Bertrand Russell whose essay "In Praise of Idleness" points out that there is far too much work done today, "a great deal of harm is being done in the modern world by belief in the virtuousness of work, and that the road to happiness and prosperity lies in an organized diminution of work." [12] The work ethic, he argues, is an anomaly in the modern world, a remnant of the slave societies of earlier ages, and must be replaced by a new morality, one that gives respect to leisure, to avoid the disaster and misery resulting from enforcing excess idleness on some and denying it to others.

It has been argued that there are certain critical preconditions to the development of a leisure of worth. One of these is that leisure must arise out of a work life that is satisfying, not degrading nor tyrannical. It must be correlated with a work life that is equally worthy. A healthy leisure time cannot develop among a "population that must respond throughout its working day to the lash of an unconsidering economic power and that must too frequently occupy its leisure time with haunting fears lest the very lash itself be withdrawn. . . . no amount of leisure . . . can ever really compensate for life that is frustrated and shot through with fear." [13]

Brightbill talks about "no job, no joy," and indicates that "humans would be badly off without the incentive, the accomplishments, and the satisfactions which come from labor. . . . Work, of course, precedes leisure which, in turn, may be our reward for having fulfilled a useful role in society. . . . Leisure and labor come as a set—a set that cannot be broken. Without work there can be no rewarding leisure and without leisure work cannot be sustained." [14]

Overstreet points out that for leisure to develop properly a new environment must be created; for man's larger body, wherein he lives, is his room, house, neighborhood, and community. "People cannot issue from sordid environments and gain cleanness of spirit in a few hours spent in a park or by the sea. Sordid home or neighborhood

---

11 Overstreet, pp. 12-13.

12 Quoted from Bertrand Russell, *In Praise of Idleness and Other Essays,* in *Mass Leisure,* ed. Eric Larrabee and Rolf Meyersohn (Glencoe, Ill.: The Free Press, 1958), p. 97.

13 Overstreet, *Civilized Leisure,* p. 20.

14 Charles K. Brightbill, *Man and Leisure: A Guide to Its Organization* (Englewood Cliffs, N.J.: Prentice-Hall, Inc., 1961), pp. 24-25.

conditions linger and prevent the development of graciousness and charm."[15] Unlivable tenements or multitiered cave dwellings of the big-city dweller, who is supposed to be better off, and the ugliness, noise, soot, exhaust fumes, smog, smoke, and such that millions must live in—these make up the environment in which man must live, and if this environment includes pathology, unhealthiness, as he says, "deformity," the individual will not easily escape being deeply influenced. This is not to say that healthy use of leisure time cannot happen before our entire life has been thoroughly reformed. Some small degree of release from some of these conditions will give men courage and strength to live, to enjoy life, and to work to change unwholesome conditions and to reconstruct the society upon a more wholesome basis.

Leisure values may be gained in release from the tempo and demand of work, and from environmental inadequacies, but leisure's best and fullest expression is based upon environmental adequacy and work fulfillment.

LEISURE TIME AS A DANGER

There are those who see in the new leisure time a grave threat to the well-being of the society, as a dangerous and destructive innovation. Some of those who argue this are sincere persons seeking for answers to the negative outcomes of the new leisure. Others may be bent upon turning the clock backwards, or, like Nietzsche or Spengler, arguing for a view that sees civilization declining and man destroying himself as his world crashes in upon him. An argument in this vein was advanced a few years ago by Cutten, who believed that the coming of the machine before man was ready for it "has forced leisure upon us, and turned us, whether we wished it or not, from a people to whom toil was our breath to a nation of idlers, little knowing what to do with our surplus time."[16] The result is a calamity, with the amount of leisure time increasing steadily and "every extra hour of leisure adds in geometrical progression to the danger."[17]

He recognized the possible role of the machine in emancipating man from drudgery and freeing him to fulfill his other potentialities.

[15] Overstreet, *Civilized Leisure,* p. 24.

[16] George Cutten, *The Threat of Leisure* (New Haven, Conn.: Yale University Press, 1926), p. 12.

[17] Cutten, p. 44.

But he argues that people, instead of learning the art of leisure and becoming interested in the cultivation of their better selves and spending time in libraries, art galleries, schools, and resting on grassy banks by murmuring brooks, will very likely increase their attendance at pool rooms, taverns, and similar places of loafing.

There are, he claims, very few people interested in religion, cultural projects, civic affairs, or education, and a tiny number, relatively, interested in science and literature. "This is a terrible arraignment of our day and generation, but means nothing more than that we suddenly find ourselves with an amount of leisure on our hands beyond the wildest dreams of our fathers and have made no provisions for the use of it." [18] The result is a commercial exploitation of leisure-time needs, encouraging dissipation and other serious public evils and providing low public amusements that debase rather than elevate the personality, and create habits more base and perverse than enlightened and sophisticated. "It seems altogether likely that most persons will devote their leisure to occupations which, if not positively vicious, will be stupid or aimless." [19]

There is grave danger that leisure time, coupled with the comfort and ease of our modern life, will result in both physical and mental degeneracy, he concludes, and he warns us to strive seriously to provide for the constructive use of leisure time, in order that these dangers and perils to the public welfare may be avoided. We must remember that Cutten wrote from a moralistic, almost puritanical point of view in the 1920's, shocked at the excesses of the flapper age and the postwar release many people found in "low" recreations. Yet there is good reason to assess realistically the threats to man's welfare that may be inherent in our present-day movement toward a leisure era.

One very sober view is presented by Durant, who takes note of the gloomy opinion that leisure time is a threat to modern social stability and asks, "why should the opportunity for the vast majority of people to have time to spend, time to enjoy, time to develop their own private interest, be regarded as a problem, one almost said a danger?" [20] There had been prophets of doom for centuries. The eighteenth and nineteenth centuries produced such views as that of Adam Smith, that the

---

[18] Cutten, p. 69.

[19] Cutten, p. 75.

[20] Henry Durant, *The Problem of Leisure* (London: Routledge & Kegan Paul, Ltd., 1938), p. 3.

dulling routine of performing simple factory operations provides the worker "no occasion to exert his understanding or to exercise his invention. . . . He naturally . . . becomes as stupid and ignorant as it is possible for a human creature to become . . . incapable . . . of conceiving any generous, noble, or tender sentiment." [21]

De Tocqueville predicted that with the coming of democratic society would come a mass leisure characterized by ease, low taste, vulgarization. Some modern prophets of doom react to the growing leisure in somewhat the same vein. Russell reacts to this point of view with the charge that "this is the morality of the Slave State, applied in circumstances totally unlike those in which it arose. No wonder the result has been disastrous." He argues for a sane organization of society to pass on to the masses all the leisure gained by technology. Instead, at present, we force some to be totally idle while many are still overworked. "In this way, it is insured that the unavoidable leisure shall cause misery all round instead of being a universal source of happiness. Can anything more insane be imagined?" [22]

There is a danger of the worker's loss of interest in his handicraft and in the wholeness of his productive work. Industry has removed the worker to industrial plants and commercial establishments where interesting work is at a premium. The unemployed person in modern society is a particularly unfortunate victim of this system, whose leisure is enforced, and is thus not normal but tormented. Leisure time cannot be pleasant, and there can be no opportunity for challenging and gracious living, if any man is not already assured of the reason for existence and has no secure and stable position in life.

Durant summarizes this predicament as follows: "Work completely fails to supply to the workman the *rationale* of his existence. . . . Living is no longer to be interpreted in terms of labour, but in terms of the hours spent away from the stool, the machine, and the plough. Instead of being relaxation, leisure has become an effort to secure the meaning and justification of life itself." [23]

He finds in the public's restless searching for new entertainments an indication of little satisfaction with the kinds of amusements available. Thus leisure-time amusements often fail to amuse, to fulfill the

---

[21] Adam Smith, *The Wealth of Nations,* 1776, Book V, Chapter I, First edition, pp. 366-367, quoted in Durant, p. 10.

[22] Russell, in Larrabee and Meyersohn, *Mass Leisure,* p. 99.

[23] Durant, *The Problem of Leisure,* pp. 17-18.

function they should. In fact, they debase the tastes of the consumer. He sees that while some persons are able to compensate for their dead-end economic existence by leisure-time creative activities, "the majority are incapable of similarly defeating the dead weight of their circumstances. Engaged in monotonous, repetitive work, which makes no demand on their facilities, they are everywhere enveloped in an environment which contains little or no stimulus to seek the more difficult adventures of life." [24]

MacIver describes the problem as one of "great emptiness" for many people who find themselves released from the necessity of long hours of work. "It is a marvelous liberation for those who learn to use it. . . . It is the great emptiness for those who don't." Habits developed during work hours have little meaning during free time. Time is available, but what to do with it? And so, as MacIver says, "leisure becomes a void, and from the ensuing restlessness men take refuge in delusive excitations or fictitious visions, returning to their own earth no more." [25]

Important questions have been raised about the relationship between the increase in leisure time and the growing popularity of certain important social problems. One of these is gambling, which has its countless practitioners, providing in some places large revenues to government and huge profits to the operating organizations. The connection between these organizations and the criminal organizations in some modern countries—the United States, for example—has been of concern, as well as the rising tide of crime in general. Parallel to this has been the increase in juvenile delinquency and illegitimacy, attributed to a complex of causes, among which are commercial amusements and their operators, disorganized family life, youth unemployment, and so on. Students of social disorganization in modern community life have identified a number of problems connected with modern leisure, which we shall study later on.

Another negative component in the new leisure is discussed by Martin, whose concern is with the psychiatric problems related to misuse of leisure time.

> Caught off-guard, unprepared, uneducated, unequipped emotionally and psychologically to make creative use of leisure,

---

[24] Durant, p. 26.

[25] Robert MacIver, "The Pursuit of Happiness," cited in Larrabee and Meyersohn, *Mass Leisure,* pp. 118-122.

> there is a consequent misuse of it. Instead of leisure fulfilling its natural, biological function of enriching life and promoting creativity; instead of serving as the parent of Philosophy and the Arts . . . a very high proportion of leisure time activities . . . are drafted into the service of various and often conflicting compulsive needs. For example, the need to conform, to compete socially, the need to escape, the need for togetherness, the need to prove superiority and uniqueness . . . [make us] now the victims of inner compulsions that make the wise use of leisure impossible.[26]

He speaks of "spiritual unemployment," not knowing what to do with one's leisure time, and he recognizes this as a critical modern problem. There is misuse of leisure due to compulsive needs such as to have to escape or take flight or take refuge, to have to prove oneself rather than wanting to improve oneself, to have to please the authorities rather than oneself, to have to prove superiority, to satisfy perfectionistic compulsions, to have to get away from people, to have to keep busy and to fill in time, and to have to conform. All of these he sees as sabotaging and destroying the opportunities for the individual freely to express his recreative tendencies.

Related to this problem is the struggle to overcome the puritan heritage that blocks many individuals' free and spontaneous use of leisure time. The guilt feeling many have if they enjoy themselves too much prevents them from freeing their conscience sufficiently to attain the "spiritual freedom" required for creative use of leisure. The urge to conform, or to act compulsively in other ways, to follow the fads, to become a good "organization man" as the means of getting ahead, all of these are part of a complex of barriers to attainment of true freedom. Ogden Nash is quoted as saying "We are suffering from hardening of the oughteries."

Possibly related to this aspect of our problem, but perhaps related also to the economic needs felt by many persons and to their desire to purchase more of the things which they are urged by mass advertising to buy, is dual jobholding. Millions of persons give up many of their hours of leisure time to "moonlight"—hold two jobs. The importance to these individuals of gaining more material possessions is certainly part of the reason for such activity. Rising consumer prices and low

---

[26] Martin, *Leisure Time as Health Resource,* p. 3.

pay levels are added factors. Shorter normal work weeks provide opportunities for taking a second job. But an added factor is the perverted value systems of many individuals, which lead them to fill their hours compulsively with work and toil and to fail to realize the leisure values that potentially are theirs.

A realistic view of the problems and negative components of the modern leisure is required of the recreation philosopher, and certainly the rise in crime, delinquency, mental illness, family disorganization, and other problems has enough relationship to the fact of the increasing leisure time as to require sober study. Some have argued, so far without sufficient empirical support, that trends in the last two decades have sufficiently proved the warnings in the thirties to have been without basis. It is claimed that America has moved significantly from watching to doing, that individual recreations, "do-it-yourself" hobbies, gardening and home-centered arts, travel and outdoor sports, aquatics, arts and use of cultural facilities, all are on the increase. Further study of both these trends and the countertrends is needed to undergird any more definitive assessments of the situation so apprehensively viewed by these competent students of leisure.

Modern society's partial loss of the work rationale, or purpose, and individuals' unreadiness to use their leisure time creatively have led to widespread misuse of leisure time, commercial exploitation of recreational illiteracy, and failure to fulfill leisure values.

LEISURE TIME AS A CHALLENGE

In any case, those studying modern society and its leisure might be expected to be concerned with the critical problems facing those for whom new leisure has brought new problems, for whom fundamental economic and social changes have brought new difficulties to cope with, difficulties that older generations were not required to face. Of these students of leisure, some have examined the situation from the point of view of the profound challenge it presents. Among these is Burns, who argued in the 1930's that we should value our spare time, take it seriously, and make the most of its treasures.

Burns was primarily interested in the impact of the new leisure on the living patterns of people. He undertook, in particular, to show that leisure time is introducing a much greater measure of equality into our lives. Thus in our daily customs, "equality is in the air. Nobody knows what structure the new society will have; but we make experiments daily in new forms of social equality." [27] He saw modern foods and food preparation, ready-made clothing of great variety of style and color, new materials and means of home construction, new services for meeting health needs, and much more in modern life to meet people's requirements for comfort and pleasurable living. And he saw these things within the grasp of wide masses, with the potential of much more equal sharing. Kaplan points out the forces at work changing some of the visible evidences of class differentiation upon which class consciousness and other class phenomena were partly based. The "style of life" of the wealthy classes can be imitated fairly successfully by the less wealthy masses by the handy devices of the department store, the supermarket, and the installment buying plan. These are the product of the consumers' revolution, which by no means has abolished social strata and class differences, but has required new ways of studying these and understanding them in relation to our leisure culture.[28]

It has been argued that family life and the home are deeply influenced, mainly for the better, in the new leisure age. The family is developing new relationships, and functioning more adequately. There is more opportunity for the wife to be the equal of her husband, in the amount and uses of leisure time, in interests and activities. Women no longer need to be tied down to demanding home responsibilities. Kaplan argues that in the leisure age "family life can be dynamic, exciting, ever-changing, growing . . . free time rather than work is the central factor." [29] Family members mean more to each other as objects of pleasurable and satisfying living together.

Burns believed that new relationships and new forms of social intercourse between people are developing, based upon a new kind of democratic way of life and good manners between equals. There is more willingness to experiment in ways of living, more ability to meet and associate with people of varying outlooks and attitudes. Especially in regard to conventions and what he calls "manners," he believed that the new leisure is causing changes that will bring a better balance with the modern environment. "The conventions of an aristocratic society

---

[27] DeLisle Burns, *Leisure in the Modern World* (New York: The Century Company, 1932), pp. 21-22.

[28] See Kaplan, *Leisure In America,* pp. 82-92.

[29] Kaplan, p. 60.

are passing away. The conventions of a community of equals are replacing those of a community of dependents and their controllers."[30]

There is emerging a common philosophy of democracy and equal rights, as represented by a mutual respect among people and a lessening of class snobbery and superiority feelings. Burns does not point out that these manners may simply cover up some very basic inequalities in social life; but this covering up does not make such conventions bad. If there is a trend toward more equality in modern life, one of the forces in this transformation or tendency can be the relationships and attitudes of men toward each other in leisure.

In the new era, leisure will not be peculiar to any particular class. Said Burns, "leisure as the basis for civilization at its best is not, in modern conditions, the privilege of a class."[31]

The masses will create for themselves a civilization of refined graces and delicacies, of skills in living, and of the understanding and appreciation of the sciences and the fine arts, which will be as great as that civilization created by the privileged aristocracies of earlier days. The new leisure will make new men and women, who will be less exhausted with work and more lively and spirited, less dull or bored, more creative and light-hearted, who will gain more enjoyment in fellowship with intimates and casual acquaintances, who will be more sensitive and humane in their recreations and enjoyments, and who will be eager to do many kinds of new things and to share in many kinds of new experiences.

Other writers have recognized the important changes in the lives of people and the structures of social groups that have developed along with our leisure age. But they doubt that the ideal "man of leisure" is emerging as surely as Burns had hoped. Efforts to understand more fully what the changes have been have led to research into the varying leisure habits of social class groups. Kaplan has pointed out the notable lack of class consciousness among the American social classes and the forces at work interfering with the historical identifications of individuals with the classes of which they might be members by virtue of their economic or occupational status. Another potent force is represented by the mass media, both for the images of modern living that are portrayed by TV, radio, and movies, and for the advertising activi-

---

[30] Burns, *Leisure in the Modern World,* p. 126.

[31] Burns, p. 212.

ties which powerfully and subtly influence persons' attitudes toward themselves and their fellows.[32]

Attitudes toward possession of leisure time and other goods are not the primary dynamics of social class, of course. Money with which to buy things is a major factor, and the style of life characteristic of social class position is another factor. White points out that use of leisure time is a function of class position, showing this with comparative data from a sample of children and youth from several class groupings. Participation in park, playground, and church activities, for example, was more popular with lower class groups, while libraries and home activities were among those less popular with these groups.[33] Clarke pointed out in another study that important differences exist between occupational groups. Lower groups enjoyed more commercial activities, more craftsmanlike activities, and more TV. Upper groups enjoyed more cultural recreations, more community and civic activity, and more reading and study.[34] Other studies have indicated other aspects of the modern situation, which finds leisure time activity as an aspect of social stratification, and differences in class patterns reflecting the distance American society must travel before it reaches the hopeful state predicted by Burns.

The ability to stand in thoughtful contemplation of the world, to reach out for an understanding of its meaning and its beauty, to attain a serenity, peacefulness, and deep inner understanding—this ability or capacity is believed to be present to some degree in all persons. With leisure time to develop it, it comes within the grasp of each of us. The quality of inner life that is developed by the common folk is the main determiner of the civilization. It develops as persons become able to hear, to see, and to feel experiences and meaning more profoundly. Some become able to record these richer meanings in poetry, painting, or song. Some may express themselves in deep scientific or philosophical insights into the nature of experiences of life, of reality, and of relations between men. Those who argue for the challenge of leisure argue that the new leisure has set in process a series of great construc-

---

[32] Kaplan, *Leisure In America,* pp. 82-92.

[33] R. Clyde White, "Social Class Differences in the Uses of Leisure," *American Journal of Sociology,* Vol. 61, No. 2 (September 1955), pp. 145-150. Included in Larrabee and Meyersohn, *Mass Leisure,* pp. 198-205.

[34] Alfred Clarke, "Leisure and Occupational Prestige," *American Sociological Review,* Vol. 21, No. 3 (June 1956), pp. 301-307. Included in Larrabee and Meyersohn, pp. 205-214.

tive changes in the lives of man, and has opened up the possibility for still greater changes in which man can create a new civilization of democracy, equality, and culture.

The challenge of leisure was visualized by Pack in another way. He argued that in earlier days man's basic creative and productive instinct, the "pioneer instinct," was put to work conquering the wilderness. But with the end of the frontier this instinct became diverted, or perverted, to an exploitation of weaker abilities and less powerful people. So we have to find new means to control this thwarted, perverted human instinct. Leisure is able to meet this challenge, "furnishing legitimate and social outlets for the human creative instinct, which otherwise is so often diverted by our modern intensive civilization into channels that are essentially predatory." [35]

He wondered at the stocking of accessible and unpolluted streams with fish so that thousands of fishermen can drive their cars out to the streams and line up shoulder to shoulder trying to catch these domestically produced breeds, "a concerted mass attack upon the fish that possesses no remote resemblance to the gentle art Izaac Walton wrote of so lovingly." [36] He pondered over the similar stocking of fields and woods with thousands of game birds so that thousands of hunters can shoot at them, and at each other, in an orgy of wholesale destruction, each person hoping to take home a trophy from his "hunt." He recognized some recreation value in this but felt that its artificiality destroys some of the fundamental benefits that come from contact with nature. He wondered whether people can be guided in their leisure time toward such things as nature photography—shooting birds and game with a camera instead of a gun, outdoor collecting and hobbying, amateur production in agriculture, and other forms of "productive amateur enterprise" which he saw as so vital for human happiness and for the satisfaction of creative urges, bringing man back into a natural cooperative relation with nature.

Pack wanted more sports played instead of so much of sports being spectated by the masses. He was encouraged by the growing interest of millions in spending their leisure time with hobbies. He saw many examples of a growing aesthetic consciousness in the United States: a music of a higher and more advanced type; dances that are

---

[35] Arthur Newton Pack, *The Challenge of Leisure* (New York: The Macmillan Company, 1936), p. 49.

[36] Pack, p. 107.

more beautiful, creative, and popular; a drama and little theater that is vigorous; continuing interest in libraries and museums; and an aesthetic appreciation of the out-of-doors. He saw the man with leisure time as a free man having the precious and at present unequaled opportunity to search for beauty. And he saw that leisure time offers an opportunity for aesthetic human relationships, for happiness and contentment, for a sharing of the healthful and psychological values of friendship.

Many writers have found in the American adult education movement, the great increase in "do-it-yourself" craftmanship, in photography, in many active sports, and the like, testimony to the creative impulses which are able to find expression in the leisure lives of millions of persons of all classes, particularly among those who work for an ordinary living.

Overstreet shared this last view, and he paid attention to two aspects of civilized leisure, which we must note. One of these is the pleasure of being sociable, of sharing things with others, which is often in sharp contrast with the acquisitiveness demanded of persons if they are to attain success in the economic field. The significance of our free-time activities, he says, "is that almost inevitably they place us in a sharing mood. . . . We issue from our isolation. We learn the fine art of companioning . . . we tend to grow the habit of wishing for others the happiness that we ourselves enjoy." [37]

He also talked about the importance of being alone, of having certain times when one can remove oneself from all others and enjoy a period of tranquil contemplation and relaxation without responding to any other person. We should, he thought, recognize "the serenity that can enter the life of the individual when, for a time, he is enabled to sequestrate himself and move quietly with his own brooding thoughts." [38] What is the significance of all this wish on our part to be ourselves, to inhabit worlds of our own making, to be not blown hither and thither by the gusts of external demands? It is to get "whole" again, to gather ourselves, and to think and put things together, to explore ways that are intimately our own. This freedom of the individual, Overstreet says, is one of life's keenest delights.

We can agree with these writers that the new leisure can function in the life of a person as he learns how to live more happily with

---

[37] Overstreet, *Civilized Leisure,* p. 28.

[38] Overstreet, p. 80.

himself, to enjoy the values and satisfactions of happy relationships with his family and his friends, to gain fulfillment in voluntary and community service and in service to his fellows, and to share in more kindly attitudes among people in general. These represent part of the challenge of the new leisure to the life habits of people, as they assimilate this new dimension of living.

One finds much evidence to support the view that there is both a danger and a challenge in the new leisure, and that man may either succumb to the danger and misuse his leisure time to his own destruction, or rise to the challenge and find a new means for fuller living. Romney points out the alternatives available to man in the use of his ever increasing leisure time,

> . . . which is time of his very own, a possession which is a rightful expectancy in a democratic society—a possession earned by and complementary to his time on the job or in school. This plethora of leisure . . . may be a great personal, community and national liability if we are simply to know the pain of empty hours[,] . . . if we are simply to seek metaphorical sedatives, time killers and pain killers. On the other hand, if the people are prepared to use their leisure time constructively and joyously and an adequate opportunity for the satisfying use of leisure is provided, then the individual, the community and the state will fall heir to a rich asset.[39]

Kaplan suggests, in the new leisure, a range of creative values and prospects available to man if he is able to organize and become educated to use them. And he judges these values of creativity to be key criteria for evaluating our leisure culture. Based upon the idea that creativity in man is part of his basic nature, this creativity may be found expressed in relations with others, both because of mutual pleasure in the association and because of sharing in a common activity, concern, or interest. It may be found expressed in our seeking of new experiences and in our passive enjoyment of experiences brought to us. It may be found in the games we play and the art we experience.

He recognizes the destructive elements in our life, but still finds the direction of American life as a whole to be increasingly humanistic and richer in aesthetic values than ever before, and he holds that a

---

[39] G. Ott Romney, *Off the Job Living* (New York: A. S. Barnes and Company, 1945), p. 18.

creative and dignified leisure immeasurably richer in values than man has experienced is within our grasp, if our society and its leadership will but take advantage of its potentialities. He hopes that the people of our country, and its strategic leaders, understanding what our whole people want in the years ahead, will work constructively in carrying out the new social tasks required in social planning and organization for a new and close-to-Utopian leisure society.

> The future hinges in part on our goals, desires, values, and purposeful application of available knowledge. The goals, in turn, can be defined only as each of us individually, and all of us collectively, sets out a position of values or assumptions.[40]

The leisure age makes possible for all a more vital family life, a more democratic community of equals, a greater share in a civilization that is refined, humane, cultured, and filled with beauty.

THE ROLE OF RECREATION

Let us now turn to some considerations regarding recreation and its role in modern life. Two alternative views must be explored regarding the role of recreation. One view is that recreation's function is a balancing function, a compensatory function, or a corrective function, operating against the part of man's life which is work, and in a therapeutic way in regard to man's tensions and strains of living. The second view is that recreation must be seen as an integrating and enriching function, a complementing function, in a wholeness of life and growth.

RECREATION AS COMPENSATION

Riggs supported the first view. He was concerned with the mental health of people who suffer unnecessarily because they neglect to establish and maintain a balanced relation between work and recreation. He rejected the belief that real happiness and emotional satisfaction can be attained in productive work, even when one has a desirable job that is interesting, ethically acceptable, with satisfactory human relations within it. "Emotional life cannot be satisfied by any job or within any job, no matter what its virtues." Man is too much a pleasure-loving person "who finds the coercions of his civilization and the demands it

---

[40] Kaplan, *Leisure In America,* p. 303.

makes upon him to modify, postpone or entirely eschew his primitive desires difficult to bear." [41]

Of course, there must be a balance between work and play. Work is important, fulfilling man's ethical need to assume a useful and satisfactory role in society. But the task is overemphasized and exaggerated into a selfish and competitive striving to get ahead economically, and this striving possesses men unduly. Also in our economic life, he said, "Unfortunately, many people are forced to work long and hard, driven by their dire economic necessity. They must work in order to keep a roof over their heads and get enough food for their bodies so that they may remain strong enough to work." It is the function of recreation "to relieve the grim struggle through rest and distraction by the wise use of the little leisure they possess." [42] It is the function of recreation to balance life in relation to work, to afford a refreshing contrast to, and compensate for, the responsibility, the routine, monotony, and the coercions. Its function is to keep one's humor and sense of proportion functioning properly, to balance one's life.

One is able to identify contrasts between work and play. Work for the most part is carried on for objectives other than the sheer pleasure of doing it. Work, further, is activity bound by purpose, whereas play, in essence, is not bound by any purpose beyond the pleasure of the moment. In play, obstacles and difficulties add spice to the game, while in work we undertake to remove all obstacles. Practicability is essential to work, but is inappropriate to play, which relishes unreality, make-believe, and fantasy. Modern civilization demands, even coerces, man to concentrate on some special vocational skill while in recreation, conversely, the individual is encouraged to enjoy and express himself with broad and varied skills and talents.

Brightbill points out that recreation allows us to play many roles: "acting out the lines of self-realization and making us as much a part of as many things in the world as is possible in the time allotted us. If our work is monotonous and routine, our leisure need not be. If there is little in our toil to make us persevere, we may find much in our leisure to enable us to be resolute. If obligation to duty becomes too burdensome in our work-day world, free time may be the outlet for uncomplicated living. . . . Here the engineer can become the painter,

---

[41] Austen F. Riggs, *Play: Recreation in a Balanced Life* (New York: Doubleday, Doran and Company, Inc., 1935), pp. 6-7.

[42] Riggs, pp. 13-14.

the lawyer the craftsman, the housewife the concert pianist. Children can be adults and adults can be children. . . . Recreation . . . is the only reliable instrument for developing the dual personality with integrating rather than schizophrenic results." [43]

Brightbill's modern view supports Riggs' earlier view. Both play and work are necessary to balance the scales of life. Radically different in character and function, and calling upon the individual for quite opposing reactions, each serves in this manner to compensate for the one-sidedness of the other in a person's life. Play, however, has a special function in this respect. Riggs concluded "it affects the very quality of life—constitutes the necessary yeast, the lightening, invigorating ferment which prevents the whole loaf from falling into a state of sogginess." [44]

This view seems to be based upon the conception that recreation must provide a compensatory function in life, that life's balance requires right amounts of these two unlike ingredients. Implicit is the conception of recreation as escape from work and work's demands and tensions. Recreation provides release from these, opportunities for action, for free and freeing expression, for acting out, for emotional catharsis. It allows one to rid oneself of burdens of fatigue, the strain of disciplined attention or demanding work.

Recreation as a Corrective

A related point of view is that recreation can serve as a means for correcting maladjustments, personal or social, and that its therapeutic uses are a major part of its function. This view holds that recreation, its activities and pursuits, give respite and relaxation and also satisfaction that may be reintegrating and reinforcing to the personality. The person at odds with himself or the world, and disturbed by anxiety reactions arising out of the real or fantasied inner or outer environmental pressures under which he is suffering, finds in his pursuit of recreation interest the means for recreating himself.

This view finds many critics among recreation philosophers. Sutherland criticizes "the idea that recreation has a sort of medicinal value as a patent remedy in curing individual and social ills. Thus it is hoped that recreation may reduce crime, eradicate juvenile delinquency, improve employee morale, or hold young people within the

[43] Brightbill, *Man and Leisure,* pp. 171-173.

[44] Riggs, *Play,* pp. 33-34.

church. . . . Careful studies are beginning to indicate how ineffectual recreation may be in shaping conduct to such ulterior designs." [45]

Martin provides a sharper critique of the "escape" function of recreation in pointing out:

> No positive leisure time program to promote growth and development can be built on the concept that play, recreation and leisure time activities are to help man to forget his world, his conflicts, and his responsibilities. Sleep, which is a natural biological recreative process, in no sense is an escape from life, although it can be used as such. Where sleep serves an escape purpose you will awaken fatigued, unrefreshed, unwilling and unable to "rise and shine." This holds for all so-called recreation processes that have to be used to serve an escape motive. . . . The natural biological function of . . . recreation is not to escape.[46]

There is a logic, however, in some elements of the compensation theory. Many writers have stressed the lack of opportunity in modern industry and urban life for creative and satisfying self-expression, and the need for man to find recreative uses for his leisure through which he may express himself. It is quite valid to assume that an individual can restore meaning to his life through recreative activity.

Recreation provides in human life a compensatory or balancing function for the coercions and stresses of work. Recreation provides release, relaxation, and freedom, is noncoercive and nonstressful, and provides the individual with essential elements of creative self-realization that may not be present in work.

RECREATION AND THE UNITY OF LIFE

There is a theory of recreation and its function that assigns a much larger social role to recreation than a role of compensation or escape. This large role is that of the central integrating force in life, from which life's wholeness is derived by the individual. One philosopher who advanced this view was L. P. Jacks.

---

[45] Willard C. Sutherland, "A Philosophy of Leisure," *The Annals,* The American Academy of Political and Social Science (September 1957), p. 2.

[46] Martin, *Leisure Time as Health Resource,* pp. 4-5.

Life, Jacks believed, must be approached as a whole, not as parts.

> The art of living is one and indivisible. It is not a composite art made up by adding the art of play to the art of work, or the art of leisure to the art of labor . . . or the art of recreation to the art of education. When life is divided into these or any other compartments it can never become an art, but at best a medley or at worst a mess. It becomes an art when work and play, labour and leisure, mind and body, education and recreation, are governed by a single vision of excellence and a continuous passion for achieving it. A master in the art of living . . . pursues his vision of excellence through whatever he is doing and leaves others to determine whether he is working or playing.[47]

Jacks saw man the worker and man the player as not two men but one. Considering work and play as separate aspects of life only divides man against himself. "His leisure occupations will not reinforce his labour occupations, but will disturb them, and his recreation, far from promoting his education, will blot it out." [48]

The danger of placing productive work, education, and the like, under one heading, and leisure and recreation under another, he said, is that recreation is then thought of as joyful escape from all the serious or grim purposes the former represent. Leisure time begins to be thought of as a vacation or vacuum separated from the rest of life, and needing to be filled with pursuits that have no relevance to the rest of one's life. But with a proper understanding of the basic unity of all life this concept of leisure would change to one in which self-education, work, and recreation together would provide such a concept of a unified life.

Jacks' philosophy is based, in part, on the idea that man is by nature and in essence a creative being, creation being an essential human function and a key aspect of human nature. Man is a skill-hungry animal; satisfaction and happiness is possible when the creative part of him is awakened and his skill-hunger is satisfied. In modern civilization the moral qualities and self-esteem of people have been determined mainly by their industry, their productive work, and its motive,

---

[47] Lawrence P. Jacks, *Education Through Recreation* (New York: Harper & Row, Inc., 1932), pp. 1-2.

[48] Jacks, p. 5.

aims, and values to the society. Driven by a common desire or passion for excellence in what he does, man has found his basic values in his work. The main ethic of workmanship lies in the quality of work done, which includes the material product of the work and the human relationships among those with whom one works. Great excellence, great workmanship, requires profound investment of oneself, of one's skills and faithfulness to the objective of ennobling mankind by one's creative contribution, both individually and with one's fellows. In the modern day, because of the decrease in the amount of work, there is an enormous release of human energy, set free to find leisure-time occupation.

Jacks recognized the need for the development of leisure-time recreational pursuits that will contain the values and rewards that previously a person might have expected to gain from a deep preoccupation with his work. Paltry rewards from what may be relatively brief hours at somewhat unsatisfying and uncreative routine productive activities must be augmented and supplemented—indeed, in some respects replaced—by those from his recreation.

Yet the greatest good for the individual, Jacks believed, comes from the rich synthesis of labor and leisure.

> Viewed from the ground of creative activity, it will be seen that the distinction between labour and leisure is not rooted in the nature of things. When either of these supposed opposites is occupied in skillful or beautiful exertion it becomes indistinguishable from the other; labour, creatively spent, furnishing the "happiness" expected from leisure, and leisure the discipline associated with hard work. . . . [Thus, the] tendency of labour and leisure to coalesce as they approach the point of skillful exertion. [This unity is found in the most creative of all of man's efforts, his art.] Play becomes art when raised to its highest excellence, its highest beauty, and its highest power. Anything that one does, from cooking a dinner to governing a state, becomes a work of art if motivated by the passion for excellence and done as well as it can be.[49]

For Jacks, recreation occurs at three stages or levels, in terms of the social values to be derived. Primary recreation is the art of bringing the whole body under the control of intelligence, so that the

---

[49] Jacks, p. 99.

body may be put to the finer uses of which it is capable. Secondary recreation would be the level at which the person would learn and enjoy the wide choice of physical and aesthetic games whose pleasures depend upon their inherent movements of body expression, their beauty, grace, vigor, and rhythm, and upon the skill developed by the player. The highest recreation is art, from its simplest form in the manual craft or hobby to the finest work of the musician, painter, sculptor, architect, and, we might add, of anyone who creates and participates in aesthetic and wholesome human relations. In these creative and self-expressive activities reside the deepest and finest joys of life, as well as important contributions to one's neighbors and the community, making the art of living more available for all men.

Guérard, the aesthetician, supports Jacks' view, defining art broadly as "conscious and disinterested enjoyment in self-expression." [50] He argued that as such it eminently could be possessed by all. "It may be in the form of sports—between the spirit of sport and the spirit of art there is but little difference; it may be in the form of homecrafts: cooking, weaving, gardening, furniture-making; it may be as the folk-dance, the folk-song, the pageant, the drama. In all cases, it means joy in achievement." [51]

Guérard urged that life's enrichment through art be made freely available to all. "Art requires no riches; it can find satisfaction in the flowers of the fields, or in the voice of a child, as fully as in gold or rubies. What art demands is *freedom of the spirit,* and *leisure.*" [52] With the expansion of leisure time, and with the significance of work for millions of persons being very limited, for the salvation of mankind's pride and zest for life, it is necessary to rekindle men's creative powers and prepare them for leisure life filled with pleasure, self-expression, and delight. As he stated it, "Symbolically at least, to wear a *lei* even when sweeping the street." [53]

It might very well be pointed out that recreation may at the same time be compensatory, complementary, and unifying. Viewed from the point of view of the individual and his needs, we would find that in one case his recreational life could beneficially be entirely different

---

[50] Albert Guérard, *Art for Art's Sake* (New York: Lothrop, Lee and Shepard Company, 1936), p. 331.

[51] Guérard, p. 332.

[52] Guérard, p. 333.

[53] Guérard, p. 334.

from his work life in order to provide a refreshing contrast and compensatory values. The total involvement in another situation with an activity that provides both work and recreation for him would offer the deepest satisfaction and he would find a profound unity of life in it. Likewise, we might think of recreation and work as being complementary to each other and both being necessary components of a well-balanced life.

RECREATION AND HUMAN SATISFACTIONS

Summarizing the argument for recreation as a dynamic element in a balanced and creative life, we may identify briefly several satisfactions fundamental to man's happiness, contentment, and good health. One of these is growth itself. Growth is a satisfying thing, in which one freely chooses some interesting pursuit, creates whatever form he wishes, and develops his skills and interests. The unfolding and quickening of pleasure in increasingly successful accomplishment is highly rewarding.

Another satisfaction comes from physical expression. In earlier sections we noted the particular pleasures, the feeling of refreshment and well-being, to be derived from physical expression. Recreation philosophers more than others have been able to identify here deep values and pleasures available to participants.

Learning and mental accomplishment or mastery belong also to the same realm of satisfactions even though in some respects education has been patterned so as to emphasize its grimness and arduousness. Yet learning can be a delightful, highly enjoyable experience. Achievement in self-expressive pursuits involving oneself in an activity gives the individual further satisfaction. Self-activity, perhaps just for the enjoyment of self, is important. The added motivation of being able to contribute to the enjoyment of others, with the reflected satisfaction of social achievement, is further satisfaction.

If there is some higher need, the satisfaction of which at the same time is "ennobling to mankind," it is the need for beauty, and along with it the drive Jacks called the "passion for excellence." Veblen called it the "instinct of workmanship." Whatever its deep source in humankind, the striving to express whatever innate artistic ability we possess, the desire for beauty in our lives, provides a base for the richest forms of cultural and aesthetic expression recreational activity may produce. If recreation may bring a measure of such beauty and joy of artistic creation into our lives, it may thereby contribute great satisfactions. There is much that is frightening and harsh in our modern day life, and recreation well may be an area where, by contrast, joy, zest, gladness, and cheer may exist to help us retain our balance and give us strength and courage to survive, even to change, the conditions of fear and grimness that press upon us.

> To develop a symmetrical body which can function in a wide variety of ways, to be capable of using one's hands in relation to the stuff of the world and finally to be able to transfer one's conception of design and form and pattern upon the earth's materials—these are marks of culture. Each of these achievements is worthy of pursuit in and of itself. . . . These activities represent current needs, not merely because technological civilization tends to discard or restrict them, but also because cultural sanity requires citizens who are physically balanced, skillful, and devoted to beauty.[54]

Finally, man's need for a satisfying social relationship, from which stems the need for friendship, for status and regard from others, for pleasurable group membership, and for the more subtle rewards from social contribution, can be met in important respects in recreation. Mental and emotional balance for most men is gained from his social relationships. Man is a natural-born cooperator, and gains immeasurably from his group membership. Young people in particular need social relations, the attainment of these being one of the trying problems of adolescence and young adulthood. Merely getting along competently with one's peers is not only satisfying but sustaining to one's morale and spirit.

In the basic social group, the family, recreation has a primary role as well. Playing together deepens the bonds of companionship and affection between family members and enriches family life. In addition to its role in meeting the developmental needs of children and youth for creative play, it contributes heavily to the adults in the family, maintains the vitality of family life, and contributes to the satisfactions to be derived from family living. A family thereby strengthened is better able to maintain a level of family functioning in other ways that

---

[54] Eduard C. Lindeman, *Leisure—A National Issue* (New York: The Association Press, 1930), p. 20.

will give children the security and guidance they need if they are to have the best opportunity for sound social development.

In the cultural arts there is a special application of this principle of social satisfactions. There is for the artist a new value when he creates for an audience. Lindeman points out that, contrary to the artist in earlier days, who was in a sense creating as a servant of the well-born and rich, the modern artist in a democracy is creating for his peers, and there are peculiar problems, as well as peculiar satisfactions, in this process.

> The artist who lives and functions satisfactorily in a democracy must have a democratic audience. More than that, he needs an audience composed of individuals who can participate in his endeavors, an audience of participants. . . . Leisure may be used for purposes . . . of allowing all the people to participate in self-expression for their own enjoyment. People who use their leisure in this fashion will in the end furnish the professional artists with genuine audiences, persons who appreciate quality because they too have striven to achieve it.[55]

Lindeman saw the great challenge to recreationists to make aesthetic participation available to all the people, and to create new democratic standards and ideals for culture.

His comments suggest that among the great social institutions created and organized by man to help him in the pursuit of his needs, recreation is becoming more and more important. Through recreation, life in the society becomes more balanced and wholesome, more directed toward meeting the needs of its members, and more productive of social values. This highly significant assumption underlies the recreation movement; it will be discussed as a primary concept in relation to our later study of organized recreation in community life.

The highest value for some men comes from the synthesis of work and recreation, motivated by a single passion for excellence, becoming, at its creative best, art. This unity, in its various expressions, contributes uniquely to man's self-realization.

---

[55] Lindeman, p. 20.

Questions for Study and Discussion

1. *What evidence can you give to support the view that leisure time is a threat to human welfare? What evidence can you give to counter this view?*
2. *What data can be offered to show that leisure time offers to most people their best opportunity for self-realization in modern urban-industrial society?*
3. *What are the (1) strengths and (2) shortcomings of the theory that recreation's primary role is compensatory to work?*
4. *What are the (1) strengths and (2) shortcomings of the theory that recreation's primary role is complementary to work, that there is a unity of recreation and work in their best expression?*
5. *How may participation in leisure and recreation assist a person in obtaining a wholesome outlook toward a creative and integrated life?*
6. *How can modern American society meet the challenge of the new leisure as stated by C. D. Burns?*
7. *Do you believe that a four-hour work day or a four-day work week would be adequately self-fulfilling to the average man in light of the idea that people "need" work and are incomplete and unsatisfied without it?*

Selected Readings

Gulick, Luther Halsey, *A Philosophy of Play* (New York: Charles Scribner's Sons, 1920).

Jacks, Lawrence P., *Ethical Factors of the Present Crisis* (Baltimore: The Williams and Wilkins Company, 1934).

Lee, Joseph, *Play in Education* (New York: The Macmillan Company, 1929).

Lindeman, Eduard C., *Leisure—A National Issue* (New York: The Association Press, 1930).

Overstreet, Harry, *A Guide to Civilized Leisure* (New York: W. W. Norton and Company, Inc., 1934).

6

A PHILOSOPHY FOR LEISURE AND RECREATION

In the preceding chapters we have examined from several vantage points (historical, anthropological, sociological, psychological, and philosophical) the nature, meaning, significance, and value of leisure and recreation in the life of man. From this exploration comes support for the major assumptions presented in Chapter 1:

1. *Recreation is a cultural universal.* All known human societies have exhibited institutionalized characteristics of recreation and man has always played.
2. *Recreation is a social function.* Man has always used it to further his goals of self-realization.

3. *Recreation creates important social forces* interacting with other political, social, economic, and other environmental forces and factors at work in every society.
4. *Recreation has a philosophical base* as seen in the efforts of man to interpret and explain its values by means of various theories.

Throughout human existence men have fought for and enjoyed leisure as part of their birthright. Philosophers through the ages, from Epicurus to Russell, have tried to understand and explain leisure and recreation in relation to their understanding of the nature of man and the values he held most precious. Educators and students of modern leisure and recreation have striven in the past century to formulate some modern conceptions to explain the greater importance of recreation in the lives of all members of a democratic society. Now a few organized efforts are underway in several parts of the world to bring together the young but growing group of recreation professionals to attack one of the basic responsibilities of any profession, the formulation of a basic philosophy for the field in which they work.

A philosophy serves the basic purpose of guiding the profession's work and development. Its concepts and value statements are derived from several sources: conclusions drawn from professional practice; observations concerning the particular culture, made from a professional point of view and utilizing the findings of relevant sciences; analysis of the nature and needs of individuals gained from other sciences and its own study and observation; and so on.

The philosophy for leisure and recreation, which we have been developing in these pages in an exploratory way, is conceived as a series of basic assumptions and philosophical generalizations that undergird the recreation movement and the profession that gives it leadership and guidance in the development of a public policy and its supporting public opinion. It can also serve as the framework for an individual philosophy, as the basis for the formulation of a set of values about one's own leisure—a philosophy by which an individual makes choices of what to do with leisure time.

It is related to what are seen as significant assumptions about leisure and recreation in the American culture. The recreation movement has grown out of and is part of the American culture. It is guided by many of this culture's basic values. The recreation profession also, because of its leadership position, has made certain assumptions that are not yet generally accepted by the rest of the society. This, of course, is one task of a profession—to help the general society to deepen its own understanding of the basic purposes and values implicit in any of its areas of broad common welfare and common concern.

The profession has another concern—the education and training of its new practitioners. Part of this training is the inculcation of students with the philosophy of the profession, its basic values, ethical and aesthetic. The profession also is involved in a constant and restless search for deeper philosophical insights and a strengthening of the structure of science and logical thought upon which it is organized. Members of the profession accept the responsibility for sharing in this search and for striving to deepen and strengthen their own philosophical understanding. These two purposes, training new professionals and strengthening the philosophical equipment of professionals generally, are also the writers'.

A recreation philosophy contains several elements: consideration of the nature of the individual, his growth, his needs and interests, his rights; consideration of the nature of relationships between individuals, between individuals and society and its groups, and between society's groups; a formulation of the purposes and goals of leisure and recreation in fulfilling its individual and social function; and a consideration of the values assumed for leisure and recreation, including individual and social ethical and aesthetic values.

THE INDIVIDUAL AND VALUE

The individual has inherent worth—the fulfillment of his individual interests in consonance with other individuals is the prime value in human life.

A consideration of value begins with the individual person. The individual's welfare, the fulfillment of his individual interests, the attainment of happiness, pleasure, and satisfaction from his existence—this is the prime purpose, the prime value, of human life. This assumption lies at the base of recreation. This assumption is that the individual has inherent worth, that he is of most importance, that his humanness gives him dignity, that he and his interests are supreme (under God, some would want to add). That which gives him pleasure, happiness, and self-fulfillment is good. That which gives him pain and unhappiness, and denies him self-fulfillment, is not good. Recreation finds its base in the assumption that a man's basic rights, so simply but historically stated, to "life, liberty, and the pursuit of happiness," define a fundamental purpose for existence. The assumptions presented in Chapter 4, "Theories of Play," are particularly relevant here, these assumptions having indicated that it is man's basic physical, emotional, and intellectual nature to engage in playful activities, that these activities are essential components of his basic interests, and are essential means to his self-fulfillment.

The individual is a living, learning, growing person. The explanation of his behavior lies in understanding the dynamics and the processes of interaction between the biopsychosocial organism that he is and his physical and social environment. He is, furthermore, a learning person, whose learning leads him both individually and collectively in a series of efforts to master his environment and to extract from it more elements that satisfy his self-interests. To do this he applies intelligence and problem-solving capacity, not necessarily innate reason nor instinctive logic, but mental resources and processes available to him as he strives to pursue his interests.

The individual strives to gain mastery over his surroundings, to turn them to his use. He labors with materials at hand in order to make them useful to him. In this way he meets the needs he feels, pursues the things that interest him, enjoys the satisfactions of creatively working with and controlling his environment. And the basic values, the basic goodness, in the individual's life are derived from or are gained in the meeting of his needs and the satisfactions he feels from it.

The individual, then, is an active organism living in a physical and social environment, utilizing his capacities, his physical and intellectual abilities, to meet his needs and interests. He is able to perceive what his interests and needs are; he gains purpose in his activity from following these interests and needs. The objects of his interests and purposes have value for him. From the needs of the individual we understand the nature of value.

Further, the individual is a conscious and sensitive being. He gains understanding of his environment as he gains mastery of it. He puts nature and his environment to his own use even as he adapts to and is changed by them. The basic order in the universe becomes known to him as he reasons it out, an order encompassing the nature of life and extending to the nature of beauty and of good. Then, as he pursues the interests that are for him the central "plus" value in his life, beyond life itself and the freedom to seek his interests, he seeks out the means for satisfying these interests, of bringing him pleasurable fulfillment. This self-fulfillment, self-realization, self-actualization, is the basic individual value.

Rader says, "The truly happy life is experienced by the man who responds with positive interests to a great range of objects and who fulfills these interests in activity that brings the full flavor of enjoyment. If we were to sum up the good in a few words, we would say that it is *the cultivation and fulfillment of positive interests* . . . in which all the sides of man's nature—the volitional, intellectual, hedonic and passional—form a community, an organic unity . . . and in which all these interrelated parts . . . are cultivated and fulfilled." [1]

Self-actualization, the fulfillment of a broad range of individual interests in recreation is a prime value in human life and a basic right of man.

RELATION OF INDIVIDUAL AND SOCIAL VALUES

The self-fulfilled and socialized individual is the product of, and the purpose of, social relationships and human interaction.

The definition of man as a biopsychosocial organism provides part of an assumption essential for us: that man is a social animal. His birth, growth, and life are all products of social interaction, influence, and nurture. He is inseparably interrelated with his society, he would not be born, nor would he survive, without relations with others.

The other part of the basic assumption is that the basic purpose of human association, of social relations, is the fulfillment of the self-interests of the individual. There is no purpose to group life other than the enhancement of the values attainable by the individual. Thus, the group, the community, or the society finds basic value and its reason to be in its activity in furthering the welfare of its individual members. So it may be said also that man seeks out relations with others in order to further his self-interests.

The essential unity of man and society has led to two opposed assumptions concerning the nature of that unity. One conception is that competition, struggle for survival of the fittest, is the essence of that unity. The individual, according to this view, like other forms of ani-

---

[1] Melvin Rader, *Ethics and Society* (New York: Holt, Rinehart and Winston, Inc., 1950), p. 166.

mal life, is in a death struggle with others of his species and with other species, in which the fittest survive and the weakest perish. The law of nature is that none should interfere with this basic process. Thus, the "laissez-faire" theory of economic and social organization might argue against any imposition of social restrictions on free competition, or any social effort to protect the weak against the strong. There is in this concept the assertion of independence and a relative ignoring of the notion of interdependence as basic in human association.

The second conception is of man as an essentially cooperative being. From the beginning, as a newborn infant, he is the recipient of protection and nurture offered by family and community. Throughout his life he lives universally in groups among which extensive and complex organization of social relationships provide the framework for group survival and individual self-fulfillment. The cooperative processes are integral, despite the particular form they might take in different societies, and attest to the basic social nature of man, the wide range of his individual interests that are satisfied through group associations, and his basic interests that can be satisfied only through these associations.

The fact of the essentially social nature of man affirms that society and the group exert on the individual powerful controlling, influencing, and determining forces, which change him from an asocial infant into a social being later on. His attitudes, consciousness, habits, thoughts, are determined by the complex of his social relations. Thus, social relationships and the society are understood to be the dominant determining factors in the development of the human individual, while the purpose, the goal, the high value to be gained in such development is still individual self-fulfillment, as a social being, with social consciousness. Thus, the individual strives for the fullest and richest development and expression of his capacities in the pursuit of his interests, consonant with and in harmony with the development and expression of all others.

This concept of "socialized individualism" implies the right of every individual to attain the fullest and most constructive personal and social development possible for himself, consonant with the fullest personal and social development of others, to be achieved through a cooperative and planned and designed social organization dedicated to and conducive to that end.

The recreation movement in its brief history has developed two assumptions of values based upon this prior assumption of the social nature of man. One is that recreation fills a need of individuals for group association in uniquely satisfying ways because of the pleasure that men get from the recreational pursuits themselves and the added pleasures they get from enjoying such pursuits in the company of others. The important role of competitive activities in recreation acknowledges the competitive strivings in individuals which define some of their social relations, and provides relatively benign forms for competitive expression. Human association in recreation also avoids much of the demand and the strain of other associations because of mutual interest and the pleasure each individual gains from the voluntary and pleasurable things he is doing with others, free from the requirements of many other associations.

The second assumption is that there is social responsibility, a common responsibility, for enabling the individual to further his pleasurable pursuits in recreation. Community responsibility for recreation, as a means of providing facilities, programs, leadership, resources of all kinds, and leisure time with which to enjoy them, is basic to a philosophy of recreation. The idea of a community planning for its recreation, of a whole society or nation planning for society or nationwide resources, is a fundamental principle that guides the recreation movement. This assumption is based upon the assumption that the function of the group is that of furthering the welfare of the individual and of satisfying his interests.

In defining basic values in terms of objects of individual interest, and in placing the individual and the fulfillment of his interests as the primary purpose of existence, one other important factor must be pointed out. The means by which individuals may gain the satisfaction of their interests are social means, that is, they require organization by the individual and his fellow beings of the instruments for the fulfillment of these interests. The individual cannot attain some satisfactions by himself, as an individual. He must do so as a part of a group, of a society. The society, its members working purposively and harmoniously toward common goals of interest-satisfaction, create the means for this. The common end, the greatest good for all, also may become an ideal-end, which inspires devotion and individual self-sacrifice of immediate "pleasures" for the sake of working for it. Rader points out, "Our social ideal should be the development of *total* persons united in a culturally rich community. Personality and community are essential to one another. . . . Self-realization, the good of the individual personality, and justice, the basic value of the community, thus tend to be interdependent. . . . Our ideal should be a dynamic equilibrium, combining integration and progress. The best social order is most efficacious in cultivating and fulfilling human interests." [2]

There is a need to ponder also the difference between the concept of the highest good being defined in terms of individual pleasure or tranquillity and the concept of good being related to the vast range of socially organized means for gaining material need-satisfactions, the social component in the creation of beauty, an activity in behalf of the common good of the whole people, that is socially significant, that is morally or spiritually fulfilling.

Another concept to ponder states that the greatest good is the good of the greatest number of people. This concept poses many problems of the levels or qualities of goods, but if one assumes an intrinsic goodness of an activity or a commodity or an idea, then the sharing in it by larger numbers becomes a greater value.

The fundamental social value contributed by recreational organization in society is in furthering and satisfying the leisure interests of the individual. The interdependence of society and the individual defines each person's right to self-fulfillment in consonance with the equal right to self-fulfillment of other individuals.

THE PURPOSE OF LEISURE AND RECREATION

Our study of theories of leisure led us to consider some dark and foreboding views that anticipate the worst for an idle and leisure time burdened mankind. We saw the increase in commercial exploitation of people's leisure time with aimless, stupid, and base amusements. We recognized the pressures of dull and sometimes loathsome work, unstable income, and inadequate homes and neighborhoods afflicting millions of people. There is reason for us to appreciate fully the impact of these conditions on the pursuit of happiness, but it may help to explain why many are content to seek pleasure at any level, rather than to undertake the longer-range and thoughtful cultivation of the arts of leisure with the fuller perspective of the great treasures of satisfaction available therein.

Yet we still can make a much more healthy and progressive as-

---

[2] Rader, pp. 238-239.

sumption concerning the challenge of leisure for the greater self-fulfillment of men. For there is additional evidence that the challenge of leisure is being taken up by millions for whom great new values are becoming available.

The goals of the new leisure are to invigorate and enrich the cultural recreations of man, to strengthen the bonds of mutual and equalitarian leisure living in family life, and to enable people to meet together in congenial and friendly relationships that are conducive to wholesome democratic community and social life. The goal of the new leisure is to permit refined living, reflection and contemplation, and creative thinking and activities, to permit an attainment of poise and well-being not possible for many before this time. With leisure there can at last come into being cultured peoples living creatively, contentedly, and with dignity.

The promise of leisure, like the promise of economic sufficiency, having now come within the reach of all men, may stimulate man to insist upon a rational organization of productive processes, an organization that would free him from fear for his sustenance. Such a condition would free him as well to work with his fellows in civic and community efforts to organize the rest of his social life on a similarly rational basis. It would enable him to establish a basically peaceful and wholesome relationship among all mankind. It would free man for a pursuit of beauty and joy and deep satisfaction of his senses during the many leisure hours he would have. A new kind of man may emerge, fulfilling human destiny better than he can now.

Our earlier study of theories of recreation helped us to see its basic assumed purpose as a primary instrument for satisfying and creative living, activities in which individual freedom and choice are emphasized; activities providing surcease of toil; activities offering the basic means for balanced personal growth. The two different views of the purpose of recreation in life were recognized as each having some base in fact. One view has it that recreation is a balancing and compensating force in life, with work meeting material needs and providing social status, and play affording the refreshing contrast, keeping one's sense of proportion and emotional well-being. The implication is that work and play are opposites, with work directed toward objective purposes, practicability, and efficiency, and with earnestness at a premium. Play may be without objective purpose beyond pleasurability, fantasy, dallying, and lightheartedness.

The second view is that the art of living is indivisible. If one's activities are governed by a single vision of excellence and a passion for achieving, then life becomes an art. The distinction between work and play therefore is not rooted in the nature of things. When, in either work or play, one becomes occupied in skillful or beautiful exertion, work and play become indistinguishable. Then one's life becomes whole, one's activities become art. The purpose of recreation is to satisfy man's creative desires. At the highest level of function a unity of life in artistic work emerges.

These two assumptions—one that recreation and work are opposites and that balance implies a share of each, and the other that recreation and work at the highest level, at the desirable level at which man should live, become an indivisible unity—both have use in our philosophy. In reality, the individual may have to use recreation to balance a relatively sterile, uncreative, and monotonous work life into which his situation has placed him. Then there are those persons whose work provides such a challenge, such deep individual satisfactions, and such opportunities for creative self-expression, that leisure-time recreation as a balancing element is much less important.

Recreation, at the same time, may provide several very fundamental satisfactions that are integral to a balanced and healthy life. One of these is growth itself, in skill, interest, or pleasure. Another is the refreshment and release of physical expression. Another is learning and mental achievement. Another is experiencing beauty and creating beauty. Yet another is doing something worthwhile and significant. These are all very much concerned with the individual himself, and each can be reanalyzed with the relation to the individual and his group, for the social factor in each of these is an important component. Affection, recognition, response, and status, enrich each of the other pleasures, and contribute further to balance and emotional well-being.

The goal of recreation and leisure often may be balancing and compensatory to stressful and earnest work. At other times recreation may be integrated with work and thus contribute to a unity of life.

SOME ETHICAL CONSIDERATIONS

Leisure and recreation base their central ideas about leisure and human self-fulfillment, the recreative processes, and the method of the recreation profession, upon certain basic ethical assumptions. One of these, as we noted earlier in this chapter, is that ideas of a good life, of right and wrong, of justice and injustice, are derived from ideas of what is involved with man's living and conditions of life. These express his needs, interests, and desires, in harmony with and rationally ordered in relation to those of all other individuals.

If the satisfaction of individual interests and needs in this way is a primary good, then the social provision for the satisfactions of human needs becomes a primary social ethical good. Individual interests range from such basic things as food and clothing to things such as joyous physical expression, pleasing sense satisfactions, creation and appreciation of beauty, contemplation and thinking of profound thoughts, and engaging in virtuous action alone or with others. Spinoza said, "I say it is the part of a wise man to refresh and recreate himself with moderate and pleasant food and drink, and also with perfume, with the soft beauty of growing plants, with dress, with music, with many sports, with theaters, and the like, such as every man may make use of without injury to his neighbors." [3]

The recreation philosopher would identify as having basic value many of the vast number of objects of human interest that make up a large part of men's pursuits in their leisure, when they might be free to seek satisfaction of their needs and explore many things of interest. Because recreation is concerned with such explorations and searches—which are sometimes called "the pursuit of happiness," but broader yet than this—practitioners in this field probably have gained considerably more depth and breadth of perspective than others concerning the vastness of the range of good things available to man were he to seek them.

For men want specific things. They want material things of a specific quality and nature, things that will give health, vitality, and comfort. They want love, friendship, respect, family intimacy, children, and parents. They want work, productive activity, satisfying contribution. They want an opportunity to develop talents and capacities and creative urges and inclinations. They want beauty in their lives. The interests of people have immeasurable richness, complexity and diversity, and they exist in countless numbers.

Rader suggests that these elements in welfare have to be understood, ethically, as a basic unity, arguing for "an ethics of the whole human organism. . . . From the standpoint of such an integral humanism, the fundamental biological values, such as good nutritious food,

---

[3] Benedict Spinoza, *Ethics,* Part III, Prop. ix, note.

rest, decent shelter, warm clothing, exercise and physical play, sex-expression, pain avoidance and health care, must be considered basic to the personality and therefore to the good life. But the more 'ideal values' of man, such as beauty, knowledge, love and cooperation, security, adventure, and creative work, are, if less basal, no less indispensable to the human organism. The two sets of values—the biological and the psychological—must be regarded as interactive, interdependent, and often coalescent. They are elements in the total organic fulfillment—the complete physiological and psychological health of the personality—which is the norm of human welfare." [4]

The recreation philosopher understands the existence of recreation as a phenomenon of individual and group behavior and as an organized social institution that results from the strivings of men together to attain some of these interests and enjoy some of these goods. He believes that the function of recreation is to satisfy these interests as man's leisure time offers opportunity for their satisfaction. He understands the basic theory of value involved, that these objects of man's recreational activities have values, are ethical goods. He sees recreation's function as enhancing these values through organized means, and also in a range of individual activities if only for brief periods.

Social ethics as a part of ethics is concerned with defining the rules, values, and guiding assumptions for social organization, in view of the basic purpose of social organization, to further the processes whereby individuals attain the satisfactions of their interests. Thus, a social ethical assumption of recreation philosophers, as of other philosophers in fields of primary human welfare, is that the community has a major responsibility for furthering the welfare of its members. Along with this goes (1) the concept of the right of individuals of access to and use of community services organized for this purpose, (2) the equal right of persons of access to the services, and (3) the responsibility to provide an adequate level or standard of service.

There is a corollary to this assumption that defines the role of the recreation worker at this point. For if recreation is a part of life that depends upon provision of social resources or community services, then the person responsible for the services is a community servant, and his relation to the recreation-bound person is that of a servant, not a master or a giver of gifts. The key to the concept is the idea of the right of the person. Such a *right* is part of the social ethical good.

---

[4] Rader, *Ethics and Society,* p. 198.

The development of recreation by public or governmental agencies has been the dominant trend in organized recreation, and in modern democratic life the idea of the right of the individual to participate in the values of the service according to his interests is well understood. Equally valid is the idea that other community organizations providing recreational services have the responsibility of accepting and respecting the right of individuals in the society to organize for and to receive such services under many forms and auspices.

The recreation philosopher accepts the basic assumption of the democratic philosophy with its emphasis upon the basic rights of the people together to determine their destinies and to continue or to change their way of life and their institutions, upon the civil rights of individuals to disagree, to be a minority, to conform or not, and to obtain equal rights to all the society has to offer. Further, the field of recreation has accepted a concept of social change that advocates the improvement of man's conditions and way of life through social planning—planning, that is, in the widest social interest. This means democratic planning, which accepts the goodness of difference and the primacy of freedom, planning in the service of the good of a whole people and cooperatively shared in by the people.

Recreation is one of the indispensable ethical goods, one of the basic value elements contributing to the welfare and good life of man.

SOME AESTHETIC CONSIDERATIONS

Among recreation philosophers the questions of aesthetic values would be most important ones. More than in any other area of life the leisure of a person may be devoted actively to the experiencing of beauty. Recreation is much concerned with aesthetic assumptions and with the wide range of interests of men that give aesthetic value to the objects of these interests.

Man begins by perceiving, by sensing, things in the world about him. He draws satisfaction from these sense perceptions. He receives sensations which are pleasurable and enjoyable, satisfying and delighting to him. These basic sensual satisfactions are simple aesthetic pleasures.

He also may engage in expressive activities that provide him with pleasurable experiences. This new level of seeking-out activity brings him enjoyment not of a passively sensual nature but of a stimulating kind, in which he cooperates with his surroundings, putting himself into a satisfying experience that fulfills his interest.

Yet another level of aesthetic experiencing, another segment in a spectrum of interests, is in enjoying beauty in activities and objects. This enjoyment may be a passive experience, in which one enjoys the beauty of a thing, or it may be an active experience.

Perhaps the part of the aesthetic spectrum that provides the most intense experience is the creating of beauty, the striving to do or make something that is beautiful. This creation of beauty, of something that also often can influence the quality of life for others, that can contribute beauty to others, is of a high order of aesthetic value.

The philosopher of leisure sees aesthetic living, the creation, appreciation of, and living by, concepts of beauty, as the central theme of man's striving for a better life. He would agree with the aesthetician that the appreciation of things of beauty, whether in nature, or created by man in dancing, drama, and diving, in poetry, painting, or photography, in sculpture or singing, in contemplation or conversation, is the means of fulfilling some of the deepest meaning of human personality. He would want to provide in the recreational life of people the maximum of opportunities to enjoy and to make beautiful things as the means of aesthetic self-realization. He would want people to enjoy deeply, with cultivated sensitivities, nature's beauties, the sunrise, the delightful vapors and the deep quiet of the meadows and the forests, the sounds and smells of the seashore. He would want them to find satisfaction in experiencing with their hands or with their whole bodies the joy of creating beauty.

The creation of beauty and the enhancement of the aesthetic qualities of human life for oneself and others then moves aesthetics close to ethics. Recognizing the power of art and beauty to influence the quality of human lives and to fulfill profoundly the interests of human individuals enables one to understand that such things are ethically good. There is ethical value in the enhancement of the aesthetic quality of life in human beings and human communities. And right at this point in this particular respect, recreation finds its basic fulfillment both ethically and aesthetically. Upon this assumption recreation philosophy also bases itself.

One of man's greatest ethical goods arises out of the fulfillment of his interests in satisfying recreative experiences which provide aesthetic values of significance to him, this enhancement of the aesthetic quality in his life being itself an ethical good.

Questions for Study and Discussion

1. *What connections can you discern between recreation and individual ethical values?*
2. *What do you identify as the basic aesthetic values that can be associated with recreation and leisure?*
3. *Give examples of group behavior that would verify the following:*
    a. *Man's belief in the law of the survival of the fittest*
    b. *The principle that man is essentially cooperative*
4. *What is the justification for saying "The recreation movement has grown out of and is part of the American culture"?*
5. *Do you believe that the fulfillment of man's individual interests, in harmony with other individuals and their interests, is the prime value in human life? Why or why not?*
6. *Does man ever do anything not motivated, directly or indirectly, by his own self-interest? Discuss.*

Selected Readings

Brightbill, Charles K., *Man and Leisure: A Guide to Its Organization* (Englewood Cliffs, N.J.: Prentice-Hall, Inc., 1961).

Rader, Melvin, *Ethics and Society* (New York: Holt, Rinehart and Winston, Inc., 1950).

Russell, Bertrand, *A History of Western Philosophy* (New York: Simon and Schuster, Inc., 1945).

Whyte, William H., Jr., *The Organization Man* (New York: Simon and Schuster, Inc., 1956).

PART 2

RECREATION IN MODERN AMERICAN LIFE

We have enjoyed an excursion into the philosophy and history of recreation; now we must get an overview of recreation in the American scene. We will look at the interaction of recreation forces and technological and economic forces in America, forces upon which is based much of the rest of our social life. We will look at the modern urban community with its vast complexity, its population explosion, its impact on the lives and leisure of urban folk. We also will look at the rural community, a community in transition and change, with problems and recreation patterns distinctively rural and yet reflecting many of the problems bearing upon the total society as well. We will then look briefly at the social institution of the modern family, at its life and problems, and strive to understand the interaction of recreation and family life.

We also will examine briefly the interaction of recreation forces with the institutional forces of education and the schools, of medicine and health, of government, and of social welfare. These several investigations will be made for the purpose of laying a foundation of sociological and economic knowledge about recreation in modern life, knowledge without which the recreation worker would be lacking in one major area of professional understanding.

7

TECHNOLOGICAL AND ECONOMIC FACTORS IN LEISURE AND RECREATION

In earlier chapters we described the impact of the acceleration of the twentieth-century technological revolution on the lives of men. We recognized that this revolution in technology, and the social changes it has brought about, are proceeding apace in the present day. A major preoccupation of modern economic leadership is the problem of how to utilize automation fully, for automation is one of the two most recent developments in the technical revolution. Atomic power is the other. Social philosophers, and perhaps most practical men in industry, are concerned with utilizing these young giants in order to free man from onerous labor, to provide him with vast new amounts of material things, and to endow him with rich new resources of leisure. We want to assess the impact of the vast technological and economic forces and developments on the leisure and recreation patterns and potentials of modern man.

AUTOMATION AND ATOMS

Modern engineering skill, the miracles of electronics, vast and brilliant scientific research, and equally competent industrial engineering and organization have combined to produce, in automation, a productive technology that has profound effects on man's living and leisure. The industrial revolution originally was based upon placing new tools into man's hands, tools with which he could produce goods better and faster. These tools included both steam, gas, and electrical power and the machines driven by this power, guided by man, which did the work. The element added in the twentieth century was not entirely new. It was, essentially, only a combination of, or a culmination of, many developments in industry and engineering, brought about in large part by a series of inventions in electronics. Engineers, with business management, in recent years have achieved phenomenal progress in finding ways to get machines to produce and do more and more things with fewer and fewer workers. Automation and mechanization not only have invaded all areas of production, but also have found applications in offices, banks, communication centers, and service industries.

The process of introducing new and more advanced machinery and automated production methods has developed under the stimulus of the driving incentive of business management, enlisting the talents of inventors, scientists, engineers, time and motion experts, physiologists and psychologists, with superintendents, foremen, and production workers making suggestions. The incentive is essentially the same: more production with fewer workers in less time, in order to cut production costs and to compete more effectively.

This development has had several important outcomes. One is an increase in the national economic product. Estimates are that in the last several decades this product per capita has increased by two or three per cent a year, which, seen over a perspective of several decades, provides significant increases in the amount of goods and services available to each person in the country. A second outcome is a rapid increase in man-hour productivity, along with a decrease in the average hours worked by employees. This change has happened unevenly, as has the distribution of the goods and services of industry. Some receive disproportionate amounts of the extra goods, and large segments of the population enjoy only modest increases in their standard of living. Some also "enjoy" too much leisure, in this case enforced leisure, and find the new leisure a bane instead of a blessing. But the average amount of leisure available to people in this country, as mentioned in Chapter 5, has increased significantly.

The rapid pace of automation and the steadily rising output per man-hour are continuing to make available both huge new amounts of goods and services and vastly increased amounts of leisure time. It will be truly a Herculean task of modern American society to manage this revolution without disastrous side effects. The new production has to be consumed by purchasers who earn their pay by work. Industry must provide for sharply decreased hours of work along with stable and high salaries if its automated production is indeed to be a blessing.

A second giant force, newly discovered and only partly put to work in the service of man, is new energy sources. Atomic energy is the furthest developed. Solar energy is a field barely penetrated by modern science. Atomic energy as a new source of power bids fair to eclipse all other means for powering the machines of industry. And, if it does, it too will help produce new goods with less work, potentially to be distributed to the people in the form of more goods and more leisure.

Until now, only a tiny part of the peacetime potential of atomic power has been realized. Experimentation with atomic-reactor electric power stations and with seagoing vessels is proceeding, but military considerations have been given priority. The use of the atom as a source of power, when available, will provide huge new resources for industrial production, home use, and other purposes.

The use of automated methods in areas other than industry are influencing these fields as well. In education, for example, television is experimenting in bringing to mass audiences resources of talent, preparation, and wealth not now available through normal methods of teaching. At the opposite extreme from mass methods, such devices (teaching machines), employing carefully and expertly programmed material and allowing individual study and progress, are opening up new approaches to education of the individual.

GROWTH IN THE AMERICAN ECONOMY

We have mentioned the perspective in this country for growth in the economy, for growth in the total national economic product. The national output of goods and services increased in the decade from 1950 to 1960 from $350 billion output to $500 billion output annually. In the sixty years since the beginning of the century the real growth of the economy has averaged about 3 per cent a year compounded. Estimating certain increases due to the rapid growth in population (and thus in the labor force), output could reach $750 billion, or three-quarter trillion dollars by 1970, and a trillion dollars by 1980.

This output, distributed about the way it is at present, would increase personal income per capita from about $2200 at present to nearly $2900 in 1970. The tremendous income increase is based upon maintaining the present rate of production increase, which implies both putting technology to work continuously and putting labor, present and future, to work successfully, without prolonged unemployment or underemployment. The estimate is based also upon continuing the process of reducing hours, extending vacation and holiday time off, and in other ways shrinking the work week.[1]

Estimates of economic growth are based upon estimates of population growth. These estimates, based upon a 1960 population of 180,000,000, give the country a population of some 245,000,000 by 1980. These people will use in personal consumption twice as much as is used presently, an increase from $330 billion a year to $660 billion a year. Tremendous increases in basic industry and manufacturing will make this possible, along with many other things such as new home construction, increased food production, and so on. Difficulty is foreseen in certain respects such as: development of adequate supplies of good water and using water efficiently; development of adequate farming areas to replace those used in the expansion of residential neighborhoods, particularly in the metropolitan areas; cleaning up and maintaining adequately clean air. For recreation planning it is important, among other things, to meet an increase of several per cent a

---

[1] Walter W. Heller, "An Economic Prognosis for the 1960's," *The Social Welfare Forum, 1960,* Official Proceedings, 87th Annual Forum of the National Conference on Social Welfare, Atlantic City (New York: Columbia University Press, 1960), p. 81.

year in the use of outdoor recreation areas by the millions of people with more time for recreation and more wish to get outdoors.

Modern automated technology has made possible great increases in economic production and income, in man-hour productivity, in amounts of free time, and particularly in the production of leisure-time goods. Production of recreation goods and services is increasing greatly, with the recreation industry becoming a significant sector of the economy.

Employment

The effect of this tremendous growth in the nation's economy on the life and leisure of its population is conditioned by two important factors. One of these is the factor of employment, and its opposite, unemployment. The economy operates largely under the stimulus of private corporation decision-making under the conditions of competitive operation of the corporations engaged in the economic processes. One of the most difficult problems for this nation is finding the way, within this framework, of keeping the millions of the nation's workers working steadily and earning large enough wages to buy the things they produce. If serious difficulty arises, and the level of unemployment gets much higher than it was through the decade of the 1950's, the entire economy will be threatened. Each unemployed person, by becoming a part instead of full consumer, threatens the stability of the markets upon which the economy is based. By being unemployed his productive energies and skills are not released and the growth of the economy is hampered.

A second related factor involves the pattern of distribution of the wealth produced, the pattern of sharing in the product. The average income of American families was estimated in 1959 to be about $6,500. This average should rise to over $8,500 in 1970 (based upon a gross national product of $750 billions). Yet radical variation in incomes still may continue, to the sharp disadvantage of millions of the nation's families. The rich might grow richer while large numbers of the poor remain burdened by the relative poverty caused by spiraling prices. Heller points out, on the positive side, that in the ten years from 1947 to 1957 the proportion of our families at the "poverty" level of less than $2,500 income decreased from about one-fourth to about one-fifth. He estimates this might fall further to about one-seventh by 1970. But, he says, "it is dismaying, even shocking, to find that over 30 million people in our supposed affluent society are living at or below the boundaries of poverty."[2] This hard core of poverty may remain relatively untouched unless the free play of market forces is buttressed by redoubled government efforts in the fields of health, education, and welfare. Crucially important policies will have to be developed and carried out to convert the economic abundance into economic and social opportunity for the whole population. He urges that we not let the "glitter of our affluence lead us to dismiss or minimize the problem of persistent poverty and the failure it reflects in important areas of social and economic policy."[3]

INCOME

One of the major questions is whether constructive use will be made of the expanded national income and wealth in the coming years. Important choices will have to be made. The investment in people, in their education, health, and welfare, including their opportunity to enjoy leisure, may be considered part of the investment in human capital, like the investment in physical capital. With increases in income citizens will expect better education for their children, improved sanitation, transit, water and air supply arrangements. All of these add up to increased investment in human beings and their welfare. It implies a thoughtful approach to the broad welfare of the individual, simply and narrowly, as a consumer of machine-made material goods whatever their value. The challenge to the nation is to develop a social policy which will search out the ways and means of directing the stream of dollars toward constructive uses, of alleviating the persistent problems of poverty; of eliminating disadvantage in obtaining and securing for all the essentials of food, clothing, shelter, medical care, education, leisure, recreation, and culture; and of providing the maximum opportunity for each person to realize the fullest of his potentiality, and to pursue his interests in life creatively and freely.

A major problem of public policy in America arises in determining how a sound and growing economy with greatly increased income and leisure opportunities can provide larger groups with more leisure time and more discretionary income, and can invest sufficiently large sums to guarantee health, education, and welfare for all.

---

[2] Heller, p. 83.

[3] Heller, p. 85.

IMPACT OF TECHNOLOGY ON LEISURE AND RECREATION

The development of a technology and an economy of the kind portrayed here has tremendous significance for leisure and recreation. First, the automated economy will produce huge floods of goods and services which with sound and socially oriented management can raise the level of living of the nation's population greatly.

Second, this will be done while the work day and work week are being steadily reduced, the work week to thirty or twenty-five hours perhaps in the next decade. Man will gain many more hours of leisure time with which to enjoy his goods and services, friends and family, his natural and man-made environment, to the extent that he has "learned" to do so. The fact of this new leisure time will itself operate as a force influencing how man spends his income in the purchase of things he must have or he wants to have. With the advent of more leisure hours it may be expected that man will want to buy more leisure goods and services. An important concept here is the concept of *discretionary income*. Heller states,

> Little discretion in spending is open to families with less than, say, $4,000 of disposable income.The necessities of food, clothing, shelter, transportation, and medical care absorb virtually all of the below-$4,000 income. Between $4,000 and $7,500, a considerable range of options begins to open up. And beyond $7,500 of family income, half or more of family spending can be labeled "discretionary." [4]

He estimates that the gross amount of this discretionary income will almost double, from $135 to $255 billion in the decade to 1970, increasing from 42 per cent to over 50 per cent of spendable income. It would be anticipated that a proportion of a family's discretionary spending would be in the area of leisure-time activities of an educational, cultural, or otherwise recreational, nature. Undoubtedly a portion would also be "status" or "conspicuous" expenditure as well. The impact of recreational spending on the recreation supply industry, upon recreation facilities and resources, and so on, could be anticipated to be tremendous. The impact on the entire life of families and individuals also will be profound.

---

[4] Heller, p. 85.

A third factor of importance is that the new situation will require both individuals and nations to consider certain basic decisions about the use of time. The decision will be whether to maintain high levels of productivity for a greater number of average hours of work in order to produce constantly larger amounts of goods and services, or to maintain such high levels of productivity but for fewer hours per person per week in order that masses of people will have more leisure hours to enjoy what is already produced.

The increased technology could work largely to the end of increasing the amount of production, as seems to have been the case in recent decades. Coughlan, in *Life* magazine, points gloomily to the idea that everyone should buckle down to work to produce, that leisure time should come second. "Mountains of television sets would be produced, a set for every room in the house. But who would have time to look at them, and with all the extra furniture spewing forth from furniture factories who would have space for them anyway? . . . In an age of automatic machinery and in a capitalist society such as ours, it is not productive capacity but popular demand that sets a limit to the amount of goods that are made." [5] He points out that the new leisure has created an industry producing in goods and services probably 40 billion dollars annually, a significant sector of the U.S. economy.

The second alternative would be that we could develop a social policy that would, in effect, "settle" for certain levels of production and provision of material goods and services in order to provide to the masses of the people more leisure hours with which to pursue their recreative interests. It is possible to stress primarily the values of greater material affluence and the provision of those things gained by work, or, on the other hand, to stress primarily the values of leisure and its full use in gaining the good life. This decision will be made, sometimes individually and also in the process of developing basic national economic and social policy. It will depend, in the new leisure age, upon the values people hold, their yearning after material wealth or after the values of leisure enjoyment. The recreation worker and his profession and the recreation institution, must be influential in the making of this decision.

Two forces are at work influencing public acceptance of a "more and more goods" policy. One is the widespread habit of spending for

[5] Robert Coughlan, "A $40 Billion Bill Just for Fun," *Life,* Vol. 47, No. 26 (December 28, 1959), p. 69.

social status, which, unlike the habit of spending for genuine individual self-realization, is concerned with the process Veblen identified in former leisure-class cultures as "conspicuous consumption" of goods. Such practices also harken back to the primitive displays of destruction of goods and wealth for the purpose of status competition practiced by the Kwakiutl Indian tribes of the Canadian Northwest, described in anthropological literature. Aided by the "hidden persuaders" of sales psychology in modern merchandising, a fair proportion of the people in the United States are caught up in this practice, to the profit of the merchandisers and the destruction or inhibition of other human values.

A second force at work is the practice in modern business of engineering built-in obsolescence in goods manufactured, and then through advertising encouraging people to be dissatisfied quickly with their possessions and anxious to replace them with new ones. Vance Packard, in his book *The Waste Makers,* describes these operations of business aptly, as in an earlier book he described the operations of the "hidden persuaders" in advertising.[6]

In his book, *The Insolent Chariots,* Keats portrays these activities at work in the automobile industry.[7] Other writers have commented also on these characteristics of modern business, striving, in their own way, to cope with an ever more productive industry.

A related modern problem is the widespread practice of employed persons of giving up most of their leisure in order to take a second job, many times in order to supplement an inadequate income, but often to be in a position to purchase more of the material goods upon which no society but the modern American society has ever put such overwhelming and influential emphasis. On the other hand, the trend toward compact cars and the successful merchandising of the Volkswagen on the basis that the model seldom, if ever, changes, may indicate widespread resistance to modern advertising's influence.

Technological changes in the areas of transportation, communication, and travel have particular significance for leisure. The rapidity of travel, the increase in roads and travel facilities by air, water, rail, and highway have influenced people's leisure habits greatly, as we

---

6 Vance Packard, *The Waste Makers* (New York: David McKay Company, 1960). See also *The Hidden Persuaders,* by the same author and publisher (1957).

7 John Keats, *The Insolent Chariots* (Philadelphia: J. B. Lippincott Company, 1958).

shall see. The economy's integrated character has grown with the growth of transportation and the mobility of people. Modern communication is an integrating factor as well. The American people have flooded into the areas of recreational travel, swamping many resources once thought adequate. The development of communication and transportation also has been a powerful force in the development of economic characteristics leading to the modern urban metropolis, whose explosive character has profound implications for recreation.

American society faces the dilemma of whether to increase work schedules in order to further increase production of material goods or to increase leisure time in order to allow the population to enjoy more leisure values.

RECREATION AND THE AMERICAN ECONOMY

In economic terms, recreation is big business in America today. A large automated industry mass produces leisure goods for millions with new hours to play and new income to spend. The interaction between an increasing capacity to mass produce recreation goods through technological advances and a rising demand for such goods and related services has pushed the leisure market into major prominence. The development of automatic pinsetting machines, the application of plastic processes to the manufacture of athletic equipment and toys, the fiberglass process for mass producing boats and fishing tackle, are prime examples of how technology is at work affecting this market.

The Leisure Market

The spectacular rise in earnings and stock values of leisure goods companies, such as Brunswick-Callander, AMF, Coleman, and Wilson, attest to the volume of sales and consumption of goods and their impact on the economic scene. Latest figures released by the Athletic Goods Manufacturer's Association show 87,044,301 units of golf sales in 1960 as compared to 41,789,127 for 1950. *Time* (July 14, 1961) reports Sears Roebuck camping equipment sales up 40 per cent since 1956 (rubber mattress sales alone rose 700 per cent in one year). Coleman, manufacturer of stoves and lamps, climbed 400 per cent in ten years and reported highest sales in the history of the company in 1961. *Printer's Ink,* a trade magazine, reported close to a billion dollars in sales of swimming pools and related equipment in 1961. A large part of the money went into home pools for family recreation.

Several hundred thousand men and women earn their livelihood producing the goods and services used in the sports, amusements, and entertainments. Billions of dollars are put into circulation annually in the production and delivery of these goods and services. Other billions of dollars flow into government treasuries in the form of licenses and taxes from recreational and recreation-connected sources.

In *Fortune* magazine it was pointed out in 1954 that "Full of vigor and promise, the leisure and recreational market today is one of the largest and most complex in the entire U.S. economy. It already measures about $30.6 billion. . . . The heart of that market is $18 billion of unmistakable leisure-recreational expenditures on spectator amusements, spectator and participant athletics, hunting and fishing, gardening, domestic recreational travel (including vacations and week-ends), foreign pleasure travel, boating, games and toys." [8] A secondary group totaling a little over $12.6 billion includes alcohol, television and radio, records and musical instruments, dining out, and so on. By 1958, spending in the "fun market" had risen to $41 billion annually, although as the editors of *Fortune* point out, consumer spending for recreation has grown no faster than consumer income.[9]

The total recreation bill in America has not been accurately calculated. Into the calculation must go the costs of municipal, county, and school recreation services, the costs of voluntary agency, church, camping, and fraternal organization expenses, the supporting services of state and federal agencies, and the vast and growing expenditures of the people for leisure goods (equipment, clothing, etc.) and commercial recreation. Estimates by the writers in *Fortune* were that the expenditures for primary recreational purposes by 1959 might amount to $23–$25 billion. Similar increases in the secondary group might be expected. The largest increases were anticipated in travel and touristing. A total recreation expenditure by 1960 of close to $39 billion was forecast and probably was attained.

The above figures very likely do not include the full picture of

---

[8] Dero A. Saunders and Sanford S. Parker, "$30 Billion for Fun," *Fortune*, Vol. 10, No. 1 (June 1954), pp. 115 and 117.

[9] Charles E. Silberman, "The Money Left Over for the Good Life," in *Markets of the Sixties* by the Editors of *Fortune* (New York: Harper & Row, 1960), p. 191.

recreation spending. No studies yet have reliably summarized the very complex economic data, but what data we do have indicate that Americans spend about one-eighth of their after-tax income for recreation. Such a figure is worth thinking about.

Recreation as Industry

Whole new industries have developed to provide the products and implements for leisure-time use. In addition to thousands of workers employed in the production of equipment, goods and services, more thousands are at work in a variety of public, voluntary, and commercial agencies serving the recreational needs of the public. It has been estimated that the amusement industry employs perhaps a quarter of a million persons; selected industries such as radio, toys, and sporting and athletic goods production employ perhaps eighty thousand persons; governmental units employ in recreation and park departments perhaps sixty to eighty thousand, and innumerable thousands in related departments.

In many states recreation is one of the two or three largest industries. Just pause for a moment and think of how firmly established in our modern day leisure-time culture are the vast amusements of movies, television, and radio; the eager interest in the sports of hunting, fishing, skiing, bowling, billiards, baseball games, football games, basketball games; the fondly pursued pleasures of smoking and drinking and socializing over a cocktail; the purchase of millions of newspapers, magazines, comics, and books; the millions who seek out ocean, lake, or stream to bathe or swim, or tennis courts and golf courses to play on, or who invent a million games and pleasurable leisure-time pursuits in the privacy of their homes.

These brief data do not provide all the outlines of a vast and complex picture. In fact, economic and recreation research have not yet produced a complete picture of the economic significance of recreation, and it is beyond our scope to do so here. We can recognize, however, from these fragments of data that in economic terms recreation is a very important part of the American scene.

TRAVEL AND VACATION—GETTING OUTDOORS

Some of the foregoing statistics tell us one thing about modern Americans; they seem to gain deep satisfactions from getting out of doors and "back to nature." Whatever the motivations, whether from physical and nervous demand for fresh air, sunshine, peace and quiet, or from culturally induced eagerness to ride, camp, hike, or get a suntan—any weekend holiday, and during the summer months when most people get their vacations, millions of people head for the out-of-doors. Touring and sightseeing, fishing, picnicking, swimming, camping, hiking, and boating are popular pastimes.

Getting Outdoors in Yosemite Park, California

The desire to see things sends millions out on the highways each year. Many spend their weekends and vacations traveling, stopping at one place for a few hours or a few days, then pressing on to other points. The allure of the horizons keeps them moving. They swarm to the mountains, seashores, lakes and reservoirs, to national parks and national forests, to historical sites and local parks. One of the motives for such travel is the desire to see the country and its beauties. One report summarizes the use of several kinds of recreation areas in the following table:[10]

Recreation area	*Million visits in last year of record (1955 or 1956)*
National park system	55
National forest	53
Wildlife refuges	8
TVA reservoirs	40
Corps of Engineers reservoirs	71
Bureau of Reclamation reservoirs	4
State parks	201
Municipal and county parks	1,000 or more

The same can be said for the great American custom of going on picnics and outings. Families, couples, Sunday School classes, lodge groups, by the millions, go picnicking. They enjoy fancy or plain picnicking facilities, provided by public and private organizations. The same thing is true of water sports such as boating, swimming, sunbathing, water-skiing, and sailing.

Boating, just to illustrate, fascinates millions. One estimate in 1957 suggested that thirty million people would have enjoyed recreational boating that year, operating close to 6,500,000 pleasure craft and spending one and one-half billion dollars on the sport.[11] This represents a phenomenal growth in a recreation that requires substantial investment in equipment, an investment that millions of people are making.

In the winter there are sports rapidly growing in popularity: skiing, skating, tobogganing, or winter-resorting, in general. Millions of new sportsmen have headed for winter vacations in the snow-covered mountains, rugged country resorts, or winter sports areas. Appreciable numbers of people take their annual vacations during the months when these sports are at their peak and when the beauties of the winter wonderland have special appeal.

What is the economic significance of this particular phase of

---

[10] Marion Clawson, *Statistics on Outdoor Recreation* (Washington, D.C.: Resources for the Future, Inc., 1958), p. 7.

[11] Joseph E. Choate, "Recreational Boating: The Nation's Family Sport," *Recreation in the Age of Automation,* The Annals of the American Academy of Political and Social Science, Volume 313 (September 1957), p. 109.

American recreation? In the first place, travel and outdoor recreations are somewhat limited for several million persons, perhaps half the total population or somewhat less. These are the ones who do not have the financial means for traveling very far from home and thus will invest their recreational dollars in nearby municipal or county or private park and resort facilities. There are many other millions who can and will travel appreciable distances, and will spend considerable amounts of money to enjoy unique and satisfying natural resources of vacation areas, parks, forests, wildlife areas, historic spots, resort sections, beaches, and mountains. Relatively more favored recreation-seekers enjoy annual vacations of three weeks or more, not the traditional two weeks. They travel by automobile, railroad, steamship, airline and bus. They not only swim and rest, but also take boat cruises, sail, fish, play golf, and ride horseback. And, as we have seen, their expenditures for these things total several billions of dollars yearly.

Without attempting a systematic statistical study of the economics of outdoor recreation and travel, we can appreciate that they are not only a very important part of American recreational life but an equally important part of the American economy. Public and private agencies are recognizing this. Many states are spending millions of dollars for publicity in the highly competitive striving for the tourist dollar. Many private organizations and regional and local bodies carry on similar promotional programs. Business groups are constantly demanding action by government to improve its recreational facilities so that vacationing can be increased in this or that area, with increased profits to local entrepreneurs.

Meyer and Brightbill summarize the economic importance of vacationing as follows:

> Literally thousands of business enterprises in scores of states flourish and grow as a direct result of the tourist industry. Hundreds of thousands of jobs are made possible by it. A large portion of the money which is spent goes for meals, lodgings, and refreshments. Millions are spent on gasoline and oil, rail, plane, bus, and steamship fares. The golf courses, theaters, gift shops, and stores benefit as do the dealers who outfit the tourist before he even starts on a vacation.[12]

---

[12] Harold D. Meyer and Charles K. Brightbill, *Community Recreation: A Guide to Its Organization* (Englewood Cliffs, N.J.: Prentice-Hall, Inc., 1956), p. 58.

These data are enough to indicate how important travel and outdoor recreation, especially getting the family car and driving someplace to do something, are to the national economy. We overlook one of the greatest economic elements in recreation, however, when we overlook the investment in the automobile itself. For although the automobile is used for many purposes, including getting to work and back, a considerable amount of all automobile travel is leisure-time recreational travel. According to the *World Almanac,* in 1960, some 87 million American drivers were buying over 6.5 million new cars (for $12 billion) and keeping running some 74 million automobiles and trucks, about three times as many as in 1935. They also were buying 57.8 billion gallons of gasoline. The bill for all this totals probably a fabulous $35 to $40 billion per year. Perhaps half, or at least a third, of this can be counted as being spent in the use of the automobile for recreation: visiting friends, driving to movies or ball games or the playground, youthful "cruising" for fun, touring, traveling, and sightseeing. This adds another 15 to 20 billions of dollars to the recreational account. Such is the economic significance to our society of "play on wheels." [13]

The urge of Americans to get outdoors and travel, along with the increase in leisure time, is bringing about huge increases in outdoor recreation, with great pressure on outdoor resources and the growth of many governmental, commercial, and other resources for outdoor recreation.

EXPENDITURES OF GOVERNMENT AND VOLUNTARY RECREATION AGENCIES

The economic role of government in recreation is large. Just how much all governmental units spend on recreation is difficult to assess. School expenditures are also difficult to estimate, and many expenditures for other kinds of government service have recreation in mind as a secondary use of the service. A public school will be built primarily for education, and then will be used in some cases seven days a week and perhaps six hours a day for recreation with most of the costs charged to education. A state will spend millions upon highways used very heavily for recreational travel, although the roads originally were thought to be farm-to-market routes or roads for business travel.

---

[13] Harry Hansen, ed., *World Almanac and Book of Facts, 1962* (New York: New York World Telegram, 1962), pp. 690 and 699.

Many federal expenditures for services such as those of the United States Forest Service have recreation in mind as one of the benefactors.

Direct governmental expenditures for recreation, including municipal, school district, county, state, and federal units, exceeded $800 million in 1960.[14] This figure can be compared to public expenditures for education of over $15 billion a year. At the community level these expenditures have taken the form of important investment in new neighborhood, district, and community-wide playgrounds, parks, and centers, and specialized facilities such as pools, stadia, golf courses, tennis courts, and so forth. An equal amount probably goes into direct program services such as professional leadership, materials, expendable equipment, and facilities maintenance. This amount has been steadily increasing through the years since the beginning of the century, much more rapidly in some communities than in others. County government expenditures in urban areas and in those where county government takes on local government functions have been growing steadily as well.

State government expenditures have been allocated for the development of state parks, beaches, forests, highways, direct consultive and supportive services, and funds for grants to communities as in Washington, Michigan, California, and New York. Other important items are recreation highways, fish and game departments, and county, regional, and state fair grounds for program use. Many federal agencies carry on recreation functions either as primary or secondary functions. They expend well over $200 million for direct recreation functions. In addition, federal government and other agencies build great power dams and flood-control reservoirs, which radically change the recreation of a whole region; new waterways are dredged out and opened up and recreational boating springs up; new highways are constructed and recreational travel increases, while motels and restaurants are built to serve and profit by the increased travel.

Recreation Income

The government not only spends money but it makes money in recreation. Units of government at all levels collect many taxes from recreation. Income taxes, amusement taxes, corporation taxes, excise taxes, hunting and fishing licenses and fees, horse racing taxes, admis-

---

[14] George D. Butler, ed., *Recreation and Park Yearbook 1961* (New York: National Recreation Association, 1961), pp. 1, 6, 15, and 36.

sions taxes, and so on, bring in revenues. These do not include indirect taxes on recreation, those on gasoline used by tourists, sales and other taxes on recreational goods and sports clothing, and so on. An admittedly crude guess would be that the government units take in approximately as much in taxes as they invest directly in recreation.

The data are not available to show the above relationship completely, but a study of the Federal Bureau of Internal Revenue tax receipts from selected and incomplete sources gives the figure of more than $1 billion from federal excise taxes. Add to this $2.5 billion from liquor taxes and $1.5 billion from tobacco taxes, and we have, in round numbers, $5 billion the federal government alone raises, not all of it, to be sure, in direct recreation levies, but much more than compensated for by the large number of items such as clothing industry taxes, which are not included but are related to heavy recreational investments.

It is impossible to estimate how much value can be placed upon the recreation facilities of the United States. One may recognize that among these resources are some two hundred million acres of federal government-owned national forests and parks, and millions of other acres owned by other federal agencies and by state and local agencies. To these can be added the billions invested in man-made facilities and it becomes apparent that many billions of dollars worth of precious resources are devoted to public use. To make these most useful to the people, and to expand and develop them to meet growing recreational needs, the combined efforts and financial developmental resources of all units of government will have to be directed toward such objectives.

Voluntary and Private Expenditures

The expenditures of voluntary agencies for recreation make up another formidable figure. If one could combine the budgets throughout this land of the Boy Scouts, Girl Scouts, Y.W.C.A., Y.M.C.A., Camp Fire Girls, Boys' Clubs, Girls' Clubs, settlements, centers, church programs such as the Catholic Youth Organization and the Jewish Centers, and many local and private youth-serving and adult recreation agencies, the figure might exceed the more than one-half billion dollars expended by local government. Voluntary agency funds are obtained in part through independent drives for voluntary contributions and in part from the great Community Chest drives or similar community efforts carried on annually in nearly one thousand American communities. These amounts, and the stimulus they give to the expenditure of vastly greater amounts in recreational equipment and clothing, add their significant bit to the total effect on the national economy of recreational expenditures.

The figures for private recreation agency expenditures are difficult to isolate, but they are sizable. In industrial recreation alone, Neer reports that approximately 25,000 companies spent over a billion dollars in 1957 in support of recreation programs for their employees.[15]

COMMERCIAL RECREATION

Expenditures for commercial recreation, and the amount of leisure-time amusement and play provided under commercial auspices, are far greater than those of public and voluntary recreation agencies. We have mentioned some commercial recreations before, travel and vacation being among them, but for the present moment let us consider the close-to-home recreations that daily attract and amuse or otherwise provide leisure-time enjoyment for scores of millions of persons. We must not forget the "stay-at-home" commercial pursuits—radio and television, newspapers, magazines, comics, and books. Not all commercial recreation is spectator amusement, although perhaps the largest portion is of this type. Movies, wrestling or boxing exhibitions, professional and amateur football, baseball, basketball, track, tennis, and other sports, attract millions of watchers of all ages each day. Still more millions of persons go bowling, dancing, swimming, golfing, ice skating and roller skating, or they play tennis, billiards, pingpong, or other games. Cultural recreations attract considerable numbers of patrons, who pay their way to symphony concerts, legitimate theaters, music or dance recitals, some of these contributing profit to some enterpriser, others merely supporting a cultural activity underwritten by interested sponsors.

Uncounted numbers find their way to bars, taverns, neighborhood drinking houses, night clubs, and similar places, which carry out their century-old function of the neighborhood club. It used to be said that "the pub is the poor man's club," but with the advent of more and more public drinking all groups and strata of the population patronize these commercial drinking places; and relatively private and "exclusive" drinking clubs have declined somewhat, although as we shall see later the lodges, clubs, and fraternal organizations still thrive

---

15 Don. L. Neer, "Industry," *Recreation in the Age of Automation,* The Annals of the American Academy of Political and Social Science, Vol. 313 (September 1957), p. 80.

in many parts of the country, operating in some places as profitable drinking and gambling clubs.

Mass Media and the Amusement Industries

These latter do not characterize more than a portion of the commercial recreation scene. We would be interested in the economics of the giant amusement industry, for example. Movies, after replacing vaudeville, a large part of the legitimate theater, and the traveling shows of earlier years, swept the country. Enough theaters were built by 1947 to seat simultaneously almost twelve million customers. Movies dominated the commercial recreation field for several decades until the tremendous competition of television in the 1950's began to be felt in smaller audiences and smaller profits. In 1929 weekly attendance was estimated by the industry to be more than 100 million; in 1939, it was approximately 85 million; in 1949, it was approximately 60 million; during recent years it has been holding its own. There has been a rapid growth of drive-in movies with a strong attraction for families, for those with babies who may sleep in the back seat, and for millions who enjoy "outdoor movies" where you can "come as you are" and be in the privacy of your own car.

The annual bill to the people of the United States for the two great media of radio and television, including sale of broadcasting time, the costs of talent, and the costs of electricity, batteries, receiving sets, phonographs, and repairs, is estimated to be $15 billion. The income to the broadcasting industry is in the hundreds of millions of dollars. The 1962 *World Almanac* reports 55.5 million television sets in use and 170 million radio sets scattered throughout 55 million homes, 42.5 million automobiles, and various business places and institutions (15 million sets).[16] Many sets have been purchased, as one wag put it, "at a dollar down and a dollar a week for life" by families with limited means, who, however, could enjoy the new amusement at a considerable saving over the weekly movie. Television and radio advertising is now a multimillion dollar leisure business, which the public supports through the prices it pays on most of the products it buys. And there has arisen a great industry of repair shops with innumerable repairmen dashing about the neighborhood keeping customers' television screens clear from jiggles and "snow."

Amusement parks have become in some areas a highly popular

[16] *World Almanac,* 1962, p. 761.

recreation resource. California's fabulous Disneyland represented an investment of $17 million, and in the first year grossed an estimated $13 million income. The new Pacific Ocean Park in that same community returned similar huge sums on an investment of $10 million. Commercial entrepreneurs are planning similar projects in other parts of the country, attracted by their profitability as a family recreation resource.

What is the economic significance of the tremendous popularity of such commercial recreations? The popularity of radio and television, needless to say, has transformed modern leisure-time living patterns of the American people. Economically, it has created whole new areas of business activity. For better or for worse, in terms of the quality of recreational experience they provide, these great media of amusement occupy many hours for the average person, absorb significant proportions of his income, and support huge and thriving industries which, while often locked in sharp competition, form an important segment of the total economy.

It would take us too long even to try to touch lightly upon the many other fields of commercial recreation which are of significance to our economy. The leisure-time function of reading has been mentioned. Customer spending for newspapers would total perhaps a billion dollars a year or more. How much of this reading might be classified as recreational is not known, but, like automobile use, a large portion of it is so.

We might look at other phases of "purchased" recreation: bowling with its 84,000 alleys and forty million bowlers, professional baseball, professional boxing, and so on. Few modern leisure-time pursuits have not been commercialized, and together they attract millions of "playing customers" and support the multibillion dollar recreation industry.

Gambling and Drinking

As, hopefully, a realistic but not too sordid footnote to this chapter, let us view briefly three other activities. The Neumeyers give us the following on gambling.

> The amount of money expended annually for gambling is not ascertainable, but estimates range from six to ten billion dollars. Of this amount, nearly half is spent legally or illegally on horse racing, including money wagered on legalized racetrack

> gambling, illicit gambling joints called "horse parlors," sweepstake lotteries, and racing tip sheets. The remaining amounts are distributed among "poor men's lotteries," unorganized gambling done on football and baseball contests, prize fights, golf, various marathons, elections, and the like . . . the increase of income during the war period greatly accentuated the amount of money available for gambling purposes.[17]

Drinking of alcoholic beverages ranks very high among the recreations of many millions of Americans. Sales by retail liquor stores in 1958 totaled almost $7 billion, and the government in 1960 collected in excess of $3 billion in taxes on alcoholic goods. Much drinking, of course, is related to other leisure-time activities, mainly of a socializing nature. It is not possible to draw any kind of balance sheet to portray the satisfactions that pleasure-seeking persons derive from modest drinking of alcoholic liquors, as laid against the by-products of alcoholism, personal degradation, and ruin of families and individual lives, which often result from intemperate overindulgence. It will suffice simply to get the picture of the tremendous significance to a particular segment of American business, the liquor manufacturing and dispensing industry, of this phase of the American pattern of uses of free time.

A leisure-time comfort of millions of adults, and unfortunately almost an addiction of many children and youth, is tobacco smoking. This particular "mild vice" has grown upon Americans through the years, and with the increase of smoking by women and young persons, the manufacture and consumption of tobacco products have increased greatly, aided by energetic advertising by the multibillion dollar tobacco industry. The comforts of a smoke appear important to many millions of Americans, and their recreational values have to be weighed against the health disadvantages of the use of tobacco, and the threat of cancer and other life-shortening diseases to the steadily smoking adult.

Commercial recreation forms a significant sector of recreation, with the mass media and amusement industries vying with many sports and

---

[17] Martin H. Neumeyer and Esther S. Neumeyer, *Leisure and Recreation: A Study of Leisure and Recreation in Their Sociological Aspects,* Third edition (New York: The Ronald Press Company, 1958), p. 301. Copyright 1958 The Ronald Press Company.

cultural recreations for a share of the discretionary income of the American public. Activities such as gambling and drinking add problems of control and other negative values.

Questions for Study and Discussion

1. *What technological advances in the past decade have had a significant impact on leisure time and recreation?*
2. *Take a community that you are familiar with and answer the following question: what is the economic significance of recreation activities to that community?*
3. *Which of these two national policies would you choose for the United States? (1) Concentration of attention on greatly increased production and consumption of material goods for all and relatively little increase in leisure time; or (2) concentration of attention on increasing leisure time for all and relatively less increase in material goods and services. Construct the argument for your position.*
4. *Wilderness areas are an extremely vital part of the recreation resources of this country, yet the same land is valuable for power, for industrial development, and for mineral and timber exploitation. How should these conflicting needs be reconciled? What would be the effect on recreation?*
5. *What should be the attitude of the recreation professional to the growth of individual commercial recreations such as television, movies, drinking, and so on? Do they detract significantly from more valuable organized recreation? Do they meet important needs in a constructive way or not? Explain your view.*

Selected Readings

Coughlan, Robert, "A $40 Billion Bill Just for Fun," *Life,* Vol. 47, No. 26 (December 28, 1959), p. 69.

Kaplan, Max, *Leisure In America: A Social Inquiry* (New York: John Wiley and Sons, Inc., 1960).

Lerner, Max, *America as a Civilization* (New York: Simon and Schuster, Inc., 1957).

8

COMMUNITY FORCES

The conclusion that leisure and recreation function as social forces implies that they are an integral part of the total web of social forces operating in American life today. And just as they are influenced by other forces, so they, in turn, influence and shape these forces and, with these forces, shape American life.

The previous chapter illustrated how technological and economic forces operate in this fashion (money, machines, goods, services, equipment, and facilities), creating the wherewithal for leisure and recreation (time and trappings for recreative use). Now let us examine where this operation occurs—the community—and the factors affecting community life to see how they interact to influence leisure and recreation and the nature of the recreative experience.

For our purposes the word *community* will refer to a group of people living together in relationships based upon common interests, working together to achieve common goals, and creating organizations and institutions to advance the common welfare. This definition does not describe the large groupings that are more accurately termed *nations* or *societies,* but it does provide sufficient flexibility to discuss both large and small groupings (urban and rural) and both total communities and subcommunities from metropolitan to neighborhood.

GEOGRAPHIC INFLUENCES

Geographic factors play a vital part, not only in the nature of community life, but also as major determinants in the development of communities. Be they rural or urban, the operation of such factors as the amount, kind, and quality of natural resources available, the climate, rainfall, and topographic features of a region, exert profound influence on where and how people live. From earliest times, the presence or absence of good soil, adequate rainfall and water, mineral deposits, an abundance of animal and plant life, temperate climate, the nature of the terrain (be it valley or plain, mountain or desert) and the existence of natural barriers of land, mountain, and water have shaped the development of community life, and through this man's own destiny.

In this country these factors encouraged our evolution from a frontier into an agricultural nation, and then into an industrial giant with roots deep in a rich and fertile agricultural economy. Their relationship to and effect on one's leisure and recreation can be demonstrated through the mental images conjured up by the following words: hunting, fishing, camping, waterskiing, swimming, boating, skiing; football in the fall, symphonies under the stars; Sun Valley, Grand Canyon, Sequoia, Miami Beach, Palm Springs. Each of these reflects the impact of geographical factors and the way they influence nearly every phase of community life. Their existence in favorable degrees or quantities is conducive to community growth and vitality; in fact, it contributes to great growth of specific communities especially endowed with such resources.

As to the effect that remoteness of geographic features from an urban area may have on leisure and recreation, one would have only to stand in Grand Central Station in New York on a ski weekend and watch the throngs surging to board a ski train for upstate or New England. The ends to which people will go to seek out leisure opportunities afforded by the existence of natural physical resources are recognizable immediately. Fortunately, through improved transportation, old barriers of time and distance and natural obstacles to the utilization and exploitation of geographic and natural resource areas for recreation purposes are disappearing daily. The flow from urban areas on holidays, weekends, and vacations to adjacent or remote geographical locales is ever increasing and in its wake emerge new communities. Leisure and recreation must be added to the list of factors creating new urban areas, resort centers (*e.g.,* Las Vegas) being a prime example.

One major reason for this development is the increasing population, which renders the existing close-in resources that helped originally to create an urban area more and more inadequate because of sheer volume of numbers. It might be well, therefore, to examine what is happening to population in this country.

POPULATION CHANGES

Every society and every period in history has had its own particular group of alarmists who have sounded a warning bell for man on a number of occasions and for a variety of reasons. The twentieth century is no exception. In the last ten years one such group, the demographers, have made it their special task to alarm the world as to what is happening to its population—and well they might. The imposing array of statistics gleaned from census studies and the analysis of what is happening to the populations, not only in this country but in every country of the world, cause one to pause and give thoughtful consideration to the population problem. The statistics point up without question that one of the major problems with which the world will have to deal in the next few years is the matter of its booming expanding population. Clark Kerr, President of the University of California, has expressed the view that population is the number one problem of the world, and that something must be done about it in the next ten years or it may be too late. Some of the statistics appear to have pertinence for leisure and recreation, for the use of resources, and for community life and they should be noted here.

The Population Boom

From 1650 to approximately 1915, the average increase in population represented a worldwide increase of about 0.5 per cent per year. This figure has now risen to 1.7 per cent per year, which may not appear to be an important increase; but at this rate, by the year 2000 there will be approximately 120 people for every square mile of land surface of the earth, and the rural community will probably have passed from existence. Actually, since World War II, population has been increasing in almost geometric progression. The number of years required for doubling the population is shortening every year. In 1925, for example, the world's population was doubling approximately every eighty-four years. By the year 2000 this time interval will be shortened to thirty-five years. The effect of this progression is both impressive and overwhelming.

This increase in population is a result of a number of factors, including the improvement of medical care and health and sanitation conditions throughout the world and a burgeoning fertility and birth rate—the latter occurring to a large extent in those countries least able to afford such an increase because of a weak economy or lack of sufficient resources. In Europe, the increase is 1.2 per cent per year; in North America, 1.7 per cent; in Asia, 2.4 per cent per year; and in South America, 3.4 per cent per year. In Red China, for example, the population presently is increasing at the rate of approximately 15 million persons per year. This means that every year China must find room, food, and work for twice the population of New York City. As Douglass points out, by the year 2000 the world population will exceed six billion human beings; four out of five will be inhabitants of Asia, Latin America, and Africa, and Africans will outnumber Americans almost two to one.[1] The implications for social planning and the development and use of the world's natural resources are apparent.

In the United States, the population increase from 1950 to 1960 was roughly 28 million people. The population for 1960 in America was 180,000,000. This represents an 18.5 per cent over-all increase in ten years. It is predicted that by 1980 the United States will have a population of 245 million people.

The nature of the population is changing also. The population

---

[1] Paul Douglass, "The Administration of Leisure for Living," *Bulletin of the American Recreation Society* (April 1960), p. 8.

is getting younger as shown by the increase in percentages in certain age groupings. The under-18 age group increased 37 per cent, whereas the 18–65 group increased only 7 per cent, and for those over 65 years, the increase was 35 per cent. Women continued to outnumber men, the ratio of men to women dropping from 99–100 in 1950 to 97–100 in 1960. Census data underline several other points made earlier. First, we are becoming more and more an urbanized society. In 1960, for the first time in American history, fewer than one person in ten in the United States was a farmer. In 1959 alone, twenty-seven cities were added to the list of cities (approximately 130) in the United States with populations of 100,000 or more.

These figures underscore the continuous movement of U.S. population from farms and small towns to an urban complex. They also highlight changes taking place in suburban fringe areas, which were formerly semirural or semiurban but are being absorbed by the sprawl of megalopolis. For example, one small city in California (Anaheim), which in 1950 had a population of 14,000, by 1960 had springboarded into the "big city" class with a population of 104,000 people. It is an almost inescapable fact that the future holds for the majority of American population the prospect of being born, growing up, living, working, and dying in metropolitan complexes—some in cities, some in expanded suburbs, but primarily in urban surroundings.

Households are becoming smaller in the central city areas, partly because of the movement to the suburbs by families with children, the establishment of new households by young married couples, and the maintenance of the old household by the parents, thus restructuring the family unit from its former combined complex of grandparents, parents, and children.

To the social scientist interested in community planning, knowledge of sheer population volume is not enough. It is essential that he be aware of the factors that relate to the nature of the population: its composition by age, sex, race, cultural background; the level of physical and mental health of people; the degree of mobility of people. The latter is affected by improved transportation, better roads and highways, the use of airplanes and smaller automobiles, and the development of transit and transport systems for the hauling of people, goods, and materials to maintain the population.

In trying to understand community life and its influence upon leisure and recreation, it is important that the student (and the planner) understand the nature of the population within any given community, be it rural or urban, and take into account the factors mentioned above. These must then be arrayed against other facts and the interrelationships must be studied. The import of these facts for the organization, planning, and distribution of welfare services is obvious.

Although urbanization has brought to the big community many economic and cultural advantages through intensification and centralization of services, leadership, and resources, it must be recognized that the process has intensified other, less desirable aspects of community life—social and family disorganization, as seen in the rising divorce rate, increasing juvenile delinquency, mental illness, and political malfunctioning at all levels of government. Population shift is one of the prime causes for many of these problems, and with the prospect of an ever increasing population one can readily see why the concern over these factors is so dominant in the minds of many today.

As population increases, the need for services of all types also increases and one of the major tasks to be met in the next ten years is somehow to find the resources necessary to meet this demand. To bring this increase down to an economic perspective, in Los Angeles, for example, in the ten-year period from 1960 to 1970, $33 billion will be needed to provide the basic municipal services required by the anticipated increase in population. One million housing units must be built, not to mention the hospitals, schools, and recreation facilities that must be provided also. Small wonder that educators, doctors, planners, politicians, economists, real estate officials, engineers, and recreation experts share a common concern for the problem.

Effect on Recreation

The effects of the population increase on leisure and recreation can be expressed qualitatively and quantitatively. The quantitative aspects are reflected in participation statistics covering a wide range of activities and interests, the type of participation (active or passive) and the kind of participant, and in the growing need and demand for services, particularly areas and facilities. As one recreationist put it, "This is the period of the land grab." It requires space for people to recreate, whether indoors or outdoors, and people apparently seek and want outdoor recreation and large spaces. The magnitude of the impact of numbers and use against land and space is tremendous.

Clawson, studying recreational land use, projects mathematically the statistics of the attendance and participation in outdoor recreation areas to the year 2000, and predicts that the demand for this kind of experience will increase some ten times over present experience. He bases this conclusion on the assumption that by the year 2000 there will be twice as many people as there are now, twice as much income per person, twice as much travel, and one and a half times as much leisure time. Then, using this index, he predicts that within forty years the demand on city and county parks will increase fourfold. The demands for land accessible to metropolitan areas by motor car will increase sixteenfold, and the demand on such resource areas as national parks and national forests will increase fortyfold.[2]

One has only to be in one of our large national parks like Yosemite or Yellowstone during the summer vacation months to grasp what doubling the population would mean in the utilization of these areas. Reflect on what Jones Beach on Long Island would be like on Sunday with twice as many people as it now has, or Puget Sound in Washington with twice as many boats. One soon feels the sense of urgency to do something *now* about securing land resources to meet the demand for recreation opportunities in the future, not only outdoors but indoors. Recreation centers require space too, as do galleries, museums, theaters, zoos, concert halls, and schools.

Qualitatively, increasing population tends to affect the nature of recreation experiences available and to highlight the need for continual development of resources and opportunities that enable individual satisfaction of needs and interests. Just as the individual can get lost physically in the "big city," with its impersonal approach, so, too, can the individual be lost in "big city" recreation and its tendency toward a mass approach, with the anonymity of passive and spectator participation (theaters, sports, other commercial recreations), large events, overcrowded facilities, and lack of personal contact between the leader and the individual. One of the real challenges in leisure and recreation is how to provide for programs and services that retain individuality and through which an individual can relate to others and thus identify himself with the community.

Increase in mobility and the will to go somewhere for recreation result in movement with both temporary and persistent impact. The rural resident, no longer dependent solely upon rural institutions, is able to transcend normal boundary lines and avail himself of the more

---

[2] Marion Clawson, "Recreational Land Resources for the Future," *Proceedings of the Fortieth National Recreation Congress* (New York: National Recreation Association, 1959), p. 71.

highly organized institutions of the urban center. In large metropolitan areas such as New York, Cleveland, and Detroit, the flow of people back and forth over political and geographical barriers and across state lines for recreative purposes is readily observable. The exodus of people from the cities on weekends, flooding the countryside on their way to lake or seaside resorts and other attractions, is evidence of the movement brought about by leisure and recreation.

A more permanent type of migration revealed in the study of population statistics is the steady migration westward. Predictions are that the population in California alone will double from 1960 to 1970. Small wonder that in light of this prospect, and of the fact that natural geographical resources—its beaches, mountains, deserts, and scenic wonders such as Yosemite—make the state highly attractive for recreation purposes, California has pushed forward with its pioneer project in public outdoor recreation planning.[3] Perhaps nowhere else is there such a wide variety of forces interacting, with leisure and recreation as the center, where recreation has become a major business, where total state resources are mobilized to this end, and where people are flocking by the thousands to work, live, and play.

There is no easy solution to the problems posed by population increase in the United States. Solutions will depend upon the degree to which understanding and interest of the general public can be developed, an interest and understanding little shown at present. Birth control, as one way of doing something about population, will receive increasing attention in the days to come. Such voluntary organizations as the Planned Parenthood Federation see this method as the means of controlling population. And just as the recreation professional must concern himself with the problems of providing opportunities and resources for more and more people, so must other social scientists concern themselves with other aspects of the problem.

Geographical factors and population changes are influential forces in recreation. Population increases have radically transformed American communities, with highly developed urbanism as the dominant pattern and increasing population pressure on outdoor recreation resources and lands.

---

[3] See *California Public Outdoor Recreation Plan,* Part I (Sacramento: California State Printing Office, Documents Section, 1960).

THE RURAL COMMUNITY

Since earliest times man has lived in groups, originally for reasons of survival—as is the case still in some parts of the world. As his life became more sedentary and an agricultural economy developed, the loose, informal group structures merged into settlements, and village communities appeared. The transition of villages into towns occurred as traders settled there and developed trade centers. There are numerous examples of such centers from ancient to modern times—Babylon, Rome, London, New Orleans, New York, San Francisco, St. Louis, Chicago.

Modern communities are classified as rural or urban according to such criteria as population density, legal status, and predominant occupations of the inhabitants. America began largely as a collection of rural communities, and in order to understand contemporary community life, urban or rural, it is helpful to begin with the heritage from which came the people who, through a will and a way of life, developed the unsettled continent into the most highly industrialized, urbanized society in the world. It is in this heritage that one finds the roots of much that shapes and directs community life today, including leisure and recreation.

Rural life in America has a deep pioneer tradition of community unity and spirit, as well as a recreation tradition as old as this country. Wherever the country was settled the pioneers tended to settle in groups, each with his own farm with plenty of space to live in, but near enough to other people to be considered neighbors. Mutual aid was necessary in many cases and a happy thing when it happened, as neighbors pitched in to help the newcomer get a spot cleared, a house raised, and a farm operation started.

The pioneer community was a cooperative work community, and recreation involved making fun out of work. So husking bees, butchering rings, harvesting, and barn and house raisings, along with weddings and even funerals, were occasions for fellowship for the whole neighborhood, occasions where all might join in a spirit of sharing, friendship, and fun.

This sense of neighborliness was a strong bond, and still remains, to some degree, a bond among those who live in the rural open country neighborhoods of America's agricultural areas. The pioneer, much like the modern farmer, stood on his own feet and thought of himself as a rugged individualist, although deep in the spirit of the farm community were traditions of cooperation and mutual aid. The isolation of the pioneer rural districts, whether the prairies of Nebraska, the wooded hills of Virginia or Missouri, or Montana's open range, urged small groups of persons to bind themselves together in very intimate relationships. Their similar economic interests and the desire for friendship were the bases for a very important neighborliness. Hepple and Bright describe it as follows: "Survival among the pioneers depended upon neighbors. They not only depended upon one another for companionship, but they rendered one another invaluable service in getting started in the new area. It was an obligation that neighbors should help neighbors. . . ." [4]

Rural people also created the major social institutions necessary for their needs. The rural church was one of these institutions. It served the neighborhood within reach by foot or horseback, which meant there was a church located within approximately four or five miles of each farm family. These closely knit congregations made the church an important part of the neighboring activity and a center for recreational life.

As schools developed throughout rural areas a similar pattern developed, with usually a single teacher hired to teach a little flock of youthful learners. Even today, it must be remembered, many thousand children still attend rural schools. About half of these are farm youth and other rural nonfarm youth living in villages and open country. The other half are small-town children, primarily. In rural elementary and secondary schools, roughly one third of the teachers are in schools of one to three teachers, and the little red schoolhouse is still very much alive in this country.

The recreational life of early rural people centered around their church, their school, occasional affairs for neighboring, and the family circle. The Sunday church meeting was often a "most-of-the-day" affair, with families bringing their dinners and enjoying a somewhat staid but friendly afternoon of gossiping, politics, and the leisure-time pursuits proper for the Sabbath. The school held spelling bees, geography and arithmetic matches, literary meetings, and "box socials" to which the entire community would come for socialization and games. The child's life, in school and on the farm, included a wide range of

[4] Lawrence M. Hepple and Margaret L. Bright, *Social Changes in Shelby County* (Columbia, Missouri: University of Missouri, College of Agriculture Research Bulletin 456, 1950), pp. 24-25.

recreations, particularly the ones city moderns now long for, such as tramping the hills, exploring the woods and following the creeks with a slingshot, rifle, or fishing rod, picking flowers in the fields or berries and nuts in the woods, and making up endless games and adventures available to those who have the whole outdoors in which to play. The family itself enjoyed much recreation together. When holidays and other celebrations came up the whole family went together to enjoy the good times. In modern times there have arisen rural leisure-time and cooperative organizations for mutual aid, cooperation, social enjoyment, and recreation. Some of these, like the Grange for the farmers and fraternal, civic, and social clubs for the villagers, have played an important role in supplementing the earlier institutions.

TRENDS IN RURAL LIFE

The relative stability of rural life, despite the industrial revolution, might be said to have continued until the last three decades. But the economic crisis of the thirties and the wars of the forties and fifties accelerated the speed of profound changes in rural life. The three most important of these changes were industrialization of agriculture, migration from the farm to the city, and increasing urbanization of the rural area. Because of these changes, basic changes in the entire fabric of rural community organization and relationships have occurred.

Industrialization

These changes were overlooked for a while because a phenomenal demand for agricultural production during the years of World War II brought unprecedented good times to the farm. The high level of prosperity in the country generally meant a heavy demand for labor, which absorbed surplus agricultural population. But in agriculture, industrialization meant agricultural mechanization, specialized farming, and the gradual disappearance of the self-sufficient family farm. With industrialized farming, farm labor and migrant part-time workers were necessary. Great corporations arose that processed or marketed agricultural production, and whose policies over several decades were the "cash crop" and heavy investment in machinery.

The trend toward mechanization and industrialization of the farm economy meant rural electrification, the automobile, the radio, the tractor, specialized farm machinery, and specialized and highly technical processes in all aspects of dairying, grain raising, cattle and hog production, poultry farming, and so on. These changes have placed the farmer more and more in the position of a highly technical producer with a large capital outlay in plant and machinery. In some measure it places him in the precarious position of depending, as an individual producer, upon highly organized urban food processers, dealers, and middlemen to market his production. And he is, as they are, placed at the mercy of economic forces of credit, finance, cyclical fluctuation of prices, and so on, very much more so than the traditional, partly self-sufficient farmer was.

In this kind of farming the farmer relies heavily on farm laborers. These laborers for the most part are from low-paid, often migrant, minority cultural groups, which equal or outnumber the owner-population in a community. They are at other times relatively permanent members of the community, staying year after year. But they are "outsiders," not part of the nucleus group in the community. They make up the lower strata who live "across the tracks" and provide the rural village or small town with an "urban" class system largely unknown in the days of the pioneers. Thus other effects of industrial revolution in agriculture are a basic change in the class structure of the rural community and a migration cityward. And the rural community changes to the degree to which industrialization goes on. As Goldschmidt says, "From industrialized sowing of the soil is reaped an urbanized society." [5] He shows that to the degree to which commercialized and specialized farming becomes dominant in an agricultural region, to that degree the traditional rural community social structure and relationships break down and urban social relationships emerge.

Migration

The rural family produced more children than could find futures in farming; mechanization of agriculture resulted in fewer people being required to do the work; farms tended to become larger, and fewer owners and permanent farm hands were needed to maintain a higher and higher level of agricultural productivity. These all sped the migratory process. In addition, the shorter hours of urban industrial work, the greater amount of leisure time, the conveniences of electric lights, inside plumbing, and the seemingly more interesting recreational and

[5] Walter Goldschmidt, *As You Sow* (New York: Harcourt, Brace & World, Inc., 1947), p. vii.

social life made city life appear more agreeable and attractive to rural dwellers.

This constant flow of young and vigorous youth from country to city has been thought by some to be draining the rural areas of their best elements. Others argue that it is the best elements who stay behind while the more unstable groups move. At any rate, the decline in rural and village population, bringing declining enrollment in schools, declining vigor in community life, and a kind of settling down or stagnation in many aspects of rural life, has given the impression of loss of vitality, which is probably due more to loss of numbers than to quality. The actual decline in population has created certain difficulties. Many rural churches have ceased to exist; some are inactive; others have difficulty in carrying out their functions adequately and are carrying on with limited programs; some have been consolidated; and others may have to be abandoned in the near future, when the slow decline in membership reduces their life to a low ebb. The rural school consolidation movement has gone on apace, with rural schools closing and declining school populations being brought together in union schools. These may retain some of their traditional functions as community recreational centers, or they may represent such widespread districts that the community center function is largely abandoned.

Urbanization

The third trend in rural life is urbanization. The telephone, automobile, electricity, radio and television, movies, high-speed highways —all have radically changed country life. Gillin says, "City style homes, city fashions, vogues, education modified on the basis of city models—even religion influenced by the currents of city life—have invaded the country. . . ." [6]

Another phenomenon is the influx of city dwellers into rural communities. Just as the rural dweller is drawn toward the city, the city dweller, with the benefit of rapid transit and automobiles, and for the sake of the space, fresh air, quiet and peace, and other real benefits of rural life, often moves into the rural area. The trend toward decentralization of urban life has led to the coining of the term "exurban" [7]

---

[6] John L. Gillin, *Social Pathology* (New York: Appleton-Century-Crofts, Inc., 1946), p. 439.

[7] A. C. Spectorsky, *The Exurbanites* (Philadelphia: J. B. Lippincott Company, 1955).

to describe the new class of community and the community dweller who works in the city, who lives in the country or as far out as commuting difficulties will permit, and who raises his children and carries on his family life there. One effect is wholesome—more people can enjoy some of the benefits of rural life. One effect is negative, in a way—some of the undesirable patterns of urban life are transferred into the rural community. But in any case the rural nonfarm dwellers constitute a large group helping to diffuse urban culture into rural areas and in a sense bridging the gap between rural and urban.

An important by-product of urbanization is the orientation of the rural dweller toward the city, which has led to the decline of the village as a service and social center. Although it is true that institutions in the rural community may still meet to some degree the needs of the farmer, the adequacy of these institutions in villages and smaller towns to serve such needs is declining. Churches, health facilities, and schools are prime examples, along with merchandising facilities. As Elliott and Merrill say: "The farmer often has to go farther than formerly to buy everything except groceries." [8] Even for recreation opportunities the present-day farmer deserts the rural community.

Disorganization

Rural community disorganization results in some respects from these trends, aggravated by positive environmental disadvantages suffered by large rural groups. Rural housing in poor areas is very inadequate, and essential modern facilities for respectable living are lacking in many rural homes. Income levels for thousands of rural families are below the level required for health and decency. Prolonged depression has hit many declining villages and small towns, towns that have been robbed by urbanization of their economic base and are quietly fading away and disintegrating. In many regions, migratory workers are needed to help with crops at certain times of the year, and in general their poverty and want equals or exceeds that of the most depressed urban classes. Extreme poverty results in poor physical and mental health. Diet, housing, education, and family life are inadequate and constitute real burdens for the growing child to bear. Add to these the inability of many rural dwellers to gain any substantial satisfaction from community relations and activities, the neglect and inadequacy

---

[8] Mabel A. Elliott and Francis E. Merrill, *Social Disorganization,* Fourth edition (New York: Harper & Row, Inc., 1961), p. 505.

of their recreational and leisure-time needs, and the stagnation in community life, and the outline of rural disorganization can be seen.

Rural Recreation

Important changes have occurred in the recreational life of rural people. The change that has taken place in neighboring is one of the more important changes, for the informal mutual aid and mutual social life that once existed among families has declined. Exchange of work and cooperation in harvesting disappears, and concern for one's neighbor gives way to concern for more efficient operation of one's own farm. Social life is changing as well. Coyle says, regarding neighboring:

> There is little of the informal activity that once existed among families. . . . Formerly, all families within a short distance were well acquainted and visited among themselves, but such is not necessarily the case today. There are fewer occasions to bring people together on a social basis. . . . Trips to village centers or outside the county absorb the time once devoted to visiting one's neighbors. Indeed, it is often said, "the only time one sees his neighbor is in town." . . . Neighboring . . . is carried on . . . rather more on the basis of selection . . . with persons of similar interest who may be contacted by our present means of communication and transportation, persons who may or may not live within the radius of a few miles. . . . Selective neighboring, which is increasingly becoming a characteristic of farm life, is the type or pattern of neighboring most often found in urban communities.[9]

The local special interest groups that existed in the rural areas or villages have continued, and some have grown to a degree. Fraternal orders, civic clubs, Granges, farm associations, and the various organizations of the Agricultural Extension Service—the latter aided by the government's extension agents—have formed the basis for considerable social activities, educational work, and recreation, and in the modern period provide the basis for continued community organization. The Grange, Parent-Teacher Associations, 4-H Clubs,

---

[9] Grace L. Coyle, *Group Experience and Democratic Values* (New York: The Women's Press, 1948). By permission of Whiteside, Inc.

and political and other purposive organizations play an important role in community life, often are the organizations that provide the leadership for needed civic programs, and along with the schools and churches continue to infuse life and vitality into the community. In the more urbanized rural towns, these community activities are almost exclusively dominated by the "business farmers" serving as instruments for organized social action and activity of these upper classes. The agricultural workers, unskilled workers, and of course the migrant outsiders, are almost completely absent.

Urbanization has had its impact on rural family recreation, too, in several ways. One of these is the growth of radio and television into major resources for communication, informal education, and recreation. A high proportion of rural homes have radio and television, and they enjoy a wide variety of programs, largely urban in their primary appeal. The village and small-town movie house has been replaced by the "drive-in theater," which operates on westerns, thrillers, and second-run features. The city newspapers and a considerable number of rural newspapers serve rural homes, and in many parts of the country recent developments of mobile libraries, as well as the devoted efforts of village organizations and book-lovers' clubs, maintain library service to those in the smaller communities and open country. The cultural life of the urban community is available to many rural dwellers, and many millions of them make use of the opportunity, whether culture means attending a big league ball game, hearing a symphony, or visiting the museum.

The recreational needs of village and farm residents in important respects are quite different from those of urban dwellers. There are in the urban communities resources for recreation that many rural areas do not enjoy—commercial, public, and voluntary. The sparse population in much of rural America discourages commercial recreation ventures except those such as small taverns and drinking places, the growing institution of the "drive-in" movie, and occasional resorts appropriately close to attractive natural features. High per capita cost limits the amount of public recreation that can be afforded by local governments, school districts, or county organizations, although this is one field in which steady but not spectacular growth is going on.

The drabness of rural life and the boredom expressed by many rural dwellers because of lack of stimulating leisure-time opportunity are recognized as reasons for the abandonment of the small communities by many in favor of a more exciting city life. Yet there are many who believe that optimum conditions for life can be created in rural America and they seek for means of vitalizing community recreational life and keeping alive the cooperative and community play spirit in the rural neighborhoods. As one rural advocate said:

> The modern small town can have most of the advantages of the modern world and few of the disadvantages of mass society and urban civilization. . . . As a place to live and as a place where children can grow and mature, the modern small community has resources immeasurably superior to anything that the great cities can offer. . . . It is only in the relatively small community that a full and wholesome relationship among human beings is usually possible . . . and that the productive or work side of life can be more integrally organized with the appreciative or enjoyment side of life. . . . Life can be whole there. It follows that the expressive arts and the humanities, as they are sometimes called, can have a far deeper and more enduring significance than elsewhere. If the small community is used as a center for participation in music, drama, dancing, poetry, conversation as interesting activities, it can become of immeasurable significance to those who live there.[10]

Brownell's challenge points up the need for rural communities to do significant planning for recreation as a means of contributing to the solution of many and broad problems of rural life, and as a significant contribution to rural welfare.

The inadequacy of recreation facilities is often cited as one of the important difficulties of rural communities. Studies of farm families' choices of recreation indicate that facilities for swimming, picnicking, fishing, and boating are in high demand by those near water facilities, and that areas for outdoor games and recreation would be welcome. In many cases these may be regional facilities, but in other cases it would depend upon local community planning and action. Although many communities throughout the country may be found at work on such projects, there is a great need for further work, to increase the attractiveness of rural recreational life and to vitalize the recreational function of rural centers, villages, and small towns.

---

[10] Baker. Brownell and others, *Life in Montana,* The Montana Study (Missoula, Mont.: The University of Montana, 1945), pp. 103-104.

The traditional rural community life is disappearing under the impact of technological change, rural population movement to the cities, urban population movement to rural areas, and modern business farming and its manager-worker class system. Rural life is reorganizing fundamentally and becoming urbanized as rural dwellers become oriented toward the cities with their urban culture.

THE MODERN URBAN COMMUNITY

The growth of the urban community has been one of the most important causes of the radical transformation in the recreation of our society. In a little more than a century in America we have changed from a society in which about 80 per cent of the people were rural farmers to one in which 90 per cent of the people now are nonfarmers, whether city, town, or rural folk.

The sociological concept of *gemeinschaft-gesellschaft* (close communal society-broad associational society) appears to have meaning in many ways in comparing the leisure characteristics of rural and urban communities, although, as Kaplan points out, it has decreasing importance as the distinctions between urban and rural life are reduced. Kaplan feels, however, that there are still some aspects of "pure" city and "pure" village life that color leisure.[11]

In general, modern urbanites enjoy positive advantages: improved transportation, better schools, better organized institutional services such as health and medical services, relatively higher standards of living, and more leisure time and resources. Still, city life affects the urban dweller in many negative ways, and when families gave up the open fields, pleasant woodlands, fresh air, and room to stretch, they gave up the natural playing places for children and relaxing and recreating places for adults. Whatever else they may have gained, they lost precious recreational resources.

Some city neighborhoods with their large yards and quiet streets provide an environment almost as desirable as the open country. But in many cities there are large areas too crowded to provide adequate play space, too dangerous for free play in the streets, and too disorganized in basic neighborhood life to provide adequate recreation

---

[11] Max Kaplan, *Leisure in America: A Social Inquiry* (New York: John Wiley and Sons, Inc., 1960), p. 135.

resources for the dwellers, especially children. The speed, crowding, and tensions of city life in general; the special problems of blighted and deteriorated areas in which social disorganization in its many forms is high and living disadvantages are numerous and acute; the great difficulty of maintaining the informal social organization of neighborhoods and neighborliness in the mobile and congested urban areas—these are some of the conditions we will touch upon as significant for leisure and recreation.

In addition to these sheer "physical" problems of space, speed, and crowding, other products of our urbanized culture must be noted. Among them is the increased mobility of urban populations, with consequent uprooting of millions of people from familiar family and neighborhood surroundings as they gain the freedom of movement to newer associations and opportunities, but lose pleasurable companionship with family, neighbors, and friends of long standing, and intimate association with others in small, homogeneous communities. The urban community provides many opportunities for association with others, but there is a predominance for many of mainly anonymous or depersonalized contacts and superficial relationships. For many persons, this depersonalization is such a great loss that loneliness, anomie, and demoralization afflict them. Riesman, Whyte, and others have undertaken to analyze some of the complex problems here involved.[12]

URBAN CHARACTERISTICS AND CONDITIONS

The basic spatial pattern of population change over the past century has been a steady growth in the number and size of cities. This trend and the pattern of any particular community's growth are resultants, as we have seen, of a number of forces—geographical and climatic factors, density of population, population movement and growth, factors of health and vitality, the level and amount of variability in economic status, total wealth, and the variation in religious and cultural composition.

To these we now add the complex of forces related to spatial or ecological growth of a community. The general or typical pattern of urban growth, and the resultant spatial structure of the urban com-

---

[12] David Riesman, *The Lonely Crowd* (New Haven, Conn.: Yale University Press, 1950), and William H. Whyte, Jr., *The Organization Man* (New York: Simon and Schuster, Inc., 1956).

munity, have been studied for several years by students of human ecology.[13] They have discovered that as a city grows, whether slowly or rapidly, it tends to move something like a glacier, beginning from the center and moving slowly outward, its population flowing toward the edges of the city while older areas rot away quietly.

Shifting Neighborhoods

This movement toward decentralization of a city and the deterioration of some segments is the result of a number of factors: improved transportation, which permits people to live farther away from the central areas of the city; the flow of economically advantaged groups to newer, "nicer" neighborhoods; the flow of lower economic groups (new migrants, unskilled labor) into the older vacated neighborhoods; landowners permitting housing to deteriorate in older neighborhoods, because land near the city's core is always potential business or industrial property, and this keeps its value high; and general unattractiveness of older industrial and business structures.

The result is that an urban population tends to distribute itself geographically into a number of neighborhoods or subsections, with the higher economic groups living on the city's periphery, and lower economic groups tending to concentrate in run-down, older, deteriorated neighborhoods generally nearer to the city center.

The growth of a city, with shifting residential neighborhoods, creates a basic pattern of disorganization. The movement of neighborhoods tends to disrupt fundamental community relationships: concern for one's neighbors, concern for neighborhood issues, loyalty to neighborhood standards and customs, and resistance to and organization against undesirable forces and influences such as vice establishments and the like.

In areas where much movement occurs, churches, schools, civic organizations, local improvement organizations, and political reform groups have difficulty "sinking in their roots" and the ordinarily vital forces of community or neighborhood cooperation and self-help do not generate much power. The decline of the neighborliness of the urban neighborhood, the increase in isolation and confusion, and the lack of integration and stability are among the losses in our modern urban communities.

---

[13] See R. E. Park, E. W. Burgess, and R. R. McKenzie, *The City* (Chicago: University of Chicago Press, 1925).

Stress and Congestion

Other characteristics of the urban community are speed, tension, and congestion, which can be seen on all sides. The movement back and forth from home to city center takes on such mass character as to be in itself highly disrupting, requiring millions of automobiles on crowded freeways, highways, and streets, loaded buses and streetcars, subways and elevated trains with thousands jammed together for the long, noisy, dusty ride downtown, and contaminated air flooding poorly ventilated central and residential areas. The pressures of high land values and for intensive land use resulted in the construction in the larger cities of thousands of tenements and, in later years, the continued construction of multiple dwellings. The result is congested living, an absence of yards, open spaces, or parks, and crowded neighborhoods and buildings.

The human being is very adaptable, and his senses can survive dirt, noise, and smells, but for millions such an environment is depressing, disturbing, and unhealthy. A grim fight goes on against dirt and smog, rodents and vermin, squalor and decay; and health departments, fire departments, and police departments spend millions of dollars trying to cope with disease, fire, crime, and delinquency, which breed in the worst areas and then spread like contagion through a community to infest and infect the total population.

Although man is adaptable to a considerable degree, the speed, tension, cumulative anxiety, insecurity, and pressure have their negative effect on the mental stability and good health of urban dwellers. Those who succumb and break down become a large part of the half to two thirds of a million persons who make up the constant-patient group in the psychiatric wards of the hospitals. A much larger group, perhaps eight million Americans, are estimated to be suffering from some sort of mental disease, and a significantly high enough proportion of these are urban dwellers to indicate that urban life is one of the causes—although, of course, not the only one. There is a critical need in the community for constructive forces that will strive to provide the opportunities for release and relaxation from some of the stresses and strains of these conditions, to allow people to come together in pleasurable association during their leisure time, for companionship, for recreational enjoyment together. There is a charge on the community as well, and on the recreational forces and similar organizations, to strive through organization and planning to meet these needs of community members.

It is important to underline two related facts at this point. One fact is that in the modern city certain groups and populations in certain areas are measurably "worse off" than those fortunate enough to dwell in more favorable neighborhoods and under more favorable conditions. The second fact is that for the entire urban community there are a number of common problems, partly because of the physical and social contagion between areas and groups and partly because of the nature of urbanism itself.

Urban Recreation

In several ways the modern city is not a good place for children and youth to play. The earliest playgrounds in this country were constructed two thirds of a century ago by worried civic leaders in order to get the children off the streets, which were becoming unsafe as play spaces. With gradually increasing speed of travel and an increasing rate of accidents to children in the streets, the degree of danger is more and more apparent. The demand that there be provided opportunities and spaces for children and youth to play comes from the recognition of the dearth of natural resources for play and adventure. Going to the movies, hanging around the drugstore, talking small talk, listening to the radio, reading, or just walking around, may constitute the major recreational pursuits of large numbers of teen-age youth who haven't developed other interests and don't know what to do. If lack of funds, of ingenuity, and of facilities limit a youth's participation in these things, ennui and boredom may engulf him and his spare time may really be "time on his hands."

The city offers the youth a fair range of choices for his leisure-time activities, but very often the less desirable ones are much more accessible to him than more desirable ones. Many cities provide only fragments of a wholesome, well-rounded recreation program for youth, and leave it to commercial entrepreneurs, to fringe elements in the amusement world, and sometimes to the underworld, to make available a wide range of poor and tawdry recreations. Some communities make only feeble and futile efforts at protective legislation and effective law enforcement to repress and regulate them.

Although the pattern varies considerably from city to city, in general there are relatively better services and facilities offered to the relatively more favored groups in the newer areas of the city than are offered to the more needy groups in the older and less well-off areas.

There are basic reasons for this difference. In the poorer areas live a lower economic and somewhat less well-educated population, with less political influence, fewer well-organized civic and community groups to demand service and provide volunteers to help, and fewer other advantages. Youth-serving recreation agencies, especially if they are under pressure to demonstrate their value to the public in terms of the numbers they serve, tend to put their available funds and personnel into those areas where clubs, groups, and organized activities can be promoted readily and where the cost of service is less per child.

Another reason is that agency administrators and personnel, not able or willing to undertake the more difficult tasks of building programs in underprivileged neighborhoods with fewer leadership resources of their own, often choose instead to operate "where the going is easier." Waltz found that the cost of services per child for voluntary agencies is three or four times greater in the poorer areas of a community because of the greater difficulty in obtaining, training, and keeping volunteer workers, the increased professional staff supervision required, and the need to maintain more building-centered programs.[14]

When among the members of these less well-served neighborhoods are large concentrations of foreign-born or minority cultural groups who in other respects may be discriminated against, patterns of discrimination and unequal treatment of groups sometimes carry over into recreation services. Segregated facilities of an inferior quality sometimes are constructed, but more generally in these older areas, with their poor future as residence areas, with the likelihood of the invasion of industrial or commercial use, recreation agencies both public and private hesitate to make heavy investments. The tendency is to follow a pattern of neglect and minimal services.

Minority groups tend to get more than their share of poor housing, economic and social disadvantage, and neglect, in important areas of basic services such as sanitation. Often, on the other hand, they receive a great deal of police service to deal with high delinquency and crime rates. And imposed on them are corrupting and degrading amusements that their more influential and active neighbors would

[14] Heny Waltz, unpublished study of relative costs of voluntary agency services by areas of social need in Los Angeles (The Welfare Planning Council of Metropolitan Los Angeles, 1947).

never permit to exist in the "better neighborhoods." For recreation to avoid this inequity in its services, the agencies must not only accept the professional commitment and social responsibility for providing services in relation to need, but they must gain the power and ability to make good on that commitment.

Cities are growing in number and size, with subcommunities differentiated economically and socially, with a high degree of congestion and critical slum conditions in some central areas, and with magnified problems of space, facilities, and opportunities for recreation in all areas.

SUBURBIA

The years since World War II, although marked principally by the mass movement of people to large metropolitan areas, have also been witness to population regrouping within metropolitan areas themselves. In the previous section, it was pointed out that as a city grows it tends to move outward and its population flows toward the edges. The name given to this process is *suburbanization.*

> Out toward the fringes and margins of cities comes a region where they [cities] begin to be less themselves than they are at the center, a place where the city looks countryward. No sharp boundary line defines it; there is rather a gradual tapering off from the urban type of civilization toward the rural type. It is the city thinned out.[15]

During the past forty years, the lure of the suburbs has replaced the lure of the city as a prime mover of America's population. Some 25 per cent of the people now live in suburbs, and this figure continues to increase. If there is such a thing as a typical middle-class American, the chances are that he lives in the suburb. The product of the automobile, mobility, and the five-day week, the suburbs began primarily as bedroom communities in which men slept, then went elsewhere to work and to engage in institutional life, leaving the wife and children to be absorbed in the small community whirl of PTA, bridge clubs, and neighborly gossip. Now we find that life in the suburb community increasingly absorbs the attention of the men as well as the women

---

[15] Harlan Paul Douglass, *The Suburban Trend* (New York: The Century Company, 1925), p. 3.

and children, and a cluster of social and civic centers within the suburb itself have sprung up—institutions found previously only in the larger complex of the city. Schools, churches, civic groups, recreation centers, and the like have mushroomed along with other services (shopping centers, government, and now even industry) to bring within the purview of the suburb community a full range of services and opportunities that make travel anywhere unnecessary except to work.

Recreation Facilities in Suburban Area

American idealization of the small self-governing community is believed by many to be the basis for much of suburban migration. And while it is true that suburbs tend to assume a uniformity of character and, as Riesman points out, a homogeneity of taste through decentralization of leisure, with the home serving as neighborhood center and the whole family acting as a force to perpetuate this homogeneity,[16] still "suburbia" is firmly ingrained in the American pattern. There is further evidence that even suburban government is managing

[16] David Riesman, "The Suburban Dislocation," *Metropolis in Ferment,* The Annals of the American Academy of Political and Social Science, Vol. 314 (November 1957), pp. 123-146.

to survive the political machinery with which it is straddled. Not cultural lag alone, but also contemporary social reality have led the suburbs to cling to their own autonomy.

> [S]mall governments . . . remain . . . to cling to the ideal of the republic in miniature, and to prevent the encroachment of the metropolis. Suburbia is brave to the point of rashness in its struggle for existence: it is resourceful, aggressive and so far successful.[17]

Population statistics for 1960 documented the shift toward increasing suburbanization. From 1950, of the fifteen largest cities in America, ten lost in actual city population, while their metropolitan areas all increased significantly. New York, Chicago, Philadelphia, Detroit, Baltimore, St. Louis, San Francisco, Boston, Cleveland, and Washington, D.C., exhibit this trend.

To some, all that glitters in the suburban sun is not gold. And to generalize too much from the studies available concerning suburban life is hazardous. As Riesman points out, we know too little about settled suburbs, and almost nothing about the suburbs of some of the newer smaller cities. The evidence of the presence of urban elements in rural areas and vice versa, and of suburban styles in many cities and urban ones in many suburbs, implies that an urban fringe is growing which is neither country, nor city, nor quite bedroom suburb, and leads Riesman to conclude, "The differences which divide Americans today depend less and less on where one lives, what one does, or who one is in terms of lineage, but more and more it depends on style and social character." [18]

In relating suburbanization to leisure, Riesman expresses concern for the homogeneity in people's reactions to decentralization of leisure (leading to reduction of specialized differentiations in leisure activities). He also is disturbed over the uneven distribution of leisure found in the typical suburb among the professions and service trades and the next-door neighbors of equal income, but far easier schedules, who do not have to bring work home at night. Within the ranks of the professional, management, and service classes are found the people with the least leisure time, who are the real victims of the leisure age.

---

[17] Robert C. Wood, *Suburbia: Its People and Their Politics* (Boston: Houghton Mifflin Company, 1959), pp. 254-255.

[18] Riesman, "The Suburban Dislocation," p. 124.

All life has both positive and negative aspects, and so it is with suburban life. The conformity imposed by tract homes and homogeneity of standards and interests, the highly organized but still somewhat aimless social life, the tensions created through commuting, indicate a less than rosy hue in suburban life, which the recreation worker and organized recreation services must consider in their efforts.

Suburban development in modern cities has produced a particular kind of middle-class culture and community life, with its conformity, commuting, and lessening contact with the wider community.

URBAN PLANNING

The problems of urbanization have not gone unnoticed or untouched. There have emerged the increasingly important roles of regional, metropolitan, and city master planners, who, with social scientists, have brought into play a philosophy and a vision designed to correct the picture so aptly described by Victor Gruen:

> Although we are the richest nation with the highest individual living standard, we have one of the lowest public living standards of Western nations. Our cities are littered with ugliness and choked with automobiles. Our parks, schools, museums, municipal buildings, and transportation systems are unattractive and poorly maintained. Our urban areas sprawl, constantly swallowing up agricultural land and ignoring the need to preserve the countryside.[19]

Evidence of urban planning and replanning is seen in the vast urban renewal program that is "face-lifting" many metropolitan and city areas today. Creation of an Office of Urban Affairs at the federal level to assist in the efforts to avoid metropolitan sprawl, reduce density, and control the area covered by people has been proposed.

The recapturing of open space is a vital and integral part of the urban renewal concept. As Wilfred Owen puts it: "In the great urban renewal efforts that have taken place during the past two decades and in the planning of new suburban growth, we have applied these lessons fairly well. We know now that parks and open spaces are needed for

---

[19] Victor Gruen, article in *Life,* Vol. 47, No. 26 (December 28, 1959), p. 172.

recreation and beauty and to make residential areas in densely populated areas more livable."[20] This author goes on to describe how, through modern technology, urban renewal can proceed at an orderly, systematic rate through the revival of mass transit systems, the role of aviation, staggering hours of work and sound community planning designed to reorganize urban areas into compact pedestrian islands that separate the areas where people live and work from traffic and transportation. As Gruen says:

> The growth of cities will not be an evil if we make them once again a pleasant place to stroll, eat, shop, sightsee, enjoy cultural amenities and live. Only then will our leisure time be worth living. Otherwise we will spend our precious hard earned leisure within our own four walls, cut off from society by the foes we have created: murderous traffic, smog, disorder, blight and ugliness. We will be trapped in our suburban or city homes, all dressed up with no place to go.[21]

Housing, of course, is a crucial issue and will continue to be so as population and urbanization increase. Architects agree, however, that with proper planning and imaginative building, run-down apartments and tenements can be replaced with modern mass housing designed to build into daily living the leisure concept of increased space and privacy of play areas in a park atmosphere.[22] Even the family home on the small suburban parcel of land would be replaced, freeing the householder from the chores of "do-it-yourself" home upkeep and providing more time for more creative hobbies and cultural activities.

Margaret Mead takes the view that technological change may take away from the cities of the future all of the functions once made necessary by war, poor communications, and the need to concentrate populations for production and consumption.[23] The improvement of communication through radio, telephone and electronics, the decentralization of goods and services, and improved mobility, render unnecessary the immediate presence of most of the factors that led

---

[20] W. Owen, "Transportation," *Metropolis in Ferment,* The Annals, p. 34.

[21] Gruen, *Life,* p. 172.

[22] For the architect's conception of this, see Ballard's design of the "Tower in the Park" in *Life* (December 28, 1959), pp. 168-169.

[23] M. Mead, "Values for Urban Living," *Metropolis in Ferment,* The Annals, pp. 10-14.

originally to the creation of community life. Probably the one exception is of interest to the student of leisure and recreation. As Mead points out, the unique functions of cities will remain that of providing contact among many kinds of people, and she envisions the city of the future becoming a center for culture, thought, knowledge, communication, and relationships through conferences between people in an informal and creative environment.

Megalopolis—Urban Sprawl

IMPLICATIONS FOR LEISURE AND RECREATION

In the final analysis, in discussing the community and its needs, one ultimately arrives at the individuals in that community and their needs. Man created his institutions in his efforts to satisfy his needs, and the foregoing analysis highlights some of the needs of individuals and how some institutions in communities are mobilizing to meet these needs, whether they be rural, suburban, urban, or metropolitan. Each of these institutions has its own unique set of demands for space, services, and resources. Competition for them is inevitable. In light of the forces at work, however, American society can ill afford to dissipate resources and energy in competition at the social institutional level that is destructive or limiting to the people themselves. To do so negates the very reason why institutions—and democracy itself—exist. We are in urgent need of the new and human science that Romney identifies as *social conservation,* a science rooted in the needs of people.[24]

Assuming that the individual's goal of pursuit of happiness lies at the heart of all of his efforts and energy, then certainly leisure life and the opportunity to fulfill and to meet one's needs, to achieve leisure through the recreative use of one's leisure time is most important. And every trend suggests that leisure and recreation must secure their fair share of the planning and resources necessary, particularly if we expect to reach the goal of freedom of opportunity for the individual to achieve leisure, regardless of age, sex, occupation, race, state of health, social class, or community.

For these reasons it becomes imperative that recreation leaders assess their communities and their resources for leisure and recreation. When we think of total community need, we must be aware of who contributes to this need, who are the people to be served, what is needed, and what is the best way in which social action can proceed. This type of thinking and planning requires leadership of the highest nature and at many levels.

Fortunately for recreation there is evidence that such leadership is emerging and that resource analysis and planning is underway. At the federal level the mobilization and the analysis of resources has been carried forward by the National Outdoor Recreation Resources Review Commission, under the chairmanship of Laurance S. Rockefeller. This commission, created by act of Congress in 1958, devoted three years to comprehensive analysis of the outdoor resources in America and recommendations for priorities in land acquisition and development for the future. "Mission 66" of the National Park Service and "Operation Outdoors" of the National Forest Service, to be discussed in Chapter 12, are examples of how other federal agencies have concerned themselves with long-range planning of recreation resources under their control.

At the state level of government there are many other examples of planning and thinking that reflect the increasing recognition of the

---

[24] Henry Romney, "A New and Human Science," *Sports Illustrated,* Parts I and II (March 28 and April 4, 1960).

importance of leisure and recreation needs and resources, the California Public Outdoor Recreation Plan being just one example.[25] The development of the concept of flexible space and area standards to meet local needs and account for varying combinations of geographic, economic, and social factors in communities is another.

At the metropolitan and local community level, recreation agencies throughout the country have been concerned with and involved in community studies and reorganization of services for many years. Beginning with a background and tradition established in the thirties by the Works Progress Administration, and continued into the forties with pioneer projects in Boston, Chicago, and Baltimore, blueprints and models such as the recreation district have developed to meet leisure and recreation needs. These blueprints and new ways of organizing and doing things undergird the premise that different kinds of services are needed in different kinds of communities, and community needs may vary widely in any given community by the nature of the subcommunities that exist within the larger grouping. Such factors as specific age, levels of income, rent and extent of home ownership, density of population, and incidence of delinquency, are significant in planning services not only for youth, but for all ages, reflecting social rank and degree of urbanization.[26] Los Angeles, using these factors within a metropolitan complex, derived nine area types or subcommunities, the classification of which was extremely useful in planning recreation services to meet community needs. The nine area types developed were (1) most advantaged suburbs, (2) most advantaged residential communities, (3) most advantaged apartment house areas, (4) moderately advantaged suburbs, (5) moderately advantaged natural suburbs, (6) moderately advantaged dwelling areas, (7) least advantaged rural areas, (8) least advantaged industrial communities, and (9) least advantaged rooming house and apartment areas. The scale in terms of degree of urbanization and rank is apparent in the terminology used. There are other examples, but this one indicates how differentiating a community and understanding the elements within the subcommunities identified can be useful in planning leisure and recreation opportunities.

In each one of the subcommunities identified, there are different

---

[25] *California Public Outdoor Recreation Plan.*

[26] See *Guides for Planning of Leisure Time Services,* Welfare Planning Council of Los Angeles Region (January 1958).

patterns of leisure-time behavior and need for recreation services that suggest how community services in the form of agencies, facilities, leadership, and programs should be mobilized to meet these needs. For example, in least advantaged areas are frequently found the groups of youth who are "hard to reach" and who tend therefore to be served less than other groups. Some of these are individual youths whose inability to adjust to the normal program, whose shyness, aggressiveness, or rejected status in the group, keeps them from participating in programs. But the key groups are those identified as "juvenile delinquent gangs," whose disruptive and destructive group behavior brings them to the attention of police and the court. These gangs, with their fights, sex delinquencies, stealing, truancy, and other offenses, have constituted a group out of reach of normal recreation.

Frequently the question arises: "Can recreation reach these groups?" One answer lies in specialized programs of intensive recreational and group work services, in which specially trained workers work directly with such gangs and through intensive and individual guidance and well-planned group recreation programs help them to enjoy normal satisfactions and stop, or at least reduce, their antisocial behavior. A second and more long-range answer lies in the development of urban recreation programs in general, to provide large proportions of youth with the values of well-operated public and voluntary programs, to encourage larger groups to participate in these programs, and thus reduce or prevent the neglect that in part has resulted in youth heading off for unsupervised leisure-time activities, out of which delinquency often develops.

In the final analysis, the yardstick that must be applied to life is how human beings are living and the kind of environment created, whether it be for work or play. At the very center of all of man's efforts, be they communal or individual, should be man's own dignity and his own welfare. Against this yardstick, no community will be any better than the leisure and recreation it affords, nor will leisure and recreation be any better than the degree to which it contributes to this welfare.

The complexity and magnitude of the problems of urban life have resulted in efforts to renew urban community life, to correct problems of unplanned sprawling metropolitanism, and to provide for basic community services, including housing, schools, open spaces, and recreation.

Questions for Study and Discussion

1. *Recreation may be identified with what significant aspects of present population growth at both community and national levels?*
2. *What differences exist between rural life in the nineteenth and twentieth centuries? Explore the relationships between these differences and the differences that were expressed concurrently in recreation. What values have been gained or lost for rural life and rural recreation in this change?*
3. *Assuming the validity of the estimate of the population theorists that the population of the United States will reach 250 million persons, mainly concentrated in huge urban centers, what will be the effect on recreation and what problems will be encountered in recreation? Suggest some means of meeting these problems.*
4. *Project a doubling of population in a community. In what ways would you as a recreation planner deal with the recreation problems this growth would create, in order to provide for an expanded and enriched recreation program in the community?*
5. *What are America's choices with respect to the increasing competition for open spaces among agriculture, lumbering, industry, residence, and recreation? What does this mean for population policy? Recreation policy?*

Selected Readings

The Editors of *Fortune, The Exploding Metropolis* (Garden City, New York: Doubleday and Company, 1958).

Metropolis in Ferment, Annals of the American Academy of Political and Social Science, Vol. 314 (November 1957).

Park, R. E., E. W. Burgess, and R. D. McKenzie, *The City* (Chicago: University of Chicago Press, 1925).

Riemer, Svend, *The Modern City: An Introduction to Urban Sociology* (Englewood Cliffs, N.J.: Prentice-Hall, Inc., 1952).

9

RECREATION AND THE INSTITUTIONS OF FAMILY, EDUCATION, CHURCH, HEALTH, AND WELFARE

An understanding of the significance of leisure and recreation in the life of the individual human being involves an understanding of his life and growth as a social being. It requires understanding the means by which he is influenced and by which his life is shaped. The individual human being, his basic nature and personality, and his attitudes, habits, and values are a product of his associations with other human beings in interaction with his growth processes.

Probably the most influential associations are those with his family, the basic social institution for the nurture and education of the child, and the one that provides for the individual the means for meeting basic needs. The relationship between an individual's leisure values and his family values is close and intimate. Family recreational life is of great significance in educating the young members toward certain expectations and values of their own in respect to recreation.

Then as a child grows up his contacts with his environment increase in scope. He comes into contact with and under the influence of institutions other than his family, which provide the framework of the society in which he lives. The first institution, next to the family, that influences him deeply in his formative years is education. Education in American society is a comprehensive and pervasive influence, with great significance in the whole life of the child. From kindergarten age on, for ten or twenty years, the child's primary task in life is to go to school and learn—to "get an education." In the leisure age this task involves getting an education for leisure as well, and the interaction of the education institution and the leisure institution is an important part of our foundation study.

As the individual's experiences broaden further and as he grows older, he comes into contact with other institutions that are influential in his life. The government, religion and the church, medicine and health, and the welfare institution are recognized as other major social institutions, which along with the recreation institution are part of the complex organization we call *society*.

This chapter studies these social institutions and their interaction as social forces, with the social forces related to institutionalized recreational activities and organizations. From this study comes foundation knowledge about the dynamics of the relationships within which recreation functions in our modern age.

CHANGING FAMILY LIFE

Family life is undergoing important changes under the impact of modern times. The family is giving up a number of its earlier functions. One of these functions is education, which after the infant years is removed from the home and given each day in the school. Another is economic production, which in earlier eras was (and still is in the farm family) centered in the family, but which in modern industrial communities is removed to the factory, shop, or office.

The family still has very important functions, some of them centering around childbearing and rearing, and a central one being recreation. The home has been called "the cradle of personality." The baby is born as a highly receptive person, not with his feelings and ideas about things already there, but ready and eager to learn. Parents are the most important persons in his life, and the ones who give him very basic and early learnings. From a warm, loving, cooperative, and playful family life the child learns that people are friendly, happy, generous, and dependable. From a family life that is cold, conflicted, unplayful, and neglectful, the child reacts with distrust, fear, and hostility toward people and unhappy feelings about himself.

Of course, many factors and forces outside the family influence the child, especially later on. But the child's family experience is primary and central. How the mother, father, and children get along together, have fun with each other, trust and love each other, will have a fundamental influence on the growth of the child, and, of course, on the happiness and contentment of the parents. Of the total experiences considered to be essential to the sound emotional development of the child, the primary one is believed to be the warm, intimate, steady, affectionate relationship with the parents. The child deprived of this relationship tends to suffer from emotional and intellectual retardation, and sometimes suffers lasting psychic damage.

Satisfying and stable patterns of family life, and a wholesome family environment, contribute to each family member important elements of a mentally and emotionally healthy experience and the basis for normal growth and development. Recreation in the family can contribute actively to this wholesome environment, as well as contribute basic values such as affectional response and joyful group activities to the family members, including the growing child. The problem in modern American family life is that profound and disturbing changes have taken place in the institution of the family which have upset the traditional family life and have required tremendous and upsetting adjustment.

Woman's Role

One of these changes is the position of women. In modern times a group of some twenty million women are working, approximately a third of the labor force. About five out of ten adult women of working age and about a third of all married women are working, many millions of them mothers. One writer points out that there are nearly 7.5 million women in the labor force with children under 18; three million have children under 12.[1]

---

[1] Georgie Anne Geyer, article in the *Chicago Daily News* (January 30, 1961), p. 21.

The number of women working is the result of several conditions: the greater freedom for women to work and improve their status, economic or otherwise; the lessened load of child care as schools, recreation agencies, and other agencies expand their functions; the economic pressure on millions of families requiring women to work to establish or maintain the level of family living; the increase in family disorganization from divorce and desertion requiring women to seek employment, whether children are neglected or not; the active recruitment of women for millions of jobs, both traditional and new ones, because of their proved ability, their willingness to work for lower pay, and other reasons.

The relative freedom of women to work and support themselves has loosened the ties of economic dependence that often tied them to unhappy marriages in earlier eras. This is one reason for the significant increases in the American divorce rate in recent years. Two wage earners in a family also provide increased family income with which food, clothing, shelter, and recreation can be purchased. There is often increased self-respect of the woman, part of the self-fulfillment that makes her a better wife and mother.

There are important problems affecting the family, problems relating to the complex of new dynamic forces at work in family life and to new disorganizing factors. One of these is concerned with the objective conditions of life within which the family must survive. The crowded conditions of urban living, the small flat or home with its congestion and lack of privacy, the deteriorated and slum character of countless dwellings, the inability to spread out—these factors are destructive to family relationships, marital morale, and one of the very central functions of the family, the raising of children to be wholesome and creative citizens of a vital community.

A national conference on prevention and control of juvenile delinquency called by the Attorney General of the United States had this to say about economic needs:

> *It is hard to be poor and good.* Many, many boys and girls have grown into fine men and women in homes that have known real poverty. They have had other things in their family life that made up for the poverty. But there is no question that it is hard to be poor and stay out of trouble. That is the great economic problem of the community and the Nation. . . . [I]t takes money to get good food and raise healthy

> boys and girls; to live in a decent house, to buy suitable clothes, to go to the movies occasionally, or to the beach together; to give a growing child even a small allowance so that he can hold up his head among his fellows. It takes money to buy the coal and pay the doctor. . . . [F]amilies who live always on the edge of debt are apt to be harassed, irritable, and often unreasonable with their children.[2]

But the crux of the matter, the real dilemma facing modern married couples, is whether to pioneer in the concept of equalitarian marriage or to try to live within the traditional inequalitarian framework and make the best of it. When the wife accepts the role of dependent and lesser person, she establishes relations between herself and her husband in which they stand to lose the deepest values of equal sharing and cooperation and instead countenance a situation in which exploitation and inferiority lead to the destruction of the basic and precious values of real shared love, and to a deterioration of the marital relationship.

On the other hand, the wife may fight for a more significant social role and an equal relationship in the marriage. The husband after some struggle may be willing to give up the dubious satisfactions of being a dominating "head of the house" to attain the infinitely deeper and more satisfying companionship and affectional mutuality upon which physical and emotional fulfillment and self-realization are based. There are many married couples who are striving to implement this equalitarian concept, seeking out an adjustment to the realities of marital life together, based upon deep and sensitive understanding of each other's needs and proper social and sexual roles, and a deeper sharing of the profound happiness of their mutual life together.

This might be formulated as an ideal toward which modern married people could work. Within such a concept of a strengthened marital relationship, children might be reared with security, steady affection, and relaxed and thoughtful attention to their developmental needs by understanding parents who are comfortable and happy with each other and similarly happy with their children.

---

[2] National Conference on Prevention and Control of Juvenile Delinquency, *Report on Home Responsibility* (Washington, D.C.: United States Government Printing Office, 1947), pp. 20-21.

But the disorganization and confusion in American family life is the other side of this picture, as millions of families struggle to meet the serious problems of surviving in changing and difficult conditions, with millions of women working, a million men in military service, disturbing social and economic problems upsetting family and personal life, and a deep conflict continuing between traditional male-dominated family life and the struggle for more equal rights for women.

Family Unity

Yet the staying power of the American family is very formidable, and the capacity of the family to link together parents and children to fulfill its essential social functions and maintain family unity is strong. One might identify three elements in family unity that function with cohesive power to link the family together in a harmonious relationship, able to deal successfully with both internal and external disorganizing pressures. One of these elements is unity of objectives, in which values and attitudes in relation to common objectives and joint activities are similarly defined by family members. A second element is unity of personal ambitions, harmony between desires and personal ideas of life organization, an understanding and sympathy for each other's desires, and a willingness to subordinate one's own ambitions on many occasions to the welfare of the family as a whole. A third element is unity of interests, the possession of many similar avocational, recreational, educational, cultural, and religious interests, which provide the basis for pleasure together, for mutual understanding, and for reciprocity in several areas of life.

Underlying these important matters of relationship are the demands and elements in self-fulfillment, which in some way influence each individual in our society. One of these demands is that children shall be born and raised and that the home shall be the center of this process. The home is recognized as the "cradle of values," the essential beginning place for the child's development of his attitudes toward life, toward himself and others, and toward life's important experiences. Here he learns many leisure-time skills and, more important, develops many leisure-time interests. Here is where his health level, through years of nutrition and health care by his parents, is fairly definitely established.

For these reasons, as well as for reasons of family relationships, the family and the strength and vitality of its life are important considerations for recreation, which assumes as one of its key functions the strengthening of family life.

Recreation and education for leisure are functions of the modern family, and are influenced by the changes in modern family life and its new requirements. In some situations, tensions, conflicts, and deprivation override the unifying forces, and disorganization and disharmony enter in.

Family Disorganization

Under the pressure of external forces, without the constantly broadening base of unifying factors, with discouragement, low morale, and nonharmonious relationships characterizing day-by-day life, family life can deteriorate, bonds will loosen, and disorganization can become more chronic and permanent. It is possible, and usually the case, that a family under such conditions will continue to exist even though it has lost some of the vitality of the family relationship and cannot meet important needs under such conditions.

The disorganized family may experience the loss and disappearance of common objectives; the cessation of cooperative effort; the withholding of mutual services and kindly, giving acts; the emergence of antagonistic or indifferent emotional attitudes; the increase in antagonistic verbal exchanges; sometimes what seems to be irreversible hostility and actual disruption; or the end of the relationship through desertion, divorce, or other means. Primary psychological and personality tensions, or a clash between temperaments, may be deeply irritating and often take on violent forms. They may clash under some conditions and eternally irritate and try the patience and good will of one or both parties. Argument, anger, and resentment flare up.

A final tension area to mention is the area of affection and sex relations. Under our highly romantic ideology of marriage, any lessening of the keen ardor and responsiveness of the courtship or honeymoon period may create dissatisfaction, anxiety, and anger. Anything that disturbs the sympathy and love between husband and wife can create concern and worry. Then, in circular fashion, affectional and sexual incompatibility, temporary or more long-lasting, can be the result. An adequate and happy affectional-sexual adjustment in marriage is a central and highly important component of total marital success. Because of its nature it tends to be deeply affected by other positive and negative forces in the marriage. Other tensions and anxieties, emotionally disturbing incidents, nagging misunderstandings and incompatibilities, and a host of other facts, each interacting on the others, can assail the marital relationship in vulnerable areas. If it is in a weakened state it can deteriorate and in the process disturb all the other aspects of the relationship.

Thus family life can exist, for a couple or for parents and children, on many different levels. Certainly many families exist, and many married couples make a fairly satisfactory adjustment, on the basis of a pleasing companionship, a sympathetic understanding, and a satisfying affectional life. For others, however, pressures, tensions, unhappiness, and despair bring one or both of the partners to the belief that it is impossible to go on trying. This is the state of real disorganization. Some families in this condition yet continue to hold together for reasons of religion, for appearances, or for the sake of the children, or because one member will not countenance breakup, and so on. But for others, the marriage is broken up, either by desertion or divorce—the final collapse of the marital relation.

Divorce legally (and desertion illegally) dissolves the marriage relationship. There are several million families in the United States with one of the partners missing, by virtue of divorce or desertion. There are, in addition, a considerable number where death of one member has left the other a widow or widower. Some estimates would indicate that children were involved in a third to a half of these cases.

This country has one of the highest divorce rates in the world, as an estimated one out of five marriages winds up in divorce courts. The total number of children involved is a national tragedy, perhaps up to five million children (under 18) in this country growing up under handicapping conditions.

The student of recreation ends up with the disquieting recognition that several million American families are in fact broken. There are at least a million children of broken homes being cared for in children's institutions and foster homes and by the federal government-supported program of aid to dependent children. This indicates one effect of family collapse on the welfare of the children. Add to these millions of children living with one parent only and deprived of the opportunity to grow up in a family with love and care and balanced attention from both parents. Add to this problem the burdens of loneliness, incompleteness, and isolation that oppress many millions of adults whose marriages have broken up. One then gets a bleak picture of marriage and family life for many millions of Americans for whom family life is incomplete, and who struggle to establish an adequate life within the wreckage of a collapsed marriage and a broken home. This information leads us to the following conclusion:

The modern American family is undergoing great changes, with a newly emerging equalitarian concept of marriage, and severe disorganization accompanying the breakdown of traditional family relationships under the impact of modern economic, social, and community conditions and forces.

RECREATION AS A FORCE IN FAMILY LIFE

The effects of this situation on recreation are profound. One effect is the demand placed on recreation and recreational organizations to soften somehow the crushing blows on the individual of breakdown in his family. It is hoped that somehow recreation and recreation relationships can partly take the place of other influences and relationships, for example, in a child's life, to sustain him and to further his healthy growth.

Recreation leaders strongly believe that recreation can be a positive force in strengthening family life. It can give family members common goals and common pleasurable experiences, and these will strengthen the bonds of family unity.

The tremendous forces, positive and negative, shaping modern family life are in some ways seemingly beyond the influence of recreational forces in the society. Recreation itself is influenced by some of these forces, and becomes something different from what it was before in the life of the family. One example is modern television, which, as we have already noted, has grown to be a tremendous recreational resource for families. Television has been shaped primarily by economic forces into a gigantic mass recreational medium reflecting the wishes of its business owners to gain the greatest profits from its operation, at what cost in recreational and cultural values it is possible only to guess. Fashioned, as one sharply critical observer, Turner, has said, as an instrument of amusement based upon the commercial exploitation of the most crass and obscene impulses in man, it in turn becomes a force stimulating such impulses, particularly in children, for whom it becomes an important educational force. He argues that the great TV networks operate on the single premise of whether the show sells, and they sell

> ... by appealing to the lowest basic instincts of the public.... Some of the shows ... are obscenities, crimes against the little children who watch them.... They corrupt. They are insulting.... I am afraid we will begin reflecting what is drummed into our senses night after night—shoot your enemy; insult your parents; play your trivial little games; buy, buy, buy; drive a convertible; sip a cocktail; strike out at whoever gets in your way; stand by while a strong man solves our problems. Great little invention, television, comes right into our living rooms.[3]

Such criticisms raise the important question of whether modern recreation contributes more to family disorganization than to family organization. There are certain negative forces at work in the modern recreational life of the family. There is little doubt that for many families recreation is a disorganizing rather than a strengthening force. At least for many urban families recreation by and for the whole family is seldom found. Elliott and Merrill say on this subject,

> Seldom does the urban family actively partake of any recreational event as a unit.... The recreational function of the family has been assumed by other agencies.... Many families, in fact, make no effort to provide recreation for children in the home. In the first place, there is no room for it. In the second place, the parents are too busy or tired. In the third place, the attraction of commercial recreation is too strong. ... Recreation in the old-fashioned sense of creating one's own good times through games, music, and conversation is becoming virtually a lost art for many city families.[4]

This is a pretty grim view. It is undeniable that some modern urban commercial recreation lends itself to a pattern of individual family members recreating by themselves. Many public and voluntary agencies' programs are designed in this way also. The movies are passive and likely to have little effect in bringing a family together. Taverns and bars, favorite recreation places for adults, usually and

---

[3] Terry Turner, "TV News," *Chicago Daily News* (February 4, 1961), pp. 3-4.

[4] Mabel A. Elliott and Francis E. Merrill, *Social Disorganization,* Third edition (New York: Harper & Row, Inc., 1950), p. 356.

properly are barred to children. Were they not, they could still hardly be recommended as family recreation centers. Television has tended to keep family members home more than before, but it does not stimulate active family playfulness together. Drinking in the home often is a source not of unity but of disunity, embarrassment, tension, and argument. The picture could be enlarged.

The Family at Play

But this is not the main picture either, by any means, for recreation can be and is a positive force in family life. The Neumeyers say,

> The home was one of the first institutions around which play and recreation activities were organized. It is still the center of much enjoyment, and many hours of leisure are spent at home. Spontaneous play, whether in the home or outside, is one of the easiest forms of social intercourse. Through genuine and wholehearted participation in home play activities, parents and children come to know each other better and lay a

> foundation for a happy relationship, which is the greatest protection against future stress.[5]

This is the positive view that recreationists in general take of family recreation—that it has a great potential for recreational satisfactions to members, and, properly and thoughtfully developed by the members and aided by outside recreational groups on many occasions, it can be a powerful and dynamic force for family organization and happiness.

THE HOME AS RECREATION CENTER

The home is the child's first and natural place for play. City dwellings are often badly planned for play activities, even though they are needed for that purpose, and some family planning for this is highly desirable. There have been many efforts to help families to create in the backyard and the dwelling some facilities for play, to make the home recreationally livable. But still for many millions of children the sidewalk, the front stoop, the alley, or the street is the playground, despite the many dangers to life, limb, and morale. With planning, a few square feet of outdoor yard space can provide the little child with a sandbox, swings, things to climb on, or kiddie cars. A lawn sprinkler converts to a great shower; a table provides a place to paint, crayon, make things out of clay, and so on. As the children grow up some of these things can be given to the neighbors and replaced with a doll house, a playhouse, bird houses, and window boxes or garden plots; a space may be needed for dogs, cats, mice, hamsters, birds, budgies, bugs, or bunnies; the side of the garage can become a ball-bouncing place; a basketball backboard and hoop can be put up.

In many parts of the country outdoor fireplaces and barbecue pits have become highly popular recreation facilities. Suburban subdivision promoters advertise the "recreation room" as an important part of the split-level ranch house being sold to eager buyers. We already have noted the boom in home swimming pools in recent years.

---

[5] Martin H. Neumeyer and Esther S. Neumeyer, *Leisure and Recreation: A Study of Leisure and Recreation in Their Sociological Aspects,* Third edition (New York: The Ronald Press Company, 1958), p. 410. Copyright 1958 The Ronald Press Company.

There is a considerable market as well for commercially produced backyard playground apparatus, including swings, jungle gyms, horizontal ladders, flying rings, and so on. Home craftsmen can copy some of these without too much difficulty. These and other developments suggest the growing awareness of the American family of the possibilities for making the home an important place for the play and recreation not only of children but of the entire family.

The home is important as a music center, with the record player and record collections providing much satisfaction to family members. It is important as a reading center when books are purchased to provide children and adults with hours of individual or group pleasure. Pictures on the wall, art objects around the house, color combinations and home decoration, and workbenches, easels, and sketching materials can make the home an art center.

In selecting toys, materials, and activities, the family has an important educational function to perform in helping children to grow up into wholesome adulthood. One problem in these years in which so much attention is devoted to war is to help children to understand about war and about peace. Many modern toys are warlike toys, and, stimulated by adult talk, television, and movies, many children center their informal games around wars, battles, and killing. The National Recreation Association made this observation: "toy shops are full of soldiers, guns, and pistols. Why play at killing?" [6] The question is still pertinent.

The Attorney General's conference on juvenile delinquency makes a similar plea, pointing out that American parents

> . . . are bewildered or afraid . . . are deeply anxious about the future. . . . if we grown-ups do not learn to keep the world at peace everyone knows how terrible the future of our boys and girls will be. Today's adults have peculiarly urgent responsibilities as citizens, as members of their communities, to help create the kind of world in which their children may live at peace.[7]

---

[6] National Recreation Association, *Home Play* (New York: National Recreation Association, 1952), as quoted in Harold D. Meyer and Charles K. Brightbill, *Community Recreation: A Guide to Its Organization* (Englewood Cliffs, N.J.: Prentice-Hall, Inc., 1956), p. 220.

[7] National Conference on Prevention and Control of Juvenile Delinquency, *Report on Home Responsibility*, p. 13.

THE FAMILY AS RECREATION UNIT

More important to the welfare of the family, perhaps, than making use of the potential facilities available in the home is making use, as a family unit, of the greater potential of other recreation activities, which can bring rich satisfactions to the members of the family and act as a force binding them together in happiness and personal fulfillment. Meyer and Brightbill say:

> Every effort should be made to revitalize the family as a functional unit of recreation and to encourage newly organized families to establish definite patterns and practices of recreation as an essential part of family solidarity. . . . Any family recreation program depends upon participation by the entire family. . . . Every member of the family should be encouraged to use his imagination in suggesting activities which the entire family might enjoy.[8]

PLAYING TOGETHER

Recreation has one unique quality that the family can capture and turn to good use: the quality of being thoroughly enjoyable, making the participants happy, happy to be with each other, and content. To the powerful attractiveness of simple enjoyment can be added the pleasure of sharing the activities with loved ones, and helping them to enjoy them as well. The fun comes in doing things together, playing together, each member sharing in the pleasures. The occasions are endless: around the table at mealtimes, in games and conversations, while planning a trip, or just in simple camaraderie. Evenings offer opportunities to make things, play games, enjoy music, and converse.

Weekends, holidays, and vacation times are times to plan for. Projects can be worked out at home, in the yard or garden or house, that will be fun for all. The family can plan trips, picnics, hikes, bicycle rides, or any one of countless outdoor recreations, which take on new spice and pleasure because the family is getting to know itself better, and is gaining in morale and good spirit because of the fun of having fun with loved ones. Other recreations with friends, relatives, and neighbors add additional pleasures and are special occasions for

---

[8] Meyer and Brightbill, *Community Recreation,* pp. 209-210.

fellowship and happiness with an intimate group in which the family and family life is still the center.

Closeness and "togetherness" can be overdone. Wanting to "pal" with their children, parents sometimes reduce their own activities to the common denominator of their children's interests and thus sacrifice their own interests and impose themselves in areas where healthy growth requires some autonomy and freedom for the child. Particularly as children grow older and strive to enjoy independent recreations, the parents, with a rich tradition of play together, are well advised to happily let them seek new friends and new pleasures free from the family. The parents may then enjoy some independent adult life of their own, yet have many opportunities to come together on special occasions and enjoy again the old and comfortable family relationships.

Courtship and Marriage

It is important to mention the significance of recreation as a means of establishing a healthy relationship between young couples in the casual precourtship dating of teen-agers and young adults, and as a very important activity of the man and woman during courtship itself and during the engagement period. The fun-filled activities of this period are useful as a means of becoming better acquainted, exploring common interests, and developing a natural and wholesome relationship with each other, at whatever point of casual acquaintance or serious courtship the couple may be.

Very important also is the recreational life of the young married couple who are in the preliminary period of adjustment, who are finding out what important changes in attitude and in development of relationships are going to be required for their marriage to grow smoothly into the deep and fulfilling experience it can be at its best. The light touch of fun and happiness in pursuing together pleasurable activities may be of importance in this period, as well as throughout the whole of married life. Married couples must always know how to have fun together.

But for husband and wife there is available a vastly deeper play experience which has the most profound significance for their marriage. This experience is love life itself. Marital love is a matter of sharing equally and fully as much as possible of life's vast fund of experiences, of encouraging the fullest maturing and deepening of the interests and personalities of each, of building countless delightful and gratifying mutual activities and habits of behavior, little things that please one another and increase the joy of living together. It is a matter of drawing closer and closer together, of enjoying each other's fine qualities, of continuously enriching the physical and emotional and spiritual life of each through the other. This, of course, does not just happen. It requires conscious, serious, loving effort on the part of both persons. And it takes time. Yet love life, gently nourished, can gradually develop, it can last and grow through the years, enriching the lives of the couple and bringing comfort, contentment, and refreshing beauty to their entire life together.

Making love is the greatest, most beautiful form of play we know. In its purest, most wholesome form it is the uninhibited and enthusiastic sharing by husband and wife in the entrancing, fascinating, aesthetic games of sexual relations. When it is enjoyed without tensions, fears, exploitation, or self-seeking, with the combination of profound satisfaction of one's own passions and the loving effort to maximize the satisfaction and fulfillment of one's mate, it becomes emotionally, aesthetically, and spiritually the most creative of games.

Recreation may function as a positive influence toward family happiness and stability, with the home a potential center for family recreation and the family a vital recreation unit. The marital relationship itself offers potentially the important aesthetically fulfilling play experience of love life.

COMMUNITY RECREATION—INTEGRATING THE FAMILY OR SUBSTITUTING FOR IT

The recreationist, with his professional concern for contributing as fully as possible to the welfare of the individual, will play an important role in supporting family recreational activities in many ways. To a degree, he may be called upon for individual counseling in the area of family life and marital relations. While his opportunities and area of proper functioning may be rather limited, a basically wholesome and sound point of view, an understanding of a valid ethical and aesthetic foundation for marriage and family life, would be very important to him.

Community recreation can play two important roles in family life. One role is to support family recreation in a wide variety of ways, to the end that families will be better able to use their opportunities for recreation together, and will have better facilities, resources, and knowledge. The recreation agencies have the responsibility to create a play spirit and teach play activities that will carry back to the home and help to vitalize family life.

Several agencies publish materials on family recreation and make them available to families to stimulate their interest and increase their knowledge. Often classes and groups will be set up in which parents will learn about activities that can be introduced in the home and in the family circle. Special events of many kinds can be planned to bring the entire family to an agency, a center, or a playground. In addition to special events, there may also be regular family nights, and so on. Many agencies have carried on family camping programs.

Some public agencies and most voluntary agencies make active use of adult volunteers to lead children's groups. The principle of volunteer leadership underlies the work of the Camp Fire Girls, Scouts, Y's, and other agencies. But more important, particularly in the Boy Scouts, the parents are expected to join in very actively in much of the program. Den mothers, den fathers, troop committees, pack committees, special committees, and so on, involve millions of families in this important part of the recreational life of the child. It is true that this is particularly child-centered, but the parents can receive important rewards as they contribute to the program. Agencies with building-centered programs often devise them to provide the entire family with the opportunity to come together, to play with their own groups part of the time, to participate in some general activities, and in ways most pleasing to themselves to participate in a common program.

The recreation center sometimes plays a second and dramatically different role, however, in the case of the weak or disrupted family. For, as we know, in the midst of our communities are literally millions of members of families that are broken or at least "badly bent," and in these disturbed and unhappy families are those who need a different kind of help. There are confused, deprived children who seek elsewhere than from their families the satisfaction of their sometimes powerful and even distorted needs. These are vulnerable children who need extra care, extra protection, extra concern, so they may grow up with healthy personalities. Some recreation agencies provide a considerable amount of their services directly to members of these families, who need particular help in surviving and growing up within difficult home conditions.

When a child from such a home seeks out a recreation agency he is, in fact, seeking out a *substitute home.* The recreation agency becomes, in some ways, this substitute home; if permitted, he practically lives there. If it were open long enough and would permit it, he would be delighted actually to sleep on the floor. Whether the program is such that the child can attach himself to a small, organized, intimate group, or whether he must cling to fragments of informal groupings in a general program, he may try to gain the satisfactions from this group that he would normally find in some manner or measure in his family life. He transfers to the group the attitudes and expectations, the feelings of tension, dissatisfaction, and so on, that he customarily might associate with his family group.

This influences deeply his way of behaving with the group. In case the deprivations and confused feelings have created emotional and behavior problems with which it might be difficult for his family to deal constructively, then the group, and the professional person working with the group, might have a similar problem. In fact, the group becomes for him, again, a kind of *substitute family.* More important, the adult person working with the group, especially if he is willing to be placed in this position and to make himself "available" emotionally and otherwise to the child, becomes a *substitute parent,* or perhaps a substitute older sibling, if that has been the child's experience. This creates a very complex and possibly difficult situation for the playground or center worker, for it requires him to mobilize a high degree of relationship skill to help such a child or young person with this problem. This subject will concern us at a later point when we discuss the professional method.

We must ask the categorical question for now, however. Is it not a proper as well as an unavoidable function, in our present family-disrupted society, for the recreation center, the recreation group, and the recreation worker—within very significant limits of ability and resources—*to accept the roles of substitute home, family, and parent?* It is our belief, qualified by many considerations of the limitations and difficulties involved, that it is both unavoidable and proper.

Recreation may have an important function also for the adult member of the broken family. For example, the divorced mother has serious problems of loneliness, embarrassing attitudes of friends and neighbors, overburdening care of children while working to support and meet their physical and emotional dependence needs. Under these conditions, she is critically handicapped in efforts to seek out an adequate social and recreational life for herself and the opportunity possibly to remarry.

Guidance in finding and developing diversional and creative recreational pursuits would reduce her loneliness, help her to make new friends, and help her better to cope with the emotional needs of her children, and her own as well. Community recreation agencies begin to meet this type of need through such organizations as "Bachelor and Bachelorette" clubs, in which such mixed groups could get together for pleasurable and constructive recreation.

Many groups in this country are aware of the special significance of organized recreation programs for special groups deprived, for different reasons, of normal family life. Thousands of the members of the armed services constitute one such group. In this respect the government and many voluntary agencies invest vast resources in providing these men and women with social recreational experiences such as the USO, the Red Cross, and other military recreation programs. Recreation in prisons and youth correctional institutions, recreation in hospitals and other treatment centers, and like programs, have some of the same basic elements.

Community recreation has a twofold responsibility in family life: to support and strengthen family recreational life and unity, and to offer relationships with other persons and with the recreation worker in pleasurable activities providing desirable elements often missing in the family life.

EDUCATION FOR LEISURE

All human societies have formalized the education and training of the young in some fashion. In our country in modern years education is a force of great importance. It encourages and guides (and also limits) youth in their basic growth toward adulthood, toward being economically and politically productive and useful individuals in the community. The function of the school in educating for leisure, or in not educating for leisure, is crucial in the present movement toward an increasing understanding and use of leisure and recreation as a means for enhancing the worth of the individual and his happiness in life. The function of recreation as a social force influencing the philosophy, content, and method of education is equally important.

One of the great impacts upon the education institution has been the fact that with the development of a society in which recreational values rank alongside work values, at least in terms of the amount of a person's conscious hours spent in each of these pursuits, educating for recreation competence as well as work competence has become a basic charge upon education. To an educational institution for centuries oriented toward an ethic of work, toward the function of educating a person to perform work, this impact has been very sharp. Education now is becoming aware that to fulfill its institutional function it must help individuals to gain attitudes and understanding about leisure time, and to develop skills in its use.

Another impact on education is the recognition that not only is an ethic of play necessary for individual self-fulfillment in the age of leisure, but also that the speed, the frictions, the pressures, and the tensions of modern urban and industrial living threaten great damage to the individual personality unless some means for release, for relaxation, for tension reduction, and for re-creativity are made available and people are educated to use them. Once this therapeutic and restorative function of recreation is understood by education, one of the important responsibilities it must undertake is to educate people to make wise use of their leisure time.

One fact that helps to define for education its function in this respect is that large numbers of the population of our nation are not educated for leisure.[9] "Recreational illiteracy" is high, partly because the leisure age has come so rapidly that institutions have not yet adapted to it adequately. This failure cannot be charged to education alone, for education for leisure must be conceived on a society-wide scale, involving all of its institutions and all of its organizations, and relating to all of the society's population of all ages and in all of its relationships. Yet education should be expected to play a central role. Further, it is recognized in the recreation field that the general level of education of a people of a country has a great deal to do with the matter of recreation participation. A people with education and educated interests and tastes will demand and choose recreational pursuits somewhat different from a people oppressed by ignorance and the conditions that accompany it.

A second fact that also contributes to the definition of function

---

[9] John L. Hutchinson, ed., *Leisure and the Schools* (Washington, D.C.: American Association for Health, Physical Education, and Recreation, 1961), p. 12.

in leisure education is that recreation is an area of life in which the individual may choose, may exercise his freedom to pursue his own interests, to act in regard to his own volition. How he chooses depends upon the set of values he possesses in respect to recreation. Education for leisure becomes a matter of helping a person to internalize certain basic aesthetic and ethical values that he will utilize when he makes his recreational choices. Thus, contrary to education in other areas where discipline, conformity, or like values are of primary concern, educating for leisure is a matter of helping a person to establish ideas about his own creative self-expression and standards about his own means for aesthetic living. These elements are present in other areas of our lives, of course, but they are central in our leisure life.

The difference between the freedom that is implied in leisure and the discipline that is implied in work poses for the school a very critical problem of undertaking in one educational process two relatively unlike functions. There is no doubt that this problem still remains primarily unsolved by the schools. It will be more adequately solved when children and youth in some future year will graduate from our schools with hungers for many kinds of creative recreations and eagerness to fill their leisure hours with aesthetic and deeply rewarding activities. The tragedy is that millions of children are being exposed to a wide range of cultural recreations in the schools in such a way that after they leave school they never engage in the activity again. The individual who "hasn't touched his trombone since graduation" reminds us of the problem for education and for leisure in this respect. Education eventually will understand its role as one of teaching school subjects with their leisure potential fully recognized and their leisure-time use one of the primary focuses of the teaching.

The leisure age requires modern education to accept a new role of educating individuals toward a new leisure ethic, while education's role of educating for competence in important fields of life activity influences greatly the emerging leisure culture and the nature of the recreational pursuits of the people.

THE FUNCTIONS OF SCHOOLS

Education is the institution primarily responsible for teaching people to make good use of their leisure time. This is not to say, however, that there are not leisure-time educational functions in several other areas of institutional life. In some of these other areas leisure-time education may be consciously directed, while in still others such education may occur indirectly or even unconsciously. For example, in the case of commercial recreation, which is part of economic institutional life, we can see how influential a bowling alley or an amusement park may be in setting standards, attracting participants, and inculcating recreation tastes of individuals. In none of this, however, is the educational purpose uppermost. Other organizations, such as government, social welfare, and religion, have specific leisure-educational functions. In each case the institutional function expands in response to the modern leisure-education requirements of the society and takes on related education functions, even though these may be merely secondary purposes.

Education, however, through the schools and adult education programs, plays a primary and influential role in recreation and *the* primary role in education for leisure. Its influence on recreation can be felt in the modern design of schools as community centers, in administrative and faculty attitudes toward recreation in the community and the role of the school, and in the all-important way in which subjects are taught. Educators have recognized the basic significance of this relationship for many years. In 1918, Seven Cardinal Principles of Education were formulated to become a basic statement of educational objectives for American schools.[10] The seven principles included health, home life, learning, citizenship, vocations, character, and leisure. Preparation for the worthy use of leisure was charged to the schools as a basic purpose of education. In the decades since that time education has accepted as well the responsibility for providing opportunities for such worthy use of leisure for children and adults and has shared in total community effort to enrich the recreational life of all persons.

Education has discovered that it shares with the recreation institution most of its other basic objectives. It is clear that recreation can provide a balance of vigorous and relaxing activities contributing to the *health* needs of participants. Recreation, as we have seen earlier in this chapter, can contribute markedly to happy and strong *home* and family life. Recreation pursuits are vital forces in the individual's

---

[10] *Cardinal Principles of Secondary Education,* a report of the Commission on the Reorganization of Secondary Education (Washington, D.C.: National Education Association, 1918).

learning. Leisure-time group recreational experiences often are directed toward the vital and satisfying activities of *citizenship* and community civic participation. Recreation often is the setting for the exploration and acquisition of interests in a wide range of *vocations*. The guided group activities of many recreational organizations are important in contributing to the *character* education of individuals, particularly children.

A forward-looking statement of the roles of public education in recreation in California defined the following six roles:

> (1) Schools should educate for the worthy use of leisure —recreation is an essential part of the educational program, with the purpose of acquisition and development of attitudes, skills, insights, and resources for the enrichment and creative use of leisure.
>
> (2) Schools should achieve maximum articulation between instruction and recreation—meaningful recreation experiences must be part of the instruction, preserving, nurturing, and strengthening the relationship between what happens in school during class periods and what happens in the recreation setting.
>
> (3) Schools should coordinate and mobilize total community resources for recreation—a basic responsibility is to help the community develop awareness of the recreational needs of its members, assisting in the organization and development of all resources that can be used to meet these needs.
>
> (4) Schools should develop cooperative planning of recreation facilities—accepting the responsibility for leading in building interagency teamwork and cooperation to develop community recreation facilities and program.
>
> (5) Education should encourage, stimulate, and produce research on recreation—providing a laboratory and research resources for evaluation and other necessary research efforts.
>
> (6) Education should stress professional preparation of recreation personnel—adequate preparation and qualification by registration and certification contribute to the improvement of recreation leadership and professional service.[11]

---

[11] *The Roles of Public Education in Recreation* (Burlingame, Calif.: The California Association for Health, Physical Education and Recreation, 1960). Pamphlet.

Thus there is an integral interaction between the institutional programs of education and recreation, with the focus of education upon a fulfilling recreational life and upon providing basic recreation services to individuals and groups and participating in community-wide efforts to develop a leisure culture.

The schools have the opportunity to contribute to leisure education and recreation in four basic areas. The first area is the formal curriculum. Leisure arts have been given a prominent place in the curriculum. Other subjects, offered earlier with a vocational emphasis, have been reorganized to be offered for their leisure use. Physical education, language arts, graphic arts, social studies, and other subjects are taught primarily as a contribution to the personal recreation resources of the student.

The second area is extra-class, recognized as informal-educational in method and content, although seen as part of the total curriculum experience. Capturing the voluntarism and spontaneity of play pursuits, these programs have recreational objectives and utilize the recreational method, recognizing their important educational product.

Third are school-centered community recreation programs directed toward meeting broad community needs for recreation services and implementing the concept that the modern school shall be one of the centers around which the community may build its life. Programs serving all ages and wide interests, during all the hours and days in which the need for recreation exists, are being offered. The adult education programs of the schools involve millions of persons throughout the country, and play a large role in the recreation of the nation.

The fourth area of service of the schools has been a relatively more passive but still important area: that of providing facilities for community recreation carried on by many other agencies and organizations. Schools are designed not only to fulfill their educational function but to fulfill highly significant recreation functions originally thought to be outside of the schools' purview.

An important aspect of the relationship between education and recreation in our modern-day life is the interaction between the professions of recreation and education. The century-old professional discipline of the educator, focusing upon the serious work of helping the individual child to prepare himself for the exacting processes of adult work, requires fundamental change to adapt to the requirements of the recreation method. As we shall see at a later point in this book, the recreation method is based upon the philosophy of the values in recreative play, the creativity, spontaneity, voluntarism, and other elements sometimes consciously set against the sober and serious attitudes and disciplines of work. These latter have been key components of the traditional education method. The awakening of education to the challenge of the leisure age and the values of recreation in human self-fulfillment has had two effects. One is the acceptance by education of the new responsibility of education for leisure. The second is the growing understanding of the dynamics of the creative zestfulness in recreation and an effort to provide some of the conditions and motivations in education that produce the same creativity and zest.

Schools and related educational organizations are adapting their philosophy and method to the requirements of their primary role in education for leisure and in meeting recreational needs for individuals through formal curricular activities, extra-class programs, school-centered community recreation programs, and provision of facilities for other community recreation agencies.

GOVERNMENT AND RECREATION

The interaction between the political institutional organizations and the recreation institution is active and continuous. In this country government increasingly has been involving itself in recreation at all levels from the national to the local. Recreation, in fact, has been for many years an acknowledged function of government, although there are many political subdivisions that have not acknowledged this function by providing services. Government, in accepting the responsibility for functioning in areas of need required by the people who determine its policies, has influenced profoundly the development of organized recreation.

The political organization of a country, the Neumeyers point out, "conditions the leisure of people. Each type of political system presents characteristic recreation phenomena." [12]

In a democracy such as the United States there is provided in government the means for the people to strive for greater attention to their leisure needs. Eventually, at all levels of government, these strivings can result in changes in government policy more adequately to meet these needs. Along with these changes goes the imposition of

---

[12] Neumeyer and Neumeyer, *Leisure and Recreation,* p. 161.

taxes for the support of public recreation, the borrowing of money, and the floating of bond issues, which governments undertake to support this function. The government also has impost taxes on commercial recreation, mainly as a means of securing revenue. The government has played an active role in controlling through legislation certain recreations judged to have harmful by-products if misused.

Some governments, such as that of the Soviet Union, more actively than that of the United States, participate directly in the leisure of their people as a matter of public policy. Kaplan points out that

> Russia provides important examples of direct state interest in the leisure time of its citizens. This is evidenced in several directions: a major program in physical education and sports, state-owned resort centers for free or low-cost vacations for workers, a vast output in literature, and an apparently genuine interest in all the arts. . . . The Soviet Constitution guarantees an annual paid vacation of at least two weeks. Many categories of workers get more. In addition to time off, the Soviet worker has access to vacation and health resorts "at very reasonable prices and in some cases without cost." This is financed by a combination of government and trade union funds. . . . Free accommodations come to about 20 per cent of all persons attending health resorts and to 10 per cent of those at vacation resorts. . . . [This] is an illustration of direct governmental interest in leisure for general purposes of control but in a positive way that uses the device of winning loyalty through a significant benefit to the person.[13]

The Federal Government in our own country has accepted continuously responsibility for more involvement in the support of recreation. Through the activities of the National Park Service, the Forest Service, the Fish and Wildlife Service, and other federal agencies extensive programs are being carried on. During World War II federal recreation programs by the Federal Security Agency carried programs into many communities. As Kaplan says, "The impact of this program on civilians during the war and upon the professional recreation movement after the war was immeasurably large." [14]

---

[13] Max Kaplan, *Leisure in America: A Social Inquiry* (New York: John Wiley and Sons, Inc., 1960), pp. 144-145.

[14] Kaplan, p. 143.

The greatest impact on recreation in this country, however, has occurred at the local level. The 1961 *Recreation and Park Yearbook* [15] reported some 2,968 communities had accepted basic responsibility for recreation functions. City planning, zoning, and taxing agencies have anchored firmly into local government fabric the idea of the essential need for public spaces and facilities. We have seen how the municipalities have fought to keep pace with suburbanization in establishing new recreation areas and facilities in outer areas. The recreation movement itself has found its main impetus and base in the public programs of the country's municipalities.

Other subdivisions of government, particularly the states and the counties, have participated in the expansion of public recreation through not only recreation and park authorities but also departments of conservation, forestry, agriculture, and others. These have provided useful recreation services and have in turn established in government policy at these levels recognition of the validity of recreation as a function of government. In some areas, special political subdivisions (special recreation districts) have been created to provide for the organization of recreation services when the public agencies that do exist do not have the resources.

Because of the fact that American government operates at several levels and through a multitude of jurisdictions, a major problem of complexity is posed in efforts to be sensitive and responsive to new and changing needs. The federal, state, county, and municipal agencies are operating among a number of other special, regional, and cooperative organizations, all of them making up a very complex structure of jurisdictions, sometimes simply struggling to maintain effective working relationships between each other, but sometimes sharply in conflict as to whose jurisdiction a given problem falls into. In respect especially to a new function such as recreation, where time-tested relationships have not yet been worked out, there are numerous problems. An example is the problem posed by the freedom of recreation-bent individuals to travel many miles from their homes to utilize a given recreation facility. A local jurisdiction can plan a desirable facility, anticipating primarily use by local population, only to find it flooded with participants from beyond its normal borders, beyond all possibility of effectively coping with them.

[15] New York: National Recreation Association, 1961.

There is evidence, particularly in metropolitan areas, that new patterns of government on a regional basis may be needed and may emerge to deal with common problems such as water, transportation—and recreation.

Thus, developments in government both stimulate recreation and, in turn, reflect the growing significance of recreation and the demand of the public for governmental action to support this social function.

One example of this pressure is at the state-government level, where greatly increased governmental activity is occurring in many states. The emergence of extensive state activity to spark recreation growth is resulting from the operation of a number of significant societal forces. Douglass lists these as:

> 1. Economic facts such as increasing disposable income, time and energy, increasing mobility, increasing populations· projected against decreasing availability of natural sites suitable for recreational activities.
>
> 2. Efforts of state economic enterprise in its competitive promotion to increase state income by recreational attractions.
>
> 3. Evolution of state policy concerning natural resources in relation to outdoor recreation and the growth of metropolitan regions, which require a new kind of planning, political leadership, and relationship between state and local authorities.
>
> 4. Increasing professional activity of the state societies operating within the American Recreation Society [and other recreation bodies].
>
> 5. Activities of commercial and trade association interests forecasting increasingly profitable outlooks in a mobile America, provided with adequate recreational facilities and attractions.[16]

Another example of this, at the national level, is provided by the United States Forest Service. The original task of the Forest Service was to provide for the conservation of vast forest reserves and to develop a forest management program for the country. As pressure for outdoor recreation space grew during the years, the government was required to reexamine its policy with respect to the national forests and gradually accepted a concept that defines several simultaneous

---

[16] Paul Douglass, "Why States Are Sparking Recreation's Growth," *American Recreation Journal,* Vol. 1, No. 1 (August-September 1960), pp. 32-34.

uses for the national forests: the multiple-use concept, which advances the idea that timber, grazing, watershed, wildlife, and recreation all have values for the nation, values that can be realized with sound management of the forests. Multiple use implies that among competitive uses of the lands there may be defined by sound management, once the objective of the owning agency is determined, a reasonable solution consistent with public policy and providing for primary and secondary needs. In fact, this multiple-use concept has provided for increased appropriate recreational use of vast resources, as this function comes into prominence in national thinking, and attention is paid to the growing need for recreation service.[17]

Serious consideration is being given at several levels of government to increased government services in recreation. Proposal for a national recreation agency and a strengthening of national recreation services are receiving close attention by the federal government. The creation of the new Bureau of Outdoor Recreation is one result of this attention. Proposals have been made for federal government support of international good-will leisure travel by United States citizens, which would foster good will among countries. The program of the International Recreation Association supports this trend also. Rapid growth in municipal expenditures, which form the bulk of present public expenditures for recreation, is expected to continue, reflecting continued response of the government institution to the needs and requirements of the recreation institution.

Government is an important force in recreation, with all levels of government carrying on recreation as one of their important functions. Public demand for government to expand many recreation services reflects increasing public awareness of recreation's value.

THE CHURCH AND RECREATION

For almost all of the Christian era the countries under Christian church leadership were given specific ethical and religious rules to live by in respect to the ideas of work and play. Perhaps in response to the demoralizing results of the forms of leisure life developed during the Roman Empire, or perhaps to make the people more seriously devoted

---

[17] See C. Frank Brockman, *Recreational Use of Wild Lands* (New York: McGraw-Hill Book Company, 1959), Chapters 6 and 8.

to the tasks of serving their lords and masters, the medieval church sanctified work and in one way or another defined play as a tool of the Devil. Although, as we saw in Chapter 2, this philosophy could not quite be made to stick, efforts of the church, particularly early Protestantism, were unremitting.

One good example was Puritan New England, where strict laws were passed against a wide range of leisure pursuits as a "misspense of time." Then as life became easier in the colonies a relaxation of these strict laws occurred, and the needs and interests of people in respect to play began to be realized. Nevertheless, the effect of religion on the recreation institution was undoubtedly important, restricting some directions of its development and permitting others. It undoubtedly played an important role as guardian of the morals of the community and waging unrelenting war against harmful or "sinful" amusements and vices.

The role of the church in respect to recreation still includes some of these elements in the modern day, but important new elements have entered in. Pieper formulates a Catholic philosophy of leisure, defining it as a mental and spiritual attitude characterized by tranquility, calmness, and contemplation, which unites man with the source of creation and causes him to celebrate his identity as a creature and child of God, the creator.[18]

Religious leaders have pondered the modern question of the ethical implications of the decline of work as a source of human values. They now ask the question, is not leisure to be the main source of man's freedom to be creative, to exercise his gifts, and to contribute of these gifts to his fellows? And the church has moved from its earlier position as primarily guardian of the ethic of work and fighter against pursuit of leisure to an institution with significant recreational functions.

Brightbill argues that leisure and recreation are closely tied to religion ideologically.

> Religion is, indeed, a means of expressing our desires for well-being and self-realization, but this is equally true of the recreative life in its most positive light. . . . Both religion and recreation are engaged in voluntarily. . . . [Both] occur during

---

[18] Josef Pieper, *Leisure: The Basis of Culture* (New York: Pantheon Books, Inc., 1952).

> leisure and both provide a chance for gain as well as for achieving balance and perspective. Similarly, religion and recreation provide the opportunity for us to satisfy and express our inner desires. Each places us at the center of our own destiny and each recognizes the supreme worth of the individual.[19]

Both argue for equality of opportunity. Both give us the chance to restore depth and quality to our lives. There is indeed, he observes, great compatibility between religious and recreational life.

The church, generally, has added significant recreation functions to its total function. Churches have introduced recreational activities into their programs. These serve as a means both of meeting socialization and fellowship needs of church members and of interesting people in the church and attracting them to broader participation in church life. The church pays attention to the needs of its members for creative activities, for social life, and for opportunities to share with others in congenial pursuits.

The church also has served community groups other than its members, often in the spirit of community service, sponsoring community-wide programs for youth or for whole populations, establishing settlement houses and other centers for service in neighborhoods without regard for religious affiliation. Sometimes the church has undertaken programs in order to attract new members and recruits to its religious life.

Another feature of the relationship between these two social forces is the influence of the recreation and informal educational method on church educational work. The church has seen the value of the creative and informal approach to the involvement of individuals in satisfying leisure programs, and has discovered in this method elements that can be applied to church educational work. Further, the church has employed trained recreation workers to carry on programs under its auspices, and has enriched many church programs with recreational features.

The interaction of religion as a complex of social forces and recreation as another complex of social forces, therefore, can be viewed in several respects. The church is contributing significantly by pioneer-

---

[19] Charles Brightbill, *Man and Leisure: A Philosophy of Recreation* (Englewood Cliffs, N.J.: Prentice-Hall, Inc., 1961), pp. 97-99.

ing interfaith and intercultural programs in camping, conferences, and other ways. The church is making a contribution in interpreting the spiritual and ethical values in play and recreation. It is playing a powerful and constructive role in creating wholesome attitudes toward recreation, opposing undesirable and unwholesome recreational influences, and offering constructive alternative choices.

There are those who believe that the church has gone too far away from its basic spiritual function and has become, in fact, almost a recreation agency. They criticize the modern churches with their recreation rooms, bowling alleys, social halls, and so on, and their "country club at prayer" atmosphere. They would have a return to a more spiritual, ascetic, worshiping atmosphere and less of the lightness and gaiety that takes away from the serious task of evangelizing the world and witnessing in the spirit of the saints and martyrs. But there are others who believe that the church finds its legitimate and basic function in furthering leisure time as a potential source of significant self-fulfillment. They believe that the church should help man find the basic good in himself, and the vastly increased leisure time makes this help possible.

Religion and recreation, originally in Western civilization sharply opposed, have drawn closer together, with religion contributing to recreational ethics and values, with recreation becoming a church function, and with the two forces closely related ideologically and supporting like goals of individual self-realization.

HEALTH AND RECREATION

The complex of medical, therapeutic, and health service and education organizations making up the health institution is experiencing a revolution. This is having a sharp effect on the health situation in the nation. One of the important changes for the recreation worker is the increase in average lifespan. The average age to which people can expect to live increases steadily year by year because of medical success in attacking the disease problems causing death early in life. Average length rose from 69.4 years to 69.7 in one year (1958–59). The child born today can expect to live almost 74 years. Vast new tools of medical science are being developed and put to use to conquer major diseases, such as polio, which earlier took their toll. New antibiotics, surgical techniques, and the wonder drugs, among others, along with improved public health administration, provide medicine with new means for raising the health standard of people.

Health Education

Health education has striven to advance the medical concept that health is not merely the absence of disease but a state of physical and emotional well-being of the whole person. Programs of health education in the schools and in the community in general have improved, being supported by public funds and huge new voluntary and foundation sources.

The impact of this development on recreation has been marked. Health and sanitation standards and programs, which have been developed for communities, have required recreation to conform and to upgrade its own standards. Health considerations, for example, stimulated the medical and physical education fields to call on recreation to guarantee in its programs consideration for the health and safety of participants. In one instance the danger of physical and emotional damage to participants in Little League baseball was pointed out to the recreation movement by these authorities, who demanded that leadership and supervision of this sport be given by the recreation authorities. This demand still has not been adequately responded to, but the influence was and is strongly there.[20]

Physical Fitness

Another area in which health considerations are stimulating recreation activity is in the area of fitness. It came as a shock to this country when researches during recent years pointed up an alarming decline in the physical strength and fitness of American youth. President Kennedy tried to increase the national concern with the statement that

> . . . despite our unparalleled standard of living, despite our emphasis on school athletics, American youth lagged far behind Europeans in physical fitness. . . . the harsh fact of the matter is that there is also an increasingly large number of young Americans who are neglecting their bodies . . . who are getting soft. And such softness on the part of individual citi-

---

[20] See *School Athletics, Problems and Policies* (Washington, D.C.: Educational Policies Commission, National Educational Association, 1954), pp. 27-32.

> zens can help to strip and destroy the vitality of a nation. . . . For physical fitness is not only one of the most important keys to a healthy body; it is the basis of dynamic and creative intellectual activity.[21]

The President identified a problem that education, recreation, and health authorities have been working on since President Eisenhower launched the program in 1956, a problem made up of objective factors such as the sedentary habits of children, spectator habits, car driving, and lack of vigorous school and recreational pursuits, and subjective factors such as a lack of national concern for health. The national fitness campaign organized under the President's Council on Youth Fitness involves millions of youth and thousands of school and recreation programs and organizations, but it is too early to determine whether the downward trend in the nation's health has been halted or reversed.

Stress and the Need for Relaxation

A third area in which the health forces in this country have been active and the significance for recreation is great is in respect to tension, and the wear and tear of the modern tempo of living. Martin points out that important increases have occurred in the medical problems of ulcers, coronary thrombosis, mental diseases, and use of tranquilizers for sleeplessness and tension. Parallel problems of juvenile delinquency, frenetic and escape-type recreations and amusements, and speeding endlessly in automobiles, are increasing. These and other phenomena point to an increasing health problem for the nation. Searching for the cause of this, he points out that our modern culture has stigmatized relaxation and glorified high-pressure industrial efficiency and an "on your toes, a get ahead" philosophy. The result is an increase of anxiety and of compulsiveness and tragic frustration over the inability to relax.

> The complete inability to relax even for a moment is a common complaint and evidence of neurotic disturbance . . . a fear of relaxation and leisure. . . [I]n those who are beset by severe after-work irritability . . . many spasmogenic conditions

---

[21] From "The Soft American," by John F. Kennedy, *Sports Illustrated,* Vol. 13, No. 26 (December 26, 1960), p. 6. By special permission of *Sports Illustrated,* Time, Inc.

> in the gastrointestinal tract, of neurotic origin, have become much worse during holidays. . . . [S]evere psychoneurotic and even psychotic episodes have occurred when an individual attempted to rest after a particularly long period of intensive work.[22]

He points out that this fear of relaxation has both cultural origins and psychoneurotic origins, each reinforcing the other to impose on the individual such compulsive tendencies that even his effort to re-create takes on unrelaxed and intense forms and the basic recreative values are radically diminished.

In making an argument for relaxation and recreation as a basic key to personal physical and emotional health, to holistic well-being, Martin points out that the problem that frustrates the maintenance of this good health for many persons is their pervasive tension and compulsiveness, and their avoidance of leisurely living because this leisure creates anxiety. He likens leisure to sleep in its best sense.

> Sleep is a positive, forward moving part of the growth cycle . . . as a means of reinforcing, promoting, growth and expansion. In healthy, wholesome sleep we are recreated. We awaken refreshed and enriched. . . . True relaxation in the sense of a surrender to one's own basic, intrinsic, unique rhythm is not an escape, but like true sleep, brings us in touch with the darker reaches of ourselves and gives us a greater sense of our totality.[23]

Recreation and Well-Being

Such insights, along with the demand upon recreation to recognize its own power as a source of and key to individual health and well-being, influence and support the idea of recreation as a basic need as well as a basic right of man. Martin stated at another time "that leisure and the recreative processes are natural, biological and innate, and an essential phase of the growth cycle; that leisure . . . comes to us as a natural blessing by the 'Grace of God'; that the recre-

---

22 Alexander Reid Martin, M.D., "A Philosophy of Recreation," *The Doctors and Recreation in the Hospital Setting* (North Carolina: North Carolina Recreation Commission, Bulletin No. 30, 1962), p. 8.

23 A. R. Martin, pp. 10-11.

ative process complements the work process . . . that leisure is essential to all creativity; that man's great imperishable intuitions have only come to him during his moments of true leisure." [24]

Recreation and leisure gain greatly in stature from the impact of such demand by health forces for the improvement of leisure as a key to well-being. The argument for leisure and health is supported also by the physiologists, who point out that vigorous physical activity stirs up the circulation, facilitates normal metabolism, increases muscle tone, aids digestion and elimination, and promotes a sense of well-being. It slows down the aging process, which is very rapid among inactive older persons. The human body was designed for action, physically and mentally, and to keep it in good condition action is necessary. The functional efficiency of any of the body's organs or systems increases with use and regresses with disuse. Muscles grow when they are used and atrophy when they are not used. Because a considerable part of recreation is active and also designed for outdoors, recreation offers opportunities for both body use and fresh air, two components long recognized as valuable for good health. The scientific evidence is plentiful, and the medical opinion even more impressive, that wholesome recreation that provides relaxation, action, self-satisfaction, and pleasure is a basic health requirement for modern man. It is also true that good health and a sense of physical and emotional well-being are needed for the fullest enjoyment of many recreations, although many recreations are available to those not able to enjoy the best health.

The health institution, coping with new health and fitness problems growing out of modern life's demands and stresses, is demanding that new attention be paid to the development and encouragement of recreation as a valuable contribution to the individual's health and total well-being.

RECREATION AND THERAPY

Recreation has been stimulated by the ideas and demands from health organizations and professions, the medical and psychiatric practitioners, the therapists, and the hospital operators. And it is in

---

[24] Alexander Reid Martin, M.D., *Leisure Time as a Basic Health Resource* (New York: American Psychiatric Association, 1958), mimeographed, p. 4.

the hospital settings that recreation has made outstanding contributions to the health, therapy, and rehabilitation movements of today. The burden of the care and treatment of millions of ill and handicapped individuals constitutes a huge task for our modern health organizations and they have sought desperately for means of managing this task and increasing their efficiency. Recreation as a direct therapeutic tool has been one outstanding contribution to the armamentarium of health and medical practice.

The basic approaches of recreation to therapy and rehabilitation can be classified according to three different kinds of therapeutic situations: (1) situations in which activities are primarily physically therapeutic, but have a recreational character; (2) situations in which activities are primarily recreational, and are used for their psychotherapeutic effects; and (3) situations in which recreational activities and periods of leisure time are provided to maintain a normal leisure component in an individual's life while he is in the therapeutic setting. In each case the basic purpose is to help the patient to maintain a frame of mind, attitude, and morale that will make him most receptive to and cooperative with the medical treatment, and eager to work to get well or to tolerate his disability or handicap more easily and enjoy life more fully despite it.

Therapy as Play

The first of these approaches simply recognizes that making a physical therapeutic exercise or required movement into a fun-filled game or a musical dance routine will make it an easier pill to swallow. Recreation therapists in this direct service provide an integral part of the paramedical service to the patient, making the therapy more palatable and increasing its effectiveness by making the pleasure in its doing a supporting aspect of the treatment.

Recreation as Therapy

The second of these approaches recognizes the role of recreation as a complex of pleasurable activities and relationships with others in which the joy, satisfaction, fun, relaxation, and self-fulfillment are dynamic therapeutic and rehabilitative agents in themselves.

Brightbill defines this type of recreation therapy as "the medical application of an activity, voluntarily engaged in by the patient during the period of treatment or convalescence, that is enjoyable and personally satisfying to him, even though the activity and the patient's participation in it are structured to achieve a predicted result beyond the patient's own personal satisfaction."[25]

The design of experiences is subject to medical direction, and meets the requirements of the other aspects of the therapeutic regime. But activities range widely over the field of recreational fun.

> Today in hospitals and rehabilitation centers the blind are bowling, the amputees are dancing, and the crippled are swimming. Music is being used as patients emerge from shock treatment; it is piped to them under their pillows. . . . Mentally ill patients are "acting out" roles in psychodrama. . . . patients are publishing and distributing their own newspapers, operating their own . . . radio systems . . . [and] governing themselves through their own patient councils.[26]

Rehabilitation literature is rich with clinical and research evidence of the astonishing curative power of recreation in respect to hospitals treating general, neuropsychiatric, and chronic disease cases. The recreation therapist has become a respected member of the medical team in the hospital, one who has added to his recreation education some basic grounding in the biological and behavioral sciences, medical and psychiatric information, and orientation toward the medical setting and its therapeutic and rehabilitative philosophy, science, and method.

The student of recreation needs to be aware of the close interrelationships and intermingling of the social institutions of which health and recreation are two. In the recreation therapy field these interrelationships are clearly and dynamically seen. The interplay between the doctors, nurses, physical therapists, occupational therapists, social workers, hospital administrators, and the recreation therapists, the close teamwork required, and the understanding required by each member of the function in therapy of the other members of the team, each in behalf of the patient, provide us with an outstanding example of the principle of institutional and interdisciplinary interrelationships.

Recreation as a Normal Life Component

The third type of situation in which recreation has a major contribution in the therapeutic setting is where the patient needs as many

[25] Brightbill, *Man and Leisure,* p. 244.
[26] Brightbill, p. 251.

Recreation Therapy

elements of a normal life as can be provided or closely simulated. Free use of some leisure time of his own in the midst of the demanding, perhaps boring, sometimes frightening routine of a hospital is one of these. A second is the existence of many camps or special units of camps that provide resident camping experiences for children, youth, or adults suffering from one or another illness or disability. Some of these are specially planned to deal with the special medical problems posed by campers, and are restricted to those with such problems. Others are designed to bring members with such handicaps together with other nonhandicapped campers in order to provide an experience as close to normal as possible. There are scores of such camps in the United States for those suffering from asthma and allergies, cardiac troubles, diabetes, cerebral palsy, emotional disturbances, epilepsy, lowered vitality, mental retardation, orthopedic handicaps, social maladjustment, speech or hearing defects, visual handicaps, and other difficulties.[27]

Special recreation programs for groups of children, youth, and adults are carried on by the United Cerebral Palsy Association and other national health agencies. Youth organizations like the Girl Scouts and the Boy Scouts have also initiated such programs. Municipal recreation departments and health agencies are attempting to serve recreational needs of many handicapped groups. Club programs, day camp programs, programs of training for parents in home and family recreation with their handicapped members, programs of home visiting by volunteer or paid recreation workers to bring services to the homebound, all of these are found in hundreds of communities throughout the country. These programs demonstrate the truth of the idea that through recreation the health and lives of literally millions of those for whom full health and well-being is temporarily or permanently impaired may be enriched.

Recreation therapy is emerging as a significant tool of modern medicine and rehabilitation: in direct therapeutic design of experiences, as a means of normalizing life in the therapeutic setting, and as a meaningful activity for the temporarily or permanently handicapped.

---

[27] Brightbill, p. 241.

RECREATION AND SOCIAL WELFARE

Of the complex of major social institutions that we have been reviewing here, modern recreation and social welfare have the briefest histories as modern institutional organizations. This is not to deny that recreation has had an institutional history as long as man's history. In some form or other, the organized efforts of men to minister to each other's needs in time of trouble have been found in all human societies as well. But modern institutionalized recreation, with its public departments, investments in facilities, and professional recreation leadership, is a relatively new phenomenon. So is modern institutionalized social welfare, with its public welfare departments, professional child welfare and family welfare agencies, probation, parole, and protective agencies for delinquents, and other agencies. These new forms stand in contrast to the long-established organizations of government, the hoary traditions of organized religion, the hundreds of years of medical science.

Kinds of Agencies

Institutionalized social welfare is identified in the grouping of agencies and organizations devoted to serving the needs of members of the community whose problems range over wide fields. Public welfare agencies serve primarily economic and insurance needs of individuals and families such as the unemployed, aged, children of families without a breadwinner, blind, disabled, and others. Family service agencies serve individuals or families who are suffering from problems of damaged relationships or other problems of personal and social maladjustment, and engage in educational and community activities. Child welfare agencies help individual children and sometimes families when adoption, foster home, protective guidance, residential placement, day care or nursery, and other service is needed. Probation and parole agencies connected with courts and penal programs serve individual youth or adults who have had difficulty that has brought them under police or court supervision, and undertake to help them make an adequate adjustment again to normal society. Group-serving agencies, such as settlements and the national youth agencies, serve children and youth, and sometimes adults, with programs of an informal educational and recreational nature and with individual counseling and like services when needed.

Common Concerns and Efforts

In respect to one basic principle, recreation and social welfare provide important supportive help to each other. The basic principle that each individual is entitled to equal opportunity for recreation and has the freedom of choice of leisure pursuit is matched by the social welfare principle that each individual has eminent worth, that he has the right to the agency's services as a member of the community. Essentially, he has the freedom to use the services or not. This principle has, in a sense, certain exceptions, but the philosophy of the agency is to guarantee as far as possible important freedom of decision and choice in using the agency's services.

In the broad sense the institutions of recreation, education, health, and social welfare are a web of closely related organizations serving closely related needs. Out of their common efforts to serve the educational, recreational, health, and social welfare needs have grown certain instruments of cooperation and common purpose. One of these at the community level is the council, often called the health, education, and welfare council, which functionally links together the several agencies for planning and cooperative approach to problems that are often too complex for a single agency.

The professions serving these several institutions find themselves bound together by many ties of common philosophy and method. We will discuss the "family of helping professions" at a later point. It is sufficient to point out that the institutions themselves form a functionally close-knit family as well, and they often have been considered to be fields of "social welfare" in the broadest sense of the term.

Institutional and Corrective Programs

Just as the health forces in the country "discovered" the value of recreation as a tool in the rehabilitation of physically or emotionally ill individuals, the social welfare organizations concerned with the rehabilitation of the socially maladjusted more and more have undertaken to utilize recreation in their service. One example of this use of recreation is in prison administration, which in its best sense is committed to helping the offender change his thinking and aspirations so they will be socially acceptable. This is rehabilitation, bringing about a successful readjustment to enable him to live in the free world.

Enlightened prison administrators introduce recreation into prison life partly because it will help alleviate the monotony of prison life and partly because it can be useful for controlling the inmate, providing a safety valve for releasing tension that otherwise might result in disturbances and trouble. But mainly recreation can be a means for giving the inmate an area in his life that is satisfying, an area in which he can achieve some peace of mind and some successful accomplishment. Upon the basis of this satisfaction, he may be able to be helped to consider other problems in his life and to work toward their solution as well.

A field closely related to this is the field of delinquency control. In relation to delinquency, opinion has ranged widely. Some have argued that recreation can be a potent tool for delinquency control; others claim that recreation has no significance in this respect. The fact is that, under skilled professional social group and recreation workers, programs for delinquent youth have been significantly successful. Recreation has been used by such workers with much success, in combination with the workers' use of a strong and steady relationship as the basis of help and counsel with the delinquent concerning other problems in his life.

For the large majority of youth in a community who are less prone to delinquent behavior, but still are potential delinquents, active and well-operated recreation programs can be attractive alternatives to just "goofing off" and getting into trouble, serious or not. Meyer and Brightbill point out that "Common sense indicates that using young people's idleness and free time for constructive recreation activities helps to forestall some delinquency. . . . The role of recreation is not eliminating delinquency but rather holding the line against character disintegration through providing the chance for positive personal development." [28]

There is a large number of young offenders committed by courts to corrective institutions of one kind or another. At this point a penal institution for youth must function essentially like a penal institution for adults. Recreation again is called upon to be a tool in reformation and rehabilitation, and society is inclined to invest resources in this kind of rehabilitation. However, in most states there are staggering problems of overcrowding, understaffing, and inadequate rehabilitative programs in these corrective institutions.

The basic recreation principles that apply in meeting normal indi-

---

[28] Meyer and Brightbill, *Community Recreation,* pp. 417-418.

vidual developmental needs operate in corrective programs as well. One of these principles is that recreation is a right of the offender, not a privilege or reward. A second is that it is a voluntary activity in which some choices must be provided. A third is that the program must be highly individualized, designed to meet individual needs as part of the individual rehabilitation program. A fourth is that normal activities and relationships should be approximated, both in the programs within the institution and in community recreation programs to be used by the offenders capable of constructive use of such experiences.

In resident institutional programs carried on by social welfare agencies, such as child welfare and aged care agencies, recreation plays an important part and its function is fulfilled usually in the congenial setting of other organizations. Recreation programs for homebound individuals, recreation programs in public housing developments as part of the encouragement of wholesome community life, recreation with elderly groups, unemployed groups, and the like, are other examples. An interesting example of one effect of recreation on the social welfare institution is provided by the following: The public welfare program of aid to dependent children in several states has accepted the principle that attendance at a summer resident camp, or another recreation program, is an important part of a child's growing up. Camping organizations and other groups accept children from such families on a special fee basis, with the welfare department granting extra financial help to the families to pay the camp fees. In many communities these funds are supplemented by monies derived through campership drives sponsored by community organizations and newspapers. The *New York Herald Tribune*'s "Fresh-Air Fund" is typical. While these are modest programs, they perhaps illustrate more clearly than other examples how the values of recreation as a developmental influence in the lives of children have become convincing goals for the social welfare institution, and a guiding policy in its program.

Modern social welfare and recreation are closely identified philosophically in their common concern for the worth of the individual; they meet closely related needs and work together in many areas of organizational services. Social welfare utilizes recreation as a basic resource for helping people in many fields in which it is working.

Questions for Study and Discussion

1. *Study a family with which you are familiar. How would you analyze the function of recreation in that family—as a positive force or as a negative force in family life? Give your analysis.*
2. *Many recreation agencies organize, for specific age and sex groups, programs that tend to encourage family members to recreate away from each other. How would you compare the positive values of such programs with possible negative outcomes in terms of family unity?*
3. *What are the main challenges facing education today in playing its role in an expanding leisure?*
4. *What are the main obstacles presently in the way of education's completely fulfilling its role in recreation?*
5. *How could government agencies in the United States best implement their present activity in leisure-time recreation?*
6. *Based upon your reading, what influences do education, the church, health, and social welfare exert upon recreation?*
7. *How do you assess the validity of the belief that worship is the highest form of leisure expression? Do you agree that the basic function of organized religion is to further leisure and raise its expression to the highest levels?*

Selected Readings

Elliott, Mabel A., and Francis E. Merrill, *Social Disorganization* (New York: Harper & Row, Inc., 1950).

Larrabee, Eric, and Rolf Meyerson, eds., *Mass Leisure* (Glencoe, Ill.: The Free Press, 1958).

Neumeyer, Martin H., and Esther S. Neumeyer, *Leisure and Recreation: A Study of Leisure and Recreation in Their Sociological Aspects,* Third edition (New York: The Ronald Press Company, 1958).

Rosenberg, Bernard, and David Manning White, *Mass Culture: The Popular Arts in America* (Glencoe, Ill.: The Free Press, 1960).

PART 3

RECREATION AS A SOCIAL INSTITUTION

A social function, by definition, is some part of a society's operation which has been created and developed as an integral part of the means for survival, for meeting common needs, and for providing for the happiness and well-being of the members of the society. In Chapters 2 and 3, recreation was identified as a social function because of its existence as an integral part of all societies. As any social function emerges, organization of effort occurs to carry on certain aspects of the function, and the framework of institutionalized practices can be discerned. Thus, recognizing recreation as a social function leads to a search for all of the forms in which it is found. It is found, of course, as an informal activity of countless individuals, families, and other informal groupings who pursue their interests without any concern for or involvement with other persons in organized groups of a lasting or stable nature. It is found, also, in a wide range of formal and informal organizational forms of this latter type.

Among the complex of these forms will be identified recreation's social institutional characteristics. This section, therefore, outlines some of the varied organizational forms in which recreation in its broadest scope is found.

AS A SOCIAL INSTITUTION

10

RECREATION IN ITS SOCIAL ORGANIZATIONAL FORMS

One of the characteristics of recreation is the diversity of its expression. It is organized in any community in a vast number of forms, adapting to the different needs of different groups and adapting to several forces that influence its organization. Among these are economic forces and governmental purposes. It adapts also to the character of its social milieu, such as the urban, suburban, rural, or other characteristic of the community.

Cities, where humanity crowds in on itself and children's games compete with automobiles and trucks for priority in the use of streets, have been the places where recreation has needed to be organized, and has been organized, with the greatest energy. The urban dweller, deprived of most of the natural means for recreative play, has had to devise means for himself. The rural community, perhaps lacking some of the more critical space needs, also has developed an active organized life, often more informal than the cities' highly structured one, but striving to obtain for its members the same basic values as the larger centers. Our primary, but not total, concern will be for the urban organizations, which comprise the major bulk of the organized recreation of the country.

The basic idea underlying the vast community organization for modern recreation is that this basic function has developed, along with the organized forms it takes, in response to important and deeply felt needs of the people who live in these communities. DeMarche states:

> Recreation contributes to the satisfaction of fundamental human appetites. The need for it stems from deep emotional drives which impel us to seek outlets for their expression. The hunger for belonging to a group, for being wanted, for self-expression, recognition, creativity, competition, security, and adventure . . . challenge[s] the individual to invest his off-duty time pleasantly and profitably. . . . [T]hese, plus urban conditions . . . are factors contributing to a greater need for community-provided recreation.[1]

A large number of books in the recreation field present in effective detail a great deal of material about the organization of recreation under the wide range of auspices in which it is found. Because the descriptions given in other books are so complete, this chapter will undertake only to indicate the breadth of perspective with which the field must be examined and some of the new directions of development at present. It will provide the student with an outline of the recreation movement, on the basis of which the rich resource material in community organization for recreation can be explored.

For our purpose, this study of organizations and settings in which recreation is carried on will review the public agency, the school, the

---

[1] David F. DeMarche, "Recreation," *Report of the National Conference on Appraising Family Needs* (St. Paul, Minn.: The Conference, 1949), mimeographed.

voluntary agencies, the commercial agencies, and other agencies. Other sections will review the subjects of organizing the community and providing state and federal supporting functions.

THE PUBLIC RECREATION AGENCY

The years since the Boston sand gardens initiated the organized public recreation movement in 1885 have seen more than three thousand cities and towns organizing public recreation agencies. This rapid growth has characterized the recreation movement since its beginning, and public recreation constitutes the core of the modern recreation movement. The furthering of municipal recreation has been a major concern of the recreation profession, and the most extensive and competent professional literature has been written in the field of public recreation and its administration. The student who wishes to enter the field of professional recreation education is urged to consult some of this outstanding literature, particularly *The Administration of Public Recreation* by George Hjelte, *Introduction to Community Recreation* by George Butler, and *Community Recreation: A Guide to Its Organization and Administration* by Meyer and Brightbill (see Selected Readings list at end of chapter).

The public recreation agency develops and helps people to put to the fullest recreational use the community's natural and constructed resources and assets. It begins by acquiring, establishing, maintaining, and operating recreation areas and facilities of all types. It promotes, organizes, and supervises activities and recreation services for the public. It administers public funds for this purpose. It takes some responsibility for coordinating into a workable whole the efforts of other municipal government agencies with secondary recreation functions such as police, water, health, street, and other departments. Democratic government accepts responsibility for promoting and providing the means for furthering the common welfare, and government has the resources, the power of taxing, policing, and eminent domain, and a permanent commitment to the people's welfare. It is therefore called upon to provide recreation much as it is called upon to provide fire and police protection or roads.

Administrative Structure

The type of agency administrative structure varies, with three forms being most popular: (1) the separate recreation agency, (2) an agency combining recreation and parks, and (3) a recreation department in the board of education structure. Recreation experts have argued that each of these has its strengths. The separate agency gives recreation the proper attention as a dynamic and active municipal function with requirements of facilities, programs, and professional leadership of its own. The combined parks and recreation department has in its favor the argument that it can integrate the indispensable facilities of a community—the parks, beaches, playgrounds, and so on—and the centers, programs, and leadership resources of active recreation. A complicated problem is that park authorities often have been charged with the conservation of places of beauty and of special historical or other significance. The conservation and recreational functions may be opposed in certain cases, requiring a skillful reconciliation of these two approaches in the department charged with both functions. The recreation department of a board of education can base its service on the philosophy of the integration of recreation and education, as well as the proper use of the extensive community investment in school areas and facilities. The school's commitment to the whole development of the child and the educational welfare of the entire community makes it ready to accept the responsibility of education for leisure. The traditional school might find itself stretched beyond comfort to accept the challenge of meeting the broad public recreation needs of the entire community, with the demand for specialized park, beach, and other facilities that schools traditionally have not provided. Yet the schools have a vital role in community recreation. In some communities, by creative planning based upon a thoughtful acceptance of the basic philosophy of comprehensive recreation service to an entire community, schools have successfully played the role of the primary municipal recreation agency.

In any case, the municipal recreation agency operates within a legal framework of specific or general enabling legislation provided by the state government and the charter and city ordinances of the municipality. These permit the local government to levy taxes and appropriate money, to acquire, develop, and control properties and facilities, to employ personnel, to operate programs and services, and to use other municipal governmental powers in support of recreation.

Program and Facilities

The provision of areas and facilities is a primary function of the public recreation agency, these to be well placed, planned, designed, equipped, and staffed. In the modern big city, with suburban movement, population growth, and movement of new rural groups to the cities all taking place at once, this poses many problems. Subdivisions spring up without enough thought being given to necessary recreation areas. Increasing congestion in the inner city areas, along with the high cost of land and construction, cannot readily be matched by facilities expansion, to say nothing of going beyond matching to creative new development to meet new needs and desires of a community in the recreation age.

The modern public recreation system undertakes to meet certain basic standards: neighborhoods shall have play lots for tiny tots and beautiful and well-equipped playgrounds for children; districts and subcommunities shall have a playground with major facilities for a wide range of sports and individual and group activities; district and regional parks with large-scale facilities, perhaps with water areas and picnic areas, shall be provided; and recreation buildings and centers shall be provided and staffed on many of these facilities for a wide range of indoor recreations.

The range of facilities in a large system is very broad, including not only standard park, parkway, and playground facilities, but beaches and pools, golf courses, specialized fields and stadiums for certain sports, zoos, museums, children's theaters and facilities for the cultural arts, hiking and riding trails, senior citizens' and teen centers, small boat harbors, and many more facilities.

All of these foregoing activities—the setting up of an agency, establishment of its legal enabling framework, acquisition and development of areas and facilities—are preliminary to the basic responsibility of the agency: providing program and leadership services. Program is often conceived of as developing at three levels: (1) a permissive program of "free play" activities, with a minimum of scheduling, supervision, and worker participation; (2) an organized program of activities, interest groups, and clubs working on a scheduled basis; and (3) a program enriched with special events to provide special "highlights." Programs are planned with consideration of such factors and forces as the varying demands of different groups to be served (age, sex, race, etc.), and the special economic, cultural, and other characteristics of a particular neighborhood or subcommunity influencing program timeliness and value.

LEADERSHIP

Professional leadership is the most important ingredient of the entire recreation service. It is being recognized that the professional recreation worker is the one who puts life, creativity, and vitality into the program and makes the service meaningful to the public. So, for superintendents, supervisors, directors, and leaders the emphasis is upon adequate professional competence and employment of sufficient staff to carry on the program. Some of these considerations will concern us later on, in the chapter on the profession of recreation.

The task of administration is to mobilize the creative and productive energies of the staff and to support them in their best professional functioning. This means guaranteeing the material means and conditions for effective work, involving the staff in the cooperative democratic process that is staff administrative policy at its best, and guaranteeing the effectiveness of the auxiliary processes of finance and budgeting, community and public relations, and supervision.

Stability and adequacy of financial arrangements, foresight in budgeting, and responsible accounting are other important elements in administration. Participating in community organization and planning, sharing in professional community relationships as a cooperative member of the community agency team, and carrying on public relations as a function of responsible stewardship and interpretation are additional elements in administration. Finally, staff supervision is looked upon as a highly responsible and important administrative-educational process. In supervision, the supervisor functions both to help the worker get the agency job done competently and as a recreation educator, helping the worker to increase his capacities, to improve on the job, and to grow professionally.

Special types of public recreation agencies are county recreation departments and special recreation districts. County governments set up recreation departments to administer facilities and programs. Some states have passed enabling legislation providing for special recreation districts to be set up by joint action of several municipalities and subdivisions. These districts may administer facilities and programs, with several smaller communities cooperating in this manner to their mutual advantage. Very often a county or a special district can perform on a decentralized basis a highly important service to local communities and school districts that would have difficulty with their funds in providing adequate services on their own. Another device sets up a matching or grant-in-aid program in which the county provides help to small communities in establishing recreation services.

The public recreation agency, possessing taxing, land-acquisition, and other legal powers, should acquire the lands necessary for comprehensive public and voluntary service, provide varied program and professional leadership for both individual and group recreation, and play a leading cooperative role in community recreation planning.

Urban Recreation Facilities

THE ROLES OF STATE AND FEDERAL GOVERNMENTS

The discussion of the government institution in Chapter 9 identified both (1) the government policy that supports active government participation at the state and federal levels and (2) the extensive activities at both levels that demonstrate the carrying out of this policy. The governmental organizations and agencies that have recreation responsibility are many and varied, and this complex is relied upon to provide basic recreation planning, consultation to governments at other levels, research, development, conservation of leisure resources, and basic service operations.

It is obvious that many of the recreation problems faced by the nation require state and federal action. They are beyond the competence and scope of authority of local agencies. In the state of Washington, a potentially disastrous collision of interests occurred between pulp mills and recreation and other interests. The sulphurous waste from the mills was poisoning the waters of Puget Sound, killing the clams and oysters, ruining the beaches, and endangering the commercial fishing industry as well. State action was essential. In Pennsylvania, steel mills dumped waste into the Schuylkill River, polluting the river for many miles and destroying its recreational values. State government began to find the solution.

The Department of Defense and its jurisdictions control hundreds of miles of coastline, navigable rivers, and lakeshore in the country, including vast areas desirable and needed for proper recreation development. Federal government action will be required if these areas are to be made available. The problem of reconciling the need of the city of Chicago for millions of gallons of Lake Michigan water for its water and sanitation needs with the needs of several states and Canadian provinces for an adequate level of water in Lake Michigan to maintain recreation, water transport, and water and sanitation needs of their own requires federal *and* international agreements for its solution.

In those states that have invested important resources in the recreation of their people, sometimes highly diverse and complex organizational patterns are found. Douglass points out that in Pennsylvania, for example, recreational activities at the state level are "distributed among 12 administrative departments; 5 independent administrative boards and commissions; 20 departmental administrative boards and commissions; 70 subunits of state departments, boards, and commissions; and one citizens' board advisory to the governor. This situation is repeated in some fashion in many other states, and the resulting chaotic, inefficient, duplicating, diffuse, and ineffective situation frustrates effective and comprehensive recreation planning and service for their states." [2]

---

[2] Paul Douglass, "Why States Are Sparking Recreation's Growth," *American Recreation Journal,* Vol. 1, No. 1 (August–September, 1960), p. 34.

STATE ORGANIZATION AND SERVICES

In searching for means of bringing administrative order into the states' recreation functions, states have explored several patterns: an interagency or interdepartmental council, a board or commission, a combined park and recreation board, a bureau within a major department, a development authority, or an integrated operating department. Most of these have been attempted, with varying values attending to the several forms. What state governments need, in the estimation of experts in the field, is an opportunity to mobilize the forces and resources of several operating agencies. The responsibilities of these agencies include recreation services and they must continue these services under their own auspices if their administration and organization itself is to be functional. Also, there should be a state agency with recreation development as its primary function, whether or not it coordinates the work of other agencies as part of that function.

Douglass says the "experience of states with the recreation commission or board is now sufficient to indicate that the pattern is politically feasible, professionally desirable, and operationally effective."[3] The combined park and recreation board has demonstrated the usefulness of this approach, along with some problems of combining functions. The bureau within a department may function successfully, depending upon the congeniality of the larger department and its administration and the clarity with which the function of the bureau is spelled out by the state legislature. The development authority has fairly limited functions, perhaps not adequate for fulfilling the broad functions of the state.

There is an argument upon the basis of administrative logic that, someday, the recreation function at the state level will require the organization of a department,[4] but authorities agree that further experience and experimentation in the organization of state services are required in most states in order to develop state recreation services adequate for the needs of individuals and the economic and social growth of the state.[5]

---

[3] Douglass, p. 46.

[4] Douglass, p. 48.

[5] See Harold D. Meyer and Charles K. Brightbill, *State Recreation—Organization and Administration* (New York: A. S. Barnes and Company, 1950).

State departments provide a vast array of consulting, planning, and direct services in recreation. Foremost among these services are the activities of park, forestry, and conservation departments in providing major recreation areas for regional use. Fish, game, and wildlife agencies, highway authorities, universities, welfare departments, departments of education, departments of agriculture, and other organizations all render services.

Federal Programs and Services

The federal government includes many agencies that are involved with recreation. In 1946, several agencies were linked together under the sponsorship of the Secretary of the Interior in a voluntary association, the Federal Inter-Agency Committee on Recreation. This Committee, striving to improve and make more effective the public recreation services of the federal government's agencies, comprises the following members:

Department of Agriculture—the Forest Service, Federal Extension Service

Department of the Army—the Corps of Engineers

Department of Health, Education, and Welfare—the Office of Education and the Public Health Service

Department of the Interior—the Bureau of Land Management, Bureau of Reclamation, Fish and Wildlife Service, and the National Park Service

Housing and Home Finance Agency—the Public Housing Administration

The Inter-Agency Committee operates as a voluntary organization to assist the member agencies in fulfilling several federal recreation functions: (1) those related to the recreation programs conducted by federal agencies for their own personnel (particularly military personnel scattered all over the world); (2) those related to the operation of federally owned properties such as parks, forests, wildlife preserves, hospitals, military establishments, reservoir areas, and housing projects; and (3) those with advisory services in connection with the planning and operation of state and local community park and recreation programs.

This latter type of activity includes (1) planning for recreation in cooperation with other agencies and organizations, (2) consulting about recreation matters with states and their subdivisions, and (3) collecting and disseminating data and information necessary to carry out the above functions.

Typical of the efforts of federal agencies to meet growing national recreation needs is "Mission 66" of the National Park Service. The fact became apparent to the nation's leaders that the American heritage of inspirational, historical, archeological, and educational resources, which are priceless and irreplaceable and which the national parks and monuments represented, was in critical jeopardy from sheer recreational overuse. The 25 million acres included in these areas, which had been obtained through half a century of acquisition and development since Yellowstone National Park was established in 1872, had by 1941 become the vacationland for 21 million visitors. At that time this use was stretching the staff and resources designed to serve adequately perhaps 25 to 30 million visitors. By 1959, however, the number of visitors had *tripled,* having swelled to 62 million visitors. The original expectation, and the instruction to the National Park Service, was to conserve the priceless scenery, natural and historic objects, and wildlife, and to provide for their enjoyment in such appropriate ways as would leave them unimpaired for the enjoyment of generations to come.

By the 1950's this picture was being shattered. Facilities and areas were being worn out, abused, and endangered. The National Park Service in 1956 responded to the emergency by planning and launching Mission 66, a ten-year plan to reach its completion in 1966, the fiftieth anniversary of the National Park Service. This plan foresaw the development of a great network of areas and facilities to meet the needs of 80 million or more visitors a year and, at the same time, to safeguard fully the wilderness and the scenic, scientific, and historic resources in these areas. During the first half of this period, a modest but useful sum of more than $100 million had been expended. Roads and trails, campsites, utility systems, and informational services were improved. Park staffs were increased to provide better protection of park features and serve the visitors more adequately. Plans are presently underway to acquire new lands, the extent of this depending upon the awakening of the American people to the need to increase vastly their common investment in this particular public resource.

The United States Forest Service faced the same critical problem in overuse and severe deterioration of recreation facilities in the

National Forests and initiated "Operation Outdoors" in 1957, calling for $85 million expenditure in five years to rehabilitate and develop recreation facilities in the 149 national forests in forty-four states with their 180 million acres, to which more than 60 million visitors come annually.

The nature of the problems relating primarily to outdoor recreation and the demands upon natural resources for recreational use led Congress to undertake in 1958 a nationwide study of outdoor recreation under the direction of the Outdoor Recreation Resources Review Commission. The purpose of this study was to determine: (1) the outdoor recreation needs of the American people in 1960 and what they will be in 1976 and 2000, (2) the resources available to meet these needs, and (3) what policies and programs should be recommended to meet these needs.[6] As a result of the Commission's report, there was established in 1962 a Bureau of Outdoor Recreation in the Department of Interior. The Bureau does not manage any land but functions to coordinate the recreation activities of more than twenty federal agencies whose activities affect outdoor recreation, and to assist state and local governments with technical aid, including a proposed grants-in-aid program to states for planning and acquisition of needed areas.

Another example of a national government activity reflecting a growing understanding of recreation and its importance in individual welfare is the work of the military services. The Department of Defense, to help maintain morale among the members of the armed forces and to maintain sound social contacts and understanding between the armed forces and the general public, has instituted programs and established facilities for recreation wherever the armed forces are stationed. Trained personnel are employed to conduct programs and community service personnel work on problems of military-civilian community relationships, particularly with respect to off-duty living opportunities for military personnel. These programs are being developed both in the United States and in scores of military bases scattered around the world. The Department of Defense on occasions provides funds to communities to pay a portion of the costs of maintaining, under community auspices, public and voluntary recreation programs offered for military personnel and others in the community.

---

[6] *Outdoor Recreation for America* (Washington, D.C.: Outdoor Recreation Resources Review Commission, January 1962).

The federal government has also responded to an expressed national recreation need by establishing the National Cultural Center. This center was established in 1958 as a bureau in the Smithsonian Institution. The board of trustees is charged with responsibility for constructing such a center in Washington, D.C., for presenting classical and contemporary music, opera, drama, dance, poetry, lectures, and other programs from this and other countries, and for developing programs for children, youth, and other age groups, which will be designed for their participation, education, and recreation. It is hoped that the center may function to stimulate throughout the nation new interest in and support for cultural arts programs encouraging expression of the leisure-time cultural interests of the nation's people.

State and federal governments should play active roles in support of recreation, since there are many problems beyond the scope of local organizations to solve, and there are many regional or national resources that require action at that level, if the future development of recreation is to be nationally furthered.

THE SCHOOL AND RECREATION

In Chapter 9 we discussed the important role of education as a social force interacting with recreation in modern American life. We recognized the importance of education for leisure and the contributions to recreation of the several areas of the schools' functions.[7]

The School's Role

In the community, the school may play an active part in providing the complex of recreation services. The school curriculum itself is being oriented gradually toward leisure-fulfillment purposes, along with vocational and other purposes. In the language, graphic, and musical arts, social sciences, home crafts, and several vocational subjects there are splendid opportunities for teaching recreational values. The extra-class program of sports, interest groups, clubs, cultural activities and social activities, operating before school, at noon, after school, and at other times, comes closer yet to fulfilling direct recreational objectives.

---

[7] For additional background on the school see John L. Hutchinson, ed., *Leisure and the Schools* (Washington, D.C.: American Association for Health, Physical Education, and Recreation, 1961).

The school-centered community recreation program attacks the central problem of community need. School facilities, particularly gymnasiums, pools, fields, auditoriums, laboratories, and the like, are adapted to both educational and recreational program needs. School and park authorities have experimented widely with the Park School, in which the areas and facilities are developed adjacent to each other and a joint education and recreation program is offered, using fully the resources of each. School camps, water facilities, and so on, provide the basis for special programs.

In some cases, particularly in smaller communities, the school may be the only public institution that has facilities and resources approximating what might be necessary to support a community recreation program. It also has the financial resources and the personnel resources to mount such a program. Under the pressure of need and public recognition of this need many schools are moving ahead to organize for a community recreation program. They have already organized summer programs emphasizing sports, social recreation, craft and cultural arts interest groups, community celebrations, and other activities. Year-round programs up to seven days a week attract participants of all ages to the school and other facilities under its auspices and to a wide range of regular groups, free play, and special events.

The administrative organization varies. In some cases a regular school department like physical education is given the responsibility for carrying on the program. Or a special department may be set up for this purpose. On occasion an arrangement will be made to assign the operating responsibility to an outside agency, using the school's facilities. A cooperative operation of a school authority with a municipal authority may be worked out.

A major task is rethinking the function of the school plant itself, adapting, redesigning, and reconstructing school facilities with the "community-school" function and multiple use in mind. Another task is making the school available to community groups through a permit plan or some other device, with or without fees. Special community recreation service units have been built, so that education and recreation programs can be operated daily, partly parallel and partly in series, using many hours of the day and night seven days a week.

The adult education movement, it has been pointed out, is one of the outstanding adult leisure-time recreation programs in the country, at least from the point of view of numbers involved. Many hundreds of school-sponsored community recreation programs for children, youth, and adults bear witness to the deep involvement of the school in this field. It is important to note the special impact of this new function on the education profession. Educators are striving to face the problem of enabling individuals to fulfill their interests and needs in the voluntary leisure-time programs under school auspices rather than the "captive-group" environment of the compulsory public school system. The fundamental differences in method, as well as some of the important common elements in method, are the subject both of careful study and much discussion.

A special educational program of importance is that conducted for the three and one-half million college and university students in the nation. Aware of the fact that these young men and women, and the several hundred thousand faculty members who teach them, need to live well-balanced lives while on campus, schools are making provision for recreation including extensive sports, cultural, social, and other pursuits. Student unions and student leisure-time centers are being built and professional staffs are developing programs and coordinating the associated activities of students. The Association of College Unions, which has a membership of almost four hundred unions, directs this program on a national scale. With one million additional students enrolled in junior colleges, the expansion potential of the student union is matched by the fact that college enrollment will double in the period 1960–1970, thus making these programs all the more significant.

The point of view of the recreation profession is that for the school adequately to undertake the community recreation function, educational administrators must recognize the need for the programs to be operated in the main by professionally trained recreation workers. Schoolteachers can provide important assistance in the program, given the elements of proper selection, orientation, and training. But the major leadership and the supervisory activities must be provided by recreation personnel. The skilled recreation administrator recognizes in the teaching staff a rich resource of leadership, both in the role of leisure-educators as well as in the general recreation program of the community.

How Large a Role

It must be recognized that the school is often the largest single public agency in a particular community, is perhaps the only one with qualified professional personnel at work, and has specific responsibilities to the entire community. For these reasons it must play a major role in developing recreation. At the same time it must conscientiously work to instill in any community the concept of cooperation and teamwork, and must set the example in its own relations with the rest of the community. There are communities where the school seems to have placed itself in a position of semi-isolation from the rest of the community's service agencies. There are communities, on the contrary, where the school is playing a vital functioning role as a leading team member in a close-knit structure of many agencies and organizations serving the community's recreation needs and participating in community organization and planning.

The argument remains whether or not the school should take the central responsibility for community recreation. Some argue that the school is best fitted for this role, and other public and voluntary agencies should play a secondary role. Others argue that the school ought to play a secondary role and stick to education, leaving recreation to another public agency. A more reasonable view than either of these suggests that there is a need today to mobilize all the resources possible to meet the expanding needs for recreation services, and that the public schools, like other agencies, must be active in fulfilling their responsibility in this area of social welfare and community life. The specific form of organization must be adapted to the particular local need as the community, aided by its educational and recreational leadership, recognizes such a need.

The school should play a major role in recreation, committing its resources to a program of education for leisure and recreation for the entire community. Its professional teaching and administrative personnel should play a role as a leading member of the community recreation-planning team.

VOLUNTARY RECREATION ORGANIZATIONS

An important part of the American recreation tradition is the work of voluntary agencies. The identifying characteristic of these organizations is their reliance upon the volunteer efforts of citizens to organize, finance, and carry on their programs. The agencies do not operate under government auspices, but instead rely upon volunteer participation of community members on their boards of directors, and upon voluntary contributions of the interested public for their support. They often raise their main funds through participation in community funds, as well as through independent efforts.

The basic common philosophy of these agencies is their belief that through guided group programs they can contribute to the healthy personality and character of the individual child, to his physical, mental, and social well-being, and to his ability to participate constructively in the community. In the earlier years of these organizations, they operated usually under the sponsorship of religious organizations, and their programs emphasized religious educational efforts and "character-building" activities. These ranged from religious study to sports, crafts, and a variety of cultural and recreational pursuits, all with the hope of obtaining the deeper values. Later on, programs began to center more on the individual and his needs, and agencies shifted away somewhat from standardized programs toward more flexible efforts to meet individual needs and to utilize a wide range of program and group situations designed to help the individual in his social adjustment and personal growth.

In a modern community there may be one or many voluntary agencies operating in schools, churches, neighborhood centers, and so on, organizing troops, groups, packs, clubs, and tribes under leadership that is, primarily, volunteer. The local agency may be a unit of one of the great national voluntary organizations. It will itself be organized with a volunteer board of directors, which takes responsibility for raising the agency's funds, supervising its financial operations, reviewing its administrative and program policies and actions, and otherwise working to keep the agency functioning productively on an even keel. As with Scouts, Y's, and similar groups, a community may have several local units operating, each under a local board or committee, and with numerous subcommittees actively at work on planning and policy making, service programs, and other aspects of the operation.

Some voluntary agencies own facilities as well as make use of other community facilities. Boys' Clubs, Y's, and Settlements base their work upon buildings, some of the space of which may be used to house young people under agency auspices, and some of which provide facilities such as gymnasiums, meeting rooms, libraries, lounges, nurseries and kindergartens, playgrounds, and activity rooms for crafts, dramatics, and other arts.

A second group of organizations go out into the neighborhoods, organize the children into groups, and then seek the use of other buildings for their programs. Scouts, Camp Fire Girls, and the Y's rely to some extent upon public recreation facilities, schools, churches, lodges, and fire stations for meeting places. Many agencies are concerned with camping facilities for their members, and campsites are acquired and developed for resident camping either during the summer months or on a year-round basis.

Voluntary Agency Programs

The recreational activity programs of the agencies are the means by which participants are attracted, and through which groups are organized and guided group programs, often progressing through several age groups, are established. Children are attracted by promise of high adventure and fun, and the meetings, activity periods, projects, hikes, outings, and so on, feed the child's love for fun with his fellows, for games, new experiences, and adventure, especially in the out-of-doors. Worked into the programs of most agencies are carefully planned activities stressing service and helping others, as well as citizenship activities and useful community activities. The serious purposes that underlie these programs, that are worked into the activities, provide many of these agencies with the main threads in the fabric of the total program.

Groups are under the guidance of adult leaders who, through the programs and by adult example, seek to inculcate attitudes and habits contributing to sound character and good social adjustment. In this conscious effort to guide children's play into specific value-directed channels, the voluntary agencies differ somewhat from those recreational agencies that rely upon learnings derived more directly from wholesome and creative group-play activities without direct indoctrination with ideals of character or citizenship. Both approaches have significant elements of validity.

The range of voluntary organizations, many of them national agencies with thousands of units and up to millions of members, can be comprehended by a quick glance at the list of some of the significant ones:

Young Men's Christian Association—organized in 1851; 1960 national membership 2,650,000 boys and girls and young adults, seven years old and over, in 202,000 groups, with 377,000 volunteer leaders.

Young Women's Christian Association—organized nationally in 1871; 1960 national membership 2,150,000 girls, young women, and adult women, twelve years old and over, in 69,000 groups, with 80,000 women leaders.

4H Clubs—organized in late 1800's and authorized by act of Congress in 1914; 1960 national membership 3,000,000 members, ten years old and over, in 95,000 clubs, with 462,000 adult leaders.

Boys' Clubs of America, Incorporated—organized in 1906; 1960 national membership 600,000 boys, seven years old and over, in 585 Boys' Clubs, with 14,200 men leaders.

Boy Scouts of America—organized in 1909; 1960 national membership 4,850,000 boys, eight years old and over, in 130,000 groups, with 1,340,000 men and women leaders.

Camp Fire Girls Incorporated—organized in 1910; 1960 national membership 675,000 girls, seven years old and over, in 45,000 groups, with 180,000 women leaders.

Girl Scouts of the United States of America—organized in 1912; 1960 national membership 2,500,000 girls, seven years old and over, in 150,000 groups, with 320,000 women leaders.

Another kind of organization, found more often in the larger cities, is the settlement or neighborhood center. The settlement is located usually in the older and poorer city neighborhoods where income, housing, and family conditions are inadequate for many. The settlement undertakes to work with all of the positive influences in the neighborhood, to provide a center where the neighborhood families can enjoy social, recreational, educational, cultural, and civic activities together, and to focus its helping efforts at the points of greatest stress in neighborhood life.

Settlement buildings house varied recreation facilities, and recreational activities make up a major part of the settlement's program. The member often becomes strongly involved in the varied activities of the settlement and comes deeply under its influence. Participating in the program and enjoying relationships with the professional settlement staff and his neighbors, also tied together in the stimulating life of the settlement, an individual finds both the satisfactions of friendly neighborly associations and the stimulus to live more effectively in the neighborhood.

The settlement functions as a recreation agency, in the best sense of the word. But the neighborhood-improvement function and the focus upon the individual and his needs underlie and change the focus of much of the work. One individual is enabled to seek help for individual social-relationship problems. Another is encouraged to put superior leadership abilities to work for the benefit of his fellows. A family is encouraged to work out problems of confused relationships. Some neighbors are helped to understand another neighbor group, to live together with them harmoniously, and to build neighborhood unity. Thus, in the settlement, recreation becomes an essential element of a larger complex of related welfare services.

Rural Programs

In rural communities, and experimented with in some urban areas, is the highly creative 4H Club program of the Cooperative Extension Service of the Federal Department of Agriculture, the state land-grant colleges, and the county governments. The county agricultural agent is a state-college employee, and he and his staff are responsible primarily for club organization, but they depend upon volunteer adult leaders in the communities to carry the major responsibility for organizing the clubs. In fact, the Department of Agriculture sponsorship of this program makes it a mixed public and voluntary agency program, but it is placed here because of its predominantly voluntary nature at the local level. The programs are strongly organized toward the goals of rural and agricultural education and improvement of rural living, with a heavy emphasis on appropriate recreational values as a secondary goal. The programs are offered to children and youth sometimes as part of the school program, but primarily as leisure-time programs. They range from deeply interesting individual and group projects in agricultural production and farm and animal husbandry to cultural and craft activities and to camping, conferences, and participation in rural fairs.

Voluntary recreation organizations have the responsibility to provide children and youth with guided group programs, to work closely with the other recreation agencies, to strive to provide this opportunity equally and freely to children, and to accent the individual development value elements in their programs.

COMMERCIAL RECREATION

Commercial recreation plays an important part in the leisure life of millions of persons. We reviewed some of its dimensions, including its economic and recreational significance, in Chapter 7. Its proper relation to the other community agencies, as well as its proper control and encouragement to provide the best experience for participants, is the concern of all of those interested in community recreation, and is our concern here. The range of its operations is rapidly growing both in number and diversity. The familiar movie, pool hall, nightclub, dance hall, theater, tavern, ball park, and race track possibly are losing some of their relative popularity to the new amusement park, bowling alley, exercise and reducing salon, swimming pool, ski resort, all-day fishing excursion boat, private day camp, coffee house, and other leisure-time activities.

The motivations of commercial recreation, and its guiding principles, are different from those of other recreation agencies. Commercial recreation is organized for profit. It has to be organized and presented to the public, so that they will pay for it. Programs are ultimately evaluated in terms of financial returns, in contrast to other recreation, which is nonprofit. Operators of the latter are motivated by a sense of values related to worthy use of leisure time and the well-being of the community and its people. Leadership and program both tend to be evaluated from different points of view by these two segments of the recreation organization.

Program Guidelines

There are, in truth, some important points at issue. The community recreation agency strives to meet needs as broadly as possible and to provide wholesome content in its program. The commercial recreation agency must make money; it cannot serve persons who do not pay for its services. Moreover, it must get customers in competition with other commercial agencies, and must use the same means for attracting patronage as its competitors use. Sometimes this competition results in throwing aside considerations of propriety, wholesomeness, and dignity in favor of sensationalism, provocation, immorality, and high-pressure appeal.

Some leisure-time pursuits have been criticized as active demoralizing and degrading elements in community life. Enough evidence has been gathered of the powerful hold of drinking, drug addiction, sex delinquency, gambling, and related vices upon millions of people to appreciate that commercial promoters and pushers must bear part of the responsibility for the misery and maladjustment that accompany these sordid recreational pursuits. The eager exploitation of sensationalism and immorality tends to a perversion of aesthetic tastes, particularly the corruption of healthy and normal sexual feelings and interests, in the process of making profits by exploiting such themes. This critical problem has been attacked by legal regulation of commercial establishments to reduce undesirable activities. Such police activities are demanded and supported by the community generally, particularly in respect to common efforts to protect youth from damage and to encourage a wholesome environment for family life.

On the other side of the coin, thousands of legitimate and competently operated commercial recreation establishments are offering millions of people a wide range of highly rewarding, health-giving, and satisfying recreational activities. Commercial promotion has stimulated the interest of the public in many new activities, and has provided many attractive facilities and programs that meet important community recreation needs. The mass base upon which many recreations have been offered has made them available to millions of people who without these programs might have to wait indefinitely for public or voluntary agency capital for their organization. Lloyd Settle, discussing the amusement park, lists the following points as guides in the planning of major commercial recreation developments: (1) large centers, based upon showmanship; (2) imagination in planning and operation; (3) family appeal; (4) clear dollar value to customers; (5) prestige value of big names and groups; (6) big promotion and honest promotion; (7) cleanliness and sanitation; (8) easy accessibility to mass population groups; (9) healthy political climate and cooperative government attitude; (10) awareness of weather as a factor and a tool.[8]

Among commercial recreations certain sports rank high. Bowling has become almost a habit for millions. Skiing in the winter and sailing, boating, and canoeing in the summer run a close second. Commercial resorts offer fishing, outdoor picnicking, swimming, and other water sports for vacation and holiday-bound folk. Amusement centers like Disneyland in Los Angeles, Riverview in Chicago, and

---

[8] Lloyd Settle, "The Future of Commercial Recreation," address delivered at the University of California at Los Angeles, 1958. Unpublished.

Coney Island and Freedomland in New York draw their share of funseekers. The public dance hall is a popular and successful recreation venture. From there to nightclubs and bars is, however, but a short step, and we leave the field of active recreations for sedentary ones. We also leave the field where community approval and encouragement are found and enter one where legal supervision and police control of undesirable activities become more important.

Spectator sports and amusements, offering primarily amusement and what exercise and emotional outlet shouting at contestants and umpires provides, are a second major area of commercial recreation. Professional baseball, football, basketball, hockey, boxing, and "wrestling" shows provide amusement for more millions of persons.

Community Relationships and Responsibilities

There are two important responsibilities of the community in regard to commercial recreation. First, by government regulation and community demand, the community must guarantee proper practice regarding safety and health and appropriate standards of taste and moral and ethical practice. Second, where responsible citizens with a proper concern for the public interest are operating legitimate and beneficial commercial enterprises, they must be encouraged to take their place in the community recreation planning bodies and assume responsibilities as members of the community recreation team. More and more frequently, individuals and commercial organizations are relating themselves to recreation-coordinating councils and participating in the planning of services for the community. There are many entrepreneurs who believe firmly in rendering a public service to the best interests of the public instead of merely for their own profit.

The view that at least the mass communication field has responsibility for public interest was expressed by Federal Communications Commissioner Newton Minow, who said in addressing the United States Broadcasters Association:

> We all know that people would prefer to be entertained than stimulated or informed. But your obligations are not satisfied if you look only to popularity as a test of what to broadcast. You are not only in show business; you are free to communicate ideas as well as relaxation. It is not enough to cater to the nation's whims—you must also serve the nation's needs.[9]

---

[9] As reported in *Newsweek,* Vol. 57, No. 21 (May 22, 1961), p. 87.

Commercial mass amusement media, discussed previously in the chapter on recreation and economic forces, might be included here as part of the recreation organization of the community. In one sense, the movies, radio, television, newspapers, and mass production of other literature are part of the commercial recreation of the community and should be assessed for their contribution. In another sense, these mass amusement media are operating far from the level of community recreation organization. This isolation keeps the recreation movement from properly undertaking their integration as cooperating organizations into the mainstream of community recreation life. It also poses serious problems and offers serious obstacles to the ordinary processes of citizen regulation and control through the instrument of local democratic government.

Commercial recreation, with motivation for profit often obscuring other value considerations, must strive to maintain basic leisure values and to accept full membership on the community recreation team in order for its great potential as a positive leisure resource to be realized.

CHURCH, HOSPITALS, INDUSTRY, TRADE UNIONS, POLICE

The Church

As we noted in Chapter 9, the church plays two roles with respect to recreation. One of these roles is as guardian of public morals, in which it opposes some of man's playful pursuits because they can do more harm than good. The other role is as a social and recreational center for its members and the community. It has recognized the values of recreation in strengthening the bonds of the religious fellowship, as a progressive and informal educational method for young and old alike, and as a feature of church life attractive to new and old members and to others in the community. Modern church structures often include selected recreation facilities, and professional religious educators are trained in recreation philosophy, method, and program skills.

The Catholic Youth Organization, the Jewish Community Centers, and several Protestant denominational organizations have undertaken extensive youth programs of a recreational nature under the sponsorship of local parishes, synagogues, or similar organizations. The Jewish Centers and a wide range of other Jewish organizations, such as B'nai B'rith, are under auspices considerably broader than simply religious groups. The Jewish community emphasizes the cultural heritage of the Jewish people and strives through its various social and recreational programs to fulfill this cultural objective rather than a narrowly religious one, although religious values and traditions are integral to the programs as well. The Mormon church community is an outstanding example of the integration of recreation programming into religious affiliation and family and community life. Church camping is growing rapidly and a sizable body of literature with recreation content (songs, dances, activities) has been built. Many of the larger churches employ full- and part-time recreation leaders.

The church, from its position as guardian of ethical values, makes several important contributions to community recreation. One contribution is its unremitting campaigns against the more obnoxious vices that attract and exploit many recreation-bent individuals. Second is its combining of two important leisure-time uses, religion and recreation, with wholesome satisfactions, thus giving added dimension to both and to the life of the individual. Another is its success in offering family recreational programs that strengthen family life and stimulate the congeniality and unity of family relations. The church also plays a positive supporting role to public and voluntary recreation organizations, and as an informal educational agency in helping people to enjoy and contribute to the richness of wholesome community recreational life.

Hospitals

In Chapter 9 a brief description of the developing field of recreation therapy was given, along with a picture of the relationship between the health movement in this country and the recreation movement. The location of much of the actual functional relationship is in the general hospital, the neuropsychiatric hospital, or the special-function hospital (such as the hospital for chronic diseases or the one for children). The rapid development of recreation in the hospitals and the equally rapid development of the specialization and training of recreation therapists bear witness to the growing importance of this relationship.

Particularly in the neuropsychiatric hospital have the medical directors realized that an important part of the total help given a patient is providing him with nondemanding but interesting and engrossing experiences, either individually or in groups, that permit normal satisfactions of desires for creative, pleasurable, self-respecting pursuits. The patient who is able to use these activities is helped thereby to enter into the more demanding, usually frightening, sometimes discouragingly slow-moving therapeutic experiences.

The recreation therapist thus operates in a crucial area of the medical complex, using his basic method and relying upon his basic philosophy of values as a guide to give meaning to recreation experiences of patients. The Special Services Sections of the Veterans Administration and the Armed Forces, the American National Red Cross, and the United States Public Health Service have established hospital recreation programs. State and local departments of mental hygiene as well as many private and community hospitals offer comprehensive recreation services.

Industry

Industrial recreation is enjoying steady growth. It began with the recognition by enlightened management that some of the tension, fatigue, and low worker morale in connection with modern high-pressure industrial processes might be alleviated by programs of relaxing recreation. Management has learned to pay some attention to the physical and mental health of the workers as factors in productivity. While there might have been some thought of recreation as a device to still the murmurs of worker dissatisfaction over basic problems of hours and wages, recreation was seen primarily as an important tool for creating a better working environment. Relaxing and enjoyable activities with other workers during rest periods, mealtimes, and off-the-job hours are recognized as being important to the physical and emotional health of the individual worker, to the improvement of relationships within the plant, to the reduction of accidents and carelessness, and to the improvement of production on the line.

Many forms of organization have been tried. Sometimes the entire program will be sponsored by management. Sometimes there will be co-sponsorship by management and workers with financing by management. Other times there will be joint financing as well. Another form will find the program operated entirely by the employees. The argument has been made for an organization that is relatively independent administratively of direct control by either management or labor. A certain basic distrust by workers of employers, with whom they may have locked horns in basic disputes over wages, hours, and working conditions, does not permit of any plan other than a forthright one based upon cooperative administration.

Programs and facilities vary widely by size and type of industry. Companies have experimented with almost the entire range of recreations, both for brief sessions during the work day and for evenings, weekends and vacation periods, often involving families of employees. The program may vary from a few special events such as "the company picnic" to highly organized interest groups and clubs, athletic leagues, dances, movies, and so on. Community facilities are being used more and more, and are thus providing a framework for public-industry cooperation. In some instances the company, with its employees, *is* the community, in which case it plays the role of community recreation agency.

Trade Unions

To many workers their union is the most important organization to which they belong. Although they have been organized primarily to improve the living standards of members, unions have expanded their activities to fulfill a concern for the welfare of their members in other ways. Recreation has been a growing function of many unions. New union centers are being built with an eye to their use as a major recreation center for members. Recreation programs range from informal, cooperatively sponsored, single events to comprehensive and well-developed programs employing trained recreation staffs and scores of volunteers such as those sponsored in the United Automobile Workers and the International Ladies Garment Workers. Among the activities and programs carried on by unions with strong leadership are extensive sports and leagues; dances, dinners, and social events; fishing, hunting, and outing activities; resident camping; bowling and archery; cultural activities such as choruses, painting, photography, dance, and music groups; and special programs for retired workers. Some unions operate their own recreation facilities—camps, resorts, clubs, and the like. Others function through local volunteer recreation committees that organize special-interest groups and secure space, equipment, and leadership for them at a minimum cost to the worker.

The leadership of the unions has only partly recognized the value of recreation in the life of the trade union. There has been an effort to understand and use recreation as a means of vitalizing and making more attractive the union meeting itself. There is the problem also of helping the union leadership to appreciate the value of recreation as a means of enriching the life of the worker and of his family and to understand the role of the union in stimulating worker interest in recreation and leisure-time interests, and the role of recreation in stimulating interest in the union. Also, union leadership could give much thought to the development of union headquarters as recreational and cultural centers for the members, with appropriate services to fulfill this purpose. For many workers, direct contact with the union occurs mainly when they are unemployed and thus have an abundance of leisure time.

Police

With the stated purpose usually of preventing juvenile delinquency, but with the additional objective of providing leisure-time activities for children and youth in a community, police departments have often undertaken recreation programs. In rural communities, law enforcement agencies have had contacts with youth in need of programs and not reached by any other agency. Law enforcement agencies have provided important service to such youth as a supplement to their delinquency-control activities. Activities may include street programs, athletic leagues, special events and trips, summer camping outings, and swimming.

A major benefit of such programs is the way they reorient the attitudes of children and youth toward law officers, whom they learn to know as friends rather than as threatening and punitive adults. Similar attitude changes are found in the police, who may find in recreation a tool for guiding youth and who may be able to help youth not only through their own programs but through referral to the recreation agencies available.

The problem faced by police agencies involved in extensive recreation programs is obtaining the professional recreation personnel required for adequate programs from within their own ranks. The hope that police officers, with their specialized training in skills other than recreation, would prove to be adequate as recreation leaders falls short of reality. Instead, it is argued, close cooperation of law enforcement agencies with public and voluntary recreation agencies will facilitate the programs of each and will result in both better recreation and better law enforcement.

Probably the police function in recreation, in addition to its highly important function of supporting the community recreation efforts through cooperative activities, will be to experiment with special limited programs with particular groups for whom such contact might be important educationally, but not to undertake programs of broad service to the community.

In Chapter 9 it was pointed out that the police and penal organizations make constructive use of recreation as part of the rehabilitative efforts of penal institutions. These activities in their best sense are thought of as recreative and therapeutic in nature. They require thoughtful adaptation to the state of morale, anxiety, and emotional disturbance of individuals and groups placed under the restrictive and protective custody of courts and institutions. We recognize that recreation in these settings still has a dynamic quality, when made available in appropriate forms and circumstances, to those in need of this kind of rehabilitation.

Recreation organizations under church, hospital, industry, trade union, and police auspices, providing important parts of the community's recreation services, should direct their efforts primarily toward those individuals associated with these organizations but must participate in the cooperative assessment of community recreation need and in planning for community recreation.

ORGANIZATIONS FOR THE CULTURAL ARTS

Under municipal or other public auspices, or under voluntary or private auspices, there operate in communities several major cultural arts organizations providing important contributions to the people's leisure. Often these organizations operate under the public recreation department, often under another municipal commission or body. In any case, they exist as a part of recreation not always closely linked with the rest of the recreation field either in the thinking of the public or of the operating groups that are responsible for them. Nevertheless, they are a primary recreation resource and fulfill a major role in the leisure life of the community. Among these organizations are libraries, museums, zoological and botanical gardens, aquariums, planetariums, symphony, opera, and ballet organizations, the little theater and the legitimate stage, dance, musical, graphic arts, and literary organizations, and others. Their contributions are of much importance in the recreation whole.

THE LIBRARY

Libraries as agencies, and librarians as professionals, are dedicated to helping people to enjoy recreational and educational reading. With the exception of certain valuable collections and collectors' items, the most important objective is to wear a book out (through proper use) as rapidly as possible. Under both public and voluntary sponsorship, libraries have been built and programs have been developed whose aims are to stimulate reading as a source of personal happiness and cultural enrichment. Libraries on wheels (bookmobiles) roam hospitals, rural communities, the suburbs, and the city neighborhoods seeking out their reading public. Libraries have made available collections of films, records, tape recordings, scripts, orchestrations for instrumental groups, and music for choruses. They have organized literary clubs, storytelling programs, tours, and exhibits. All of these move the library close to the broad community and encourage millions to seek enrichment in life through reading and cultural pleasures.

The Museum and Planetarium

Whether for social historical collections, natural historical materials, art collections, scientific materials, or meteorological exhibits, museums in the modern day are important community recreational and cultural resources. The emphasis of the great collections, often gathered at tremendous cost and representing priceless cultural treasure, is to make the best art available for the leisure-time study and pleasure of the community as well as the leisure education of the young. Museumobiles and historymobiles are designed to take small collections out to the community. The modern curator and astronomer-director must be a cultural-recreationist himself, as well as a scientist and artist. Some of the outstanding museums such as the Field Museum in Chicago and the Metropolitan Museum of Art in New York have developed the skill of presentation and display to a high art form. In the space age, the planetarium, with its costly equipment, meteorological displays, and scientific demonstrations, comes even more into its own as a community resource.

An important problem presents itself to the directors of these institutions. Some of the collections include treasured items of great value that are impossible to replace. To reconcile the important task of preserving these items with the equally important task of encouraging the interested public to share in their enjoyment requires much thought. The first task requires great scientific skill, as in the preservation of noted historical documents, treasured archeological remains, or priceless paintings or sculptures. The second task focuses therefore on the problem of full use without misuse or overuse.

The Aquarium, Zoological Garden, and Botanical Garden

The collections of live things in these great organizations offer unending pleasure as well as educational benefits to people of all ages. There is much creative work going on to make the collections meaningful and interesting to the public. Children's zoos, traveling zoos, and the highly effective presentations of the collections in their natural surroundings, increase their value. And, like the staffs of the museums, the staffs of these organizations must wage a daily struggle to keep animals and other things accessible, safe for the viewers, with safety for the exhibits. Both the public and the recreationists, who may think of facilities, equipment, and supplies as expendable and who try to maximize their appropriate use and to replace them when they are worn out, must learn to understand the dilemma of the curator who wants the public to enjoy his treasures but who must post "don't feed" or "don't pick" or "don't trample" or "stay on the trail" signs, who must put things behind glass, who must put fences around California's redwoods, for example, to keep visitors from trampling the roots and killing the trees.

The Music, Drama, Dance, Graphic Arts, or Literary Organization

This wide range of cultural organizations should be brought into the community team of leisure-time agencies so that their contributions to community recreation may be fully enjoyed. Some of these organizations may be primarily commercial, but for the most part they are carried on by groups of individuals on a voluntary basis in order that their activities might enrich the cultural life of a community. Sometimes activities are publicly sponsored; more often they are under the sponsorship of individuals who contribute to their maintenance; and in some cases they are sponsored by a foundation. Often they provide programs for children. Many communities have thoroughly competent professional artistic personnel employed in major producing companies. But often the companies who band together are semi-professional artists or professional artists who offer their services to the public on the basis of minimal, if any, compensation. Their contribution to the community's cultural life is significant. Their participation in these cultural activities is a profoundly self-satisfying recreation for themselves as well. The community's opportunity to be the beneficiary of these cultural efforts depends usually upon the dedicated organizational and artistic effort of those whom the community can count upon as its cultural leaders.

Important cultural contributions to the recreation of a community must be made by special organizations under municipal, school, voluntary, commercial, or other auspices. These organizations—operating libraries, museums, music and dance groups, and a great variety of other cultural activities—should play an important cooperative role in the community's recreation.

CAMPING

Brief mention must be made of camping, which is a part of the recreation and education program of many municipal, school, and voluntary agencies, industry and union organizations, and commercial and therapeutic agencies. It runs the gamut of agencies and organizations, yet stands as a movement of its own, in some respects, with a national association—the American Camping Association—and many practitioners who count camping as their profession.

The powerful appeal of the out-of-doors and America's pioneer and Indian tradition have encouraged the growth of the organized camping movement, which directs its energies to providing opportunities for millions of campers, mostly children and youth, but including adults and families, to spend some time enjoying the high adventure of camp life. It should be noted that this country, nevertheless, may well be lagging behind several other countries in camping opportunities. In Sweden, for example, practically every child is guaranteed summer group camping experiences as part of his educational life. The philosophy of resident camping emphasizes interest in the out-of-doors, the self-reliant way of life for the individuals. The essence of camping is the highly cooperative living experience of a small group working, playing, and learning together in a natural environment with varying degrees of primitiveness.

A major community investment is required for most camping, in order to provide safe and adequate facilities. The American Camping Association has developed standards that require competence in program planning and direct leadership of program groups by trained personnel.

It was pointed out that in 1958 there were 7,377 camps providing camping activities for children 9–16 years of age. It is estimated that 20 per cent of the children of this age want to attend camp, a conservative estimate in relation to standards in this country and several European countries. On this basis it was estimated that to provide two weeks at camp for these children by 1980, 16,319 camps of the present average capacity would be needed to meet the need.[10]

Even for a short period of a few days, camping is for each person an intensive experience. The closeness of his relations with nature and with his fellows and leaders day and night is an opportunity for a special kind of education. A variety of recreational programs can also be utilized for the benefit of the camper. Camping is fun. For these and other reasons, recreationists have estimated that, for the healthy growth and development of the individual, the camping experience for a few short days might be the equivalent of many months of ordinary intermittent club or group experience. This notion needs testing by research, but there is little argument with the point that camping is a highly significant experience, and one to be offered in community programs to broad groups as an adjunct to other programs.

In recent years, day camping has developed as an outgrowth of the overnight program. Day camping is camping on a daytime basis and has assumed major proportions in the over-all program of most public, voluntary, and private recreation agencies. The familiar station wagon full of kids is the badge of operation. Although some skeptics may question just how much actual camping or camp-program activities are included, the usual program of playground-type recreational activities is modified to introduce the "flavor" of camping.

INFORMAL GROUPS

Finally, among the organizations interested in recreation, we must take note of the contribution of a large number of informal and private organizations whose concern may be primarily for themselves, but whose concern often is turned toward the area of community recreation service. There are thousands of clubs and groups whose almost exclusive concern is providing recreation resources for their own members who organize and support the programs. Among these are athletic clubs, golf clubs, tennis clubs, country clubs, beach

---

[10] American Camping Association, "Resident Camps for Children—Present Status and Future Needs," a study for the National Park Service (Bradford Woods, Martinsville, Indiana: 1960).

clubs, and such. A second category of groups are lodges, fraternal groups, and similar groups such as the Elks, the Eagles, and the Masons. The American Association of University Women, the League of Women Voters, and similar organizations pursue cultural, educational, and community-service objectives along with other objectives.

Another group of organizations—the service groups—claim as their primary function important civic and service functions. These groups—the Junior Leagues, Rotarians, Kiwanis, Lions, and Optimist Clubs—contribute often to important recreational objectives. They study community needs, particularly in the area of child and youth welfare, civic improvement, and enrichment of community life. They carry on many projects directed toward community improvement. In many smaller communities, they often become the mainspring of community effort directed toward improving community recreation.

The important recreational functions of these informal groups are not the same as those of public and voluntary recreation agencies. The latter are the permanent operating organizations. The former function as supporting, activizing, stimulating, auxiliary forces in the community, and they can be counted upon for important assistance when called upon. They are truly the citizens in action. Strong community organization for recreation depends upon the active functioning of both the formal organizations and these informal organizations, united in striving to enrich community leisure life.

ORGANIZING THE COMMUNITY FOR RECREATION

As we have seen, community recreation activities are organized by a wide range of organizations. Programs under public auspices, either municipal or school-centered, are often the major services available. Programs under voluntary auspices are found in a great number of organizations and often constitute a large part of the community program. The programs under commercial auspices, seen in their widest scope, involve more people, more investment, and more expenditure, probably, than all the other programs combined. Many commercial activities, however, are not thought of as part of the basic recreational complex, particularly in planning, and thus one segment of the community's program is relatively unrelated to the rest.

Police, trade unions, industries, and a large number of private organizations have involved themselves in recreational activities, and are an important part of the organizational whole.

The important question at this point is, how can the community mobilize and utilize most effectively these many resources to meet its needs, and what are the organizational principles involved? The range of organizations involved is not the only variable. Another variable is the range of ages of participants and the variety of needs and requirements they represent. A third variable is the range of economic and social class groups, racial and cultural groups, religious groups, and geographically differentiated groups. This poses for organizers and planners important problems of varying needs as well as of principles of equal rights and opportunities. Some of the sharpest conflicts in communities, posing some of the most difficult problems for community leaders, have grown out of the growing belief that segregation in recreation and special privilege for certain groups are intolerable according to the democratic American concept of community, and that recreational opportunity ought to be equally shared by all. This provides the principle underlying community planning for recreation—that all resources should be used to the fullest in meeting the needs of all groups in the community.

In most cases, the governing organization in a community in modern years will have taken some steps to organize a publicly supported recreation agency, and as this agency undertakes to fulfill its public function it will find itself involved with many previously established voluntary and other organizations similarly at work fulfilling this community need. These groups of agencies have tended to work out a provisional division of labor among themselves. The public agency, with its considerable financial resources and its capacity for establishing special claims to land areas in the name of the public welfare, has accepted as a primary function the provision of the major material means for recreation, the basic land and water recreation areas, and some basic community recreation building facilities.

The commitment of a city to acquire adequate areas for recreation has led to very difficult and frustrating experiences of cities experiencing the great decentralization and suburban movements discussed in an earlier chapter. The effort to plan properly in these new areas, and to maintain properly in the old areas, sufficient land and facilities for the proper development of recreation has run contrary to the economic interests of residential and commercial developers and others.

A new and challenging idea has been advanced by students of scientific and humanistic city planning—that planning, housing, recreation, school, commercial, and other interests must be coordinated to the end of functional and happy modern living in the great urban areas of today, both the new ones and the renewed ones. This means devising functional organization of space so that several community services and community processes can operate effectively, in a congenial relation to each other, and in direct relation to community need.

An equally vital problem in mobilizing the total resources of a community for effective recreational service is to determine what groups of agencies shall take the primary responsibility for each of the several areas of service. There are several criteria for determining this division of responsibility: which agencies have the logical legal position to accomplish certain things; which have the resources to carry on in certain areas of function; which have the competence and specialized training and skills to undertake the operation of certain programs; and which have the ability to guarantee sound standards and the maintenance of basic human values in the programs they carry on.

Several principles have gained general acceptance in the field of community organization for recreation. The first of these principles is that the public, tax-supported agencies should provide the foundation of basic community-wide facilities and services under qualified leadership. A second principle is that these public agencies have the function of providing the leadership and special equipment for a broad, organized recreational-activities program in many fields of common leisure-time interest. Voluntary and private organizations provide important services in this area as well, although their role might more properly be to explore special activities programs and to develop new areas of service and programs for new or special groups rather than undertake to provide such programs for a whole community.

A third principle is that provision of leadership and program opportunities for smaller, self-determining groups, who may need help in organizing, developing leadership, and enriching their experiences, may be a responsibility of both public and voluntary agencies but eminently of the latter. Both groups of agencies may have an important area of responsibility in serving special groups who may need help in developing satisfying recreation.

A fourth principle relates to the development of social treatment programs, originally located in some specialized voluntary organizations but found in present days being developed by both public and voluntary agencies. Important experimentation in several cities presently going on in delinquency-preventive recreation and group work with teen gangs and groups is being carried on under both voluntary and public auspices.

A fifth principle is that the community must pay special attention, and provide an intensification of services, to the areas that need the services the most because of the economic and social disadvantages found there. A sixth principle defines the responsibility of the community for integrated and comprehensive planning of all organizations and agencies in order properly to coordinate services and cooperatively to approach the problems of functional recreational organization. This latter principle has as a corollary an emphasis on planning as a creative democratic process, one which brings together for cooperative effort all the organized forces in the community concerned with recreation, one which integrates planning by citizen-participants at all levels, from the neighborhood to the highest levels of community-wide decision making.

The question of who has the primary responsibility for community planning is of much importance. There are many in the field who agree with Hutchinson that, in this respect, "At the center of the coordinating level *the public agency acts as the hub around which all other recreation efforts evolve.*" [11] The public agency, as the one most certainly belonging to the entire community, may claim this leadership role. But there is a second view, that the field of recreation is as broad as the whole society, and for its proper coordinated development each community agency must accept an equal share of the responsibility for the cooperative effort.

Whatever view one may hold, it is expected that there would be broad agreement with the principle that community planning and organization efforts become significant to the degree to which there is a profound identification with and commitment to the total effort by each of its parts. Through the processes of cooperatively hammering out policies, reconciling differences, committing oneself to the whole, and operating upon the basis of democratic convictions and upon the development of principles and priorities for effective service, community agencies and organizations learn to work together for the common good.

A community welfare council, council of social agencies, com-

---

[11] John Hutchinson, *Principles of Recreation* (New York: The Ronald Press Company, 1951), p. 281.

munity council, or other planning or coordinating body is usually found in a modern community functioning as the organizing center for the social welfare efforts of the community. Some of these councils are linked with the official social planning organizations in communities. In some places there are recreation planning councils that coordinate the operations of all agencies involved in just this area of social welfare. The Metropolitan Recreation and Youth Services Council of Los Angeles is such a body, in which city, county, school, voluntary, and other agencies are officially linked together.

Because community recreation is the job of many organizations ranging widely in philosophy and commitment to community welfare, community planning is of great significance; there is a requirement of all organizations to maintain communication and to plan together, with the purpose of maximizing leisure values available to community members.

Questions for Study and Discussion

1. *Discuss the organizations in your community that help provide recreation facilities for members or the whole community. How do these organizations decide what to provide? What is the nature of the planning processes and coordinating processes?*
2. *What are the comparative advantages and disadvantages of commercial and noncommercial recreation in contributing to human welfare?*
3. *How does the organizational set-up of a recreation agency influence its goals and contribute toward their realization?*
4. *What is the trend in state and federal responsibility for supporting the leisure movement in the United States? What evidence is there of this trend? What are the strengths and weaknesses in this trend?*
5. *What are the important differences and similarities in emphasis between the recreation programs offered by public and voluntary organizations?*
6. *For any of the types of organizations presented in this chapter make an estimate of its peculiar contributions to the leisure values of the community. Use specific examples if you wish.*
7. *What should be the attitude and responsibility of recreation professionals toward commercial recreation?*

Selected Readings

Butler, George D., *Introduction to Community Recreation,* Third edition (New York: McGraw-Hill Book Company, 1959).

Hjelte, George, *The Administration of Public Recreation* (New York: The Macmillan Company, 1940).

Hutchinson, John L., ed., *Leisure and the Schools* (Washington, D.C.: American Association for Health, Physical Education, and Recreation, 1961).

Meyer, Harold D., and Charles K. Brightbill, *Community Recreation: A Guide to Its Organization* (Englewood Cliffs, N.J.: Prentice-Hall, Inc., 1956).

PART 4

RECREATION AND HUMAN NEEDS

Any consideration of values in recreation must be concerned primarily with values of individual self-enhancement and self-realization. The contribution of recreation to these values is the central criterion for judging its worth. The professional worker in recreation draws from this fact the primary focus for his work. He sees his function as helping individuals meet basic needs and achieve primary satisfactions through leisure-time recreative experiences.

This function requires the worker to attain competence in one of the important foundation areas of professional knowledge, the area of individual behavior, development, and needs. The synthesis of biological, psychological, and social scientific knowledge about individual behavior and the knowledge of recreation's potential means of meeting human developmental, maintenance, and self-fulfillment needs becomes part of the core knowledge of the professional worker.

Material in this section reviews the facts concerning the range of needs of the individual child, youth, and adult and the relationship between play and recreation and those needs. It is intended that this consideration will contribute to purposive exploration of the subject of the method of the recreation worker as he sets about meeting the needs of recreation-bent individuals.

11

RECREATION AND THE NEEDS OF THE CHILD, THE YOUTH, AND THE ADULT

The professional recreation practitioner above all must understand deeply the relationship between play and recreation and the processes of self-actualization of the individual. He must understand the significance of play and recreation as developmental influences in the growth of the child. He must know about the physiological, emotional, and social needs of the individual at each point in his development. He must study the interrelationships between, and the unity of, the biological, psychological, and social processes in individual life and growth. He must learn to be able to facilitate the use of the types of play and recreation that are best adapted to the needs of the individual.

He must become skillful in devising and designing for individuals and groups play experiences that will most effectively meet particular needs at particular times.

In this chapter we propose to look at the individual and his needs during three periods: childhood, roughly the first twelve years; adolescence, the teen years; and adulthood, from the twenties to the nineties. We shall focus, in turn, on four categories or areas: physiological, psychological, social, and aesthetic. We recognize that each of these areas is not independent of the other areas, and that other categories could be used. But because recreation writers have not written much in this field there is no standard set of categories, and the ones proposed will do for our purpose.

Throughout this analysis we must think of the individual as a *whole person,* even though we separate "parts" of him for the moment for study—a *whole person* with a concept of self, which through the influence of his perceptual field directs his behavior toward the maintenance and enhancement of that self.[1] As our second task, we must think about a problem about which much less is known, that of designing play activities and relationships with particular concern for these complex and interrelated needs at each point in the individual's development.

THE CHILD

Physiological Needs

During his first year the child does most of his physical growing at an extremely rapid rate, which decreases during the following years. Skeletal development is rapid, but the soft and pliable bones are subject to both deformity and malnutrition, against which the child should be protected. Muscular and motor development and organization have parallel growth, with the fundamental big-muscle development occurring more rapidly. This development gives the infant the ability to kick and wave his arms; later to sit, crawl, and then walk erect; and to pound, throw, and keep his balance. The neuromuscular-motor development and coordination present in all of this shows steady improvement during the childhood years. At age one, the child

[1] See A. W. Combs and D. Snygg, *Individual Behavior* (New York: Harper & Row, Inc., 1959), for elaboration of the perceptual approach to behavior.

sits, crawls, and handles and inspects and tastes things. At two he is throwing, toddling, climbing, and pounding. By three and four he is running, climbing, riding tricycles, throwing balls, and beginning to grasp crayons and chalk.

By the time the child is ready for kindergarten or school he is physically able to do many things. His legs are increasing in length. He is energetic and active, although his muscular and motor development is still incomplete and uneven, and the eye muscles and small muscles such as those of his fingers are yet only partly developed. Precise motor accomplishment or sustained periods of quiet and concentration are difficult and cause strain. The child is getting his second teeth by about age six; postural problems may develop, and girls are somewhat ahead of boys in physical development. The child will be constantly on the move and yet susceptible to overstrain. He requires rest and relaxation and protected convalescence after illnesses and childhood diseases.

The child of nine or ten shows vastly greater muscular skill and motor-muscular coordination than his younger brother. There is great individual variation, and differences in maturity equal to two or three years of growth can exist between two normal ten-year-old children. The heart still lags behind the development of the rest of the body. The child is stronger, more robust, and better coordinated, but still needs rest, protection against fatigue and overstrain, and protection of the growing skeletal system from shock or undernourishment.

At twelve the child often has attained more than half of his adult height and half of his weight. He is approaching adult levels of coordination of much of the body. Girls are usually in a growth spurt which increases their advance in maturity over boys by several years. There is still need for protection from overstrain and adequate nutrition for their rapidly growing bodies. Activities requiring great muscle control are now valuable, whereas earlier they might have been harmful.

Play is a prime requisite for healthy physical growth of the infant through childhood—properly designed play, that is, that avoids misuse and abuse of the child's body. Especially in the earlier years the child needs an abundance of exercise adapted to his skills, energies, and strength. Modern physical educators estimate that the child from infancy until puberty requires four or five hours a day of vigorous big-muscle activity for normal development.

The child is provided with the organic potential for a huge amount of energetic physical exertion. These strenuous play activities have an important function in stimulating the circulatory, respiratory, digestive, excretory, and nervous systems. The child's health at this point will have much to do with his ability to stand the wear and tear of later life. The random infant movements gradually take on meaning as play activities, and the child begins to learn about his environment. He grasps anything he feels, and eventually he finds out what to put in his mouth and what simply to hold on to or throw away. He continues for months his exploratory movements of pushing, moving, waving, and pulling apart as he "gets the hang" of the things around him.

At one year a baby can crawl around, empty waste-paper baskets, roll a basketball, throw blocks, splash the water in his bath, and close doors; and all of these things seem to be very meaningful to him. At two years, he is toddling around carrying his toys, climbing on the couch, spilling sand out of the sandbox, and pouring drinks of water for himself. At three and four, his play requires manipulative and riding toys, pushing and lifting and throwing equipment, and more space to run and play in. At five, six, and seven, his ability to run, ride, climb, throw, pound, push, and jump increases, and in respect to sheer physical exertion he will benefit from games and toys, and also from group activities of a very simple nature which will stimulate but not overstimulate his natural vigorous expression. From eight to twelve, his games and toys and groups become more complex and will require more complex coordinations. Wise leadership still protects him from physical stress and strain beyond his ability, and from gradations of skill demands suited to his small-muscle development. The child is developing his basic viscero-neuromuscular-motor "tone," coordination, and vitality. Family, school, and recreation agency team together to guide and guard his growth.

Children in this period, we can see, are developing basic vitality and physical health. They also are developing manipulative skills and the coordination of hands, feet, eyes, and the rest of their bodies. At each stage of development they eagerly begin the play activities at that level—both those activities requiring sheer big-muscle activity and those activities in which coordination and intelligence join—and children are active in building, creating, and putting together. Slavson calls this early phase the "manipulative or play phase. . . . The activities in this stage may be described as manipulative-exploratory. . . . [T]he child manipulates, builds, shifts things around, changes things. His interest is to keep busy and handle objects." [2]

To help them in this development, little children's toys should include things to handle, pile up, push around, and mold. They need blocks, boxes, and construction sets. They need clay and sand. A few years later they need scissors, paper, crayons, paste, and paints. They need hammers, saws, and other tools, as well as balls, bats, and mitts. They need chalk for drawing hopscotch courts. These playthings encourage the development of manipulative skills, and of the small muscles as well as the big muscles. The children's well-rounded physical development is thereby enhanced.

Psychological Needs

A child's psychological development, more obviously perhaps than his physical development, is powerfully influenced by the experiences planned for him, or to which he is exposed, by adults. The earliest need of the infant is to have the warmth, security, and love of his parents to help him over the difficult hurdle of making his initial adjustment to the strange outside world into which he is projected from the comfort of the womb.

Beginning as a completely dependent bit of humanity, he is destined to become through the years an interdependent human being. It is hoped he can make the most of whatever his hereditary endowment is, that he may enjoy strong and wholesome ego development, may gain self-understanding, may enjoy adequate superego development, and may develop his thinking, feeling, and relationship potential.

The infant, in what has been called the *oral* phase of his development, is possessed with one major need: to satisfy his recurring hunger pains. He usually learns that food is supplied by loving parents, and he learns to trust these people and to trust his own power to get help. Later, driven by intense curiosity and his feeling of omnipotence, he sets out to explore his environment and to test its response to him. This relentless exploratory urge leads him into innumerable reality-testing experiences, in which, inevitably, he experiences some frustration, some conflict with limiting parents, and a resulting ambivalence, or the presence of both love and hatred for his parents.

If the child receives from his parents the needed reassurance and

---

[2] S. R. Slavson, *Recreation and the Total Personality* (New York: The Association Press, 1948), p. 51.

satisfaction of his oral or hunger needs, freedom to explore his environment, and the necessary limitations reality imposes on him, he happily launches forth to explore his world and all of its sounds, tastes, tactile and visual sensations, and so on. Parents patiently introduce him to these things with a minimum of traumas, and encourage him to learn how to do things, to satisfy his curiosity, and to learn about life. He is encouraged and helped to succeed and to enjoy the satisfactions of accomplishment.

Erikson describes these growth periods, and the area of experiences they have for the child, as "nuclear areas of conflict," major areas of life adjustment and growth. He thinks that the child must necessarily suffer some trauma in working through them, with the possibility of either a largely positive or a largely negative outcome in terms of impact upon personality and ego strength, in relation to the particular personality attribute under development at that time.[3]

Through his playful and exploratory activity the little child finds ways as well to work out tensions that arise in his adjustment to life's realities. Much of this life is beyond his comprehension, and he needs support and protection against the fears and the strangeness. He also needs help in accepting the limits reality places upon him. He needs the opportunity to be himself and to act out his feelings in a permissive atmosphere. He needs the security of sensible limitations so that his activities are anchored to reality. He needs toys and materials that he can use to express and project his feelings and impulses. He needs freedom to go at his own pace, to do things his own way, to think creatively and expansively, to experiment to his heart's content, to speak and act as a child of his age feels, and to be accepted and loved as a person of worth and a member of his first group, his family.

The child of two or three years enters into another stage of development which, in relation to our culture, has been described as the *anal* stage. The child becomes conscious of his anal and excretory functions, and at about the same time undergoes toilet training, at which time he is encouraged to control his immediate anal pleasure in excreting to gain the pleasure of socially approved toilet behavior and self-control of one's bodily processes. Hopefully the child will accept this new pattern of orderliness and control with a minimum of struggle,

---

[3] Erik Erikson, *Childhood and Society* (New York: W. W. Norton and Company, 1950).

and will build along with it a personality component of orderliness, cleanliness, and organization. This, again hopefully, will not be overdone to the point of compulsiveness, resistance, and anxiety over his behavior. Some of the other components of personality—such as generosity or parsimony, and aesthetic qualities such as awareness of cleanliness, beauty, and decoration, and so on—probably have their beginnings in this stage of development.

From the age of three to six the child works through a third stage of development called the *genital* stage. Hormonic changes bring to the child some consciousness of sexual feelings, and he is attracted to the parent of the opposite sex in a generalized way. At the same time his primary self-centeredness expands or grows toward an ability to give love as well as to receive it. Yet his attraction to his opposite parent tends sometimes, at least in his mind, to bring him into rivalry or conflict with the other parent, and out of this may grow anxieties and fears in the child, and evidence of hostility toward the parent, efforts to claim the opposite parent, and so on.

The healthy resolution of this conflict for the child is the tendency, finally, to identify with the parent of the same sex, to assert control over his or her impulses by channeling them into playful affection toward other children, and to gain the respect and affection of both parents by learning to act like the parent of his or her own sex, to be more manly or more girlish. At about the time a child enters school, this process of growth takes place, and the sexual feelings are controlled and channeled into acceptable interests and creative pursuits where satisfactions of good workmanship and accomplishment are available goals. Sexual elements are thought to be essentially latent, although there is disagreement between authorities on this point. First concepts of self are established at this time, and provide the basis for self-development during the next few years, until adolescence requires a basic reshaping of the personality structure.

Through childhood years, parents, teachers, recreation workers, and those interested in his healthy growth all play important roles in helping the child to develop and maintain emotional balance and poise, to effect as untroubled as possible an adaptation to the demands of his environment and an inner stable balance between his several impulses and drives and his controls. The child must be helped to come to a realistic relationship with the environmental forces and pressures to which he is constantly exposed and must develop a concept of self that is sufficient to manage his inner tensions and adjustments to his environment if he is to attain an adequate personality integration.

Play can contribute very positively to the psychological and emotional growth and well-being of the child. For one thing, the child's insatiable desire to explore life can be satisfied in play and provide opportunity for him to exercise his intelligence. Opportunities for scientific or cultural explorations, for sensing and thinking about all of life, properly adapted to his age and developmental level, can be provided in fascinating recreational activities for the child from infancy to adolescence.

The insatiable curiosity of the baby is satisfied as he explores, mauls, manipulates, tastes, and tries everything he lays his eyes or hands on in his own house or anybody else's. The child of three or ten is still curious, though more restrained. Things such as clay, puzzles, noisemakers, chemistry sets, books, cooking materials, dad's workbench materials, or mother's cosmetics drawers, and the limitless opportunities for exploring by microscope or "going places" are means of satisfying this curiosity.

Play can help the child to achieve success, giving him experiences in accomplishing satisfying things in a situation where there are few economic, formal educational, or other demands made upon him. Play gives him the opportunity as well to attain release and inner peace again after an exhausting siege of trying to live with adults and trying to learn something they want him to learn. Play permits him to compensate, in some way or other, for failure to meet adult standards, with its accompanying feeling of inadequacy. In play he can often achieve success, which is important in giving him a positive, healthy concept of himself. And when a child encounters negative responses at home or in school, in his play life he can find achievement and prestige and thereby a sense of real worth, of hope, and of courage to continue to live and learn.

One of play's greatest powers is the ability to stimulate exuberant spirit and cheerfulness, for play is joyful activity. The zest in spirited play, the spontaneity, the buoyancy and exultation so often enjoyed, are very positive influences in a child's mental health. Excitement and adventure find their expression in many forms of recreation. In each case, the joy of doing contributes to wholesome feelings of satisfaction and well-being. The social games of all ages—music and dancing, reading and listening, sports and active play, the play at being cowboys and space pilots and pioneers—all of these and many others pro-

Free-Form Play Structure

vide either physical or emotional stimulation or both and include valuable ingredients of excitement and zest.

Today, with insecurity, tension, stress, confusion, anger, and rage frequently characterizing family and other human relations, the child needs opportunities for protection against or retreat from these violent and disturbing moods, for the calmness and peace of mind that can be gained in reflective and quiet pleasures. Play activities and relationships, if removed from the strain and violence of competitive conflict, can provide protection and peace to a child, and to older persons as well. Reading, painting, fishing, sunbathing, and such activities, can be precious opportunities for such peace.

In quite an opposite way, many games provide competitive experiences that in some measure prepare the child for the realities of modern American life, for striving to win and to do one's best against an opponent. The greatest challenge exists for recreation to provide such competition in constructive and helpful "doses" or measures that will not overwhelm him with the tensions and insecurities of conflict, and which will help him to gain an adequate and comfortable perspective in life and a sound balance between its competitive requirements and its cooperative requirements.

The child under six or eight probably has little need or capacity for competitive activities. This would suggest that he not be hurried into such situations. He also can manage only the beginnings of competitive teamwork and high organization games. To expose infants and younger children to planned interpersonal competition, to winning and losing and beating and getting beaten, is to project them into situations that could be damaging and harmful rather than wholesome. Gradually the older child may be introduced to the thrills of competition and be helped to manage the emotionally disturbing components.

Another value of play is that, potentially, it can offer safe and wholesome expression of the emotional feelings of anger and the "fighting impulses." It permits catharsis, the discharge of aggressive feelings and hostilities in acceptable ways in vigorous imaginative activity. Direct interpersonal striving can be structured into acceptable games that will provide positive outcomes.

A child is permitted to regress occasionally to more infantile emotional behavior without criticism. This regression permits him to express himself at other times on a more mature plane when he is able to do so. Through good sportsmanship and team spirit these expressions have acceptable and positive channels, providing both catharsis and examples of more mature conduct. From the standpoint of catharsis alone, if the child has an outlet for venting otherwise repressed and inhibited feelings through some expressive activity there will be some gain. And if he is given help to understand these feelings, he is given a chance to learn to use such emotions constructively and to attain a firmer feeling of well-being.

Henry C. Schumacher, Medical Director of the United States Public Health Service, points out in this regard that

> . . . psychological theories of play stress [that] through playful repetition of painful events the child can, as it were, relieve himself of too tempestuous expression of his pent up feelings on the one hand, or, on the other, through a playful change from the passive, suffering role to the active, inflicting role, take a symbolic revenge on people who make him suffer.[4]

A final contribution that play can make to the psychological needs of the child is in the opportunity it provides for the free use of his imagination. The child imitates with great happiness his parents, siblings, or others, gaining understanding of their nature by being anything or anybody that interests him. By dramatizing in play whatever he strives to understand he gains a valuable and necessary means of mental development. In imaginative games the child constructs a more simple reality for himself out of the complex and confusing environment by imitating the actions of those about him. His imagination moves readily from reality into fantasy.

The imaginative free play of children is highly stimulated by all they see and hear on television and in movies, and their play-acting is apparently one way they have of expressing their feelings derived from these programs. The child should be encouraged to dramatize, to interpret his feelings and attitudes in play-acting, and to play out his happy and disturbed moods, fantasies, real situations, resentments, and inhibitions. Such activities may have important mental hygienic ends.

Slavson summarizes some of these considerations as follows:

> Healthy emotions and a vigorous intellect require full release of the play impulse in early childhood. . . . by denial

[4] Henry C. Schumacher, in a speech to the Second California Recreation Conference, California Recreation Commission (Sacramento, 1950).

> of play, aggressiveness, which can be turned into curiosity, is stunted. . . . Through play the child not only develops body and intellect, but also drains off excess energy that otherwise would be turned into himself and create tensions, making him restless, irritable, and anti-social.[5]

He lists a number of ways in which recreation can contribute to a healthy emotional state, including provision of complementary and compensatory experiences, discharge of aggressive drives, attainment of aggressive values, attainment of escape from reality, satisfaction of social hungers, and enjoyment of resources for solitude as well.

The positive contributions of play activities to the emotional needs of children can be negated in play activities that are unwholesome or destructive. The requirements of some games may threaten a child and he may suffer much from the cruelties or the excessive demands of play situations. Guided play activities hopefully can avoid the negative and destroying experiences to which the child potentially can be exposed, and instead can be the steady and positive force that the child needs for healthy growth.

Social Needs

A child must grow up to be an individual, but he must also grow up to be a socialized individual. The fact of the dependence of the individual human being upon the human group or the human society for his development, particularly in the early years, simply underlines the tremendous social needs of the individual. He must develop into an adjusted and functioning member of groups, he must learn about his culture and have much of it become habitual with him, and eventually he must become a member of adult society.

It is in groups that affectional needs of the individual are met, in groups in which he can give and receive love and friendship. Related to this need is the need for belonging, for having common ties and interests and the support of others. Another need is for achievement in groups, for contributing to and participating in groups and gaining the approval of and status in the group. The self-centered, completely selfish infant, through group experiences, can be gradually transformed to the generous, sharing, participating group member. Appropriate

---

[5] Slavson, *Recreation and the Total Personality,* pp. 3-16.

maturity at any given age level will have as one of its criteria of measurement the degree of socialization of the individual. It is in groups that the largest measure of the educational process for the individual goes on.

Group membership is a basic source of both security and insecurity for the child. He has a deep need for group identification. Membership in the group, depending upon whether it is a positive or a negative experience, provides either satisfaction or frustration of the child's needs. His experiences of success and failure, of satisfaction and dissatisfaction, are related directly to the group's acceptance or rejection of him and his actions.

Group membership may not of itself always be a positive learning experience, both because the individual at a given point may not be able to use a particular group experience that would be desirable for other individuals in a different stage of development, and because some groups are characterized by negative and destructive interaction that may destroy individual integrity and growth.

The group also demands some degree of conformity of behavior and attitudes, and sometimes conflicts between group and other loyalties create inner conflict in the individual. The individual therefore has to develop independence and self-reliance, and he must be able to make correct decisions about particular group values and behaviors. He must also learn to take his place in groups as a positive member, to be able to play a role in making group life positive and constructive for its members.

These qualities of personality are sometimes called *character*. Good character is thought to be made up of mature emotional behavior, acceptance of the highest ethical, moral, and spiritual values of a society, and independence of judgment and thought. There is in America today considerable confusion over what are the highest ethical values. Sociologists describe them as "conflicting value systems." We talk with difficulty of characterological needs of children and about individual attributes that go to make up character.

But even with such difficulty we recognize that the child needs opportunities to experience the satisfactions of moral or ethical behavior, to show integrity, courage, independence, and self-reliance. Character is a highly social quality, and such attributes as respect for others, kindness, unselfishness, honesty, and courtesy are important elements of this quality. Citizenship, which involves loyalty, cooperation, and adherence to group morality, may be another important ingredient of character.

The infant, of course, is born without any character or perception of self. These have to be learned and acquired. Different levels or stages of such development are normal for a child at different ages.

Play activities potentially offer a child an important opportunity to develop such capacities. Play provides learning situations in which character can be developed. There is an opportunity, within the intrinsically interesting play activities that attract a child, to introduce concepts of fair play, cooperation, honesty, and so on, and to reward the child for learning in this field. Sports have long been justified partly in the belief that good sportsmanship—the ability to win honestly and be a modest victor, and to lose graciously—is basic to the activity. Although from the fields of professional, school, and amateur sports come many examples of the corruption of the basic ethics of sportsmanship, many examples of the finest sportsmanship may also be cited. Certainly the child can find many models to imitate, and many sympathetic teachers of sportsmanship, among professional recreation workers.

These concepts about social and characterological needs are much too briefly mentioned here, but even this simple and inadequate mention suggests to the recreationist some very important principles of guiding group play. For example, children need an opportunity to learn early and in a friendly and secure group relationship some of the important elements in group living, such as the common bonds of friendship and affection, the sharing and working together, the getting along together, and the giving and taking.

The infant's participation in the group will be very self-centered. Hearn points out that in group situations the child develops a feeling of security and acceptance that

> . . . is a necessary prerequisite for the establishment of the healthy interpersonal relationships which will be the foundation in the future of his democratic participation in groups. . . . [The preschool child] loves to play, and the patterns of his play show both imitation and imagination. Although he likes to play in the presence of others, his play patterns are solitary rather than cooperative for the most part. Several children of this age will play with various play objects in a parallel rather than an interdependent fashion. Each will play

> independently with a toy if there are sufficient to go around. If there are not, they will compete for the toy rather than share it. Each wants what he wants when he wants it. . . . Democratic behavior which implies interdependent pursuit of common goals cannot and does not exist at this age.[6]

Hearn goes on to point out that, around elementary school age, children play with others in informal contests designed to test their skills or strength. A group of friends provide very important experiences for the child, although relationships within the group are loose and changeable, in the form of pair relationships. The group, instead of the parents, begins to assume dominance as a source of the child's ideas, and he begins to assert some independence of his parents. He will have a strong sense of justice mixed with selfishness, and will argue endlessly about any apparent infringements of the rules in hopscotch or baseball. Sharing is possible at this stage, and some concern for the interests of others, so that democratic behavior can have meaning for him, although there is little or no evidence that "naturally" he grows democratically.

There are many other implications in this for the recreation worker. The parent, as the child's first recreation leader, begins playing "peek-a-boo" with the infant before his first birthday. He also delights in the baby's imitative behavior and realizes how powerful this drive is. He tussles and sings and goes through endless antics to get the baby's first social responses. When baby gets a year or two older and wants more playmates of his own age, his parents satisfy this desire, and fortunate is the four-year-old who can enjoy the guided group activities of nursery school or parent-organized neighborhood play. Cooperative play with toys and make-believe games are now needed, and the child responds eagerly when the child next door asks, "Can Johnny come out to play?" Hartley says,

> When he is about four, the child becomes much more social. "Let's play" is the byword. He still loves to climb, to swing by his arms, to pedal a tricycle fast, but he likes to do these with other children. Equipment that calls for cooperation is right

---

[6] Gordon Hearn, "Democratic Behavior," in the 1951 Yearbook of the American Association for Health, Physical Education and Recreation, *Developing Democratic Relations Through Health Education, Physical Education and Recreation* (Washington, D.C.: The Association, 1951), pp. 41-42.

> for him now: boards to use as bridges and catwalks, packing cases for houses, and garages, are fine for outdoor play.[7]

Games when the child is four or five must be built upon the acceptance of a very elementary group consciousness of the child, and upon his need to be involved in only the simplest and relatively undemanding group relations. The school-age child, however, plunges, ready or not, into a major group experience. He spends much of his play life gaining and maintaining his place in a group of children. Game skills become very important to him, and the indirect competitive games of cops-and-robbers type involve the children in pseudo-conflict situations with important socio-emotional components.

The child of six or seven can play many types of teamwork games, but still not the kind that require, for example, a great deal of losing and taking defeat, or a highly complex kind of sustained cooperation, for the demand upon him in each case is great. Low-organization games calling for cooperation and immediate group satisfactions are more suitable than those placing undue strain upon the competitive relationships.

The child of nine or ten is powerfully attracted to group life. He needs to enjoy such experiences, he needs help in learning which group roles are constructive and acceptable and which are destructive and not acceptable. A place in the group that gives him status, experiences in being a good group member, and experiences that help him to be sensitive, considerate, and cooperative with other group members to advance group aims will be basic in meeting his social needs.

His group life often takes the form of clubs.

> Clubs reach their zenith at this point. Even when they break up today and are patched up—with new "laws"—tomorrow, there must always be one. Ball teams often serve as the basis for clubs, as do Scouts and similar organizations. Some clubs are simply social groups with names, emblems, and special purposes. Whatever form the clubs take, visual signs of membership are important. A cap, a lapel decoration, an arm band will do. These signify for all the world to see that a youngster has been accepted by other children his age and is loyal to his group.[8]

---

[7] Ruth Hartley, "Children Grow Through Play," in *The Encyclopedia of Child Care and Guidance,* Sidonie Gruenberg, ed. (New York: Doubleday and Company, 1956), p. 870.

[8] Hartley, pp. 873-874.

The activities of the group involve gradually more competitive games and sports, as well as quiet table games of skill and luck. The ten- to twelve-year-old is ready and eager for competition, for active sports, and for a rich mixture of all the dynamic processes of group play life. He needs, also, opportunities to be alone and to be able to enjoy solitary play and private relaxation.

Aesthetic Needs

Recreationists know a great deal less about the aesthetic needs of individuals than about their physiological and psychological needs. In our materialistic and science-minded modern day much stress is placed on vitality and mental health and very little stress on the development of the ability to appreciate beauty.

D'Amico states the case for aesthetic experience in his study of art experiences for boys and girls:

> . . . art is essential to their growth and well-being. Psychologists point out that many emotional disturbances of later years originate with childhood difficulties and that children are often able to work out such difficulties, at least in part, through creative expression. Creative experience, however, is much more than an agreeable safeguard against mental and emotional illness. It is a means toward full personality growth . . . all children need equal opportunity for creative experience. . . .[9]

Educators and play school specialists have recognized the significance of aesthetic needs and have experimented with various artistic activities that appeal to children of different ages. They have designed toys and games and materials appropriate for different age levels, and have studied the development of aesthetic appreciations and abilities.

Certainly the recreationist is much concerned with play and recreation as a means of meeting an individual's need for experience with beauty of form and movement, for participation in creative activity, for enjoyment of music and song, plastic and graphic arts, drama and dance, nature's beauty, and all else that is of aesthetic worth in man's life.

A child's need for creative activity requires resources that give

---

[9] Victor D'Amico, "Art Experiences for Boys and Girls," in *The Encyclopedia of Child Care and Guidance,* p. 889.

him both opportunities for understanding and appreciating beauty and opportunities for manipulating materials and creating things. If the child has many opportunities to enjoy the beauty of decorative things, well-built things, and pleasant surroundings, there will be a stimulus to his sense of beauty and good taste.

A child needs to be encouraged to enjoy creative art experiences and to express his imagination freely and sincerely, in accord with his own wishes. Someone has suggested that "creative self-sufficiency" is a meaningful aspect of wholesome personality. Further, a striving for greater perfection in one's art, at whatever level one is functioning, is a wholesome striving.

In much of art, an individual creates or appreciates something by himself. It may be an individually satisfying activity, or it can become a group experience as well. Both forms of expression have important values, and recreations are varied enough to meet both types of need. Recreation researchers will do well to examine carefully the studies of educators in the arts and learn as much as they can about the various kinds and levels of aesthetic experiences such as dancing, dramatics, painting, and crafts, which children are capable of enjoying at different ages, so that through the important years of childhood these experiences can be provided in a way to enrich the cultural leisure of individuals, and to teach them what great beauty in our world can be experienced by one whose sensitivities are sharpened and whose mind is alert. For the creative child ever new beauty can be created, new things can be imagined and then made with materials at hand. The creative, beauty-loving individual is likely to strive to bring beauty into his life and into the lives of those around him; this striving shares with religion a contribution to aesthetic and wholesome human relations.

The infant of one year already has many aesthetic interests of a primitive sort. In the graphic arts he will begin at a very simple level. Water, mud, sand, clay, and dough are materials with tactile fascination. He will manipulate and feel everything he can touch. At two or three he will love the colors of fabrics or flowers or paints, and will splash and mess enthusiastically with paints and colored clays, with crayons and chalks. He will squeeze and pound the clay, and make many objects of much meaning to him, although they may be unrecognizable to others. He will make collages and constructions like clay masses or mobiles, gradually building his power over materials and giving his work more meaning.

The young child's art is a means of expression, and may be just masses of color or materials to others but deeply meaningful and expressive to him.

> The child is discovering things for himself, gaining independence of action, and finding out his potentialities in certain directions: and all of this is valuable to personality development. . . . To the young child art is a personal language charged with emotion and meaning, and easier for him than words. . . . [In his art] the child is not merely becoming more skilled at drawing or painting. He is interpreting in his art work his growing awareness of people and life.[10]

By the time a child has reached school age he can often, with the proper encouragement, use crayons, pencils, paints, clays, and other materials with confidence and creativity, and he enjoys these forms of artistic expression enthusiastically. Through the childhood years, improvement in technique and greater confidence give him the foundation for possessing a very satisfying medium of self-expression.

Music has a similar role to play, and a similar power. The infant will bounce to music, will beat out a rhythm with a spoon, will sing his monosyllabic songs, and will delightedly join a musical or rhythmic game with anyone who invites him. The family can play an important role in developing musical interests, mainly because much of music is social—singing, dancing, or playing musical games together enhances the activity. The little child will try musical instruments and will listen happily to the playing or singing of another person. From the pursuit of his rhythmic or vocal efforts in infant years he can progress gradually to the point of taking lessons, joining organized musical groups, and so on, as he gets into the later years of childhood.

Another area of aesthetic interest is drama, and perhaps related to it, reading and storytelling. The combination of creative use of imagination and of acting out and fantasying is potentially both aesthetically and emotionally fulfilling. So dramatics, playing-out and acting-out games, storytelling and listening, and reading, in many forms, are valuable opportunities for imaginative play and fantasy. A child can be encouraged to dramatize, to act out his feelings and attitudes, happy and disturbed moods, fantasies, frustrations, and hopes.

A considerable range of rhythmic play activities can be fascinating for children of all ages and a field of creative endeavor. Dancing,

---

[10] D'Amico, pp. 891-893.

singing, and rhythmic games seem to meet deep human needs. They are found among all ages in all societies, and are rated high in the scale of values by most groups.

The aesthetic needs of children may be partly met if at home, school, and play the child has pictures, flowers, and displays of his and other children's work as a stimulus to further work. If he can have a phonograph and musical instruments to enjoy, and can see and hear music, drama, and dancing, it will stimulate his interest. And if he can have at hand the materials, toys, and equipment for creative work, then all that he needs is guidance, stimulation, and understanding by parents, teachers, and recreation workers, out of which hopefully will come wholesome eagerness to enjoy these creative and satisfying activities.

Recreation should meet the developmental behavioral needs of the child with creative, self-initiated, manipulative, and large-muscle activities and games, encouraging exploration of new things, success in imaginative and creative aesthetic experiences, and enjoyment of gradual involvement in group play activities calling for ethical teamwork and competition and understanding and expression of self.

THE YOUTH

Physiological Needs

Adolescence is a time of vital physiological change and growth for both boys and girls, and the recreation worker has a particularly important task in meeting their developmental needs in his design of play programs. At the onset of adolescence the girl tends to develop more rapidly and earlier than the boy. In this adolescent "spurt" she gains in height and weight. There is rapid skeletal and muscular growth, growth of the heart and lungs, and new hair growth. The menstrual cycle begins, the female sex glands become activated, and the sexual organs begin to develop their adult form. Particularly important in physiological growth is the change in the female pelvis, part of the whole growth process that prepares the female for childbearing, and which reduces in some measure free, straight-ahead leg action, making a girl less able to run at a boy's pace and freedom of movement.

The boy also grows rapidly during this time, beginning usually somewhat later than the girl, and with a wide range of variability, pace, and timing of developments. He gets heavier and taller; he doubles his strength; his heart and lungs grow rapidly; his voice changes, new areas gain hair growth; and, unlike the girl, his hip girdle area becomes more narrow and more powerful. While the girl's muscles, hips, and breasts grow round and soft, the boy's body develops power, hard muscles, and strength. The boy also develops internally, with the complex chain of glandular development setting off both over-all growth and the development of the male adult sex organs.

The adolescent, because of the activity of the organs and glands in this period of growth, may have imbalances, largely temporary, which result in skin eruptions, overeating and overweight, and new activity of the sweat glands.

The physiological needs of these young people are many. One is the real need for large muscle activities for their growing bodies, for vigorous and energetic games to play; however, they must show particular care to guard against overstrenuous participation. Short sessions of active games are suggested. Separate activities for boys and girls are often organized in recognition of the physical differences between men and women, partly in order to protect the girl from the temptation to compete as she did as a child directly with boys in all physical activities. Corecreational activities, which are highly popular with youth, especially in the later periods of adolescence, can be designed to be of eminent value in recognizing sexual differences and helping youth to accept and enjoy them.

Physical educators have been alert to point out that although vigorous play is essential to healthy physical development there are dangers from activity that overtaxes the youth's strength. Frequent change of activity helps to avoid fatigue, and games requiring high development of skills challenge and attract youth at this point. Teamwork and team activities are perhaps most attractive to people at this age. There has been criticism of emphasis on contact sports for boys in the earlier adolescent years due to the state of rapid development of the long bones and their vulnerability to shock damage and other harm.

A statement several years ago of one official body pointed up this problem clearly:

> Inasmuch as pupils below the tenth grade are in the midst of the period of most rapid growth, with the consequent bodily weaknesses and maladjustments, partial ossification of the

> bones, mental and emotional stresses, physiological readjustments, and the like . . . leaders in the field of physical education should do all in their power to discourage interscholastic competition at this age level because of its strenuous nature.[11]

Other medical authorities have stressed the importance of strictly limited body-contact sports and highly competitive sports to prevent strain and exhaustion.[12]

The recreation worker is aware of these factors. He organizes some games separately for boys and girls; he plans strenuous activities only of short duration; he avoids extremely competitive situations; he carefully plans rest and relaxation periods; he is sensitive to the extreme range of differences in individuals at this age and strives to accommodate these differences; he also recognizes the rapid changes and the differences in interest among youths of this age and is prepared to be permissive and flexible in the design of his programming.

Psychological Needs

The adolescent period is one of tremendous importance for the emotional and intellectual development of the individual. For it is during adolescence that several major emotional conflicts are resolved by the individual, in the process of moving toward adulthood and emotional maturity. The testimony of parents, teachers, pastors, recreationists, and many others interested in adolescent youth has clearly emphasized that the needs of youth at this point are seemingly more difficult to meet, and that there remains a tremendous challenge yet for workers with youth to find new ways to be of help to adolescents struggling with their emotional growing pains.

The major change from childhood to adulthood is involved in sexual maturation, becoming a man or a woman with the ability to marry and have children. The lag between the time when the modern person becomes ready to produce children and the time when he is socially ready to marry and support children is at least several years. So even if the young person is able easily to slough off the dependence

---

[11] Statement of the Society of State Directors for Health and Physical Education, American Association for Health, Physical Education and Recreation (Washington, D.C., 1946).

[12] Charles Lowman, "The Vulnerable Age," *The Journal of Health and Physical Education,* Vol. 18 (November 1947).

and irresponsibility of childhood and to accept the new role of adult, the social arrangements do not permit it. Most young people have a considerable struggle in preparing themselves to accept this new role.

The child is primarily dependent upon his parents, and growing up involves becoming independent of one's parents, giving up childhood attachments, and attaining emotional freedom from one's parents. What has been called "adolescent revolt" reflects this strong and steady drive in the normal youth to assert his independence of his parents and to establish an adult identity of his own. He also frees himself to make new attachments to a marital partner. This is positive movement, but often markedly traumatic for both child and parents. There may be zig-zagging, moments of retreat, moments of strong advance, and often confusion as to what is really happening. Fundamentally the child needs support in his striving for independence. Many adults, including the recreation worker, can play a very important part in this.

The process of emotional growth during adolescence can be described as a dual process. One aspect is the abandonment and breaking down of the childhood-based concept of self, made up mainly of dependence on parental values. Adolescence sees an essential dismantling of these adult-enforced rules. The second aspect, developing after a period of confusion, fluctuation, and experimentation with opposing values, produces a more adult perception of self based upon a new set of identifications with peers and new adult figures. Important during this period is the nature of the adult figures with whom to identify, and the peer relationships that help define the values being integrated into the new perceptual field.

It seems true that the child, to accomplish his escape from parental attachments, develops temporary attachments for another adult with whom he can identify. This development permits this other adult, who is often a coach or favorite teacher, to be of profound influence, if perhaps only briefly. These opportunities are important. Many youths seem to strive to fight free of all adult attachments, and we find youth completely loyal to and accepting of teen peer-group members and rejecting of most adults. This leads many adults to throw up their hands over a seemingly hopeless task of "getting through" to adolescent youth. But the process underway is basically normal.

Teen-age recreation must be adapted to this emotional need of the youth. They are ready for, and respond most positively to, activities and pursuits in which they have a great deal of autonomy and self-government. They crave activities that are at least something like adult activities, which help them to feel like adults. At the same time they need and often indirectly ask for adult help and supervision of their activities, recognizing their unreadiness to handle entirely their own affairs. The skillful worker offers teen-agers considerable opportunity for self-planned and self-run activities. He calmly keeps the youth in contact with the realities of socially required limits. He handles with a light touch the dramatic changes in moods and tempers and accepts both regressive and progressive behaviors as part of an active growing process. He plays parent-substitute and nonparent adult figure flexibly as the need requires. And he is prepared to ride buoyantly the storms and stresses of emotional disturbance as teen-agers occasionally boil over, act out some of their tension, and vent their feelings.

A second major area of struggle is the area of sexual activity and impulse itself. The youth, involved in a struggle for emotional independence from his parents, also must learn to understand the powerful sexual drives within himself, which naturally urge him to mate with one of the opposite sex. The society places around the mating and marital relationship many protections, one of which is that in general two persons should be able to marry and establish an independent family life. Jobs, home, and eventually children are the normal goals of marriage, and although there are many variations on this theme, it is still the central theme.

So the youth has to learn to control and channel his sexual drives in accordance with social custom and tradition, and must usually spend a considerable number of years partly in maturing and partly in preparing for an eventual role as marriage partner and parent. The youth often goes through a series of struggles here and must adapt his sexual impulses to social customs. These adaptations or compromises range from masturbation to tendencies toward sexual interest in another person of one's own sex. This homosexual phase normally is transitory and harmless, as two or three teen-age youths develop powerful loyalties to and inseparability from each other. Related to this are teen-age love, loyalty, or admiration for an adult, the parent-substitute we have mentioned before.

> There is purpose in all this[—] . . . a safety valve for all the unmanageable feelings with which the young person may be beset. Love his parent he may not. Love himself he must not. But to love another . . . may offer a compromise. . . . If we

> understand all this, there is little to disturb us, little we must oppose. The inner requirements are being met, the problems are being solved somehow. . . . Usually the period is self-limited and lasts a relatively short time, giving way before the steady push to achieve real adult satisfactions.[13]

The older adolescent normally has been successful in working through these problems and arriving at an understanding of himself and his needs for mature sexual behavior. And extensive pre-courtship behavior, perhaps with a wide range of experimentation and interest in many persons of the opposite sex, leads to a selection process and finally, normally, to the acceptance of responsibility and the rights and delights of marriage and marital love.

The recreationist working with teen-agers has a more complex and difficult group to work with than those with any other age group, in some measure because the emotional needs of the adolescents are extremely urgent and yet not at all simple to comprehend and plan group life around. But a number of simple implications can be indicated. One is the desirability of recognizing the very transient nature of adolescent interests and patterns of behavior, and the sharp fluctuation from cooperation to resistance, affection to hostility and criticism, deep spiritual feeling and blasphemy, and so on. We have mentioned flexibility in programming and the wisdom of sharing planning responsibilities with adolescents. We also have mentioned the desirability of sympathy, affection, regard, and a stable, calm, attitude reflecting a benign but ordered segment of the adult world.

Another very important requirement is opportunities for activities with groups both of one's own sex and of a corecreational nature, for at no other time are guided group activities for mixed groups of both sexes more in demand and more potent as means of meeting needs and providing an opportunity for crucial guidance in socially desirable heterosexual social relationships. Corecreational programming must have top priority in all teen-age recreation. And it should be designed, leaders should be selected and prepared, and resources should be mobilized to provide the atmosphere, the structure, and the pattern for an experience in wholesome pre-courtship heterosexual social relationships. This goes beyond games and music and lights. It is involved

---

[13] Marynia F. Farnham, *The Adolescent* (New York: Harper & Row, Inc., 1952), p. 27.

in the adults who provide the example, and the deeper challenge to help youth to understand the meaning of love, relations between men and women, and—the most significant of all social relationships—marriage.

Teen-age Recreation in a Popular Form

Social Needs

The adolescent, in the process of becoming an adult, strives to enter the adult social world and to establish an identity as an adult person. He is not accepted fully in the adult world in our modern day, but is expected to function as a kind of marginal person, half child and half adult, until age brings adult status. The teen-ager is striving for security in his social relationships, for acceptance in the new role of at least half-adult and as a person independent of parental authority.

He is anxious and insecure about his newly developing independence and seeks assurance generally from his own age group rather than only from often-criticized adults. He tends toward a strong identification with and loyalty to a group of his own age along with indecision and confusion about adult relationships.

The tendency of teen-agers to develop close cliques and gangs is evidence of this need. Perhaps the most effective work with teen-agers is done in those recreation programs that recognize the natural gang group as the working unit and find the ways to work with it. Until one is working with the gang or the clique one is likely to be working at a very superficial level of relationship.

Of course, there are important values in providing youth as well with large group and mass activities, for here they can sense the freedom of anonymity and can gradually become comfortable with the idea of being a member of a society or a community that is very numerous and in which one must function as a responsible, self-motivating adult member.

The adult sexual role becomes very important to the youth. The related social need is for opportunities for heterosexual contacts and for sexual behavior and a sexual role that are sufficient to meet the standards of his peer group. For example, it is of importance that girls have some degree of popularity among boys and have dates, and that boys be successful in making dates and managing the affair skillfully.

Problems of healthy human relations, of ethical sexual relations, of honesty and integrity in personal behavior, all are involved in the group relations of adolescents. There are an infinite number of ways in which situations can be contrived to help a teen-ager to gain insight into himself and his relations to others on an adult level. This might be classed as character education. But, in contrast to the receptivity of children to the teaching of adults, the teen-ager, whose needs may be just as urgent, will show much less receptivity. Involved as he is with the struggle to throw off adult domination, he is less likely to listen to words of adult wisdom. He is more likely to search in his experience with his peers, and hopefully with others whom he doesn't reject as he does the parent figure, for concepts to guide him.

Several studies have pointed out that the adolescent peer group and peer culture have a powerful influence on character formation. The many experiences that adolescents have together—those that are relatively free from adult supervision—are powerful learning experiences in how to behave socially and morally. The adolescent gang or clique often will be the instrument through which this influence functions. The group will be important sometimes mainly as a friendship group, "just to have fun with," but along with that it will give the individual status as a group member. It will give him outlets for his interest in members of the opposite sex. It will give him support against persons of other groups or against society in general if at times it appears to be threatening. These are thought to be major factors, mostly positive unless perverted into antisocial channels, in helping the youth to work through the troubled adolescent years toward mature adult participation in the community.

The recreation worker recognizes the power of the peer group in the life of the adolescent. He strives to harness that power to productive purpose and to guide the group's real power toward satisfying members' needs in the best way possible and providing group experiences that help the individual to grow toward good adult standards. An example can be found in coed volleyball, where the necessity, or at least the opportunity, arises for considerations of politeness and good manners to modify competitive practices. It provides a natural opportunity to get across an idea about wholesome relations between men and women and respect for the differences in their capacities. The planning of a dance is a natural opportunity to consider dating etiquette, pleasurable and wholesome relationships, and so on. The issue discussed earlier, of sportsmanship in athletic play, is equally relevant in regard to planning and carrying on athletic contests for fun in recreational programs. Many other examples are easily called to mind. The recreation worker must be sensitive to the needs of the adolescent to become aware of and to have an opportunity to experiment with his own behavior when guided by considerations of ethical adult social standards of behavior.

Aesthetic Needs

What has been said about the aesthetic needs of children is true in general of the needs of youth. An ability to look upon life's experiences as an opportunity to seek and gain appreciation and enjoyment of beauty is important to a full life for any person. Adolescents can experience beauty sometimes very deeply. With a wide range of aesthetic media available to them, they can experiment and explore, probe and wonder at, with much more understanding and ability to enjoy satisfactions from these media than younger children can.

D'Amico points out that

> The teenager reveals increasing ability to learn facts and to master techniques, but most of all his ideas become more profound and complex. He wants to express all kinds of things about himself, his friends, his experiences, about society and the world. . . . In his desire to be adult and become successful, the adolescent himself often loses faith in personal expression . . . [and yet] . . . The adolescent period should be the most fruitful of the entire span of growth because the individual at this time is at his greatest potential creative capacity.[14]

McElheny points out a similar principle in regard to music. He points out that adolescence is a time when most children seem particularly interested in learning to play musical instruments. "For the adolescent, playing to improve one's individual skill and to express in solitude one's inward emotions may provide deep satisfactions." [15] He points out, too, that group musical activities are means of maintaining interest among youth, and that they provide much satisfaction to teen participants.

In some fields, such as high school music, there is little doubt that numerous youths have the best aesthetic experience of their lifetimes. It is tragic that with the completion of school hundreds of youths blow their last horn, play their last fiddle, sing their last chorale, act in their last play, and perhaps read their last good book. These cultural pursuits many times do not carry over into adult life. The lack provides recreation with a very important field for study and planning, for it is probably true, and often has been stated, that America, at least adult America, is still at primitive levels in organizing and supporting the arts, which should be enjoyed by millions of people.

To meet the aesthetic needs of youth would require a fuller recognition than now prevails of the importance of aesthetics in human life. It would require some extensive organization of resources for production and distribution of culture. It would require a continuing educational process so that people's tastes would be educated and become more sophisticated and discriminating. And it would require a change in attitude toward aesthetic things on the part of the public. For if the

---

[14] D'Amico, "Art Experiences," p. 894.

[15] Hugh K. McElheny, "Music for Children," in *The Encyclopedia of Child Care and Guidance,* pp. 905-906.

aesthetic needs of youth are to be satisfied, a new aesthetic culture will have to be built in this country, which has great potential cultural vitality, but which is remarkably barren in many important respects.

The recreation worker, who is actively interested in developing our recreational culture and expanding the participation in it by our people, would seek for every opportunity to interest youth in all the cultural fields. And through the contagion of his own enthusiasm for and interest in the beautiful things of life he will attract youth to these things and help meet an important and often unsatisfied aesthetic need.

Recreation should meet the developmental needs of the youth by physical activities challenging maximum strength, vitality, and grace, by experiences encouraging understanding, appreciation, and responsible enjoyment of heterosexual, corecreational relationships, by a variety of creative social, aesthetic, and cultural experiences, and by experiences encouraging the maturing of attitudes toward self, group, family, and civic relations and responsibilities.

THE ADULT

To cope with the problem of too much to say and too little space to say it in, we have grouped the discussion of adults into the same series of subsections as the other groups and are considering them as one group. This ignores a very important fact—that while the childhood age span upon which we concentrated might have been ten years, and the youth age span might have been eight years, the adult age span might be as much as fifty years, and the differences between the younger and the older adults are so great that it is quite impossible to consider their needs as in most respects similar. So within each subsection we shall try to deal with both younger and older adult groups, as we recognize that the term *adult* describes widely varying individuals, each with many special needs.

Physiological Needs

The needs of young adults are much like those of youth. In the vigor of their bodies and in their strengths and energies lies the potential for great pleasure and value from energetic activities. Most of their growth has been completed by the time persons are twenty, but for ten more years they may possess undiminished vitality. Their need is for strenuous and yet relaxing activities that will refresh, invigorate, and maintain muscle tone and functioning of the bodily organs. The question at this point is usually not so much one of developmental needs as it is one of maintenance needs.

Middle-aged adults have an even greater need to maintain their physical health and vigor through mildly vigorous sports and games that are refreshing and relaxing, but do not strain a body that hasn't quite the spring and the recovery speed of younger bodies. Regular vigorous activities, properly planned to provide relaxation and energetic use of the big muscles, are of much value in stimulating the bodily organs to normal functioning. Wide use of alcohol and tobacco, lack of rest, inattention to nutrition, sedentary and specialized occupations providing no opportunity for balanced exercise all impose nervous tension and strain. These combine to diminish the bodily vigor of many individuals. They also lessen resistance to diseases and illnesses, especially cardiac and nervous diseases, ulcers and digestive disorders. It is this deterioration, a portion of which is normal lessening of vigor and energy, accelerated by bodily misuse, which poses a particularly important need. This need is for mildly vigorous and energetic recreational activities to counteract excessive physical deterioration and maintain fitness and good health.

The elderly person has still another need. Medical science and geriatric research have shown that during the last two or three decades of a normal person's life his physical processes slow down, his energies decline, and his bodily organs such as the heart are not well able to stand extensive exertion or strain. Yet it seems that the average person of today at retirement is in better physical condition than was the average person of several years ago. He has a considerable capacity for enjoying life. The older person who has engaged regularly in some physically active pursuit will be ready to carry on that pursuit, less actively certainly but still with much pleasure. The pleasure from even a slow and faltering game of golf, horseshoes, shuffleboard, bowling, croquet, or a session of square dancing will be accompanied by positive physical gain. And the physiological decline accompanying sheer boredom and a sense of uselessness is recognized as one of the harmful influences causing senescence, which must be guarded against. The elderly person, with many years of useful and pleasurable life before him, must protect himself from diseases that will prevent him from enjoying the full use of his body. Through relaxing, pleasurable, mildly active games and activities he can contribute positively to his own physical health and well-being.

Psychological Needs

The young adult has several specific psychic needs. In this period, most men and at least half of the women are making their major effort to establish themselves in the economic life of the community. Each is searching for a mate or building a marriage and a family. Each is establishing a home and a place in the community. All of these things provide the young man or woman with a tremendous challenge and require energetic and demanding use of his or her total energies. Psychologically and emotionally, young men and women have an important need for relaxation and re-creative activities that will renew their energies, give release from stress and tension for awhile, and restore emotional health and well-being. The normal adult is able with a little help to seek out such recreations, and they may be of real value in meeting his needs.

A second need of young adults arises out of the preoccupation of many of them with seeking out a mate, with entering into the intimate union of marriage. Under good conditions recreation may play an extremely important role in meeting this need, for it is through having fun together that many phases of pre-courtship and courtship can take place. It is through recreation as well that many marriages get off to a good start and the proper foundation for family life is laid. All the joyous activities of playing with a loved one, doing things together, and most important, making love itself, make up one of man's most delightful recreational activities. Man's urgent need to express himself sexually with a loved mate may be satisfied deeply; and a resultant self-fulfillment as parents caring for children is important also. The elaborate re-creative pleasures of being together and playing together are of the greatest importance. This is more certainly true of this age than of adolescence, where experimentation and exploration must be hedged about with social restrictions, and sex activities are accompanied by guilt and confusion rather than free and uninhibited joy.

For the middle adult group this same need, the sexual-emotional need, is still of much importance and can be satisfied with deep and lasting pleasure and satisfaction to men and women. Somewhat related to this, the whole family becomes a recreational unit, and parents and children find together the satisfactions of playing together. Playing together is fulfilling to parents and, as we have seen, a very positive developmental influence on children. The adult in the middle age group is much in need of stable, warm, human relations with the marriage partner. Contrary to some beliefs, he can prolong and develop soul-satisfying affectional relationships for many years, attaining one of life's most rewarding pleasures. Some recreationists have mistakenly thought that man's strongest "instinct" upon which recreation best should be based is the "competitive instinct." But probably the most aesthetic and deeply satisfying recreations in life are based on the quite different "lovemaking instinct"; and who is to doubt its potentialities?

Adults in the middle age group have another important psychic need, similar to that of young adults but probably more important—the need for relaxation from nervous tension and strain and for escape from the pressures and demands of economic and domestic life. The increasing incidence of nervous diseases in the middle age group is evidence of the inability of many persons adequately to balance their work and relaxation so as to maintain mental health and equilibrium. There is a crucial need for recreations that encourage these persons to cast aside their cares, to relax from the tense, alert, driving, combative posture in which one's whole glandular-nervous system is, in primitive terms, ready to do battle. Quiet and peaceful pursuits, a peaceful inactivity, which will rest and relax one's nerves and give one a chance to re-create nervous and emotional energy, are of major importance at this age.

Persons in the elderly age group have a somewhat different problem. For them, idleness and nonproductivity is often the common complaint. They have too little to do, and the let-down results in a direct decline in mental and emotional health, a feeling of uselessness or demoralization, and isolation from the real meaning of life. The psychological need of elderly persons is to have a creative and useful role in life, to be involved in activities that take them away from a lonely contemplation of their limitations, and to have a chance both to learn new things and to gain new happiness with familiar pleasures.

Elderly people have more leisure time than other groups, and often time hangs heavily on their hands. They need involvement in active affairs, and recreation can be built around self-planned and self-operated programs that provide them with pleasurable pursuits and give some of them important responsibilities for planning, organizing, and leading activities. Such responsibilities challenge their talents and often permit them to develop new skills and abilities they never knew they could develop.

The older person also needs security and an opportunity to relive familiar experiences and to enjoy familiar satisfactions. Recreation has an important opportunity to be centered on the culturally familiar pursuits of groups, and to provide the setting and the facilities for groups to enjoy well-remembered games and activities. This group enjoys food, a characteristic not radically different, however, from other groups, but one that suggests programs in which the emotional satisfactions of delicious food are provided.

Social Needs

The young adult has social needs of prime importance, as do other age groups. The self-centeredness of the youth normally is expanded and developed to the maturity of self-identification as a part of a larger social whole. The social relations of adult marriage, of adult productive life, of neighborhood community and civic life, all make demands upon the person to reach this new maturity, and his need is for learning experiences that help him to assume this adult role.

In the area of personal self-respect and integrity, of basic honesty, individuals and groups may have a real need for help in setting standards for adult ethical behavior. Recreational activities provide a valuable medium for lessons in personal integrity. To win honestly, to lose graciously, to cooperate generously, to compete with courtesy and friendliness, all of these elements of sportsmanship are positive values that can be built into games and leisure pursuits.

In the area of courtship and corecreation there are important needs for those qualities of character that can contribute best to happy marriage and family life. A person may be challenged to learn the kind of enlargement of one's idea of self to the "we" idea that is so important in marriage. Sharing, mutual trust, unselfishness, thoughtfulness, tolerance, kindness, loyalty—all of these are personality attributes that contribute to marital happiness and represent adult maturity. The young adult, concerned with laying the foundation for a life-long marital partnership, is very much in need of experiences that will widen and deepen his understanding of these elements in character.

An important additional need of young adults grows out of the fact that upon leaving school they leave the organized groups that naturally grow up there. School and neighborhood peer groups and associations dissolve. This dissolution leaves the individual often with few group associations to hang on to, and recreational groups into which the individual can come provide an important means of solving this problem. The adult needs a feeling of social status; he needs groups from which he can gain friendship and fellowship; he needs social recognition of his worth; and he needs the comradeship of others in his search for new experience and his enjoyment of familiar pleasures. Recreational activities can provide many of these things as well as situations in which adult behavior in many ways can be "practiced" and more adequate social adjustments can be learned.

Members of the middle adult group have much the same needs as the younger group, with the exception that their lives are more firmly established. Habits growing out of inadequate social adjustment are more fixed and less subject to change. On the other hand, habits of adequate social adjustment and the need to play a positive adult role in the community can be expressed and satisfied in the wide range of family and community leisure-time activities.

Some of the lessons of ethical behavior are learned slowly, sometimes not at all, and often an advanced age is reached before real depth of understanding is attained. The need persists, therefore, for opportunities for persons of all ages to practice in enjoyable and playful pursuits self-discipline, sportsmanship, courtesy, respect for others, and similar ethical qualities. The ability to participate and share in the activities of groups is a fundamental part of a balanced adult life. The needs for social expression, for social fellowship, for social participation, and for group response are all important social needs that can be satisfied in recreational group life.

An additional need exists in the middle age group, for it is from this group that a large part of the leadership in most of society's organized activities comes. Social cooperation, taking responsibility for participation in community and civic activities, giving unselfishly of time and energy to the infinite number of activities requiring volunteer leadership are elements in adult personality which adult recreation and leisure-time activities may require. The individual has a need to be identified with such activities, and participation in them helps him to establish a balanced adult life through contributing what he can to the social good.

The elderly individual has a somewhat different need, for with age there is a tendency to drop out of active social relationships, to rest from community responsibilities, to lose social contacts to some degree, not only from a desire to slow down but from retirement or even a feeling that one's life is over, one is unwanted, particularly among younger groups, and so on. These feelings are part of an anxiety of an older person over his growing sense of isolation from his fellows, his dependence, his nonproductivity, and his inadequacy in dealing as well as he could have earlier with the confusions and changes going on about him.

Senior Citizen Center

Elderly adults need experiences and activities in which they can maintain self-respect, and a sense of worth, value, and usefulness. Their problem is a nagging feeling of being left out, of being useless and worthless. Recreation can be a powerful antidote to such feelings, for they can find their place in helping the larger group to enjoy satisfying recreations, in giving of their talents, in taking responsibility, and in giving leadership. These activities, more readily introduced into recreation than in many other areas of activity for elderly people, have positive contributions to make to their sense of adult identification and personal integrity.

Recreation for older people can and should be group-centered, self-guided and self-respecting; it should provide an opportunity for community participation and concern for its welfare; it should be rich with friendships and pleasurable interaction. The older person's preoccupation with himself lessens when he has an opportunity to know others his own age, to develop new friends, to talk with them, to participate with them in activities. And the challenge to the older person of mildly competitive activities where he can test his skills and capabilities and gain the thrill of winning at checkers, croquet, bridge, or cake-making, helps to keep him interested in life and mentally healthy.

Aesthetic Needs

Adulthood is the major creative period in a person's life. The world admires the young artist, but most of the great artists are mature adults. Adulthood and maturity must be reached, it would seem, before one may be freed for the creative work and appreciation so important in a balanced life. Adults need opportunities and outlets for creative work. Young adults, in particular, need such opportunities so that skills developed in younger years will not become rusty through disuse and so that interests will not lessen.

Recreation can provide adults with their major opportunity for aesthetic expression. Many millions of persons who work at uncreative jobs have little opportunity in their work life to think of or work at creating something of beauty. Their leisure time must provide them with such opportunity. Young adults, preoccupied with and required to concentrate on the job of earning a living and getting an economic start, particularly need the opportunity in their leisure to be creative, to enjoy things of beauty, to deepen their aesthetic sensitivity and appreciation. Thus, they may attain a balance with the rest of their lives. The aesthetics of human relationships, in marriage, in neighborhood life, in personal friendships, are highly significant for young adults as well, because they set the patterns for a long, creative, satisfying life ahead.

The aesthetic needs of the middle age group of adults are part of their whole need for opportunities to be creative, and to be stimulated by beautiful things. We have pointed out several times that man's urge to express himself in body movements, in the media of expressive materials, and in musical sounds, seems to be basic to his personality. Fulfillment seems basic to his happiness. The nature of modern mechanical society is such that man's work more often than not gives him no such opportunity. It remains for him to seek out ways of expression, creative work, and appreciation during his leisure hours. Recreation is able to meet this need as it makes available, through informal and organized means, the infinitely varied ways of aesthetic expression.

Self-improvement can be encouraged, a wider range of means of expression can be introduced, and whole new areas of appreciation can be discovered. The cultural objective of an aesthetically enriched personal life for each individual is one of recreation's greatest challenges.

Life magazine told the story of a group of some thirty middle-aged people in the small town of Attica, Kansas, population 622, who for several years had been painting together—doing pictures of the town on the sidewalks, painting landscapes in the fields. They stimulated the entire town to enjoy their art with them. *Life* says, "These activities have given Attica's artists, who are mostly middle-aged, a new outlet for their energies. 'I'd walk the floor,' declares one, 'if it wasn't for this painting.' " [16] Each member not only is obtaining the deepest satisfaction for himself, but is immensely enriching the life of the entire community as well.

The elderly person can share in this aesthetic life more richly, in some ways, than others can, for he has the age and depth of experience and understanding to appreciate beauty, more so than youth. Also, he has the leisure time that few younger adults possess. Well known is the challenging and heart-warming story of the painting career of Grandma Moses, who, at a very advanced age, took up painting as a pleasurable pursuit and created some of America's finest painting. This has encouraged many persons, especially older persons, to try their hand at creative work that they never thought they could do, and to do better at it than they ever thought they could.

A booklet issued by the Los Angeles County Recreation Department listed scores of artistic and creative activities in which older people engaged in the public parks, ranging from square and folk dancing, gardening, oratory, dramatics, orchestra, and singing, to copper and woodcraft, stone cutting, ceramics, painting, leather carving, model building, photography, sewing, lampshade making, and many other activities. There were a begonia society, gladiolus society, orchid society, fuchsia society, and herb society, to indicate just one area in which love and creation of beauty can draw elderly people together for mutual pleasure.[17] In ways such as these, elderly people can pursue and find satisfactions of aesthetic desires which never seem to diminish as long as one lives.

---

[16] "Art Conquers Attica," *Life,* Vol. 39, No. 8 (August 22, 1955), p. 82.

[17] "An Official Invitation to Elder Citizens," Los Angeles County Department of Parks and Recreation, Los Angeles, 1951.

Recreation should meet the needs of the adult individual with a range of stimulating, pleasurable, refreshing, and relaxing activities providing maintenance of physical health and vigor, release and renewal, congenial and interesting social and group relationships, sophisticated creative aesthetic experiences, and activities fulfilling civic responsibilities.

Questions for Study and Discussion

1. *What are the arguments for and against competition for the six-year-old? for the ten-year-old? for the adolescent?*
2. *How would you define "span of interest"? How would you adapt your programming to this? Relate this to different age groups.*
3. *For the adolescent, what activities should be coeducational? Which should be confined to one-sex groups? Which might be suitable in either instance?*
4. *Discuss "teen-age crush" and "hero worship" as directed toward favored adults. Of what significance are these to the recreation worker?*
5. *What is meant by "carry-over value"? List activities that could properly be included in such a classification.*
6. *What reasons would you give for poor participation by adolescents in some agency recreation programs?*
7. *What are the important values to be gained by elderly adults from participation in social recreation programs?*

Selected Readings

Allport, Gordon W., *Personality and Social Encounter* (Boston: Beacon Press, Inc., 1960).

Anderson, Harold H., ed., *Creativity and Its Cultivation* (New York: Harper & Row, Inc., 1957).

Murphy, Gardner, *Human Potentialities* (New York: Basic Books, Inc., 1958).

Slavson, S. R., *Recreation and the Total Personality* (New York: The Association Press, 1948).

PART 5

RECREATION AS A PROFESSION

One of the systems of relationships within which recreation is understood, as we indicated in Chapter 1, is as a profession. The development of a modern institution of recreation is matched by the development of a modern recreation profession. Any profession is identified by its philosophy and ethics, its basic body of operational knowledge, its operating principles, skills, and understandings that make up its methodology, and its self-discipline and responsibility. So, too, is recreation identified as a professional organization.

This section is made up of three chapters devoted to three tasks. One of these tasks is to describe the nature of a profession—the elements in its life and function and the status of the recreation profession at present in respect to these elements. The second task is to review briefly a sampling of the important findings in several scientific and applied fields which contribute to the scientific foundations for the professional method in recreation. The third task is to summarize briefly some of the important methodological principles that presently form the basic framework for the professional method in recreation.

The recreation method is emerging out of experience in the field, in applying and testing scientific principles and theories in the practical processes of helping people to achieve leisure, and out of thoughtful adaptation to the special conditions in recreation of the methodological findings of related professions such as education, social work, and therapy. The synthesis of learnings gained from these sources into a sophisticated professional methodology for recreation is underway as a long-term process, which in important respects is still in its infancy, owing to the relative newness of the recreation profession itself.

Two more points regarding this section must be made: First, these chapters on recreation method are included in order to acquaint the student with this important dimension of the subject and to sensitize him to the ultimate importance of his role as a skilled professional practitioner. These chapters present only the barest outline, and there may be a danger that a student will mistake his understanding of this information for professional competence. No mistake would be more catastrophic for him and for recreation. Be sure about this—a sophisticated professional methodology is hard to teach and hard to learn. For students from related fields, for whom contact with one course at present is the limit of their "education" for recreation work, this section is envisaged as a small but useful guide to some of the principles that can help the worker in his approach to this new area of service to people.

The second point is that the principles formulated here are designed primarily for the use of the professional worker "on the firing line," in direct face-to-face relationships with recreation-bound individuals and groups, and for the use of the program leader or volunteer in similar work. These principles also are significant guides to the recreation supervisor and administrator who, as they approach individual staff members and staff, board and community groups, do so as enabling individuals, helping these people to fulfill their responsibilities in recreation agencies and organizations. Many recreation workers also must develop competence in the special methodologies involved in research, business administration, physical and functional planning, and so on; however, these methods are outside the scope of this book.

12

RECREATION AS A PROFESSION

Chapter 11 described how society has organized leisure-time activities for the purposes of fulfilling recreation's social function. The pattern of this organization makes up the institution of recreation in its variety of agencies and settings. Society also has authorized special groups of people to carry out the functions of the institution. These people constitute the recreation profession. A profession, among other things, takes responsibility for renewing and improving itself through organizing and directing professional education. One objective in professional education of the new person, therefore, is to acquaint him with the nature of the group of which he aspires to become a member, to make him conscious of an identity with his profession, and to sensitize him to his obligations to society and the codes and standards established for his profession. For the student considering entering the recreation profession, the person preparing for professions closely allied to leisure and recreation, and the recreation worker in the field, this chapter describes the profession of recreation.

The authors' view is that recreation is an emerging profession. It is a new profession without the maturity or the stable organization that marks an established and older profession, but a profession with a distinctive social function, a specialized body of knowledge, and a distinctive methodology. In respect to its philosophy, its guarantees of standards, and its maturity of professional practice, recreation has not yet attained full professional status. Sorenson challenges recreation to strive for full maturity as a profession.

> Do we want to forge out a philosophy, goals and techniques required of a profession? Do we want to realize full professional preparation, admission, and standards? Do we want professional societies which contribute fresh professional insight across institutional lines? . . . Do we want to strive for the role behavior of a mature professional marked by the motivation, human relations, mental discipline, work excellence, play spirit, moral integrity, and personal adequacy worthy of professional spirit and behavior? . . . A profession is in the making; it is not yet formed. In our generation we are favored with exciting, pioneering, creative work to do to mature our profession.[1]

BASIC PHILOSOPHY AND PURPOSE

Theories about the nature of leisure and recreation and about their goals and values make up basic components of the recreation philosophy, and provide a conceptual framework for action. Such a philosophy defines the terms, presents the theories, reviews the foundation of scientific knowledge, and indicates the values and objectives that guide and direct the action of the recreation profession.

Recreation is still in the process of developing this philosophy.

---

[1] Roy Sorenson, "Professional Maturity," *American Recreation Society Quarterly Bulletin,* Vol. 5, No. 1 (May 1953), p. 16.

Modern writers have made a number of contributions for perhaps the last century. This book in part represents an effort to define, briefly but systematically, a recreation philosophy. But to say that there is *one* coherent philosophy upon which most professional workers in the field agree would be ambitious. The reason for this disagreement is, in part, the diversity of interests of the various people working in recreation, the varying professional backgrounds from which they have come, the organizations to which they belong, and the setting in which they work. There is agreement, however, in the foundations for a philosophy that depends upon general goals, particularly upon the belief in the democratic way of life, the values of recreation in the life of the individual, the significance of leisure time in the life of the individual, the community, and the society, and the importance to society of organized effort to guide and direct recreation.

Recreation professionals must define more clearly specific aims and objectives, not only for themselves but for the general public, whose support is essential. The profession is actively trying to prescribe its boundaries and horizons. For many years, the profession has tried to make recreation explicit and distinct, separate from education, medicine, social welfare, and other related areas. The hazard to avoid, of course, is making it so general that it has no meaning, or so specific that we fragment and splinter and lose effectiveness. The result of either would be lack of public understanding and support for aims and objectives. Lay participation on boards and commissions and in the organization of community coordinating and recreation councils is doing much to build public understanding, but this must be broadened considerably if the profession is to have full support of the general public for its philosophy and goals.

CODE OF ETHICS

The transition from the conception of the worker's role as just a job to that of being a professional perhaps can be most clearly marked at that point when an individual establishes standards for himself and subscribes to a code of ethics to govern his behavior and conduct. Certainly among the so-called "helping" professions, the personal standards a group establishes for itself determine to a great degree the status the group will achieve as a professional body.

Codes of ethics have been developed by most professional groups. Social workers, doctors, lawyers, and teachers have all adopted guiding principles in the fulfillment of their personal responsibilities. Usually these are developed through professional society committees and, once adopted by the official body of the organization, become ethical behavior goals for their members.

The American Recreation Society, the Group Work Section of the National Association of Social Workers, the National Recreation Association, and the American Institute of Park Executives have adopted codes of ethics; numerous state recreation societies have followed suit. These codes are fairly similar in nature and spell out the recreation worker's responsibilities to (1) *participants,* through belief in and treatment of them fairly as individuals, (2) *society,* through promotion of democratic processes, loyalty, and improvement of community life, (3) *the profession,* through giving of best efforts to it, participating actively in professional organizations, and contributing to its advancement, (4) *self,* through objectivity, maintenance of fitness, and respect for others, and (5) *agency,* through loyalty, adherence to rules and regulations, cooperation, and maintenance of a professional level of service.

Another hallmark of professional growth is the extent to which a profession reaches out to set goals that lift the individual worker above the commonplace and give deeper meaning to his efforts, joining him with all others engaged in like work of improving the quality and dignity of man himself. Douglass, in his "Guide for Leisure Leaders on the Space Frontier," suggests these goals:

> Grow intellectually to a fuller understanding of the age by carefully selected reading and thoughtful discussion.
>
> Mature spiritually by rethinking the goals of living in the context of the leisure-space age.
>
> Elevate programs from routine insignificance and let them speak the idiom of the age.
>
> Develop teamwork in mind-outreaching, soul-satisfying projects which combine the resources of libraries, museums, craft centers, discussion groups, and value defining activity.
>
> Have courage to budget your time and resources to the significant.
>
> Elevate the standards of the profession by active participation in professional societies.

Strengthen the channels of public information so that people will understand your goals, the resources which you make available, and the satisfactions which they may enjoy.

Realize that the learning process may function at its best in leisure pursuits, the recreation leader being thus the most responsible of all teachers.

Look to the future with personal expectation and work to make the "ought to be" the "is."

Be imaginative in encouraging growth in the habits of participant citizenship.[2]

SPECIALIZED BODY OF KNOWLEDGE

Fundamental to professional status is the accumulation and development of a specialized body of knowledge, complex enough to require special education and with sufficient intellectual content that scholarship is necessary to master it. This criterion separates a craft from a profession. As Sorenson says:

> There will always be a large place in recreation for the craftsmen. We will use a large number of non-professional people as coaches, assistants on playgrounds, instructors, and in other ways. But those on the leadership level who need to know why as well as how, require a more complex body of knowledge.[3]

What is the professional body of knowledge in recreation that requires scholarship? The foundations for the body of knowledge are found primarily in the natural and social sciences and the humanities. They include: (1) the facts and understanding of biology, psychology, anthropology, philosophy, and sociology, which are related to the development of man; (2) facts and understanding about man's physical environment (physical and biological science) as it relates to recreation and leisure; (3) facts and understanding of the ways (the arts) through which the individual releases his creativity; and (4) facts and understanding of society and social institutions, and of community organization and structure. Borrowing from other disciplines is

---

[2] Paul Douglass, "Guide for Leisure Leaders on the Space Frontier," *California Recreation News and Previews,* Vol. 13, No. 2 (February 1958), cover page.

[3] Sorenson, "Professional Maturity," p. 16.

not unique to recreation. It is the means whereby any new discipline arises and develops. Another example of this borrowing is geophysics, which emerged out of geology and physics, and is now recognized as a distinct area of study.

The specialized body of knowledge in recreation arises from the application of the foundation facts and understandings to the leisure setting. This body of knowledge comprises: (1) the history, philosophy, and theories of leisure and recreation; (2) facts and understandings of the role of leisure and recreation in the development of the individual; (3) the social significance of leisure and recreation as a conditioner of culture; (4) people's patterns of recreation and leisure; (5) understandings in the areas of planning, organization, administration, and leadership related to programs of recreation; and (6) facts concerning the dynamics of groups in meeting basic needs of individuals.

One of the challenges for the recreation profession is to extend the volume and depth of its specialized body of knowledge, but the necessary scholarship has been all too scarce within the ranks of the profession, primarily because professional education is still a new idea, and also because most practitioners have been satisfied with mere "know-how" rather than "know-why." Outside of the field, most research has been done by sociologists, psychologists, and therapists, as the literature reflects. The literature also points up the stress on organizational, administrative, and activity education. There is a need to encourage and support research directed to recreation theory and method and to validate the methods and techniques used by the worker.

Recreation Research

The major focus of research efforts in past years can be grouped generally into six categories: (1) physical and mental health (experimentation with the use of recreation as a therapeutic tool and the adaptation of activities for therapeutic purposes), (2) evaluation of leadership-preparation programs, (3) outdoor recreation and the use of land and water areas for recreation purposes, (4) design of recreation facilities, equipment, and areas, (5) measurement of the effect of participation upon the individual (primarily within the industrial setting, and related to improving worker effectiveness on the job), and (6) development of measurement tools and devices for determining the effectiveness of recreation services.

The techniques employed most frequently are the normative survey and the observation interview. If recreation is to move ahead, however, its practitioners must engage in more and more creative experimental and evaluative research to determine the validity of efforts.

Research is conducted primarily by colleges and universities, special centers and institutes established by philanthropic foundations (for example, Resources for the Future), and by governmental agencies and community health and welfare agencies. Professional organizations have been steadily attempting to correlate these separate efforts into a unified systematic and organized research effort. The national research committees of the various professional organizations make annual compilations of studies and projects either completed or underway in the major institutions known to be conducting recreation research. The search for new knowledge and the testing of hypotheses must be done within the disciplined environment of the research process and mainly in institutions of higher education. The number of graduate students and institutions offering graduate education has increased sizably in recent years and the transfer from the rule-of-thumb approach to the slide-rule approach is underway.

METHODOLOGY

Any profession, in order to achieve full maturity, must develop a methodology appropriate to its own unique function. It must have its "own way" of doing things. In recreation, this uniqueness grows out of the nature of the recreation "climate" and the special goals of individual welfare and creative self-fulfillment which have emerged for leisure and recreation.

The recreation environment usually is informal and playful, the attitude of the participant is one of freedom, and opportunity for choice exists. In almost no other social institution does this kind of environment prevail; the setting tends to be one of compulsion rather than of freedom. But in the recreation setting, the worker normally deals with people who want to be there and who have purpose. The worker's task is to help the individual achieve the special goals of leisure time, particularly seeking to guarantee creativity.

Out of this environment emerges the core method of working with individuals and groups in recreation. In certain areas of professional responsibility this methodology may vary in degree. For the face-to-face worker "on the firing line" it is the major component of his leadership tools. For the supervisor, specialist, or administrator it is an integral component, but it is supplemented by other methodology not necessarily unique to recreation. The specialist may use primarily a teaching methodology. The executive would use an administrative methodology primarily. All of these individuals work with people, however, and they have a common base or generic method.

There is some confusion over recreation methodology. Many workers tend to relate their title, agency, and level of function to a level in methodology, with the impression that different methodologies exist and are used in different settings and in different jobs. Such distinctions are artificial because fundamentally almost every position—regardless of level, title, agency, or function—embodies administrative, supervisory, and face-to-face worker responsibilities. The public playground leader's generic methodology would be little different from that of the social group worker in a settlement house, the recreation therapist, the director of a senior citizen's center, the Boy Scout executive, or the supervisor of cultural arts.

Since in starting positions most of the activities would take place in face-to-face relationship with clients, it is important for the recreation student to understand what this primary methodology is, what its roots are, and how it is applied. This methodology will be explained further in Chapters 13 and 14.

The recreation profession, to fulfill its responsibility, must develop a philosophy for the field and a code of ethics for the profession, a specialized body of scientific knowledge related to its helping function, and a sophisticated methodology by which professional practitioners work with recreation-bent individuals and groups.

PROFESSIONAL EDUCATION

True professional education for recreation is a relatively new development. Prior to 1926, schools and colleges gave it only meager attention, but with the establishment of the National Recreation School by the National Recreation Association in that year the first real recreation curriculum came into being. During the 1930's, professional courses were introduced in a few colleges and universities, and following the first college conference (1937) on training recreation leaders, real emphasis was directed to the professional preparation of recreation personnel. The growth and expansion since then has been steady. In 1937 there were only five institutions offering recreation programs; by 1944 there were nineteen; and, by 1960, there were sixty-two, with thirty-nine institutions offering graduate instruction and fifteen conferring the doctoral degree. In some states, junior colleges now offer professional and general education courses in recreation.

The number of students engaged in programs of professional education increases steadily. In 1960, Sessoms reported, 2,673 students were preparing for recreation careers and 684 degrees were granted.[4]

The thinking of professional leaders about the nature of professional education has been guided primarily by recommendations growing out of national curriculum conferences sponsored by colleges and associations that have established frameworks for desirable undergraduate and graduate preparation.[5]

Varying patterns of organization have characterized the development of recreation education. The introduction of recreation courses into the physical education curriculum was the first step. Educators then experimented with an interdivisional or interdepartmental approach, in which existing courses in physical education were broadened to incorporate offerings available in other departments, schools, and colleges.

One approach, widely employed, was the development of curricula and courses around specific skills and abilities required for employment and on-the-job performance. The advantage of this approach was that curricula could be geared directly to demands in the field and for specific agencies or levels of leadership. In view of the rapidly broadening scope of leadership opportunities, however, it was an impractical approach because, as the recreation profession grew and matured, concepts and descriptions of the worker's task changed. The current approach is functional, one wherein the problems met by the worker in the performance of basic roles have been identified, the competencies needed to solve these problems have been delineated,

---

[4] H. D. Sessoms, "Recreation Education in American Colleges and Universities Today," *American Recreation Journal,* Vol. 1, No. 7 (April 1961), pp. 8-9.

[5] See *Professional Preparation of Recreation Personnel,* Conference Report, American Association for Health, Physical Education, and Recreation (Washington, D.C.: The Association, 1957).

and curricular experiences have been planned to develop these competencies.

There is increasing utilization of recreation courses by other disciplines. Examples of this are the addition of recreation education courses to physical education credential requirements, and the provision for recreation background in preparation programs in home economics, nursing, elementary education, and social welfare.

Undergraduate Preparation

It is generally accepted that undergraduate professional preparation for recreation should have three emphases: (1) A broad, liberal, cultural emphasis encompassing foundation study in the humanities, social sciences, communicative arts, and the natural sciences, which would be designed to provide the student with a better understanding of himself and his relation to others in a constantly changing society. This is the general education content for the professional recreation worker and consensus is that it should constitute about half the curriculum. (2) A general professional emphasis directed to development of basic understandings and competencies in the fundamental areas of educational psychology, sociology, human growth and development, public administration, evaluation and research, group processes, and principles of administration and supervision. (3) A specialized professional emphasis geared to developing the specific competencies required in the worker role. In this area are the foundation experiences in the history, philosophy, and principles of leisure and recreation, program areas and methods of leadership, and organization and administration of services, supplemented with directed out-of-class field experiences designed to provide the preprofessional student with working knowledge of the tools and methodology of the professional worker. Specialization at the undergraduate level should be minimized and should focus primarily upon the development of the skills, understandings, and knowledges common to all recreation workers.

Graduate Preparation

Increasing attention and emphasis is being given to graduate preparation in the field of recreation, owing to the need for advanced study and research and the demand for preparation of leadership for higher-level positions in supervision, teaching, research, and administration. Graduate preparation presupposes that the student already possesses competence in the actual working relationship, developed through sound undergraduate preparation, field work, and experience on the job. Graduate study should build upon this background and national conferences have recommended three emphases: (1) further emphasis in the foundation areas of the history and philosophy of American culture, the impact of modern leisure on the lives of people and the understanding of the institutionalized forms that leisure and recreation are assuming; (2) emphasis upon increasing skill and understanding in the use of fundamental tools of evaluation and research and their applications to problem solving; and (3) opportunity for specialization in such areas as hospital, industry, and camping, and the development of competencies necessary for administrative and supervisorial positions. Field work at the graduate level is invaluable and internship programs have been developed to provide this.

The amount of graduate education necessary and the level of the degrees offered vary. Few public or private recreation agency positions throughout the country require advanced degrees although the job to be done may deserve it and demand it. If recreation is to gain full professional status, however, the professional education program must continue to raise its status within higher education, particularly at the doctoral level. This is critical for the development of an adequate research program and the enrichment and upgrading of college teaching faculties.

Tasks in Professional Education

Of major concern is the recruitment of sufficient members and the selection of the right kinds of individuals for professional education and entrance into the profession. In 1958 there were approximately 3,000 positions available and less than 2,000 students engaged in professional preparation. The assurance of a flow of students adequate to meet demands for leadership is a responsibility of the total profession and is shared by all workers, including those responsible for the educational process.

In some instances, colleges have developed intensive specializations leading to separate curricula at the undergraduate level. The development of too much specialization at the undergraduate level, however, tends to work to the disadvantage of the broad, general preparation considered necessary for entrance into the profession at large. There must be proper balance in the curriculum between skills and theory. However necessary the acquisition of individual skills in a variety of program activities may seem to an individual or to recreation agencies, the development of a sound philosophy and science of recreation constitutes more basic professional education content and should receive major emphasis.

The accreditation of programs of recreation education and of the institutions preparing recreation workers is a necessary step. In the rapid growth of the recreation movement in the United States, some institutions initiated programs of recreation leadership preparation that now may not possess the qualifications essential for sound professional education. The requirements of adequate resources of library, classrooms, laboratories, professionally qualified instructional staff, breadth of course offerings, and community laboratory and field opportunities for internship have to be met. The profession is demanding a process of accreditation to ensure adequate standards in the professional preparation process. Major leadership in this direction is being given by the professional organizations. Joint national committees and conferences have developed evaluative guides that have been incorporated into the materials of national accrediting agencies, but much remains to be done.

A final task is the utilization of professional education to elevate and improve personnel standards. One way this is being done is through more careful definition of those functions of the worker which are truly professional. Technician duties should be the focus of junior college and terminal education programs, and to mix the professional worker's role with the technician's role confuses not only the educational process but also the services rendered. A second aspect of this task of definition concerns those individuals employed in recreation who have not had adequate preparation in recreation or in allied fields or are seeking to upgrade themselves professionally. Present leaders come from diverse disciplines and backgrounds and have required orientation and reorientation as the profession moves ahead. Add to this number the great multitude of volunteer and part-time workers who staff playground, center, and agency programs all year, during the summer, and on weekends, and the implications for recreation education are obvious. The extension of educational services and curricular opportunities through in-service education, workshops, institutes, and conferences is evidence of the professional effort being put forth to satisfy these needs.

Continued cooperative action among schools, colleges, and universities and the profession and its organizations, flexibility in curricular patterns, balance in offerings between general and professional education, and higher standards in the experiences provided—these represent the contribution recreation education can make to the profession.

The recreation profession and the nation's colleges and universities are working to expand and improve the undergraduate and graduate curricula for the professional preparation of recreation personnel. Recruitment, accreditation, curricular organization, and in-service and extension training are major continuing problems.

PERSONNEL STANDARDS

The formulation and refining of personnel standards have received major attention from recreation professional organizations, agencies, and individuals for many years. The establishment of sound employment practices with adequate salaries, working conditions, job descriptions, educational requirements, recruitment, and identification procedures is part of the standards-implementation process.

Leadership Functions and Titles

The assumption is that recreation standards are based upon the functions the leader performs in achieving his major objective: assisting individuals to attain leisure values through recreative uses of their leisure time. What are these functions? Butler identifies the following as typical:

> 1. Guide and encourage individuals to acquire new interests and to gain greater satisfaction from participation in familiar activities. 2. Help to organize recreation groups and to assure successful group operation. 3. Attempt to expand and equalize recreation opportunities. 4. Teach people to acquire new or more advanced skills. 5. Provide and maintain places in which individuals in groups may engage in activities. 6. Assure safe and healthful conditions and practices. 7. Furnish equipment and supplies essential for the enjoyment of many types of recreation.[6]

These functions can be (and are) stated in other ways, as leadership literature indicates, but they are sufficient for our purposes here.

---

[6] George D. Butler, *Introduction to Community Recreation,* Third edition (New York: McGraw-Hill Book Company, 1959), p. 96.

In Chapter 11, the various settings in which these functions are performed were described. Like most professions, the range of opportunity in terms of organization and the nature of the setting is quite wide. Professionals are found in urban and rural settings, in public and private agencies, in the United States and abroad, with all different age and cultural groups.

The exact number of professionally employed recreation workers in Amerca is rather difficult to ascertain. Estimates have ranged from twenty to twenty-five thousand. These statistics were based upon projection of regional recreation studies that included leadership. Another picture has been provided through a national social-welfare manpower study made in 1960, which reported 116,000 social-welfare workers employed in the United States. Of these, 10,450 were recreation workers in government and voluntary agencies. Of these workers, 64 per cent were found in government agencies—52 per cent in state and local agencies and 12 per cent in federal agencies. The remaining 36 per cent of the workers were employed in voluntary agencies. These figures were derived through sampling and probably do not include the commercial fields or fully reflect either the public or private agency.[7]

These individuals are employed under a variety of titles. For example, the National Recreation Association, in its recruitment booklet on choosing the right college for a career in recreation, identifies the following positions:

Superintendent of Recreation
Assistant Superintendent
Recreation Director
Consultant Field Representative
Executive Director
Hospital Recreation Supervisor
Campus Recreation Coordinator
Extension Specialist
Service Club Director
Girls' Worker and Boys' Worker in a private agency
District Recreation Supervisor
Recreation Leader
Supervisor of Special Activities
Recreation Therapist
Recreation Educator

There are full-time and part-time opportunities in these positions for general practitioners and specialists.

---

[7] W. Sutherland, "The National Social Welfare Manpower Study—1960," *Recreation,* Vol. 54, No. 8 (October 1961), p. 411.

LEADERSHIP QUALIFICATIONS

The establishment of civil service procedures, primarily for personnel in governmental organizations, and the efforts of the various national, state, and local professional organizations through conferences, workshops, and study committees contributed much to the development and standardization of personnel terminology, classification, and qualifications. The general education experience and personal qualifications required for initial placement are basically the same, whether the agency is public or private, large or small. The differences and variations occur in salaries and in scope of responsibility.

The personal qualifications require that the potential recreation leader be enthusiastic, dependable, and of sound character; that he have a sense of humor, enjoy good health, be flexible, creative, and personally attractive; that he have broad interests, be friendly, like people, and be energetic and cooperative. That these characteristics are important in working with people and are essential for successful leadership requires little explanation. However, they are so general and have become so accepted as criteria for selection processes that it is more upon other bases that standards in the recreation profession are being largely determined. They are, in effect, the base point from which the other standards operate.

The most important standards are the educational requirements set for entrance into professional service in the field. The minimum essential is graduation from a recognized institution of higher education with a bachelor's degree, a major in recreation or in a closely allied field such as physical education, group work, education, or sociology, and including supervised field work in the recreation setting. Graduate study is necessary for persons preparing for or seeking advanced positions that also require experience. There are opportunities for specialists with degrees in the program areas of art, music, drama, and the like. Deviation from this standard has been dependent largely upon the supply of personnel available. Because of the relative newness of programs of professional recreation education, agencies are sometimes unable to secure leadership that meets these standards, but progress is being made. A survey of the education of these recreation workers showed that 53 per cent possessed bachelor's degrees or higher degrees. Fifty-one per cent of those in state and local governments had degrees, 38 per cent of those in federal service had degrees, and 61 per cent of those in voluntary agencies had degrees.[8]

Personnel Practices

Beginning salaries for recreation workers are comparable to the beginning salaries of allied professional groups—nursing, teaching, social work, and so on. The exact amount is usually dependent upon the size and type of agency and the part of the country in which it is located. By and large, public recreation agencies tend to pay higher salaries than private agencies, and salaries are higher in larger cities than in smaller cities, regardless of whether the agency is public or private. The salary scale in recreation reflects the local market. A study of salary levels showed that the median annual salary for all recreation workers was $4500. The median salary for those with bachelor's degrees was $5240. The median salary for those holding master's degrees was $6900 annually.[9]

Several of the professional organizations have developed personnel practices codes that spell out for the profession desirable employment procedures and working conditions. These codes include recommendations on such matters as: selection on merit procedures, including examination processes; classification methods and salary ranges; appointment conditions, including length of probationary period and basis for discharge; registration or certification requirements as a qualification; performance evaluation and rating system to be used; advancement and promotion procedures, including length of service and merit ratings; fringe benefits such as vacations with pay, sick leaves, professional advancement opportunities, pension and retirement plans, medical benefits, and overtime pay; and working conditions in terms of number of hours. There is no more important task for the profession than wise selection and effective use of leadership personnel, and such codes contribute immeasurably to this effort.

Recruitment

The concept of what the recreation worker should be has been undergoing change. There is increasing recognition of a broader role of the worker than just program responsibility. Professional groups

[8] Sutherland, p. 411.
[9] Sutherland, p. 411.

are giving more attention to projecting what the leader of tomorrow will need to be like if he is to serve the interests and needs of the masses of people who will be seeking recreation experiences. More and more, recreation standards are reaching out to encompass the concept of the worker as a person who understands the role of recreation in the lives of people, who is able to integrate not only the what and the how of programs and facilities, but also the why, through research and fundamental grounding in the discipline and theory of recreation.

The recruitment of this type of leadership is of major concern to the profession. The development of standards and their application in the employment process requires there be sufficient supply of recruits to make selection possible and encourage further elevation of standards. One of the major challenges the recreation profession faces is to make more young men and women aware not only of the opportunities but also of the significance of the field, at that crucial point when they are considering the selection of a life career. Part of the information they need relates to the adequacy of working conditions and salaries and whether they enable a person to practice his profession with freedom from distraction and economic insecurity, the scope and nature of professional positions, and the values of the service that the professional person can render to his community and society.

The average college campus is the scene of intense competition among several professions and fields for the kind of leadership they vitally need. Industry, medicine, social work, law, and science, among others, are appealing to talented youth in every way possible. The recreation profession is striving for its share of the highest type of leadership available. The task of recruitment is a shared responsibility and is being borne by schools and colleges, by professional organizations, by employing agencies, and by professional workers themselves in their face-to-face relationships with people. The community at large is being tapped also through lay participation, parent groups, and other community organizations.

Identification

The development of standards for the competent and qualified professional workers is only one part of the professionalization process. It is essential that there be some way to identify those that are so qualified. This identification process, when it is established by definite criteria, serves to assure the public of the quality of service, helps the employer in the procurement of qualified leaders, and provides protection for the individual worker who has prepared for the profession. A system of identification can be initiated at various levels and by several kinds of groups. In some instances, the professional organizations and societies have been responsible for the identification process, whether it be through registration or certification. To some extent, colleges do this with the granting of degrees. In other cases, a governmental agency is assigned responsibility for this function. It is generally agreed, however, that responsibility should be assigned to an agency that has the function of registration for other types of professional personnel. The criteria normally used for identification include meeting standards covering individual qualities and personal attributes (health, personality, and the like), professional education, job experience, tests of knowledge, competence, and so on.

Recreation has been experimenting with several types and plans of identification, including both registration and certification. The procedures for these two are somewhat different. Registration involves a licensing process, whereas certification represents a formal statement by an official, usually public, which confirms that an individual possesses certain required competencies. At least one-third of the states have voluntary registration plans, and the American Recreation Society has established a national voluntary registration program. At least two states (New York and New Jersey) certify recreation workers, primarily because recreation is closely related to education in these states, and the certification plan parallels that for teachers. The over-all purpose of both approaches is much the same; namely, to establish minimum standards for the profession, to clearly identify professionally employed recreation workers, and to certify the qualification, training, and experience of the recreation worker. Those individuals currently employed at a certain level who fail to meet the standards established in such plans are "blanketed in" as an initial and temporary device in some states, notably California and North Carolina.

Identification is essential, and employment practices conforming to political pressures and patronage-dispensing traditions will be replaced as professional recognition of the importance of the establishment grows and as adherence to standards becomes more widespread in the effort to meet the increasing demand for recreation services and leadership.

The recreation profession devotes much attention to the development of personnel practices codes, job description and classification plans, recruitment and selection procedures, identification processes, and means for raising the qualifications and the standards of work of recreation personnel.

PROFESSIONAL ASSOCIATIONS

Organized interest groups made up of people who specialize in the same kind of work constitute a large number of the organizations found in America. So it is with every profession that, in its evolution, has organized when there was evidence of common interest of many of the workers and support for efforts to form a professional organization. Carr-Saunders feels that mere interest in the subject matter of the profession is not enough to justify the presence of associations and identifies three other powerful motives for association: (1) the desire to distinguish those who possess a certain skill from those who do not, (2) the desire to associate with and include in the association all practitioners who qualify, and (3) the maintenance of high standards of professional character and practice and the elevation of the status of the professional group concerned.[10]

In expressing these motivations, the recreation profession has organized itself into many professional societies and associations. This organizing is due in part to the scope of the recreation profession and to the various facets of recreation services which vary not only in the kind of agencies involved but also in the historical development of professional leadership and relationships with allied professional groups. Considering the settings in which recreation occurs, the professional worker could logically consider himself an educator, a group worker, an artist, a musician, a therapist, a physical educator, or a manager. As one writer put it, if mere evidence of the number of organizations were sufficient, recreation would surely meet the criterion of a profession.[11] Each of the major organizations has members who identify primarily with the area of concern of the organization.

---

[10] A. M. Carr-Saunders, "Professions, Their Organization and Place in Society" (Oxford: Clarendon Press, 1927), as reprinted in *Social Foundations of Education* by W. O. Stanley and others (New York: Holt, Rinehart and Winston, Inc., 1956), p. 584.

[11] Sorenson, "Professional Maturity," p. 19.

Major Organizations

The major groups are: (1) the American Association for Health, Physical Education, and Recreation, composed chiefly of physical educators and school recreation personnel; (2) the American Camping Association, composed of individuals and agencies interested in private and organizational camps and camp programs; (3) the American Recreation Society, composed primarily of public recreation workers; (4) the American Institute of Park Executives, made up largely of park personnel; (5) the Association of College Unions with institutional memberships, including those individuals responsible for the operation of college union programs and facilities; (6) the Group Work Section of the National Association of Social Workers, consisting mainly of private agency workers; (7) the National Conference on State Parks, composed essentially of state park executives; (8) the National Industrial Recreation Association, with a membership made up largely of individuals and companies with employee recreation programs; and (9) the Society of State Directors of Health, Physical Education, and Recreation, with a membership of past and present staffs of state departments of health, physical education, and recreation.

In addition, there are two major service organizations; namely, the Athletic Institute and the National Recreation Association. The former is a nonprofit organization whose purpose is to promote and encourage participation in the field of athletics, recreation, physical education, and health education. It is supported by the manufacturers and distributors of athletic, sports, and recreation goods. The National Recreation Association has long been identified as one of the major leaders in the recreation movement and performs many functions common to professional societies with membership open to both organizations and individuals, and has a full time professional consultant staff that renders nationwide field services.[12]

Some of these organizations were in existence before the recreation movement was sufficiently advanced to be identified as a separate movement of its own and to which professional alliance and identifi-

[12] For a more complete description of the scope, purpose, and function of each of these organizations and their publications see Harold D. Meyer and Charles K. Brightbill, *Community Recreation: A Guide to Its Organization* (Englewood Cliffs, N.J.: Prentice-Hall, Inc., 1956), pp. 433-450.

cation was important. The word *recreation* was not added to the title of the American Association for Health, Physical Education, and Recreation until 1936, and the American Recreation Society was not founded until 1938.

Naturally confusion arises over this range of association and organization, particularly for the young new recreation worker, for it is difficult to decide with which group to establish primary professional orientation. Most recreation professionals in the field today maintain membership in several of the organizations, for varying purposes and needs. Some believe it is important and necessary that these organizations be joined into one common society. Examples in other professions indicate that such a merger is not essential. The American Medical Association may serve as the official spokesman for the medical profession, but there are still separate societies—such as the American Psychiatric Association and the American Public Health Association—that maintain independent status and work together through joint committees. This is no less true for recreation. Each of the several societies identified above have their proper place within the perspective of the recreation profession at this time. Perhaps all professional associations can best achieve the one objective they have in common—namely, the improvement and upgrading of the profession—by continuing their independent autonomy, along with creating and providing liaison opportunities and interorganizational relationships that permit a joint approach to problems that concern the whole recreation movement.

Federation of National Professional Organizations for Recreation

There have been efforts to establish cooperative relationships. One of the more prominent attempts was the creation of a National Recreation Policies Committee, which concerned itself with the development of policy statements relating to recreation. Two thirds of the members of the committee were elected by professional organizations in recreation but did not represent formally the respective organizations and were free to take independent actions. This group is no longer active, and a more recent effort was the creation of a Federation of National Professional Organizations for Recreation. The Federation was organized in 1954 for the purpose of establishing a means for various national professional organizations for recreation to work together, the specific goals being sharing information, studying common problems, developing public understanding, raising professional standards, and generally furthering the aims of the total recreation profession. Membership in the Federation is open to all national professional organizations concerned wholly or in part with recreation. Its members are contributors with voting privileges. All of the organizations identified above are members of the Federation, with the National Recreation Association and the Athletic Institute serving as consultants. Projects of the Federation include (1) developing a statement of national policy on land encroachment for parks, recreation, and camping, (2) exploring the future role of the federal government in the field of community recreation, with implications for the establishment of a federal recreation service, and (3) helping to organize a National Conference on Leisure. An appointed representative and the executive secretary or director from each of the respective organizations constitute the working membership of the Federation, and they meet semiannually.

Whether one strong national professional organization can be developed from all of these separate groups with which recreation workers identify and associate themselves remains to be seen. It appears to be a long range objective and will best be accomplished through evolution, not revolution. Meanwhile, the major objectives are to avoid conflict of purpose, objectives, and approaches, and to join together in a unified search for understanding and purpose, with mutual respect for each other's unique objectives and functions. The real purpose of organization and association is to further the profession. More and more recreation workers are finding that they have more common attributes than they have differences. Evidences of this are found in the joint sponsorship by several professional groups of national, regional, state, and local conferences and meetings (e.g., the National Recreation Congress), the organized efforts to merge organizations, and the existence of joint committees on legislation and research. These underscore increasing recognition that no one of the organizations can do the whole job. More important, they indicate growing ability and desire to cooperate and work together. Every sign points toward increasing maturity in this aspect of the profession.

International Relationships

One of the newer trends in professional association has been the establishment in many professional organizations of channels for international liaison. Most of the professional organizations in recreation have international committees that relate to parallel organizations or counterparts in other countries and nations throughout the world. This fabric of societies and organizations concerned with recreation on the international level has developed over the years rather informally, primarily stimulated through international conferences and special events such as the Olympic Games.

The National Recreation Association through its operation and sponsorship of International Recreation Congresses for many years has given major direction to international relations and professional association in recreation. This direction culminated in 1956 in the creation of the International Recreation Association, with offices in the United Nations Building in New York City. One of the major activities of the IRA is the community recreation exchange project in which leaders are exchanged between the United States and other countries for the purposes of recreation study and training. Since 1956, more than thirty-five representatives of the Association have given "on-the-ground" service in fifty-nine countries on six continents. By 1961, more than fifty-nine men and women from thirty-one different countries had visited and studied recreation in the United States on programs administered by the International Recreation Association. Affiliated with the International Recreation Association are a number of national recreation associations in other countries, such as Pakistan, India, and Japan, as well as many other federated sports and recreation groups.

The recreation profession includes several professional associations whose wide diversity reflects the various fields and settings in which the profession practices. The means by which these organizations can communicate and cooperate are being worked out, with high professional standards and appropriate professional discipline and responsibility being the goals.

Questions for Study and Discussion

1. *Do you believe recreation would be served best at present by one professional organization or by the several different organizations presently existing? Give reasons for your belief.*
2. *What would you list as the important parts of a code of ethics for recreation workers?*

3. *What would you identify as the major areas of responsibility that the recreation worker must assume?*
4. *In what respects do you believe recreation has developed a base of scientific knowledge? In what respects do you believe recreation is lacking this scientific base?*
5. *What would you consider to be important questions for recreation research today?*
6. *Why may recreation be termed a profession? Give your arguments.*

Selected Readings

Brightbill, Charles K., and Harold D. Meyer, *Recreation: Text and Readings* (Englewood Cliffs, N.J.: Prentice-Hall, Inc., 1953).

"Recreation in the Age of Automation," *Annals of the American Academy of Political and Social Science,* Vol. 313 (September 1957).

Wilson, Gertrude, and Gladys Ryland, *Social Group Work Practice* (Boston: Houghton Mifflin Company, 1949).

13

CONTRIBUTIONS FROM RELATED DISCIPLINES

An important possession of the professional recreation worker is his *method*—the knowledges, understandings, insights, skills, and techniques that make up his professional work tools. This professional method is based upon the findings of the modern sciences of human behavior, such as physiology, psychology, and sociology. It borrows heavily from the related applied fields of social work, psychotherapy, and education.

The first workers in recreation were individuals possessing some special personality attributes and equipped with program skills and some leadership or teaching abilities. They were assigned to recreation centers and worked with individuals and groups, building relationships and affecting group life so as to enrich each individual's experiences in his group as well as to enrich the life of groups as a whole. The recreation worker found himself working with certain conditions somewhat unique to his field. For one thing, his relationship with groups differed radically from that of the school teacher. The teacher worked with individuals who were in compulsory attendance. Pupil reaction to the loss of freedom had to be dealt with, often by reinforcing compulsions.

The recreation worker, however, found himself working with free groups. They could come or stay away, and in other ways exercise their right to freedom of choice. He had to rely strongly upon making the group experience or the activity attractive and rewarding. Playground and recreation center leaders were called upon to supervise free play activities, to lead in low-organization games and activities, to teach and coach sports activities of a relatively low demand. They also conducted a range of groups in crafts, dramatics, and so on, in which "fun" was the attraction—freedom of choice was a main feature.

A second feature of the situation in recreation groups was the unique set of purposes and goals that were defined. For children, educational and developmental purposes that were similar to those for education were defined, with recognition of the informality and the permissiveness of the atmosphere. For adults, goals were defined in terms of enhancement of the individual, of pleasurable self-realization in leisure pursuits, of relaxation and personal reintegration and re-creation, and of the satisfaction of personal needs for responsive human contacts through social relationships.

Group Work

In the past two decades, study and experimentation with methods of work with informal educational groups have been carried on in many agencies whose work we reviewed earlier. Professional workers in these agencies have focused much attention upon providing important values through small primary group experiences. Members are believed to gain such values when the group life develops the qualities of cooperation, democratic behavior, friendly interpersonal interaction, intimate fellowship, and common interest in activities. The method of work with such groups in the professional leisure-time social agency is called *group work*.

There are two mainstreams of professional practice in group

work. One is *social group work,* one of the major methods in the profession of social work. Recreation draws heavily upon the principles of professional practice in social group work as it is found particularly in voluntary agencies such as settlements, community and youth centers, the Young Women's Christian Association, and others, and also in public recreation practice in a number of municipal systems. Several principles of social group work will be introduced in the next chapter for what they can contribute to basic recreation method.

In pointing out that social group work is an important base for the recreation method we should point out also that the method in social group work has received its primary components from the developing method of professional social work. The social work method has been thought by many writers to be made up of three identifiable methods: (1) social case work, (2) social group work, and (3) community organization (some might add administration and research). Some would rather call these processes than methods. But in any case, among social workers there is wide agreement that these several specializations, having characteristics of process unique to each of them, possess their basic processes as generic to all of them. There is a core of knowledge and a skill generic to all social work practice. Social group work is based upon that core, and has many important special components.[1]

The second stream might be called *educational group work.* This method is based upon the same scientific foundations as social group work, and upon many of the same principles. It finds its base also in the modern study of group dynamics, of human relations research, of the principles of group process in education. But it is oriented not only toward application in the informal education of such agencies as the Young Men's Christian Association, but also in the programs of schools, many public recreation systems, and other settings. The principles in this stream of group work practice will be studied in the next chapter as well.

The two developments in group work method, one anchored firmly in the professional practice of social work in group-serving organizations and the other being explored and experimented with in a wide range of organizations serving groups, are closer together in

[1] For a description of the background and the fields of social work practice see Arthur Fink and others, *The Field of Social Work,* Third edition (New York: Holt, Rinehart and Winston, Inc., 1955).

respect to their basic principles and practices than one might perceive at first glance. They also are closer than some educators and practitioners in group work might care to admit. The foremost practitioners in each field are moving gradually toward a synthesis of a generic base for the group method, a base upon which can be developed a sophisticated professional method adapted to a wide range of professional group-serving functions. Among these functions, in a central position, is recreation. We can derive from these developments the following principle:

Modern recreation workers in both public and voluntary agencies should integrate the developing science of group life and methodology of group work into the professional recreation method.

The Professional Recreation Method

The public recreation field has little basic literature of its own on professional method. But many practitioners are studying the growing literature dealing with group work methods, and are becoming acquainted with the extensive experimentation in related fields of group psychotherapy and education. Recreation, as it develops a deeper awareness of its own professional needs, is moving toward the adaptation, in the main, of the methodology of group work as the foundation for its professional method.

At the same time, in each of these fields and in the scientific fields most closely related to them, the results of extensive experimentation and research are being made available. Their applications to the field of recreation are being studied and made use of by more advanced and professionally trained practitioners in the field. The recreation worker is deepening his understanding of the values of informal education and recreational pursuits in meeting basic needs of individuals. He is developing a greater understanding of the complex structure of human personality and growth patterns, especially the processes of socialization and the satisfaction of his developmental needs. As was discussed in Chapter 11, the focus of recreation work is on design of program activities and experiences in order to meet biopsychosocial needs of the whole individual.

The recreation worker is learning to understand the meaning of the complex streams of social and psychic interaction which make up the dynamics of group life, the nature of the processes of movement and relationship in groups. He is learning to analyze them and to function knowingly and skillfully in relation to them so as to maximize the constructive values of the individual's experiences in these groups. It is highly important for professional growth and advancement that this process continue. The new data from several important scientific fields must be integrated with practice, and the contributions of new research and discovery from experimentation in several fields of related practice must be taken and translated into more effective professional functioning. Let us look, in turn, at some of these fields.

CONTRIBUTIONS FROM INDIVIDUAL PSYCHOLOGY

From individual psychology we learn the nature of human personality and its development. Our review of individual growth and development in Chapter 11 shows us that as the individual grows through the periods of childhood, youth, and adulthood his needs vary as his growth processes interact with his environment. We learn to understand individual behavior and recognize the drives, developmental needs, and interaction processes that determine behavior. We learn the means by which recreation can help the individual to satisfy his behavioral needs.

THE HUMAN PERSONALITY

Study in the field of psychology has given us gradually a more adequate picture of the human personality. Murphy, in his classic study of personality, indicates several points of vantage from which to view personality:

—as a biological system or organic complex, developmentally influenced by heredity and environment
—as a learning process through the interaction of the individual constitution and a specific environment
—as a structure of one's sense perceptions, imagery and feeling; as a cognitive-affective system
—as a conception of self, and possessing dynamic means of attaining, maintaining and defending selfhood
—as a genuine unity or wholeness
—as a flowing continuum of organism-environment events [2]

[2] Gardner Murphy, *Personality: A Biosocial Approach to Origins and Structure* (New York: Harper & Row, Inc., 1947), pp. 18-21.

This opens up many areas of study of the forces at work in the development of personality, each of which is significant. Erikson's study of individual growth from infancy to adulthood, as we noted in Chapter 11, identifies eight successive phases through which the person must go, eight "nuclear areas of conflict," which the individual must attempt to resolve.[3] The degree of success with which, and the manner in which, earlier conflicts are resolved determine in some measure the resolution of later problems and the degree of personality maturity or the "self" development the individual will possess.

A similar formulation of this growth process as one of meeting and solving problem situations, the concept of "developmental tasks," is given by Havighurst.

> A developmental task is a task which arises at or about a certain period in the life of the individual, successful achievement of which leads to his happiness and to success with later tasks, while failure leads to unhappiness in the individual, disapproval by the society, and difficulty with later tasks.[4]

It has been understood that personality develops within a framework of situations that act upon persons. Just as important as the organism that responds to situations is the nature of the situation, its structure and dynamics. This is the essence of the field theory of personality—that personality is a continuum of organism-environment events, and that while the inner organization of an individual may resist environmental pressures to some degree, there is still a basic relationship between the environment and the individual, the individual growing primarily in response to the complex influences of his total environment. This must be seen as a continuum through time, with the individual living within this complex of external stimuli through the years and interacting with them.

An important facet of this, the creative thrust of human nature, is identified by Murphy in his description of human nature. Murphy points out that human nature may be understood as a synthesis of three things: (1) the original raw distinctive humanness, emotional

---

[3] Erik H. Erikson, *Childhood and Society* (New York: W. W. Norton and Company, 1950), pp. 219-231.

[4] Robert J. Havighurst, *Developmental Tasks and Education* (New York: Longmans, Green and Company, 1952), p. 6. Courtesy of David McKay Company, Inc.

and impulsive equipment, sensitivity, capacity to learn, to change, to adapt, all of this a product of biological evolution; (2) a thing molded by culture, personality evolving under the impact of culture into a human cultural product; and (3) the creative thrust of the need to understand and to discover, the creative forces of curiosity and of artistic and scientific endeavor always remaking the culture and demanding growth, freedom to create, freedom to think or do something different.[5]

Individual Differences

Psychologists recognize as well that the individual and his growth within the environment can be understood only by recognizing individual differences. From conception there are differences, both in the genes, the inherited potentialities, and in the prenatal environment. There are differences in activity, vigor, temperament, and tolerances, which remain with the individual. These differences suggest that from the beginning each child must be treated as a unique individual if he is to develop optimally.

There are differences in sensitivity among infants, some being so flooded with perceptual stimulations that actual discomfort can result, while others are almost imperturbable and readily adjust to light, sound, touch, and motion. There are differences in tempo and rhythm, not necessarily related either to basic intellectual competence nor to success in life, but important for the worker to understand if excessive demands for speed, patience, or thoroughness are not to be made. There are differences in physiological reactions, in nervous resilience, and in vulnerability to disturbing factors. There are differences in kind and in amount of intellectual endowment. The amount is often emphasized too much by teachers and parents and the differences in kind are not understood at all adequately at present.

The Self-Concept

The integration and unity of physical, mental, and emotional factors is just now beginning to be understood. We now recognize that each person perceives himself and his "culture" in relation to this organization of factors. This is one's perceptual field, one's perceived self, and man's goal is not just the maintenance of that self but also

---

[5] Gardner Murphy, *Human Potentialities* (New York: Basic Books, Inc., 1958), pp. 15-19.

the development of a more adequate self. This is what has been termed as man's basic need, "that great driving, striving force in each of us by which we are continually seeking to make ourselves ever more adequate to cope with life." [6]

Psychology has identified a number of important mechanisms and processes involved in the growth and defense of the self. These are related to the continuous struggles and strivings the individual undergoes, psychologically, for a stable balance between needs and satisfactions, and for the enhancement and defense of the self. In physiology Cannon describes this balance as "homeostasis." [7]

All of these processes take place within a dynamic environmental field. These adjustments are adjustments not only to the external situation but to a perceptual whole of which the self is the center, a self-in-situation field. Psychologists have recognized that the conflicts within the person reflect conflicts, unreliabilities, and confusion in the society and in the person's immediate environment or field. In our culture, the child is bound to feel the contradictions, disturbances, and insecurity to some degree, and his personality is shaped by his effort to establish behavioral goals that enable him to cope with these forces. He may fight them, accept them, evade them, harmonize them, but he relates them to his perceived self in some manner.

Freud made psychology and psychiatry aware of the powerful influence of unconscious forces on this process. Following his lead, psychologists conceived of the individual as possessing powerful internal drives, mainly sexual in nature, which Freud called the *id,* which strive for expression. Opposing these drives in response to outside demand is the urging of the conscience, or the *superego.* The guiding, controlling, organizing force is the *ego,* which controls the irrational energies of the id and reconciles the conflicting strivings. Without enlarging these concepts further here, we simply underline their importance in modern psychology, even though they are being gradually replaced by the concepts of self and perceptual field, which include outside forces and conscience.

In the effort to enhance the self, the individual employs many techniques and mechanisms. In describing these mechanisms, we may

---

[6] A. W. Combs and D. Snygg, *Individual Behavior* (New York: Harper & Row, Inc., 1959), p. 46.

[7] Walter B. Cannon, *The Wisdom of the Body* (New York: W. W. Norton and Company, 1939), p. 24.

cite very simple examples from behavior readily observable on the playground or in a recreation center to point out the interaction and relations among the processes.

Identification—viewing oneself as one with, or like, an admired person and accepting that person's qualities as desirable. It may be selective; that is, one defends the self by an appropriate choice of objects with which to identify. *Example:* boys copy the language, body motions, and attitudes of the coach as part of the process of playing the baseball or basketball game. The recreationist-coach (knowingly or unknowingly) wields one of his most powerful influences at this point.

Projection—attributing to other persons, real or imaginary, one's own traits, attitudes, and other subjective feelings, both pleasant and undesirable. *Example:* in dramatic play, children will attack with great determination those devils, spirits, witches, and other representatives of evil who most accurately manifest their own wrongdoing. On the other hand, children attribute to parents their own tastes and feelings about things, and are often disappointed to learn otherwise.

Rationalization—discovering an acceptable or partially reasonable explanation for one's behavior, thus not being forced to perceive the whole or real reason for it. *Example:* "the other side was unfair, they cheated" as an explanation of defeat, rather than lack of practice, skill, or determination.

Regression—as a result of having experienced tension, difficulty, frustration, defeat, or failure in some situation or relationship, returning to a behavior or relationship represented by an earlier age level, striving to find there some measure of security, relaxation, or satisfaction. *Example:* temporary or playful regression by adults in gay and carefree parties, dancing, singing together, childlike splashing in the water, and in many games and sports that "make us feel young again." It provides one of play's most useful opportunities for healthy expression if it is not habitual or extreme.

Repression and *suppression*—blocking impulses by counter-pressure of will or conscience, as an important means of self-control and adjustment; such blocking often contributes to frustration and tension. *Suppression* is usually used to mean conscious repression. *Example:* many recreational activities—especially competitive games—provide opportunities for acting out repressed feelings and impulses and relaxing tension thereby.

Displacement, substitution, sublimation, and *compensation*—with one's normal means of expression or functioning being blocked, finding a satisfactory means of expressing feeling or behavior in regard to some other object or in some other way. (These four terms refer to different ways of accomplishing the same end.) *Example:* the pursuit of excellence and skill in many sports, creative arts, intellectual games, and so on, often may make up for deprivation, failure, or lack of satisfaction or opportunity for expression in other areas of life, such as one's occupation or marriage and family life.

These processes as they occur and are evidenced in play must be understood as primarily *normal* means for maintaining individual self-regard and stability. With an emotionally disturbed person whose ego is seriously threatened, recourse to these mechanisms of self-enhancement might be compulsive or inappropriate, and would be symptomatic of maladjustment. Certain of the means would be appropriate at certain ages but not at other ages. The worker's ability to diagnose and deal constructively with these behaviors will depend in part upon his ability to discriminate between normally healthy and abnormally unhealthy behavior.

A competent recreation worker would recognize and encourage in play behaviors the healthy expression of these familiar mechanisms. He would recognize the needs that underlie such behaviors. He would recognize the need for a person to express his feelings, and could provide in group life and play activities suitable opportunities for this. He would understand how he might help the person both to express and to understand the expression of his feelings, and gradually to learn more appropriate behavior and gain more normal satisfactions. Thus he might help the person to work out satisfying identifications, to create a valid level of aspiration, to secure satisfactions in activities and group life, and so on.

Motivation

There is an issue in psychology that bears on this point. Some psychologists hold that human motivation is primarily influenced by innate, unlearned, and universal instincts, which make up the element of personality that Freud named the *id*. The *ego* tends to be relegated to the status of a relatively passive coordinator between the id and the *superego,* or socially-derived conscience.

Other psychologists, among them Gordon Allport, hold that human drives are primarily viscerogenic states of excess or deficit stimulation, and sensitivities to external stimulation. These are radically modified and changed during the years of growth of the individual within the field of environmental forces. A complex of acquired traits may become the primary motivational units in the ego. The ego or self structure, including intelligence, perception, contemporary motivation toward self-actualization, and so forth, functions as a strong, active, organizing and controlling force unless it is damaged or weakened by conflict and draining off of its energies. The self is seen as the organizing center for the drive for self-actualization. This describes more accurately than a concept of *instincts* the dynamic operating whole that Murphy and others have written about.[8]

It matters a lot to the recreation worker whether his conception of the individual grows out of one or the other of these views. One view sees a person primarily subject to the overwhelming drives of instincts, with which the self comes to terms as a relatively passive compromising agent. The other view sees a person with a self which is itself dominant, the organizing force in personality, with motivations, interests, and drives for self-actualization being the result of environmental conditioning. The latter view, more influential in psychology today than it was in the past, provides the worker with the concept of personality that is dynamic and subject to education and other influences.

Role Fulfillment

Of importance to the recreation worker is another subject that psychologists have explored: the social nature of the individual. A human being is made "human" by human contact; no other means will suffice, and socialization of the individual is essential to his development. Further, an individual's personality in a major sense reflects his roles in social life. Murphy makes five observations relating to roles: (1) society requires from people the enactment of specific roles; (2) many roles require effort and put a strain on the individual; (3) a person must enact several different roles at once, and the integration is

---

[8] Gordon W. Allport, *Personality and Social Encounter* (Boston: Beacon Press, Inc., 1960), pp. 137-151.

no simple matter; (4) roles derive not only from primary obligations, but also from one's response to the roles of others; and (5) the individual develops balancing or complementary roles, complementary both to others and to himself.[9] Individual self-maintenance factors, socioeconomic factors, and the interaction and interdependence of individuals in the social situation operate as significant forces in role development. The relationship of satisfactory social roles to healthy individual personality is recognized as intimate and continuous.

PSYCHIATRY

A valuable source of data to the professions working in helping situations with people is psychiatry. Like psychology in that it is concerned with the individual and his mental and emotional life as well as his physical life, psychiatry is a field of medicine concerned with mental and emotional disorders. Psychiatry applies its medical science to problems of neuroses, psychoses, psychopathic personalities, behavior disorders, and mental defects. The etiology, organic pathology, psychopathology, and processes of diagnosis-prognosis and treatment constitute the data of psychiatry. A constantly growing literature provides rich contributions of insight into both the pathological and the normal attributes in individual behavior. Many of the contributions here credited to psychology could more properly be credited to psychiatry. A number of outstanding books are available from which the recreation student may gain information about this field.[10]

We can see, even from such a light brushing over of this important field of scientific study and practice, that the recreation worker must have a competent grasp of the facts of individual behavior if he is going to function adequately in relation to individual needs.

Recreation methodology should be based on key psychological concepts such as the nature of personality, individual differences, the nature

---

[9] Murphy, *Personality,* p. 794.

[10] Franz Alexander, *Fundamentals of Psychoanalysis* (New York: W. W. Norton and Company, 1948); Anna Freud, *The Ego and the Methods of Defense* (New York: International Universities Press, 1952); Sigmund Freud, *A General Introduction to Psychoanalysis* (New York: Liveright Publishing Corporation, 1920); J. McV. Hunt, ed., *Personality and the Behavior Disorders* (New York: The Ronald Press Company, 1944); Lawson Lowery, *Psychiatry for Social Workers* (New York: Columbia University Press, 1950); and Karl A. Menninger, *Love Against Hate* (New York: Harcourt, Brace & World, Inc., 1942).

of the ego and the self-concept and their functioning, and the psychodynamics of role fulfillment.

CONTRIBUTIONS FROM SOCIAL PSYCHOLOGY

The scientific study of group dynamics, group process, sociometry, and other subjects has produced for the recreation worker important facts concerning the nature of groups and the processes of interaction among their members. Experimental data provide insight into methods of group work; these insights can enrich the experiences of members, help groups to function at better levels, and move them toward individual and group goals more readily.

Social psychology is the psychological study of three classes of social phenomena: (1) behavior of the individual in the social field, (2) behavior or dynamics of social groups, and (3) behavior within social institutions or social organizations. In Part 1 and also in Chapter 10 we discussed some of the findings in the first field. We learned that man is a social being, that his early survival and later normal growth depend upon life in a group. We noted that one of man's strongest wishes and greatest needs is for relations with other persons; man identifies with groups; he appropriates the group members' conduct as his own; he internalizes its values in his personality. This is not accomplished without difficulty, for there is a conflict between an individual's desire to gain a secure place in the group and his unwillingness to give up some of his freedom from conforming and from paying attention to the needs of others.

As Montagu suggests,

> To conform means the willingness to forego certain satisfactions in order to obtain others, to suffer a certain amount of deprivation and thwarting of satisfactions as a discipline which may ultimately lead to what are socially esteemed as greater rewards. A certain degree of conflict, repression, and aggressiveness are the consequences of such experiences both in the family and in the group in all cultures.[11]

His suggestion is that the sense of belonging or security that comes from membership in a group and the love and respect and fellowship

---

[11] Ashley Montagu, *On Being Human* (New York: Henry Schuman, 1950), p. 94.

that go with it are of eminent value to the individual. Originally dependent upon the love and care of another, a person given an adequate opportunity for growth continues to develop a more mature form of love and cooperative behavior characteristic of well-integrated adult personalities. The society, and the groups to which the person belongs, when they function best, serve to maintain the security of the person by the assurance of nonfrustrative, cooperative support based upon mutual love and helpfulness.

Montagu argues that the dominant principle of social life is not competition but cooperation, the interaction between persons for mutual support in such a way as to confer survival benefits upon one another. When social behavior is not cooperative, he argues, it is diseased.

> Men who do not love one another are sick—sick not from any disease arising within them but from a disease which has been enculturated within them by the false values of their societies. Belief in false values which condition the development of the person, in competition instead of cooperation, in narrow selfish interests instead of altruism . . . represents man turning upon all that is innately good in him.[12]

This argument is important for the proper understanding of how the individual may gain values from recreation groups with which he may be associated, and of how these values may vary in response to different group situations. It is recognized that group membership is a source of both security and insecurity for the individual. It may provide both satisfaction and frustration of various of his needs, and a member is bound to be somewhat ambivalent about his membership. A group demands of its members some degree of conformity in behavior, attitudes, and values; some groups permit members little freedom to pursue personal goals.

Experiments have shown that group life characterized by tension, aggressiveness, and internal conflict influences deeply and probably mostly negatively the emotions and feelings of the individual. Group life characterized by strong friendships and great security for members has been found to reduce negative emotionality and encourage cooperative and constructive individual behaviors. These findings show that it is possible to help recreation groups to develop that form of

---

[12] Montagu, p. 100.

playful group life that will, for its members, minimize tensions and conflicts and maximize opportunities for acceptance and other positive values.

The Nature and Study of Groups

Careful study has been made of the nature of groups, and different classifications of groups have been attempted. Early classifications into primary and secondary groups explained that primary groups are likely to be natural, intimate, small, relatively more permanent, face-to-face groupings with profound influence on individual personality and behavior. Secondary groups are in general more casual, impersonal, formal, shorter-term groupings with particular reasons for association but with much less general influence on the individual. Another classification has the primary group meeting friendship and response needs of the individual and the secondary group providing the means for gaining some objective goal held in common.

It is an important fact that groups vary widely in respect to length of life, number, quality of interaction, degree of intimate or formal relations, purpose, and function. In general, *group* has been defined as any number of persons in reciprocal communication. But some students have undertaken to define "when a group is a group" by suggesting that a coming together of people constitutes a group only when individuals identify themselves with the group and play a role in it, when they recognize that by joint action they can solve problems and pursue mutual interests and common goals. Group workers have tended to rely upon the latter more limited, but sociologically less accurate, definition.

Any group takes on a *structure* of relations between members, or a system of solutions to the functional problems of interaction. Intensive research in group structure has been done by the sociometrists led by J. L. Moreno and his associates. They have created devices, available to the recreation worker, such as the sociometric test and the sociogram for picturing internal structure of groups and subgroups, and they have analyzed the effects of positions of isolation or leadership, or of patterns of mutual attraction, on the emotional and mental health and attitudes of members.[13]

---

[13] J. L. Moreno, *Sociometry; Experimental Method and the Science of Society* (Beacon, N.Y.: Beacon House, 1951), and *Who Shall Survive?*, Revised edition (Beacon, N.Y.: Beacon House, 1953).

A review of social psychological research in relation to group work indicates the practical questions the group worker might ask the sociometrist. For example, is it better to group children so as to have a high acceptance pattern, or should we get a wide variety of children in the group and help them to learn to like each other? Similar questions are being studied with reference to groupings with different purposes and goals, to groups of children of different ages, and so on. Further study will help to show what can realistically be accomplished with a group with a given structure, what might be accomplished with skillful initial grouping, and to what degree subgroupings and other patterns of relationships can be guided into the most constructive and meaningful patterns.

Of primary importance in the study of groups is a study of the dynamics involved in the interaction of their members, and the processes that go on in the life of the group. The concept of the "life cycle of the group" has been advanced, that a natural group, unless it is interfered with, tends to experience the stages of infancy, youth, adult maturity, and senile decline. Group workers have differentiated between natural groups and formed groups, and have been very interested in the processes involved in the growth of groups out of "infancy" into "maturity," and how this movement or growth can be facilitated. Preliminary to gaining these insights, much basic study had to be made of the nature of the basic interaction within groups and the nature of the group process.

Group interaction is recognized as growing out of the association of individuals possessing needs, some of which they hold in common and from which they derive some common goals. Yet they experience tensions arising out of the uncertainty and unpredictability of the action of the members, and the social and emotional relationships created in their contact with each other within the pressures of the environment in which the group exists.

Communication between individuals is the basis for interpersonal relationships. Communication is conditioned markedly by the particular background or perceptual field each member brings with him. Plant describes the individual as possessing a sort of psycho-osmotic envelope through which he shuts out disturbing sectors of his environment and translates those parts he takes in into material that is acceptable and understandable to him. Each member in a conversation "hears" a different thing, each "is possessed of a selective, osmotic membrane which allows him to hear only what he can afford to hear." [14] This explains the varying perceptions of members of the same event. These perceptions are developed as a product of the individual's own development within his culture. The latter we shall explore in the next section.

The concern of researchers has been with two groups: (1) those in which various processes of interaction continue relatively undisturbed by outside influences and (2) those in which these processes are influenced by a "change agent," an "outside" person, one who is not a member of the group, but is skilled in the helping process. In regard to both types of groups, study has been made of the conflict and frustration growing out of the differing goals of different members or subgroups, those conflicts that grow out of the reactions of individuals of different status to their own status and that of other individuals, or those conflicts that grow out of the behavior of members unable to accept the behavior of others or to play a group role satisfactory to themselves.

The dissociative processes of competition and conflict, and the associative processes of cooperation, accommodation, and assimilation have been defined and studied. Change and resistance to change have also been studied. Change is a transition of a system of behavior from one equilibrium level to another, and can be upsetting to group stability, but not always negatively upsetting. Resistance seems to arise from a sense of comfort or satisfaction with the status quo and also from a sense of fear occasioned by uncertainty and instability. The phenomena of resistance have been studied from the point of view of the need of a group to organize itself and attain unity. Such unity often is accomplished by conflict with some object outside of the groups, perhaps the adult leader, another group, or an outside person. Some interesting hypotheses have been advanced concerning group growth, likening it in some ways to individual growth, and noting such phenomena as infantile dependency, adolescent revolt against the parent figure, and sophistication and integrity of adult functioning.

Group Process and Dynamics

The experimentation with guided groups provides for recreation workers perhaps the most useful and important data. The term *group process* is used to describe a complex of dynamic group behaviors that

---

[14] James S. Plant, *The Envelope* (New York: Commonwealth Fund, 1951), p. 3.

in their best expression represent successful patterns of democratic and cooperative living, working, and learning together. The group exists to accomplish specific purposes or goals that fulfill common needs of its members. This focus on goals of individual value is an indispensable element of the democratic group process. "If the fulfillment, creativity, productivity, and sense of personal worth of the individual are not augmented through group process the process is not operating democratically." [15]

Factors involved in group process include: possessing realistic goals; building a sense of common purpose, loyalty to and confidence in each other; having a desire to help the group succeed; deciding upon an orderly procedure for getting things done and for involving in the planning and decision making those persons to be affected by the plan.

In addition to solving problems and attaining objective goals, group process aims at changes within the group itself. One of these aims is increased cohesion, mutual respect, and feeling of "we-ness." Such group solidarity or morale is reflected in members' efforts to understand and support each other. Conflicts are resolved in a focus on common problems and objectives and in a wholesome give-and-take of equals. Communication between members improves steadily. Each assumes more responsibility for improving group action and becomes more skillful in playing constructive roles.

Roles have been defined in terms of their specific contribution to the group's welfare and include those designed to strengthen the group's democratic processes and those that build group-centered attitudes of the members. The former include roles of seeking or giving information or opinion, evaluating or clarifying views, criticizing, coordinating views, while the latter include roles of encouraging others, compromising or harmonizing views, setting standards, and so forth. Negative roles as well have been identified: the aggressor, blocker, recognition-seeker, self-confessor, playboy, dominator, help-seeker, or special interest pleader, whose self-centered behavior distracts the group from its problem-centered functioning.

The role of leadership has been studied experimentally by group dynamics researchers. In several classic experiments Lewin, Lippitt, and White and their associates compared group atmosphere, emotional

---

[15] Hilda C. Kozman, ed., *Group Process in Physical Education* (New York: Harper & Row, Inc., 1951), p. 109.

climate, and group productivity with three types of leadership patterns: autocratic, democratic, and *laissez faire*. In each case group responses were integrally linked with leadership patterns; a given pattern of leadership could be counted upon to yield certain consistent types of responses. Autocratic leadership with a leader giving orders and making plans resulted in heightened aggressiveness toward scapegoat members and submissiveness to the leader, and to idleness, apathy, and a decline of production when the leader was absent. Democratic leadership, with a leader assisting in group planning and with members active in their own behalf, resulted in greater "we" feeling, friendliness and respect for individual members, and in responsible behavior and good production with the leader present or absent. *Laissez faire* leadership, with the leader inactive, resulted in only short-term production and cooperation, followed by idleness and frustration.[16]

An outstanding contribution to the study of the theory of small groups was the publication *Small Groups,* edited by Hare, Borgatta, and Bales, in which a considerable number of researches were brought together, along with some brief analysis of a number of problems including social perception, systems of interaction, equilibrium, role differentiation, leadership, and others.[17] The research findings in these and related areas provide important data for the recreation worker. In another volume, Cartwright and Zander do a like piece of work in analyzing group dynamics research available for study by practitioners with small groups. In respect to the concept of leadership they point out that "Leadership is viewed as the performance of those acts which help the group achieve its objectives . . . aid in setting group goals, moving the group toward its goals, improving the quality of the inter-

---

[16] See Kurt Lewin, Ronald Lippitt, and Ralph White, "Patterns of Aggressive Behavior in Experimentally Created 'Social Climates,'" *Journal of Social Psychology,* Vol. 10, No. 2 (May 1939), and Ronald Lippitt and Ralph White, "The 'Social Climate' of Children's Groups," in Roger Barker, Jacob Kounin, and Herbert Wright, *Child Behavior and Development* (McGraw-Hill Book Company, 1943), pp. 485-508.

[17] A. Paul Hare, Edgar F. Borgatta, and Robert F. Bales, *Small Groups Studies in Social Interaction* (New York: Alfred A. Knopf, 1955). Mention might also be made here of Homan's outstanding effort to explore a fresh approach to conceptual instruments for describing the nature of groups and group life: George C. Homans, *The Human Group* (New York: Harcourt, Brace & World, 1950).

actions among the members, building the cohesiveness of the group, or making resources available to the group." [18]

Recreation methodology should be undergirded by the contribution of social psychology, including such concepts as the group needs of the individual, the nature of groups and of group growth, the patterns and dynamics of group interaction, and group membership and leadership roles.

CONTRIBUTIONS FROM CULTURAL ANTHROPOLOGY AND SOCIOLOGY

Anthropology and sociology are two relatively modern sciences. The important contributions these two fields of research have made to our understanding of recreation were discussed briefly in very early chapters. Their contributions to the recreation methodology are also of much importance. Witmer and Kotinsky point out that professional workers working with children and their families must take into account

> . . . the ways in which people of various cultures differ in ideas and customs and values. . . . The aim of all professional workers is to provide constructive experiences for the people they serve. The findings of anthropologists make it clear that this aim cannot be fully accomplished unless the cultural meaning of these experiences to particular individuals is understood and utilized.[19]

The Cultural Basis of Behavior

The anthropologist tells us first that in one sense personality is the product of the interaction of the individual, driven by his own needs, and a very complex cultural and physical environment which is somewhat different for different individuals and different groups. Murphy describes the approach of the anthropologist to this subject as follows:

---

[18] Dorwin Cartwright and Alvin Zander, *Group Dynamic Research and Theory* (Evanston, Ill.: Row, Peterson and Company, 1953), p. 538.

[19] Helen L. Witmer and Ruth Kotinsky, eds., *Personality in the Making,* The Fact-Finding Report of the Midcentury White House Conference on Children and Youth (New York: Harper & Row, Inc., 1952), pp. 172-173.

> . . . though the nature of human personality is to some degree defined by the very fact of social participation, even before any specific human culture has been described, most of the meaning and richness of the social approach can be grasped only when attention has been given to a comparison of various primitive and advanced societies, in order to see the personality pattern characteristic of each set of social arrangements, and, within each such *generic* pattern, the way in which the *individual* copes with the generic problems which the culture defines, the way in which he learns to make use of, adapt to, and bend to his own uses, the cultural situation and the roles he is called upon to enact.[20]

He devotes much attention to this approach to personality, which sees personality as a continuum of organism-environment events, a "structured organism-environment field." He describes the economic and self-maintenance mores, self-perpetuation mores, self-gratification mores, and self-regulation mores, which define the values and set the rules in any society. The individual personality is, in general, guided and controlled by these mores. This is the point of view from which the anthropologist begins his study of the individual, the view that culture is powerful and pervasive, changing the character of our biological drives, affecting our thinking, emotions, and perceptions.

Examples are plentiful of the principle that the individual can be understood only if one is able to understand the culture in which he has grown up. The variability in cultural background is one force influencing the variability in individual behavior that faces the professional worker. In different parts of the United States and among groups of varying national or ethnic backgrounds there exist different ways of life, each representing traditional and, to them, meaningful ways of behaving. That these ways of behaving may differ sharply from group to group makes them no less important to the members of each. They cling to the attitudes and ways of their parents, rearing their children according to their own upbringing, instilling in them the values of their own culture.

Each experience of a group of children may mean quite different things for the individual members, depending upon their cultural backgrounds. And from this same experience will be drawn sharply

[20] Murphy, *Personality,* p. 772.

different meanings. The example has been given of two groups playing basketball. To one group, educated in cooperation, the game was stimulating and exciting because they loved the teamwork involved. But they could not get interested in keeping score because it was unimportant. To another group, the score was the important thing, giving incentive and spice to the game. They learned cooperation and teamwork only incidentally and in a framework of competition.

The anthropologist helps the professional recreation worker appreciate the meaning of these differences, to have insight into his own motivations and assumptions, and to learn to view these different behaviors as having equal validity to different groups.

Although American society is recognized as possessing many subcultures, there is a central or dominant culture pattern which anthropologists have studied and which needs to be understood as well. It has been pointed out that in this country a concept of progress and opportunity has existed, based upon important historical conditions. As Lerner says: "These—the expanse of space, the mixture of race, the pluralism of region and religion, the fresh start, the release of energies, the access to opportunity, the optimism and pragmatism of a society in motion, the passion for equality—were the crucial shaping forces of the American heritage." [21] The international "race to the moon" and the emphasis on the challenge of the space age added new elements to the competitive pressure on individuals in this country. The child in America particularly may be expected to feel this. He is looked upon as the hope for the future, and great stress has been placed upon his education and training for the competitive battle of life.

Abernathy points out that practically as soon as the child can walk he begins to be placed in situations of rivalry and competition. If he shows more fear, less initiative or more placidity than is deemed suitable, his parents fear that he may be turning into a sissy. The demand is upon the child, especially the boy, to achieve, and he must strive to success in competitive struggle at all points. "The boy is expected to prove very early that he is a 'he-man.' He has to be more strident, fight more, shout more and boast more." [22]

---

[21] Max Lerner, *America As Civilization* (New York: Simon and Schuster, Inc., 1957), p. 48.

[22] Ruth Abernathy, "Meanings in Cultural Patterns for Health Education," *Professional Contributions No. 1* (Washington, D.C.: American Academy of Physical Education, 1951), p. 64.

The result is often a desperate striving, a lack of security, and sometimes despair and hopelessness because the stresses are difficult to survive without emotional damage. Anthropologists, along with mental hygienists, educators, and recreation workers, have been concerned with the impact of cultural stresses and strains on the mental and emotional health of Americans and their children. The cultural forces contributing to modern problems of emotionally disturbed children have been discussed extensively in mental health literature. The recreation worker must be keenly aware of the responsibility he has of mitigating some of these tensions by providing recreative pursuits in relaxing and nondemanding situations within which the individual can gain, for a while, release from demand, tension, and stress.

Subcultures and Social Classes

Another important area of anthropological and sociological research is the study of class and status differentiation and the relations between social classes. Contrary to popular "classless society" mythology, American social scientists have identified major social and economic groupings: the small, powerful, and wealthy owning and managing class; the larger, heterogeneous middle class of small owners, professional persons, and like groups; and the largest group of workers in industry, commerce, and the trades, the poorer farms, and so on. The relative positions of economic influence and power, political power, social status, and privilege possessed by these three groups have been studied, and each group has been accordingly subgrouped in several different ways. It is recognized that the "culture" of each of these groups, in important respects, may differ from that of the others.

Many writers have pointed out that attitudes and values differ among these classes. The professional worker would have to be sensitive to these class differences in behavior, to be aware of his own class-determined attitudes, if he is to be successful in building, with individuals in all classes and groups, a relationship based upon respect for and acceptance of their cultural differences, and upon sympathy and understanding for the relative difficulty each group has in "making its way" in our modern society.

Finally, there are the anthropologists' explorations of prejudice, the emotional and attitudinal reaction to the present differences of race, nationality, religion, and class in our society, and discrimination, its accompaniment. Prejudice has been defined as a negative attitude of hostility, distrust, or depreciation directed toward ethnic, racial, or religious groups. Discrimination is differential treatment of individuals who belong to a particular social group. Both terms usually express attitudes or actions against groups relatively disadvantaged and unable to protect themselves or to fight back from a position of equal status.

Study has been made of the effect of being stigmatized, of having one's trust in all human beings betrayed, of being required to curb initiative and accept hostility and rejection by one's peers, of being segregated, unwanted, and so on. The radical contradiction between our democratic ideology and the reality of unequal treatment is confusing. It destroys confidence and trust while it creates resentment and counter-hostility, which, however, may not be expressed freely for fear of retaliation. There may be loss of self-esteem and considerable frustration and anxiety unless suitable constructive means can be found for expressing the feelings and participating in actions in some manner designed to solve the problem.

Studies of the personalities of prejudiced persons indicate that prejudice and discrimination are more or less accepted ways of behavior in our society, and that they provide certain individuals with an outlet for hostile feelings and a projection of their tensions in "scapegoating." There are, however, persons who are prejudiced largely, it seems, as a matter of conformity to the standards of their group. These persons stand in contrast to the more vigorously prejudiced person, who has been called an "authoritarian" personality. Witmer and Kotinsky describe this person as "an emotionally maladjusted individual who has achieved social adjustment by taking pleasure in obedience and subordination. . . . His inability to see people as individuals, his need to stereotype them, results . . . from deep emotional need. He must have somebody to punish, for his own overstrict conscience holds him to such severe account." [23]

The social impact of prejudice has been assessed in terms of its influence in inhibiting social progress, in maintaining destructive social tensions and conflicts and draining energy away from the task of constructive solution to other social problems, in functioning to distort, constrict, humiliate, and, in extreme cases, destroy the personalities of the victims.

We shall see in the next chapter how essential to the helping process is the capacity of the professional recreation worker to know himself. He must be aware of his own values, attitudes and prejudices,

---

[23] Witmer and Kotinsky, *Personality in the Making,* pp. 148-149.

aware enough so that in his work with his group members he can see that these attitudes and feelings do not get in the way of his effort to understand and work empathetically with members on their problems and in the direction of their interests. Prejudice and unconsciously held biases and attitudes might interfere seriously with the feeling and expression of acceptance, which is at the heart of the helping process in recreational work.

Recreation method should incorporate from anthropology and sociology understanding of the cultural basis for human behavior, the demands of a culture upon members for conformity to its norms and values, the functioning of racial, ethnic, national, religious, and class subcultures, and the phenomena of cultural differences, prejudice, and discrimination.

CONTRIBUTIONS FROM GROUP PSYCHOTHERAPY

Group psychotherapy is a method that uses a group, usually a recreation activity group or a discussion group, as the setting for psychotherapy with mentally ill or emotionally disturbed persons needing help with their problems. The material that follows, which describes how this method is employed, should not be interpreted to mean that the beginning recreation worker is necessarily qualified as a therapist or should attempt to use the methods described. This requires special training, experience, and study. For that reason we use the term "therapist" purposely. But there are contributions from group psychotherapy that are extremely useful in the recreation method, and they should be understood by any recreation worker, particularly such methods as sociodrama and role-playing.

Psychiatrists, psychologists, counsellors, and others engaged in psychotherapy began with methods requiring all of their concentration on one individual, but they have since discovered that the skillful therapist could take advantage of certain dynamics present in group interaction and make good therapeutic use of them. There were positive gains to be made:

> (1) in the interaction of the patients with each other; (2) in a lessening of fear and a realization that others have similar problems; (3) in encouragement and often a beginning of a "bond" which strengthens the individuals; (4) in the special

relationship between group therapist and members of this group.[24]

Therapeutic Groups

Group methods in recent years have been explored as a special use of the dynamics of relationships between individuals, guided skillfully by the therapist, permitting the individual under favorable circumstances to experience again emotional situations that he previously could not handle, and, by helping him to understand and deal with these problems encouraging therapeutic movement toward strengthening the self-concept, and increasing socialization capacity.

Study has been made of the original structuring of therapeutic groups. Groups may be formed in whatever structure creates the greatest psychological advantage to the participants. Natural leaders are used, advantageous subgroupings and clique-formations are devised or encouraged, and feelings that may be expressed and communicated by contagion to other members are used to therapeutic advantage. In activity groups, individuals with varying problems are grouped together so that each may be helped to overcome his specific difficulties. In discussion or interview groups, individuals with common problems seem to be most helpful to each other.[25] The special planning of such groups receives much attention. In activity group therapy, the activities are used as tools, just as are the relationships within the group and with the therapist. In interview or discussion group therapy, discussion among the members, led by the therapist, is the major activity.

The general objectives of group therapy are to re-educate behaviors and attitudes toward becoming acceptable to group life, and to help the person to become more adequate in dealing with reality and the problems of life. The group is important because the individual has become isolated and the sense of loss, resentment, and insecurity contributes to his unhappiness. The group, and its sympathetic leader who helps to set an atmosphere of friendship and acceptance, permit the person to make up this loss, to relieve himself of some of his hostilities and aggressions, to gain security and response, and to make more

---

[24] Gisela Konopka, "Group Work and Therapy," in Charles Hendry, ed., *A Decade of Group Work* (New York: The Association Press, 1948), p. 40.

[25] S. R. Slavson, *The Practice of Group Therapy* (New York: International Universities Press, 1947), p. 30.

and more adequate adjustment to his group members, as a preliminary to succeeding more generally in his social relations.

To this end the therapist will devise a therapeutic group experience in which, at the start, the individual group member will identify the group members and the therapist as a family and will tend to behave as he did in earlier family experiences. This *transference* is accepted, as is the related process of *identification.* In the group, the members not only identify with the worker, but also with each other. The members become aware of the similarity of their experiences, needs, and feelings, and this awareness helps each one to see himself more objectively, to support other persons in the group, and at times to build group unity in conflict with the therapist or others. The therapist skillfully copes with negative and hostile transference and identification and supports positive relations of sympathy, understanding, and friendship among group members.

The mechanism of catharsis also functions in group therapy. The therapist and the group encourage and permit discharge of pent-up emotions, tensions, and aggressions by the individual. With support he may express these feelings in a friendly atmosphere; he may "blow off steam" in verbal or bodily acting out and then have the opportunity to take the related steps, to gain insight into his feelings, to objectify his problems and understand them better, to see them in relation to the problems of others, thus reducing his feeling of isolation, guilt, and remorse.

Related to catharsis is the process called *abreaction,* the release of psychic tension through verbalizing or acting out a recollection of a formerly repressed traumatic experience with the appropriate emotion or effect. The friendly group climate and the understanding therapist encourage these behaviors and the individual finds support in his effort to reveal to himself and to others—and then to face and handle—his feelings in relation to such experiences. The person then can be helped to reshape his attitudes, undertake a *reintegration* of his personality, overhaul his concept of self, and gain means for dealing with his life and his problems in new and constructively satisfying ways.

It is apparent that the group plays a critical role in this therapy. The person in whom change is desired must wish to make the change himself. The change must come from within. The focus is upon what he can be helped to achieve, what he can do himself, with help. The relationship with the group and with the therapist is highly important. But the focus is upon the individual and how he may increase his capacities and gain a more creative acceptance and use of himself. Yet, that self is primarily concerned with effecting harmonious relations with the realities of social living, and so the group becomes the primary external reality with which he begins to relate. Therefore, essentially on his own, in his own way, supported and assisted, but without prompting, coercion, or excessive pressure, the individual strives for the changes he desires in himself.

Psychodrama and Sociodrama

Other experimental methods are psychodrama and sociodrama. Psychodrama is used in general as a therapeutic method; sociodrama is used more generally in education and other group problem-solving situations. In psychodrama, the individual is helped by the therapist and other group members spontaneously to act out his feelings around some experience, each participant obtaining a better understanding or diagnosis of the problem and its emotional components and helped to gain a better understanding of his feelings about the problem.[26]

Sociodrama is an intensive, vivid, *living through* of experiences of common concern to the group members. It has value in bringing into the group the therapeutic influence of dramatizing of common situations, an active playing out of the feelings with one's entire body, exposing in intense portrayal many things with which the group members can identify and together face and objectify. Another value is in practice and training in free expression and spontaneity. Recreation and group workers are just beginning to realize and to make use of the tremendous potential in creative dramatic play, in acting out many problems as part of the problem-solving method, and in dramatic games as both enjoyable and therapeutically valuable. The important use of these group dramatic methods is just beginning to be understood.

The careful attention paid to the role of the therapist in group therapy has produced information of much value to group workers in learning how to use themselves in the group. He is a kindly, unpunishing, friendly, positive, yet neutral, individual. He receives or absorbs with a steady, neutral, and kindly manner the varying and changing expressions toward him of the group members, and in this way he provides an object with whom to identify that will of itself assist the member in his therapeutic change. To the degree to which the group member feels trust in the therapist, gains confidence in his stable help-

---

[26] See J. L. Moreno, *Psychodrama* (Beacon, N.Y.: Beacon House, 1946).

ing attitude, and finds their relationship solid and durable, to that degree will he risk himself in the therapeutic situation.

Changing Roles of the Leader

Solomon's study of children with different personality problems showed the need for the therapist to play different roles with each of four groups: (1) the aggressive-impulsive, (2) the anxiety phobic, (3) the regressive-reactive, and (4) the schizoid-schizophrenic. With aggressive children, who may show active hostility or active demands for attention or affection, the therapist must show a fair degree of firmness and set limits as to how far these aggressions may express themselves. The anxiety phobic group feel frightened, and must be helped to feel protected; the therapist must be calm, objective, and nonpunishing. With the regressive-reactive group, an approach should be made through play objects, the therapist maintaining a warm, affectionate interest and alertness to seize upon a child's creative abilities, and give him satisfaction from real accomplishments rather than from fantasy and infantile behavior. The schizoid-schizophrenic child is withdrawn, most difficult to reach, and even then only on an emotional level. Through entering into his fantasy world and maintaining a continued interest in the child, the therapist slowly may help the child to accept a relationship that can move from the unreal world to the real one.[27]

This thumbnail sketch of but one of several dimensions of variability in children's behavior and the related variability in the therapist's behavior gives some indication of the value of such insights to the recreation worker. The worker, judging his members' needs and his timing, chooses between a wide range of behaviors, ranging from a highly permissive and nondirective role, almost withdrawal, to a highly authoritarian or interfering one. In general, however, the need for a permissive and accepting role is paramount.

The recreation worker is a symbol of the adult world, and many children resent their treatment by adults.

> Recreationists have the job of counteracting hostile and destructive attitudes, as well as establishing new ones. . . . Children have to be convinced that not all grown-ups are unfeeling, peremptory, and repressive. Freedom of choice and

---

[27] Joseph C. Solomon, "Play as a Therapeutic Medium," *The Nervous Child,* Vol. 7, No. 3 (1948).

action, a warm personal relation, and respectful attitude toward them cannot but convince children of our basic friendliness.[28]

Play Therapy

The closely related field of play therapy is based on the fact that play is the child's natural medium of self-expression. Play therapy gives the child an opportunity to "play out" his feelings. The therapist uses the child's activities in planned play sessions to diagnose his emotional problems. The therapist enters into the play situations to help guide the play activities and interpret them to the child. He helps him to face the problems expressed by the activities and to make constructive adjustments to them. There has been experimentation with both directive and nondirective therapy. In directive therapy, the therapist assumes major responsibility for guidance and interpretation, manipulating the play environment more actively in the child's behalf. In nondirective therapy, the therapist makes more use of the assumption that the individual has within himself not only the ability to solve his own problems satisfactorily but also the will or the impulse that makes mature behavior more satisfying than immature behavior. The therapist plays a role designed to permit the child much more self-direction and autonomy in relation to his growth and development.

The play therapist recognizes the powerful cathartic value of play. He understands the opportunity it gives for ventilating feelings, for relieving nervous tensions, and for imaginatively reliving disturbing experiences in a safe and supporting environment. He recognizes that the children with whom he deals are miserable, unhappy children who have not been given enough of the love, security, and happiness that is the right of every child. Such children need help in achieving status in their own eyes, in what seems to be a hostile world. The therapist works for an accepting group atmosphere within which the therapeutic processes may be furthered.

The recreation method should be based upon significant insights from group psychotherapy into the role of the group in supporting individual problem-solving efforts, the dynamic interaction in therapeutic groups, the role of program with therapeutic objectives, and the function

---

[28] S. R. Slavson, *The Practice of Group Therapy* (New York: International Universities Press, Inc., 1957), pp. 142-144.

of role playing and the group therapist in his adaptation of roles to the needs of persons with different personality problems.

CONTRIBUTIONS FROM MODERN EDUCATION

The last field we shall examine briefly in this chapter is the field of modern education. The United States, in the last two centuries, has pioneered the effort to develop an educational system that would educate all of the society's youth to be productive, adjusted, creative persons and active citizen participants in our democratic life. At no time has there been any more keen interest than there is now among educators in the search for the means of implementing these objectives by the development of a modern method of education which utilizes the dynamics of individual and group learning and advances the goals of creative and democratic living.

THE WHOLE CHILD AND LEARNING

The central concept in education is the concern for the individual and his growth and development toward maturity in our complex and changing society. This child-centered concept considers the whole child, the total organism, as being involved in learning; education thus pays attention to all of his interacting needs and designs educational experiences with these needs in mind. Emphasis on the feeling-doing-thinking relationships in behavior stresses this interaction. Modern educators accept the concepts of the uniqueness of the individual child and of individual differences, and they recognize the necessity of providing learning experiences adapted to each individual's requirements. Less regimentation and more individualization are required.

Understanding of the mental-emotional life and needs of children is growing among educators. In the book, *Fostering Mental Health in Our Schools,* it is pointed out that new research on human beings has produced important information that must be applied in educational settings to further children's mental health.[29]

> Every child has problems of growing up. Some of these problems can be serious and crippling even for the emotionally

---

[29] *Fostering Mental Health in Our Schools,* 1950 Yearbook of the Association for Supervision and Curriculum Development (Washington, D.C.: National Education Association, 1950).

> robust. . . . We could only be perturbed by the amount of anxiety, hostility, and guilt (those feelings so destructive to the individual which he in turn projects destructively upon others) which exist among the "normal" in our population.[30]

The learning process itself has been studied and an increasing body of knowledge is being acquired. The concept of the learner as a unitary, integrating organism we have already noted. His striving to attain success, meaning, and satisfaction from his endeavors is important. Vital also is his restless, exploring, active, goal-seeking nature, his individual pattern and rhythm of growth, his unique personality, values, and habits, and his strong social needs. These provide a set of dynamics with which the competent educator "cooperates" in providing learning experiences with constructive results.

With this effort also comes the need and opportunity to practice and develop discipline, both in the self and in the group. Discipline is at the core of everything we do. It is particularly important in the educational process, in the relationship of teacher to pupil and class and of recreation worker to group. As Hymes says, "You cannot have a decent family or a decent business or a decent school or a decent town without discipline." [31] Thus, the recreation method builds on the knowledges and understandings gained through educational research of the use of rewards and punishments, and the development of moral and spiritual values as exemplified in such ethical standards of behavior as honesty and fair play.

The Teacher

Much research has been done concerning the teaching process itself, the role of the teacher, and the person of the teacher. One study focuses on the processes of learning in groups under the helping influence of the teacher, and describes the teacher's responsibility in understanding the child and his learning processes, providing examples from records of classroom behavior and providing working analyses of the teacher's role.[32]

---

[30] *Fostering Mental Health in Our Schools,* p. viii.

[31] J. L. Hymes, *Behavior and Misbehavior* (Englewood Cliffs, N.J.: Prentice-Hall, Inc., 1955), p. 21.

[32] *Learning and the Teacher,* 1959 Yearbook, Association for Supervision and Curriculum Development (Washington, D.C.: National Education Association, 1959).

A thoughtful study of the function of the teacher at the point of contact with the child is contributed by Prescott. He says that teachers interact with children an enormous number of times every hour. The educative process is in functional operation when teachers and pupils interact and individual pupils react to these contacts. The teacher's vast number of decisions at these points of contact are the fundamental bases of the educative process. She must understand the child, help the individual child, analyze the group and its life and dynamics, and use the group creatively on the individual's behalf.[33]

One example of a penetrating study of the teacher is Jersild's book, *When Teachers Face Themselves*. He identifies the concern of teachers with the meaning of teaching and of life for them; the concern with anxiety, holding it to be a pervasive problem and an essential element in life and growth; the concern with loneliness; the concern with compassion as a reward in teaching.[34] This effort to help the teacher to know himself, and through self-knowledge to mobilize his resources to fulfill his teaching function, has many cues for the recreation worker.

Education for Democracy

A central objective of recreation and group work finds its parallel in modern education, along with significant experimentation in its attainment. This objective is education for appropriate behavior as a cooperative citizen-participant in the processes of democracy. Such behavior rests upon an understanding of the responsibility of the individual in participating constructively in democratic groups. It also rests, in education, upon the opportunity for practice in self-determining, cooperative, democratic, group life. The highly significant experimental evidence that cooperative and democratic groups provide optimal opportunity for the individual to learn and to exercise his creative energies and social skills, has supported efforts to introduce extensive cooperative group experiences into education.

In the field of democratic liberties, "Democratic education respects the basic civil liberties in practice and clarifies their meaning

---

[33] Daniel Prescott, *The Child in the Educative Process* (New York: McGraw-Hill Book Company, 1957).

[34] Arthur J. Jersild, *When Teachers Face Themselves* (New York: Columbia University Press, 1955).

through study."[35] Widespread apprehension of educators and other professional groups over threats to these liberties has led to struggles for their defense, and gives meaning to the broader challenge to group members to help maintain in the total society "those economic, political and social conditions which are necessary for liberty."[36]

The broad objectives of the effort to establish a new and better way of life for all races and cultures of mankind take on particular relevance today, and provide a common basis for unity among all professional groups engaged in furthering democratic human relations and strengthening the values of democratic living.

Democratic education is committed to the use of democratic methods in the classroom, in administration, and in student affairs. This requires cooperative planning processes, teaching democratic rights and responsibilities, and creating reality situations for practice of democratic planning, participation and evaluation skills, including taking responsibility for one's own acts. In this way, fundamental democratic beliefs become the result of living democracy in group experiences. The individual, as the Educational Policies Commission states, learns to be loyal:

> First, to himself as a human being of dignity and worth.
>
> Second, to the principle of human equality and brotherhood.
>
> Third, to the process of untrammelled discussion, criticism and group decision.
>
> Fourth, to the ideal of honesty, fair-mindedness, and scientific spirit in the conduct of this process.
>
> Fifth, to the ideal of respect for an appreciation of talent, training, character, and excellence in all fields of socially useful endeavor.
>
> Sixth, to the obligation and the right to work.
>
> Seventh, to the supremacy of the common good.
>
> Eighth, to the obligation to be socially informed and intelligent.[37]

---

[35] National Education Association, *Learning the Ways of Democracy* (Washington, D.C.: The Association, 1940), p. 35.

[36] *Learning the Ways of Democracy,* p. 35.

[37] Educational Policies Commission, *Policies For Education In American Democracy* (Washington, D.C.: National Education Association, 1946), p. 113.

With such objectives, education demonstrates its central membership in the family of helping professions. It contributes to its fellow members valuable experimental data concerning (1) the individual child and his developmental needs, (2) psychologically and ethically valid methods of teacher participation in learning and growth processes, and (3) ways of strengthening democratic ideals and practices.

The recreation method should be based upon modern education's insights into the child as a unitary organism, its concern for the individual and his welfare as a central democratic concept, the concept of the enabling role of the teacher, and the significance of learning experiences enjoyed by cooperative participants in democratic group life.

Questions for Study and Discussion

1. *Why should leaders in the field of recreation be concerned with studying carefully the principles and concepts of related disciplines? What influence do these principles have on recreation?*
2. *Personality development and formation is a synthesis of many factors and influences. Through discussion bring out as many of these as you can and explore their possible effect on persons and their recreational life.*
3. *Which specific disciplines or fields of study have the most to contribute to recreation work or the recreation worker?*
4. *Develop hypothetical situations in which class members may use the technique of role playing to illustrate the applications of the concepts presented in this chapter to the field of recreation method.*
5. *Select five key concepts of group dynamics and indicate their relevance to the recreation method.*

Selected Readings

Allport, Gordon W., *Personality and Social Encounter* (Boston: Beacon Press, Inc., 1960).

Hendry, Charles, ed., *A Decade of Group Work* (New York: The Association Press, 1948).

Learning and the Teacher, 1959 Yearbook, Association for Supervision and Curriculum Development (Washington, D.C.: National Education Association, 1959).

14

WORKING WITH PEOPLE IN RECREATION

People engage in recreation either by themselves, enjoying an individual leisure pursuit, or as members of groups, bent upon enjoying some common interest. In seeking these opportunities they often come to a recreation agency (public, voluntary, or otherwise) that employs recreation workers to help them to use the agency's services. This worker, the person on the "firing line," is the person whose basic methodology is the focus of our present concern.

To help individuals and groups to find self-fulfillment in their pleasurable pursuits and their associations with others, the recreation worker utilizes his professional recreation method. We have pointed out that this method is made up of some philosophical assumptions, some relevant scientific knowledge, some specific attitudes and motivations, and some practical knowledges, techniques, and skills. Together they provide him with diagnostic ability, disciplined sensitivity, trained judgment, and operating skills. The settings in which he applies his method may vary widely, but the method is of value wherever he works. What are the elements in this professional method?

The worker in general spends his time giving help in the following three situations, listed in order of probable frequency:

1. The group together is pursuing a common recreation interest;
2. The individual is a member of a group which is recreation-bent;
3. The individual is recreation-bent as an individual.

THE RECREATION WORKER

The professional recreation worker builds his professional method upon three basic elements: personality attributes or qualities, philosophical convictions, and the scientifically disciplined, trained, conscious, skillful use of himself in a helping relationship with fairly identifiable recreation participants. The first of these elements includes qualities of normal mature personality. Among these might be listed emotional stability, some capacity for self-insight, sensitivity, self-confidence, warmth, patience, a fairly high threshold of tolerance for irritation, sense of humor, integrity, and capacity to give help to others. These qualities would be supported by certain attitudes toward people such as acceptance of and respect for individuals despite cultural and other differences, and convictions concerning the basic worth of every human individual. These convictions need to be communicable, part of an outgoing personality. Enthusiasm, energy, freedom to enjoy play, and ability to interest others in creative, aesthetic, playful pursuits are relevant capacities for a worker when the participant exercises self-determination as to whether he participates or not.

Second, the professional worker's philosophy includes an acceptance of a responsibility for being of service to others. Some call this a "ministry," others might define it as part of emotional maturity, an inner-directed rational altruism. Others might simply accept a responsibility for making themselves available as a helping person to others, recognizing in it a source of sophisticated self-fulfillment. Another part of this philosophy is an enthusiasm for an aesthetic and recreative approach to life itself. Recreation, as one of several fields of organized helping services to people, shares in the common definitions of these fields as the "organized concern of people for each other," or "the ministry of men to each other." The recreation worker believes also that each human being has the right to choose how he shall enhance his leisure-time enjoyment and thus live more creatively and happily. Each individual has the right to secure the satisfactions of his material needs and to enjoy beauty, love, play, fellowship with his peers, identification with spiritual and ethical values, and participation in the cooperative building of a better life for all. In the process of engaging in the pursuit of happiness, and in the values inherent in leisure and recreation, the individual has the right to get help in fulfilling himself in this pursuit. To give this help is the function of the profession.

Third, the professional person is educated and trained to be a competent helping person. Underlying all principles of the professional technique in which he strives to be competent is the principle of *conscious use of the professional self*. The worker needs to possess scientific knowledge about human behavior as it reflects needs. He needs to understand this behavior in himself and in others. He understands himself, his needs, feelings, biases, and values in order that these may be used in a disciplined way in his relation to recreation participants. He needs to offer himself as a helping person without being blocked by his own conscious and unconscious demands and needs that have to be met. He also must understand his own feelings and handle them so that he will be free to be sensitive to the needs and feelings of the group members. He needs to be able to diagnose the needs of the group members with an awareness of the biasing influence of his own attitudes, values, or prejudices.

The recreation worker's basic function in the group is helping. Hearn says the professional person "has the position in the group of a *servant-enabler* by which we mean that he performs in the group the service of which he is capable and which is necessary for the group's present welfare. What is also important, he performs this service by group sanction."[1] This idea has two implications. One is that

---

[1] Gordon Hearn, "Democratic Behavior," in *Developing Democratic Human Relations Through Health Education, Physical Education, and Recreation*, First Yearbook, American Association For Health, Physical Education and Recreation (Washington, D.C.: National Education Association, 1951), p. 59.

it recognizes the right of the participant to use the worker's service or not, and to be free to participate or not, as he chooses. The second is that it charges the worker with the responsibility of maximizing the area of participant self-determination, of freedom of choice, which we have identified as a basic recreation right. This is not to press on the recreation worker an inactive or *laissez-faire* role, for in many groups, particularly in children's groups, individuals have not yet developed fully a capacity for responsible self-functioning. In any case, the worker's suggestions and his belief in the values of recreational activities must be shared. The worker's responsibility will also involve helping participants to come to terms with rules and limits. The worker also may be active in designing and manipulating experiences so as to maximize important values to participants.

The worker, therefore, is a sensitively functioning person, aware of his helping role, aware of the basic knowledge of human behavior which guides him in his analysis of the needs of participants and the means of meeting those needs. And he does this during the process of helping group members gain joy and pleasure out of their play activities. He strives, say Wilson and Ryland, "to create an atmosphere of freedom, relaxation and the light touch of play. . . . Behind this atmosphere of freedom, relaxation and fun are skill, knowledge, imagination, planning. . . . The worker provides an atmosphere in which the imagination can be given free rein and the members are helped to stretch themselves and accomplish more than they ever thought they could." [2]

The worker functions as a responsible representative of the agency that employs him. Recreation service is provided through the program of organized agencies, each of which is responsible to the community for providing certain kinds of services. The worker has the obligation of understanding the philosophy and purpose of his employer, and he must be able to accept this philosophy and purpose as his own. He is responsible as well for maintaining in his work the integrity of his professional function. In some cases there might develop a difference between these two. The professional worker in this case strives to reconcile the difference between what his professional responsibility requires and what his agency requires. If he cannot succeed in this reconciliation he should have the right and the duty to make his

---

[2] Gertrude Wilson and Gladys Ryland, *Social Group Work Practice* (Boston: Houghton Mifflin Company, 1949), p. 159.

professional contribution in some other agency more congenial to his professional integrity.

Before leaving this introductory note let us make explicit one point that has been implicit throughout this discussion. It is clear that the first element in our methodology is the worker himself, his self-understanding, his personality and its relevant strengths. These might be elements a recreation worker has worked to develop, or very fundamental personal qualities or characteristics the source of which would have to be sought in the complex of his own life experiences. The second element we would identify as his learned attitudes, his philosophy and professional value assumptions about himself and about human life in general. Along with this would be his knowledge, his scientific discipline, and his foundation of scientific information. At this point the worker is, we might say, "equipped," and we can discuss with some certainty the identified elements of this "equipment."

Finally, the third element identified is composed of the principles which he undertakes to follow as he puts himself in motion and tries actually to work skillfully with groups. These principles can be identified as general principles, but we recognize that their application must be adapted to an infinite number of unique situations with unique groups and individuals. At this point his application of professional methodology becomes *art*. The motions the worker goes through are *his* creative effort to meet the need of a situation and function constructively and helpfully. At this point any words written or spoken on methodology, while they may be helpful and written out of great experience and knowledge, are only guiding principles. The worker is at that moment working as creatively as he can, with himself, his behaviors, as the instrument. And at this point he is not a scientist or a philosopher but an artist, and what he does cannot be reduced to formulas, skills, techniques, or "gimmicks" without oversimplifying the basic complex art he practices.

The recreation worker, in addition to his knowledge and philosophy, must have a mature personality, be capable of sensitive empathy, know himself, and be able consciously to direct disciplined and unhampered attention and energy to the enabling process in a leisure-serving agency.

BEGINNING WITH THE RECREATION GROUP

At the beginning a recreation group comes together to a playground or center for recreation. The worker offers his and his agency's help to the group in fulfilling its purpose. If worker and group agree his services are to be used he initiates two simultaneous processes: (1) he helps the group and (2) he diagnoses its nature and needs in order to plan his work with them and to determine how he will be of most use to them.

He begins with the group with three aspects of group experience in mind. The group provides for its members self-fulfilling experiences (1) when relationships are built between members that are friendly and responsive, (2) when purposive behavior directed toward group goals is adequately organized, and (3) when the program activity itself is satisfying. The recreation worker strives to encourage the development of all three of these elements, the friendly interaction of the members, the goal-directed organizing activity of the members, and the specific program activity itself. The first two elements concern us at present.

The worker recognizes that the friendly interaction between members is based upon an initial acceptance of each other, and that a workable helping relationship between himself and the group depends upon mutual acceptance of the worker and the group. The worker takes the initiative in expressing and demonstrating warmth, friendliness, acceptance, and regard for group members. This attitude is based upon his respect for each member's individual worth and his recognition that an atmosphere of mutual regard in the group, regardless of individual differences, will be a positive force in building satisfying relationships.

The worker's demonstration of acceptance also has the effect of offering a way of behaving to the group members, with the possibility of a general development among group members of acceptance of each other.

Concerning the worker's acceptance, Wilson and Ryland point out that the worker "who has developed professional regard for those with whom he works loses his former attitudes of blame, disgust, impatience, and intolerance toward those who differ from him and replaces these attitudes with interest in and appreciation of the factors which are responsible for the difference . . . [learning] that the problems of personal growth and social development are similar in all people, including himself, no matter to which grouping in society they belong." [3]

A teen-age member of a group said this about her worker: "She may not approve of what we do sometimes, but she always is our friend and acts like we are worthy of respect and consideration. She never says anything mean to make us feel cheap. She always is the same, whatever happens, and she tries to understand us and help us understand ourselves. When somebody gets mad she always stays calm and helps her to work out her 'mad' without hurting anybody else. She is a kind of quiet conscience for us. We can always depend on her to tell us about things, what her opinion is, what she thinks is right." [4]

The worker simultaneously demonstrates friendliness and warm regard for group members, a willingness and capacity for accepting initial expression of distrust or hostility or coldness of group members toward him, and a businesslike and purposeful approach to his helping function with the group.

The worker's action in placing himself at the service of the group results in mixed and ambivalent responses from the group. Group members tend to relive in group experiences other previous group experiences, particularly family experience, assigning to other group members and to the worker roles of parents or siblings. The worker can expect to be tested by group members to see if his expression of regard is sincere, if he is strict or permissive about rules, effective or ineffective as a teacher, just or unjust as an arbitrator, democratic or autocratic in regard to reaching decisions, and so on. The worker will be prepared for some hostility or aggression, testing of limits, clinging dependency, and other behavior that reflects the members' needs, their habits of behavior toward other adults, and their efforts to use the help he has offered.

The worker's offer of help to the group includes not only the affective element of interest, friendliness, and concern, but the purposeful and businesslike approach to the negotiation of a contract. The working relationship is based on a common understanding of the issue "what are we doing here together?" The members' responsibilities and tasks and the worker's and the agency's functions and responsibilities are defined by the worker in an effort to define clearly the terms of agreement to work together. This serves the basic purpose of helping

---

[3] Wilson and Ryland, p. 16.

[4] From an unpublished group record of the authors'.

the worker to guard the focus of the work and of helping the group to best use his help.[5]

In the beginning phases of work with the group the foundation of this purposive working relationship is established, and the group begins to use the worker's help in pursuing their recreational aims.

The worker's beginning relationship with the recreation group should include his demonstration of warm acceptance and regard for group members, willingness to accept possible initial distrust of him by members, and a purposeful approach to the negotiation of a recreation service contract with the group.

DIAGNOSIS

Parallel with the worker's beginning efforts in building his relationships with the group and its members and helping them to pursue their goals constructively goes his development of a working diagnosis of the group and its members. This is a highly complex professional task, requiring him to use first his competence in sensitively observing and feeling with group members as their problems and needs are expressed, and as he identifies both the reality aspects and the emotional response aspects of situations. Second, he calls upon his scientific knowledge of human behavior gleaned from the resources of the behavioral sciences and the fields of professional helping endeavor identified in the previous chapter. This diagnosis is a working one, tentative and subject to change and development as the worker learns from his experience with the members, gains new insights, and adapts his own behavior to new elements.

He has two tasks in this regard. One task is to develop his working diagnosis of each individual member. He studies the use each individual makes of the group and its activity. He observes the individual's skill or competence in the activity being engaged in. He also observes the individual's behavior in relation to other group members and the needs and problems they represent. He studies the attitudes and actions of the member directed toward himself and the underlying needs which this behavior represents. As his work with the in-

[5] See William Schwartz, "The Social Worker in the Group," *The Social Welfare Forum, 1961* (New York: Columbia University Press, for the National Conference on Social Welfare, 1961), pp. 146-171.

dividual progresses, he analyzes the changes and trends in these elements and reconstructs his diagnosis as he goes along, learning from the members and maintaining flexibility and open-mindedness to new insights and the effect of change upon the member and his situation.

The second task is to develop his working diagnosis of the group itself. This second level of analysis requires that he study the processes of group formation, the patterns of status and acceptance, the system of group control, the means developed for decision making and planning, and so on. Considerable research material is available on types of groups and the characteristics of goal-directed behavior of varying groups. Recreation research has identified several of the motivations of groups for different recreations and some of the characteristics of group behavior in various play situations such as, among others, combative sports and cooperative group games or group projects.

The worker should analyze his role with respect to the group type. The group might be an intimate friendship group, a primary interest group, a national program agency group, or another type. He would analyze the structure of interpersonal relations in the group, the subgroupings developed around friendship, status, acceptance, or use of each other. He would analyze the patterns and processes of dynamic interaction between members, determining how he might work best to enable members to develop satisfying and purposeful relations with each other. He would analyze the group climate, the morale, the *esprit de corps,* the cohesiveness. He would analyze the basis for loyalty and attachment to the group, noting both positive and negative factors of this loyalty, and the trends in the growth and decline of group life as the natural life cycle of the group takes its course. At the outset he might study how he could best encourage the use of bonding and belonging symbols and rituals to encourage the growth of group morale and "we-feeling." He would undertake the analysis of his own role in supporting the group's efforts to deal constructively with its problems and difficulties.

The worker's diagnosis of the group organization, its system of controls, and its decision-making processes would focus upon strengthening the group's capacity for democratic group organization and decision making. Recognizing the existence of both formal and informal systems of organization and control, the diagnosis would focus upon finding the means for helping the group: (1) to produce responsible leaders and participants; (2) to share responsibility; (3) to give the several members constructive satisfactions; and (4) to survive conflicts and differences.

The analysis of the decision-making processes would focus upon the means required for helping the group to move from dependence upon a natural leader (or the worker himself) to independence, skill, and efficiency of democratic functioning, along with an acceptance of and commitment to democratic values and practices by group members.

The worker develops a flexible working diagnosis of the changing behavior and needs of the group and its individual members, to which the design of his helping activities is adapted.

HELPING THE GROUP

A lilting jingle was coined by Wilson and Ryland to describe the role of the professional worker with groups, which we can put to work at this point: "Love them and limit them and help them to achieve." We already have discussed the idea of "love," which is really, for recreation's purposes, professional regard and acceptance. This regard is basic to the relationship of the worker with the group. Equally important is limiting.

> The two functions go hand in hand. The worker who loves is able to limit without being judgmental or punishing, but he who does not love is incapable of setting constructive limitations. . . . [He is] impotent rather than strong when the members need his strength to help them in their struggle between the positive and negative forces within them.[6]

The group's use of the recreation agency's services requires that the two come to realistic terms with the contract of services. In addition, groups may destroy or endanger their real interests through inability to cope with negative actions. Some of these occasions can occur through hysterical behavior, overstimulation, conflict, or contagious negative activity. Redl and Wineman say:

> In that case the problem of the group leader is to stop the behavior . . . in order to avoid contagion and disaster, or to

[6] Wilson and Ryland, *Social Group Work Practice*, p. 91.

solicit or mobilize opposition to this behavior in some of the more reality-related children in order to develop a group-cohesive counterblock.[7]

Setting Limits

The worker, as the agency representative and a symbol of authority, must present the limits within which the group and its members must function. He does this in a way that is not disruptive or poisoning to the basic developmental goals of the group and its members. He explains the objective basis for the rules and the importance of a successful acceptance of the rules, of a mature adjustment to the reality of the limits. Understanding the difficulty individuals experience in accepting limits and anticipating the expression of dissatisfaction and hostility that may arise toward himself, he is prepared to accept these expressions with calmness and tranquillity. He expresses in turn the basic regard he has for the members, from which they can draw protection and get encouragement of their own ego strengths, even in tense and negative situations.

The worker has several means at hand for limiting, in addition to direct verbal forbidding. He can change the program, use a touch of humor, regroup the members, use physical proximity or signals like a gesture or look, an arm around a shoulder or a hand on an arm; and many other devices are available. In any case, the limiting behavior is designed to be as constructive as possible, objective in its nature, that is, directed toward an action and not being rejecting of the individual committing the action. The goal of authentic discipline is voluntary and mature self-discipline and self-control by an individual, ability and willingness to subordinate his individual wishes to the welfare of the group as a means to his own ultimate self-fulfillment as a group member.

Achieving Through Self-Determination

The third item in our jingle has to do with achievement. In deciding what to do, in planning and doing the thing, and in evaluating how well it was done, the group truly achieves; it is *successful.* The group has goals and purposes that are important to its members. The

---

[7] Fritz Redl and David Wineman, *Controls From Within* (Glencoe, Ill.: The Free Press, 1952), p. 155.

worker helps the group to formulate and pursue these goals, and he strives to guarantee the right of the group to be self-determining to the fullest extent of their resources and abilities. This professional goal, particularly well-identified with groups of children and youth, is defined as helping people to learn how to function in a democracy. The goal of democratic citizenship implies healthy attitudes, skills, and experiences in decision-making processes.

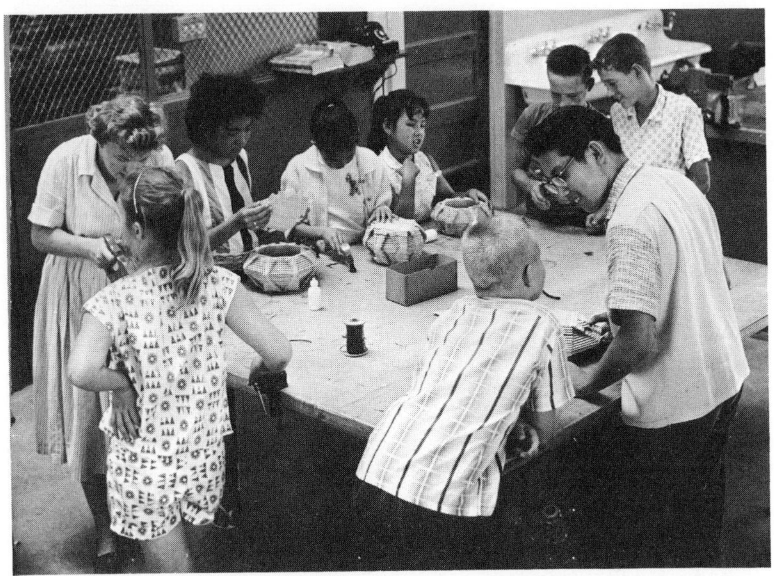

Youth Group Leader in Action

The effort to maximize the area of democratic decision making and self-determination in the group is an effort to maximize the learning experience and the growth of these democratic attitudes, expectations, and skills. The worker will encourage and nourish the capacity of the group members for responsible democratic action. They will discuss problems and issues, review alternatives and the consequences of each alternative. Each member will have important rights and responsibilities as a participant. Formal organization devices will be used soundly and with increasing skill. Leadership training will be continuous. Rights of minorities and the opposition to have their say will be guaranteed. The principle of striving for consensus by compromise and negotiation as the basis for maintaining group unity will be followed.

The concept of group growth recognizes that with a series of successful experiences a group can grow in its ability to fulfill the needs of its members and increase the satisfactions members gain from their participation in the group. The worker works within this dynamic and mobile situation, striving to help the group experience positive growth appropriate to its defined purposes. He functions differently at different points in the group's development, their needs requiring different help from him at different points. The principle that guides the worker in this is to begin where the group is and to go at the group's pace. The group has to be studied to determine at what point in development it is, and the worker must adapt his helping activities to that reality. Then he must stay with the group as it changes, and continuously adapt his own helping behavior to the changing situation. In general, groups at an infantile and dependent stage of development or caught in certain group pathological difficulties will require worker action directed to that stage of need. They will understand his function less, test him more, possess fewer stable controls and fluctuating morale, have less tolerance of planning and organizational demands, depend more upon impulsive behavior, may need more limiting and more directive intervention. Groups at more mature stages of development will use the worker differently, will depend upon him less and will be able to use other kinds of help.

In any case, the worker will move with the group at its own pace of development. He will recognize that the rate of group movement is controlled and determined primarily by the members and only secondarily by the worker. His primary role is to cooperate with this growth and help it. His skill is in adapting his behavior in his helping role to the "place" the group is and the pace at which and direction in which it is moving.

The helping role of the recreation worker requires presenting the focus and the limits of the agency's help to a group, helping the group to operate within these limits and focus, and helping the group to achieve its goals of leisure satisfaction through self-determining and self-realizing processes.[8]

---

[8] For general discussion of principles of group work method such as are discussed here see: Harleigh Trecker, *Social Group: Principles and Practices,*

INDIVIDUALIZING

The individual recreation participant is the concern of the recreation worker. The member may come to him for help, or he may offer help that he diagnoses is needed. Help may be needed in regard to some group task for which the member is responsible. Perhaps problems interfere with his best use of the group experience or the program activity. At any event, it offers the worker the chance to give a different quality of help to the individual than it is possible to give to a group.

Helping individuals calls for the development and use of the worker's basic skills: understanding of the principles of human behavior, sensitivity to the surface behavioral phenomena symptomatic of individual emotional or social adjustment problems, ability to relate to the individual at a level of emotional involvement required for a working relationship in which the worker can be helpful, skill in interviewing and counseling, and so on.

The individual who has problems may ask for help in different ways. He may simply ask, or he may behave in some unusual or bizarre fashion in order to attract attention or demand individual attention. He may seek help in dealing with a problem of which he is quite conscious, or there may be other problems of which he is not clearly aware. He will ask for help or show that he needs help, but in relation to some other problem. The worker may then help him to look at elements in the problem and gradually uncover and come to grips with the real problem. He may even resist an offer of help, but be able with encouragement to face his problem and gradually use the help which is offered.

The worker who is sensitive to the behavior of individuals will catch behavioral clues to underlying problems which may be blocking the achievement of true leisure goals. He will recognize the existence of objective problems and the subjective or emotional problems for the individual related to the objective ones. The worker, just as specifically and purposively as he does to the group, offers help to the individual. The individual is offered the chance to use the worker's help, and is

---

Revised and enlarged (New York: The Association Press, 1955); Grace Coyle, *Group Work with American Youth* (New York: Harper & Row, Inc., 1948). Dorothea Sullivan, ed., *Readings in Group Work* (New York: The Association Press, 1952).

free to use it or not to use it. This puts the helping process on a sound basis, in that the member is able to trust to this relationship as much of his problem as he feels he can; he is helped to understand that the problem is his to deal with, and yet he knows that help from an understanding and competent person has been offered.[9]

INTERVIEWING

The basic skill in individual work is interviewing. The complex of skills involved has been developed to a considerable degree in social case work and in clinical counseling as well as in psychiatry, and their basic elements can be adapted to effective work with individuals in recreation. The worker will observe carefully both what the individual is saying and the emotional accompaniments such as bodily tensions, excitability, and dejection, which will indicate some of the feelings he has about the situation.

The individual would be encouraged to express himself; questions are asked with a friendly and reassuring attitude. The member is helped to talk about himself in his own way and to take as much responsibility as he can for carrying on the discussion. Relevant material is asked for, however, and blocking, omissions, and the like are carefully noted. The worker undertakes with the individual to clarify the nature of the matter that confronts him and helps him to deal with the reality of it. He helps him to cope with manageable parts of a problem and gradually gain confidence to work on other elements. The worker helps the member to understand his feelings about himself and his problems and the source of those feelings, objectifying them in order to help the person to cope with them. All of this the worker undertakes with the client in the security and safety of a helping relationship in which the firm commitment of the worker in his offer to help is the anchor to which the person clings.[10]

THE INDIVIDUAL IN THE GROUP

While the focus of the concern of the recreation worker is with the best use of leisure-time experiences of the individual group mem-

---

[9] See Helen Perlman, *Social Casework* (Chicago: University of Chicago Press, 1957).

[10] See Annette Garrett, *Interviewing: Its Principles and Methods* (New York: Family Service Association of America, 1945).

ber, the group is a major tool of the member and worker. While working with the group, the worker is absorbed with both data of individual behavior and data of group behavior. His major attention, as well, must be on his role with the group as a whole. Individual help given in the group should not interfere with the worker's relationship with other members and with the group as a whole. The worker exercises care in drawing attention to the individual and his problem by his own action, for being "made special" may hamper the member's use of the group.

In general, the worker helps the individual member to join in group recreation activities. He helps him to choose activities and groups that are interesting to him. He gets him started by introducing him to other members. By his own activities he shows how other members may begin to get acquainted with and accept him. He helps him through the period of newness; he helps him to learn how to function as a good group member. He helps the member who has leadership abilities to gain sound experiences in group leadership. He helps him to plan meetings, to build the group stronger and further its purposes, and to influence other group members in constructive ways.

Another area of work is with the individual who has difficulty in becoming a good group member, whose individual problems are so great that he has difficulty using the group experience constructively. He may try to dominate or take over the group. He may be aggressive and always in conflict with other members. He may be passive and withdrawn. He may be dependent and unable to operate on his own.

The worker's diagnosis provides him with insights that indicate the kind of action he can undertake to help the individual with such problems. The help given must be related to the question of what the behavior and the helping activity do to the group itself, so that the group and its functioning are protected at the same time that the individual is helped. Whether the group is strong enough to stand for much destructive individual behavior is an important question. Is the group so important to the member that great effort must be made to help him and the group to survive each other so that he can get the benefit?

If Mary is a real irritant to the others, the worker might get two or three girls who are friendly to work on something with her and thus give her status and security with at least a few group members. She might be able to exploit some special ability Mary possesses. She can help other members to understand her behavior and give her help, or at least to leave her alone. The worker might have to take many steps to protect the group from Mary's overaggressive and disturbing behavior. And she might likewise have to protect Mary from the group's counter-aggression and rejection.

There are important means the worker possesses for helping the individual member in the group, some of these having been mentioned in the previous sections in connection with beginning with the group, limiting the group, and so on. These means can be utilized with individual members effectively in the group situation. Important as well are the means available for encouraging and activizing behavior of individuals, means that will be constructive for them. This activity in behalf of the individual needs to be carried on essentially with the tacit permission of the group in order that feelings of jealousy, favoritism, and loss by other members are avoided.

PRIVATE COUNSELING

An important concept involved in asking for and accepting help needs to be underlined. A person may ask for help and still have strong resistance to, and guilt feelings about, using help and thus admitting his dependence. These ambivalent feelings will be expressed in antagonism and conflict. These have to be accepted by the worker, who can help also by stressing the responsibility of the member to handle as much of the problem as he can and commending him for any successes he has in this.

An additional point is that the individual has in our society the right to receive help in pursuing his life objectives and in solving his life problems. Feelings of guilt over lack of success in coping with some area of life function are likely not to be constructive but destructive. In undertaking to help an individual to help himself one lays a sound foundation in making clear the right of the person to such help as the worker is able to give.

There are recognized limits to the help the worker can give to individuals. No recreation agency allows sufficient time for all the individual conferences and like activities that are needed. In most cases individual work would be directed to immediate problems and limited to manageable problems within the agency's resources. The best service to an individual in need of intensive individual help is to know the resources in the community available for such help and to learn how to refer him to these resources. The referral process itself is demanding of the worker's time in order for it to be successful. The worker would undertake to obtain a sound if limited understanding of the individual member's problem through his diagnosis, understanding the problem in the context of the member's life in the recreation group, then helping him as much as is appropriate, and referring him to further help when indicated.

The Individual Conference

The optimal conditions for individual work will be away from the group, in private conferences. These occasions can happen in many places, on the playground, in the office, in the craft room, on a hike, on the sidewalk. It has aptly been called "curbstone" or "locker room" counseling. Conferences may be long or short, may be initiated by either person, may be single affairs, or part of a program involving many occasions. The worker by all means avoids getting too deeply into a therapeutic relationship with a person who needs intensive individual help beyond the worker's or the agency's function or resources.

The following "story" illustrates the help that could be given by a competent worker in such a conference:

> Tonight Pete was more than usually disruptive and finally the president told him to shut up or get out. Pete wanted to argue, and I suggested in a friendly but serious voice that we had a lot of planning to do for the dance and that he had better do what Tom said and wait outside. He went out sullenly. After the meeting he was waiting in the hall for me, and I lingered a bit in my office while the others left. "You kicked me out, Coach," he greeted me sulkily. "Yea," I said with a smile, "sorry you couldn't get in on our planning." I sat down on the steps, proceeded to give him a thumbnail sketch of our plan, and invited him to come down Saturday and help make posters. "What was bothering you tonight?" I asked quietly, looking directly at him. He burst out that he had got kicked out of class that day and that they were going to make his parents come to school, because it was his third time. He thought his folks would be real mad at him. I reminded him that he had done some good things with the club in recent weeks, like the job he had done two weeks ago when we had our clean-up day, and I asked him, "Do you think I could help, like calling up the principal or something?" At that his

face got a little brighter and he said, "Well, if things don't get too rough, I'll be all right." I said, "Well, if you need help, come on in and we'll talk it over." Pete answered, "Thanks, Coach. Well, I gotta go now," and he ran down the stairs.

The individual conference gives the member the opportunity to talk over his problems with a friend whose judgment he respects, of whose respect and friendship he is confident, and whose business it is to help him with problems like his. And he learns that the worker is a listener, not mainly a person to out-talk him, that he has concern for his problem and is ready to help him.

Wilson and Ryland summarize the worker's role in the following terms:

> He learns . . . to be a sensitive listener and to ask questions and make comments which will help the individual to tell his story, ask for the help he needs, or share his confusions. If the individual comes to the worker to discuss a personal problem, he is helped to analyze it, factor out the issues, and see its parts. The worker helps him to recognize that it is his problem, and that his is the responsibility, with the worker's guidance, of working it out. He helps the individual to tackle the parts of the problem with which he feels ready to grapple. . . . the individual is able to disclose his feelings of anxiety without fear of loss of respect from the worker. The worker gives the individual the support of assurance when such assurance is justified.[11]

The worker concentrates on the individual recreation participant, helping him to enjoy individual recreational experiences, to participate in and make use of group experiences, and to solve individual problems that inhibit his best use of recreation experiences and the achievement of leisure goals.

PROGRAM

A highly important part of the substance of individual and group recreation experience is the activities themselves. These activities are significant in the lives of group members, and how they are used makes

[11] Wilson and Ryland, *Social Group Work Practice,* p. 74.

a great deal of difference in how meaningful the recreation experience is to the participant. Part of the function of the profession is to study each activity or recreation experience in terms of its contribution to the individual and in terms of its potential for enriching individual experience.

Some confusion over the concept *program* requires clarification. *Program* and *group recreative activities* are not always synonymous. Program in one sense must be thought of as the total of the individual's experiences in the agency. The total experience of the individual, the involvement in group relationships and ongoing life, the relationship with the worker and the agency, the participation in activities, must be thought of as a whole. Within this totality the activities and expressional media are recognized as a central program element, as well as a central concern of the professional recreation worker.

An important consideration in program activity design is whether the needs and interests of the participants are being adequately met, as measured not only by criteria of numbers participating but also by the depth and richness of the values gained by participants. The worker knows that there also is a difference between interests and needs. Interests represent a concentration of conscious attention upon some activity which is attractive, and these interests are the basis for mobilizing activity. Needs, on the contrary, are thought of as deeper requirements for individual welfare and fulfillment, not necessarily conscious, but nevertheless motivating need-meeting activity. The professional's responsibility is to help the group to pursue its interests and exercise its right to responsible self-determination concerning its chosen recreational interests. On the other hand, the worker takes the responsibility for guiding the group and suggesting and designing activities and program features which contain the greatest need-meeting values for members.

Programming thus seems to be guided by two somewhat opposing principles. We might draw an analogy by contrasting a cafeteria and a guided nutrition program. A cafeteria makes guesses concerning what will be attractive to the buyer, then food is made up attractively and set out for one to pick and choose. By contrast, basic dietetic values are studied in a school or hospital nutrition program and a diet that will meet the client's needs is prescribed. Similarly, we often organize a "cafeteria style" program on a public playground, leaving it up to the client to choose as his interests dictate and striving only to have a wide selection. By contrast, in a recreation therapy program, knowing that the client needs a wholesome and nutritious recreational "diet," emphasis is placed upon guided selection of items from a more restricted list of experiences.

In defense of the first principle we might repeat our belief in enlarging the area of self-determination and decision making by the client to the maximum degree. One might defend the second principle as well by pointing out the professional worker's responsibility for helping the clients to enjoy play experiences which are positive and wholesome in their effect, and for functioning actively to guarantee the best use of such experiences.

The worker can gain cues from considering some of the basic values which are intrinsic to the recreation of individuals. The value of free creative expression; the attractiveness of and the self-fulfillment in recreational activities; the basic satisfactions from fellowship with others in funful pursuits; the adventure, new experience, variety, surprise, achievement, and accomplishment—all of these describe elements in recreation which are part of their intrinsic worth.

Another element of importance in program design is the consideration of the cultural backgrounds of participant groups. Programs must be related to the culturally familiar and comfortable play habits of members and to the unique social and cultural needs of neighborhoods and groups, as well as the central stream of social custom and tradition. Within a community there may be several cultural groups, in each of which there are established patterns of leisure-behavior. In planning activities full use would be made of such culturally determined interests. Particularly in respect to recreation's goal of strengthening family life, the peculiar family culture of a participant group would be an important element in determining the choice of recreation activities in order to provide for families opportunities for satisfying and culturally familiar recreational expression.

DESIGN OF ACTIVITIES

The recreation worker is an expert in the creation, design, and use of activities as tools for gaining the end of individual benefit. Considering the broad sweep of program activities—the arts and crafts, dancing, dramatics, literary activities, music, nature and outings, social events, sports and games—the worker should ask, in each case, what this activity is doing to the person. Is it producing the maximum in values for the individual? It is recognized that certain activities will meet different physical, emotional, intellectual, and social needs at different times. An understanding of the particular inner significance of an activity in respect to certain needs constitutes an important professional insight to develop.

From another point of view, one might analyze activities with respect to their function in serving several purposes. These were discussed in Chapter 5. We noted these purposes: (1) to achieve mastery or control over oneself or one's environment; (2) to enjoy the release and freedom in self-expression; (3) to enjoy creative experience and exploration; (4) to escape reality temporarily through fantasy and make-believe; (5) to enjoy fun, laughter, and humor; and (6) to find security in familiar enjoyments and people.

Competitive and Cooperative Activities

In each case, the activity may be designed with regard to needs of individuals, not with a formula expected to fit all situations or all needs. An example is the use of competition, mentioned earlier, which some leaders automatically undertake to introduce into every activity and others strive just as assiduously to eliminate from every activity. Those who argue for it claim that competition is the law of life and the law of society and that people are simply expressing natural interests and drives when they carry their competitive desires into play. Further, it is argued, competition in recreation simply prepares the child for more effective competitive functioning as an adult. Many in recreation have concluded that competition properly may be an ingredient of many recreational activities and that values are added thereby.

The opposing view argues that in modern times there has been an unwholesome overemphasis on competition that has negated fundamental recreational values. It is argued that competition is rather more a cultural than a biological phenomenon. In growth toward emotional maturity one places under control selfish and competitive drives and builds creative motives and a sense of responsibility for the welfare of others, which contributes to self-confidence and mature self-fulfillment. It provides the basis for altruism upon which family, community, and social survival depend.

Society and the social good in our highly interdependent and interrelated modern life require that people develop the qualities of cooperation, understanding and respect for others, and capacity for mutual aid. Cooperative recreation groups have been found to be dynamic influences in developing such elements as morale, socialization, democratic leadership skills, and altruistic behavior. Many recreation professionals would support the principle of moderate use of both types of activities, according to the requirements of a given situation. It is important to note that from the point of view of mental and emotional health there are specific values to be gained, and hazards to be avoided, in designing activities appropriate to the tolerances and capacities of individuals. The damage of overcompetitive demand, for example, can be matched by the damage of highly frustrating activities. Activity designed to avoid frustration and provide for impulse drainage, catharsis, or tension discharge, is of much importance. Activities or experiences that may vary from being nearly frustration-free or simply designed to present frustration only in amounts manageable by participants are desirable. Activities providing appropriate channels for vigorous physical or emotional expression and acting-out serve to drain off excessive impulsiveness, discharge muscular or nervous tension, and leave the individual with a relaxed and free feeling.

The same principle of programming can be applied at the level of group growth. A group has the capacity at different points in its life to make use of specific levels of experiences. Activities requiring a high level of planning activity, of self-discipline, or of creative and cooperative thinking together, should be avoided in the group's life when the strengths to manage these activities have not been developed. A group may enjoy activities at a very simple level of social organization at one point in its life. At later points it will be able to enjoy much more sophisticated gratifications derived from more sophisticated activities when group strengths and capacities have developed. Then the higher demands of group organization can be accepted as a means of attaining enjoyment of deeper satisfactions.

Rules and Regulations

Another principle in activity design is the creative use of rules and regulations as a means of maximizing the values to participants of a given activity. The structuring of teams to make them even, the changing of rules to improve a game for a particular group or situation, are all part of sound protective or preventive intervention by the worker. Without neglecting rules which arise out of concepts of fair play and sportsmanship, and "built-in" traditional rules that are culturally familiar and sound, the worker can protect group play from deteriorating into activity with limited values for the participants.

TIMING AND ENTHUSIASM

Two more principles should be touched upon. One is the sound use of timing, in order that participants can have a full measure of satisfying pleasure, and then can be helped to break off the activity leaving a good feeling and an eagerness to engage again at another time. Poor timing can result in an activity being stopped before it has developed its potential or stopped long after it has run its course and is being misused. Skill is required in changing over to other activities of a nature to neutralize and diffuse negative by-products of the old activity.

Another principle is the worker's show of supportive enthusiasm for an activity, encouraging contagious interest in an activity. The worker might support a suggestion made by a group member about a new activity and thus interest other group members in trying a new and desirable activity. Or he might propose an activity and by his interest and enthusiasm create interest among group members in giving it a try. Thus, he provides some satisfaction for members in some activity, and uses memories of past fun and successes as motivation for renewed activity. He encourages creative exploration of new activities and expands horizons of members to new vistas of leisure-time pleasure.

SETTINGS

How can these principles of professional method be put to work in the typical areas in which the recreation worker operates? Can the playground program, the center program, the interest groups, the clubs, the mass activities and special events and community affairs of traditional recreation program use these principles? We say the principles of professional method are generic to all of these, although some situations allow more intensive work with individuals and more specific values to be attained than do other situations.

THE PLAYGROUND

The playground is the most familiar recreation facility in America. The playground director or worker is likely to be assigned often to general supervision of informal and casual activity, with some group program under direct professional leadership offered. The free play activities of individuals of all ages is a healthy and desirable feature of playground program, although it should not be the central feature. But even at this level of free play the worker has two important functions. One is to provide help in getting group activities started and keeping largely autonomous groups going along lines of their interests. The second is to provide guided group experiences, even of an informal and short-term nature, that will interest individuals in the playground's basic program of guided group activities, from which level individuals and groups may be drawn into group activities of a higher organized form, with greater recreational value to them.

The organization of activities on the playground, the sports tournaments and leagues, the special events from time to time, with their preparatory activities, the sports clinics, coaching programs, and instructional programs all provide the worker with his best opportunities for putting his group method to work. The informal supervisory activities offer the worker opportunities to do the highly useful and important kind of individual work with which we have been concerned in this chapter. In the group programs of the playground the worker can exercise the range of his methodological competencies actively and to good purpose, and in so doing he can fulfill the needs and interests of many participants more surely and more adequately than free play activities can.

The Center—Interest Groups and Clubs

The building-centered recreation program offers to the recreation worker not a completely different opportunity for constructive work with groups but simply an expanded opportunity, with new variations. The building facilities normally offer opportunities for a wide variety of recreational interest groups. The worker begins with the common base of interest among members, with their goals of acquiring new knowledge and skill in the activity and enjoyment of the satisfaction of participating in this interesting pursuit. The worker can help members to enjoy these satisfactions. He also can help them gradually to enjoy the other satisfactions of group life, as groups discover in their common interest in an activity the basis for other satisfactions in their associations with each other. This is not to play down the great satisfaction of creative participation in a particular leisure art. Recreation experience has documented fully the fact of the profound satisfactions to be gained from many forms of creative expression in recreational interest groups.

The club program found in many recreation agencies offers another dimension for group experience and another opportunity for the recreation worker to exercise his helping skills. The club, or friendship group, offers members a range of recreational activities that can be varied to meet the members' needs and interests, and fulfilling relationships with other group members. The focus of the worker is upon providing the fullest possible opportunity for group relationships with all of its rich values of democratic group experience and a range of recreational activities that will enlist the interests and meet the needs of members.

Program Planning

The professional worker has at least one more dimension to his professional function upon which his methodology is brought to bear: program planning. It has already been pointed out how program planning within the individual group is an important part of group life and the source of basic values. Within his agency, program planning on the basis of intergroup representative bodies is another aspect of planning. It brings together representatives of several groups. The problems of feedback to the constituency groups, of representation, and of democratic functioning are important problems. This level of program planning also offers to the worker and the agency the opportunity to help some individuals to obtain a more sophisticated and more rewarding quality of education in democratic group functioning and to anchor the agency more firmly in a broader community relationship.

From the council in the agency it is just a step to the community advisory council or "playground parents association," which might be organized around the recreation agency to integrate more fully the agency into the community and its life and to enable it more adequately to function in response to community needs and interests. The functioning of the community council, in which the recreation agency is a participating organization, gives the agency its proper place in the constellation of civic organizations participating in the leadership of the community. It also provides the professional recreation worker with the opportunity to fulfill his function as a part of the professional team that shares in the responsibility for community leadership in behalf of the health and welfare of the community and its members. The same principles of enabling leadership which the recreation worker applies with his recreation groups are put to work in his function at the community level. He fulfills both an agency and a professional function in participating as a professional worker in this relationship.[12]

The program-focused role of the worker is to help the recreation-bent group or individual to gain maximum leisure values from recreation experiences, and to help them to choose and use recreations and recreation settings that best fulfill their needs and interests.

Questions for Study and Discussion

1. *In your judgment, what are the most important elements of knowledge, attitudes, and skills needed by the recreation worker?*
2. *One of the elements of a professional recreation worker's method is his personality. As you think of the recreation workers you have come into contact with, what are some of the aspects of personality that you believe are important?*
3. *Do you think that Hearn's concept of the "servant-enabler" fits the recreation worker more, or less, than the concept "leader" does? Why?*
4. *How much should the recreation worker "push" a person to participate in some recreation that the worker feels is good for him?*
5. *What are some of the possible learning experiences gained by group participation that will contribute to an individual's capacity for successful democratic living?*
6. *As a recreation worker in beginning work with a group, describe what important elements you would try to introduce into the life of the group and its relations with you.*

---

[12] For further discussion of processes and principles in community organization see: Murray Ross, *Community Organization—Theory and Principles* (New York: Harper & Row, Inc., 1955); Campbell Murphy, *Community Organization Practice* (Boston: Houghton Mifflin Company, 1954); Wayne McMillen, *Community Organization for Social Welfare* (Chicago: University of Chicago Press, 1945); Ray Johns and David De Marche, *Community Organization and Agency Responsibility* (New York: The Association Press, 1951).

Selected Readings

Combs, A. W., and D. Snygg, *Individual Behavior* (New York: Harper & Row, Inc., 1959).

Hearn, Gordon, "Democratic Behavior," in *Developing Democratic Human Relations Through Health Education, Physical Education, and Recreation,* First Yearbook, American Association For Health, Physical Education and Recreation (Washington, D.C.: National Education Association, 1951).

PART 6

CHANGING PERSPECTIVES IN LEISURE AND RECREATION

This final section gives the authors one last chance to "speak their piece," and to attempt, for a moment, to turn aside tomorrow's veil for a look into the future. Last pages of books and last acts of plays are for these purposes—for "moments of truth"—when authors distill for the reader and listener some conclusions, offer some criticisms, and then in sincerity reveal their hopes. These few following pages are no exception.

Our nation is moving rapidly into an "age of leisure," an age marked by unparalleled opportunity for substantial fulfillment of major needs and interests of all of its members. The possibility exists of a great leap forward, toward an era when individual welfare can be served at levels unbelievable a few centuries ago. The whole world is stirring mightily with the struggles for the same self-fulfillment of millions of other human beings. In scores of countries men are throwing aside bonds of control by others and forging new means of self-government and self-determination as the basis for developing economic technology and social organization to guarantee education, health, and welfare to themselves at new high levels of individual self-fulfillment. One of the fundamental elements in this self-fulfillment is creative leisure.

Yet all of the understanding, and all of the means to gain this better world for all, man has not yet developed. Years of struggle, experimentation, and perhaps·floundering lie ahead, that is, once we accept the hopeful view that nations can avoid the searing war that would destroy our hopes and our future. In this struggle to define sound goals and to work to attain them, recreation has an important role to play. In our own country significant re-evaluation of our goals must include a re-evaluation of the means we can provide for helping the individual toward genuine self-actualization, to which creative leisure is central.

The hope is that life, leisure, and labor may be brought into a realistic perspective. The hope is that the stresses and tensions, the fears, hysterias, and anxieties, the war neuroses, the poisoning from radioactive dust and carcinogens in food, the diseases of overeating, malnutrition, and bodily misuse, and the environment and way of life which produces such pathology, can be diminished. The hope is that an environment can be created by our efforts, based upon ideals of health and tranquility and profound concern for the welfare of each individual, by a nation whose policies may be firmly based upon principles of ethical human relations.

The hope is that we shall become more free of competitive status buying, that we shall escape perpetual victimization by the hidden persuaders and waste makers and shall emerge as creative leisure-seeking and recreationally sophisticated people, loving aesthetic culture, loving nature, loving creativity, loving life and its material and spiritual components in proper perspective. The hope is that we shall turn to the work of building and organizing our communities and institutions so as to realize these values for all men and to limit the effect of those damaging and harmful practices that frustrate these values through sound leisure education and firm and thoughtful controls.

For these hopes to be realized for this nation and for this world, a vast mobilization of the constructive forces in the communities and the nations must take place. Among these constructive forces must be an enlightened public interest and an alert and forward-looking recreation profession that will work to advance education for leisure, community organization for recreation, and a public policy in support of such broad human values. The hope is that the growing recreation profession will dedicate its efforts to these goals and, in a small way, this book hopes to make its contribution. This section undertakes a brief consideration of a number of relevant trends and issues.

15

TRENDS AND PROBLEMS

This chapter represents the authors' attempt to underscore what appear to be important trends in organized recreation in America, and to indicate significant problems and issues arising out of these to which the public, and the recreation profession, must address themselves. They arise out of broader modern social trends, particularly the trend toward more people with more disposable income and more leisure time. They should be viewed against that broad backdrop.

MAJOR TRENDS

Principal documentation of these trends is to be found in the foundational material developed in specific chapters. For example,

Chapters 9 and 10 highlight the trend of increasing community acceptance of public responsibility for recreation. The few sentences here are merely to help describe the trend and suggest implications. The chapters which treat the basic subject matter in more detail are identified for each trend.

Trends in Planning and Organization

1. *Greater investment by society in people* (Chapters 7, 8, 9, 10). The increasing concern of American society, in general, for the over-all well-being of its people and others, their health, education, and leisure, can be documented in more than just economic investment terms. Welfare and volunteer services are expanding tremendously, along with huge sums for education, medical research, improved living conditions, and recreation.

2. *More planning for leisure time* (Chapters 7, 8, 9, 10). As leisure time has increased, the number and type of organizations, agencies, individuals and institutions concerned with planning for leisure-time have grown too. This trend will continue, and there will be increasing attention devoted to joint planning at all levels.

3. *More planning for population growth* (Chapter 8). The demographers have joined hands with the social scientists, the physical planners, and others to meet the problems arising out of the rapid growth and shifts in population.

4. *Continued expansion of community services for leisure and recreation* (Chapters 9, 10). Recreation is now recognized as an integral community function and accepted as being important and meaningful. In 1950 there were some 28,000 communities in America in which recreation services were provided. By 1960, there were 36–38,000 communities with recreation programs. This expansion will continue.

5. *More community planning for recreation* (Chapters 8, 10). Although there has been a trend toward more separate departments of recreation and identification of the public agency as having the major responsibility in the community for recreation, at the same time there has been no trend to delegate all responsibility to one agency, but rather for many agencies to share this responsibility through total community planning. In keeping with this trend, more and more

agencies are recognizing their part of the total community program. This recognition is bound up with the degree of social mobility existing at present not only from one part of the country to another, but also within a community itself, and with the unique roles agencies play. As people move, so do agencies and services. A program service such as the Boy Scouts' volunteer leadership, for example, may no longer be available in a specific subcommunity. The people capable of serving as volunteers have moved and the agency has moved, creating a gap which some other agency must now attempt to fill. This requires constant assessment and integration of community services through planning.

6. *More public recreation services and assignment of a larger role to the recreation function in governmental agencies at all levels* (Chapters 9, 10). The United States Forest Service is just one example of how increasing demand for many years has resulted in an agency assuming much stronger responsibility and a more positive attitude toward recreation as an agency function, along with the expansion of the recreational use of forest resources. The number and type of governmental jurisdictions operating recreation programs increases steadily.

7. *Broader services to more groups* (Chapters 9, 10, 11). Recreation services have grown beyond the concept of just a summer playground program of play activities for children and youth to keep them off the streets and "out of mischief." There are year-round services that now reach out to encompass all age groups from preschool to senior citizens. Program services are broader in scope and purpose, extending to special groups such as the ill and handicapped, the homebound, and those in penal, mental, and other types of rehabilitative institutions. The consulting service for the ill and handicapped operated by the National Recreation Association and their project for the homebound in New York City is an example of this trend.

8. *Broader emphasis in program* (Chapters 10, 14). The content of recreation programming has been broadened from primarily a physical base of active games and sports to encompass science, art, music, drama, literary expression, hobbies, crafts, and dance. Special emphases are being developed in response to the current needs and interests being identified in the mainstream of American life. For example, the National Recreation Association selected three fields for program emphasis for 1961–1965. The first of these fields is the per-

forming arts in the effort to increase opportunities and to upgrade direct experiences in the performing arts for a larger group than just the professionals or the little theater, dance, or music groups. This effort is being made in cooperation with the Music Educators and the American Educational Theater Association. The second emphasis is science, and the third is family camping, reflecting the utilization of the widespread interest in "space" and in outdoor recreation as a basis for adding new dimensions to programming. Cultural and leisure education programs of all types are receiving greater attention.

9. *Broader sources of recreation program and a redefinition of the role of the recreation worker* (Chapters 9, 10, 12, 14). For many years, the recreation program was seen as centered in or on a specific facility (playground, center, or park). A newer concept is that recreation program exists wherever people are spending their leisure time. This is being accompanied by the redefinition of the role of the worker and the methods he uses to fulfill his function. The idea of the recreation worker being a whistle-blowing custodian who unlocks gates, issues equipment, and counts noses is as passé as the horse and buggy. The modern worker is a catalyst, an individual who brings together the resources of people and opportunities, who works with people as well as things in the recreation process.

10. *Greater mobilization of aesthetic and cultural groups* (Chapters 9, 10). With the recognition of the need to broaden recreation program content and to utilize more fully the total leisure opportunities of the community, there has been increasing mobilization of aesthetic and cultural resources. The stress placed on creativity has brought to the fore the important role of the arts in life. More and more cultural groups are being identified with the recreation program, with a much broader audience and participant range.

11. *Increased attention to education for leisure* (Chapters 9, 10, 11). Many organizations and groups share in the educative process—the school, the family, the church, the youth serving agency. The emphasis on recreation in their programs is evidence that they are assuming responsibility for education for leisure in a variety of ways. But to the schools falls the major burden for the formal aspects of education for a revolutionary and quantitatively different concept of leisure time and leisure fulfillment. They are recognizing this and

are expanding their role through direct teaching, provision of leadership and facilities, and the operation of extensive programs.

12. *More commercialization of leisure-time opportunities* (Chapters 7, 9, 10). The phenomenal growth of bowling and other commercial recreation centers since World War II reflects the expanding leisure-time market and the operation of the free enterprise system. With this, of course, come the commercial pressures of advertising and promotion, which may tend to obscure participation values or imply the presence of values that do not exist.

Trends in the Profession and Uses of Leisure Time and Recreation

13. *Improved status of the recreation profession and its members* (Chapter 12). To claim that recreation has achieved full mature professional status at this stage in its growth is wishful thinking, but there is definite progress toward this goal. Voluntary registration plans, improvement of personnel standards and practices, rising salaries, specialization, growth in professional education, and development of a code of ethics are hallmarks of the positive professional growth and development underway.

14. *Increased rapprochement with other professional groups* (Chapters 10, 12, 13, 14). As the recreation profession has grown in maturity and in its capacity to render its unique social function, so have the lines of relationship between recreation and other professions. This is particularly true with medicine, education, and social work, where the working interrelationships are most clearly seen in the number of joint conferences and committees, in the frequency of participation in each other's conferences, and in the improved channels of communication.

15. *More stress on leisure time as a basic health resource* (Chapters 5, 9, 10, 11, 13). Statistics have revealed the low level of general physical fitness of both youth and adults and the increasing incidence of mental illness in the United States. These facts, when coupled with increasing longevity of the people in general, point up the necessity of seeing leisure time as a major factor in the health of all ages. The development of recreation as both a preventive and a rehabilitative tool is evidence of the larger emphasis being directed toward the use of leisure time for these purposes.

16. *Greater utilization of recreation as a tool for communication and understanding* (Chapters 12, 13, 14). One has only to examine one's own life to realize how much of our understanding of someone or the nature of our relationship to someone has resulted from sharing the recreation process with that person. Everywhere recreation and people's leisure-time pursuits are serving to break down barriers between individuals and groups, culturally, geographically, and nationally. The Olympic Games and the International Recreation Association with its student and leader exchange program are just two examples of recreation serving as a very strong tool for communication between people.

PROBLEMS AND ISSUES

The trends in leisure and recreation suggest a dynamic future for the recreation movement and profession. As promising as this appears, however, some basic questions must be answered before the potentials in leisure time can be realized. These questions carry with them the implication suggested before, that there are problems and issues that the profession and the general public must resolve if recreation is truly to serve its social function. We make no pretense that the questions raised are all of the questions requiring answers, nor are they necessarily listed in order of importance. They are pertinent to foundational study in recreation and relate directly to concepts identified throughout this book.

1. *How can the recreation profession develop a forward-looking philosophy and a conceptual framework based upon a scientifically determined body of knowledge?* Much of the present philosophy and theory, as Myron points out, is undocumented belief, inadequate or untenable in light of modern changing conditions and forces.[1] Although a few writers have proposed one or another framework, there is no common acceptance of one. Although the individual professional worker or agency may be able to express his or its philosophy, the profession in general seems to be unable to do so, in a coherent and consistent fashion.

---

[1] Harold G. Myron, "Needed: A Conceptual Framework for Recreation," *American Recreation Journal,* Vol. 1, No. 8 (May 1961), pp. 8-10.

2. *Given such a framework, how can the recreation profession agree upon a set of objectives that will give meaning to program, purpose to agencies, direction to workers and opportunity to participants?* Inability to do so has led to duplication of services, unfulfilled needs, variations in terminology and job performance, confusion in the profession, and lack of understanding and support by the general public. To answer this question, the profession needs a philosophical framework and a clarification of specific values and goals to be sought.

3. *Within the perspective of total free time, how much time should be devoted to recreation?* Recreation activity is not the only use to which free time is put. There are other needs to be met during free time. There are, at times, larger issues of life which must be resolved, individually and nationally. To put leisure and recreation into their proper perspective, therefore, major study is essential. This is not to suggest the perspective held by some who think that one of the problems in America is that there is too much recreation and not enough work.

4. *What is the role of the recreation profession in solving such social welfare problems as poverty, housing, delinquency, vice, discrimination, ill health, mental breakdown?* Some individuals in the recreation profession say it is not the task of recreation to solve any problems, that they are the responsibility of health, education, and social welfare. Be that as it may, institutionalized recreation, and the recreation profession, must be concerned with the over-all problems of society and contribute to their solution. Recreation has contributions in most social welfare fields, and how the recreative uses of leisure time can contribute to these fields is the primary province of the recreation worker, working closely with other professions and citizens in community organization and social planning.

5. *How can recreation preserve individuality and leisure time's democratic quality of the individual's opportunity to exercise free choice, in the face of population trends, increasing commercialization and promotion through advertising, and the tendency toward mass recreation events and activities?* The recreation profession must meet this challenge or fail in its most basic goal and responsibility.

6. *Who should organize recreation at the community level?* Should it be the municipal government, the county government, the

schools, the voluntary agencies? There are many who say it is a matter of local autonomy. The pattern of organization should reflect community needs and desires, the best mobilization of resources possible, and cooperative effort. But within the ranks of the recreation profession there is disagreement. It may be that new patterns will emerge, particularly along regional bases, with state and federal government playing larger roles.

Inadequate Facilities

7. *What is the best method of financing the provision of recreation services and opportunities?* Public financing through taxation, by the individual paying for the service, through a system of fees and charges, by philanthropy or by contributions to United Funds are all methods employed singly or in combination by different types of organizations and agencies. With rising costs, greater demand for services and increasing competition for the tax dollar and disposable income, along with huge increases in disposable income and potential revenue for financing services, this problem grows more complex yearly.

8. *How can recreation planners secure and retain the land resources necessary for adequate facilities and areas?* The squeeze of increasing population and decreasing land space for a variety of purposes, of which recreation is only one, is already gripping most urban areas and the nation as a whole. And it is not what is needed today that is important, but what will be needed fifty or one hundred years from now. The decision must be made now and, unfortunately, yardsticks to justify recreation's need and demand are all too few.

9. *How can the profession establish standards that will ensure the development of leadership, capable of helping to answer these questions and to determine public policy on them?* A process of certification of recreation workers, such as exists for teachers, nurses, doctors, and lawyers, is vital. This process will require the establishment and acceptance of and adherence to the accreditation of standards for professional education. There is wide variation in professional education, and recruitment programs are grossly inadequate.

10. *How can the recreation profession build a sound program of basic and applied research?* Every question raised in this chapter cries out for the systematic formulation and testing of hypotheses, the development of reliable and valid evaluative criteria, and the extension of the body of knowledge.

11. *How can more creativity be developed through the recreation program?* Too little is known of the nature and operation of the creative process and how to develop creativity in others. Although the recreation worker may be creative in his approaches to people and the activities he directs, the final test is the degree to which he can assist others to be creative. If recreation is to serve its purpose in helping individuals and groups to achieve the goal of creative leisure, then this process must be diffused through programming at all age levels and for all groups.

12. *How can sufficient time be secured in the school day to educate adequately for leisure?* Local, national, and international demands on American education for "hard" education, financing pressures, changing and expanding curricular emphases, demands for elimination of "frills," make the task of securing support for education for leisure to the degree required a monumental task, which, however, must be accomplished. Of all the challenges to the recreation profession this is one of the most crucial.

13. *How can the efforts of the professional and service recreation organizations be coordinated and cooperative working relationships established that will produce the unity of purpose essential for a mature profession?* An external structure is not implied, but independent unilateral action by associations and societies on many problems is inefficient and may be ineffective, thus impeding the progress of the profession itself. The Federation of National Professional Organizations for Recreation is making progress in the effort to develop liaison,

Wilderness—How Long?

understanding, and common study projects, as are several of the individual professional organizations.

A CHALLENGE

The philosophical issue continues to be important in recreation, whether the main thrust should be on developing individual recreations and individual recreation competence, or recreation in its social forms and as a means for obtaining socialization values for the individual. Our view is that both of these are valid goals, that recreation is a primary means of gaining, through individual creative activities, leisure values, and also, through group activities, other important values. There is confusion over the proper relationship of these two goals, and the recreation profession must be clear on its responsibilities in respect to each of these goals.

The leisure age is just unfolding, and the prospect of a nation of two hundred million people working twenty hours a week and flooding any and all recreation facilities in their leisure hours is frightening and yet challenging. The nation, the recreation movement, and the recreation profession, all must respond to the demand for a completely different and profound leisure concept based upon a vastly increased leisure opportunity.

For the leisure age to find its fulfillment, surely the basic problems facing our people must be solved in important measure. Poverty can and must be largely eliminated, for this still considerable group is denied leisure opportunitiy as long as poverty weighs on individuals day by day. Any set of valid goals for America, goals by which the American way of life can be measured against other ways of life, will include creative leisure for the people, along with economic security and challenge, satisfaction of basic needs for food, clothing, shelter, health care, as well as a resolution of the problems and anxieties of international relationships.

There must be evolved, as a matter of basic public policy, a concept of the proper balance of recreation under public, volunteer, and other auspices of a nonprofit nature, and under commercial auspices of a profit-making nature. The question for the nonprofit agencies is to accept a commitment to the fulfillment of their function creatively and with imagination and energy. The question for the profit-making sector of recreation is to fulfill basic leisure values and not to let exploitation and vulgarization of public tastes take place for profit's sake.

The above, in effect, outlines a blueprint for action for the recreation profession. Further work is needed to develop a philosophy and conceptual framework, compatible with today's forces, that identifies recreation's relationship to leisure time and to leisure, that identifies the recreation worker's competence to deal with broad social problems in leisure time along with other helping professions—medicine, religion, government, social welfare, education, and so on.

The profession needs to formulate this philosophy in terms of specific short-term, intermediate, and long-range goals, capable of deriving support of several publics and enabling progress from one objective to another. Competition for the attitude, opinion, and action of people is too great today to expect support without a clear definition of recreation and its objectives that has meaning for these publics. Once this support is assured, then priorities of timing, resources, and goals can be established.

The recreation profession needs standards for, and a flexibility in, leadership capable of meeting the challenge of changing times and forces. It needs leadership that can help individuals to attain leisure values through recreative uses of their leisure time and thus give meaning to their life, purpose and direction to the United States, and impetus to improved understanding between peoples everywhere through recognition of this common goal.

If this blueprint challenges or inspires the student and the professional, then it will have met our purpose and Pindar's criterion:

> Forge thy tongue on an anvil of truth
> And what flies up, though it be a spark,
> Shall have weight.

Questions for Study and Discussion

1. *Which of the major trends that have been presented in this chapter would you consider to be the most significant? Why?*

2. *In what order would you rank the major trends that have been listed?*

3. *What changes have you made in your own philosophy of recreation during your study of this book?*

4. *What is your reaction to each of the questions presented in the issues and problems section of this chapter? Criticize the point of view presented by the writers in each case and give your own view.*
5. *What do you think is the major challenge facing the recreation profession today? Give your reasons.*

Selected Readings

Ernest, Morris, *Utopia, 1976* (New York: Holt, Rinehart and Winston, Inc., 1955).

Soule, George, *The Shape of Tomorrow* (New York: New American Library, 1955).

INDEX